KICK-ASS

S0-ADB-198

KICK-ASS. Contains material originally published in magazine form as KICK-ASS #1-8. First printing 2011. ISBN# 978-0-7851-3261-5. Published by MARVEL WORLDWIDE, INC., a subsidiary of MARVEL ENTERTAINMENT, LLC. OFFICE OF PUBLICATION: 135 West 50th Street, New York, NY 10020. Copyright © 2008, 2009, 2010 and 2011 Mark Millar and John S. Romita. All rights reserved. $19.99 per copy in the U.S. and $21.99 in Canada (GST #R127032852); Canadian Agreement #40668537. KICK-ASS, the Kick-Ass logo, and all characters and content herein and the likenesses thereof are trademarks of Mark Millar and John S. Romita, unless otherwise expressly noted. The events and characters presented are intended as fiction. Any similarity to real events or to persons living or dead is purely coincidental. This work may not be reproduced, except in small amounts for journalistic or review purposes, without permission of the authors. ICON and the Icon logo are trademarks of Marvel Characters, Inc. **Printed in the U.S.A.** ALAN FINE, EVP - Office of the President, Marvel Worldwide, Inc. and EVP & CMO Marvel Characters B.V.; DAN BUCKLEY, Publisher & President - Print, Animation & Digital Divisions; JOE QUESADA, Chief Creative Officer; JIM SOKOLOWSKI, Chief Operating Officer; DAVID BOGART, SVP of Business Affairs & Talent Management; TOM BREVOORT, SVP of Publishing; C.B. CEBULSKI, SVP of Creator & Content Development; DAVID GABRIEL, SVP of Publishing Sales & Circulation; MICHAEL PASCIULLO, SVP of Brand Planning & Communications; JIM O'KEEFE, VP of Operations & Logistics; DAN CARR, Executive Director of Publishing Technology; JUSTIN F. GABRIE, Director of Publishing & Editorial Operations; SUSAN CRESPI, Editorial Operations Manager; ALEX MORALES, Publishing Operations Manager; STAN LEE, Chairman Emeritus. For information regarding advertising in Marvel Comics or on Marvel.com, please contact John Dokes, SVP Integrated Sales and Marketing, at jdokes@marvel.com. For Marvel subscription inquiries, please call 800-217-9158. **Manufactured between 6/1/11 and 6/20/2011 by R.R. DONNELLEY, INC., SALEM, VA, USA.**

10 9 8 7 6 5 4 3 2 1

KICK-ASS

Writer & Co-Creator
MARK MILLAR

Penciler & Co-Creator
JOHN ROMITA JR.

Inker
TOM PALMER

Colorist
DEAN WHITE

Letterer
CHRIS ELIOPOULOS

Assistant Editor
MICHAEL HORWITZ

Editor
JOHN BARBER

Collection Editor: JENNIFER GRÜNWALD
Assistant Editors: ALEX STARBUCK & NELSON RIBEIRO
Editor, Special Projects: MARK D. BEAZLEY
Senior Editor, Special Projects: JEFF YOUNGQUIST
Senior Vice President of Sales: DAVID GABRIEL
SVP of Brand Planning & Communications MICHAEL PASCIULLO
SVP of Business Affairs & Talent Management: DAVID BOGART
Book Designer: SPRING HOTELING

Editor in Chief: AXEL ALONSO
Chief Creative Officer: JOE QUESADA
Publisher: DAN BUCKLEY
Executive Producer: ALAN FINE

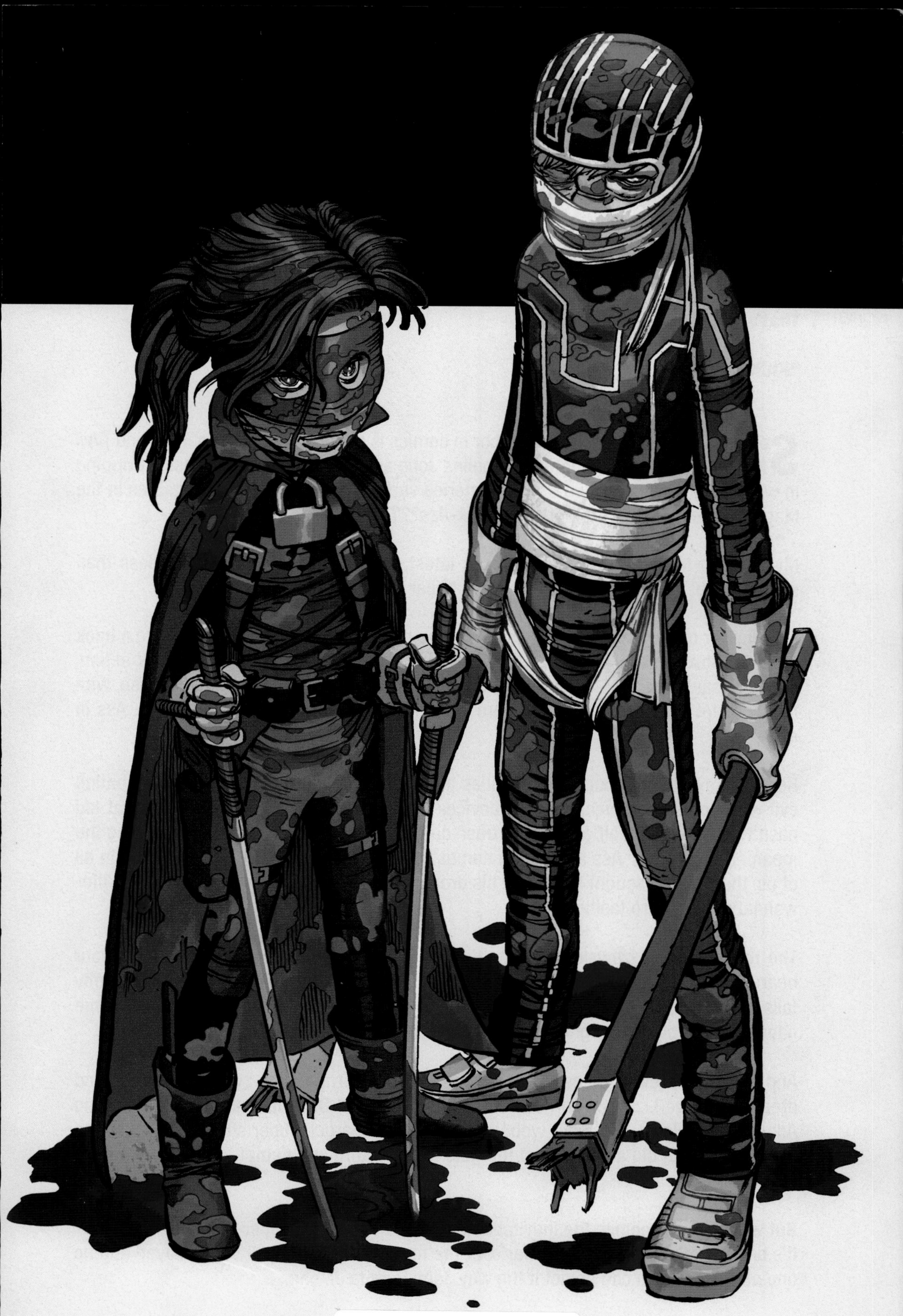

"KICK-ASS?"

Yup.

"KICK-ASS??"

That's it.

"KICK-ASS????"

So this is how the best-selling author in comics is going to follow up *Wanted* and *Civil War*? The guy that brought us Angelina Jolie as a naked, ruthless assassin dripping in wax, the guy who gave us Captain America versus Iron Man for all the marbles in the Marvel Universe? His next work was *Kick-Ass*???

My reaction to the title of Mark Millar's latest, greatest magnum opus was less than stellar. But he just smiled. Because Mark Millar gets it.

As a matter of fact, Mark got it way before the rest of us. See, If you're gonna do a book featuring the most Kick-Ass writing, the most Kick-Ass art, the most Kick-Ass action, then you can't afford to be shy, you just call it the way you see it. And in this case, with this concept and these creators, there was no doubt this comic would be Kick-Ass in every way.

Here's a story about a kid who imagines himself as a real life crime-fighter, combating evil with homemade weapons and devices available at your local Wal-Mart. What kid hasn't imagined himself grabbing a trash can lid and a baseball bat and wandering the mean streets Kickin' Ass and taking names? Dave Lizewski IS THAT KID! That kid in all of us, the kid who sought to live out his dreams and bust some bad guy ass in real-life-wannabe-superhero fashion.

The minute Dave Lizewski becomes Kick-Ass and steps into the neighborhood, your heart leaps with hope as he confronts local gang members. Your heart subsequently falls and is crushed as Dave receives his first serious beat down at the hands of same gangstas. The blood, the grit, the bloody failure. It drew us in, we couldn't look away.

And as Dave Lizewski rises again with renewed determination, so do our hopes and dreams. If Dave Lizewski can overcome, than so can I! Dave has no super powers, no Adamantium claws, no spider webbing, no gamma charged super strength. He just has a heart twice as big as yours and the guts to see it through no matter what. This is the heart of Kick-Ass!

But with courage comes the inevitable Mark Millar-imagined hyper-real super-violence. It's brutal, it's messy and it's so far over the top it has to be seen to be believed and no one on planet earth can depict it the way John Romita Jr. can.

John Romita Jr. has drawn every Marvel character imaginable. He's the ace, the closer, the go-to guy. He's the closest thing to clutch that exists in the comics biz. A few years back, he and Millar combined for the first time to bring us the super-charged epic *Wolverine: Enemy of the State*. Sales soared and fans demanded that these two team up again as often as possible. When they answered the call, was there any doubt it would be as Kick-Ass as possible?

Romita Jr's. storytelling in *Kick-Ass* is the most cinematic, widescreen, high-def he's ever attempted. The pacing, the drama, the violence in these pages is as brutal as any you will ever find. It makes you cringe and wince and ultimately leaves you with your slack-jawed mouth scraping the bottom of the floor. John Romita Jr. leaves it all on the page, he holds nothing back here and in doing so produces the seminal work of his career. Millar and Romita Jr. are peas and carrots, bees and honey, cookies and cream. Simply put, they are irresistible.

HIT-GIRL! RED MIST! BIG DADDY! It's all KICK-ASS, all the time, as only two of the brightest stars in the history of graphic novels could depict it.

When *Kick-Ass* hit the stands, fans hit the streets talking about the best damn comic to come down the pike in a long damn time. *Kick-Ass* is courageous. *Kick-Ass* is contagious. You had to get *Kick-Ass*!

It used to be that you had to be grim and gritty in order to grab everyone's attention. Now you most definitely have to Kick-Ass.

So what the hell are you waiting for? Turn the page and prepare to go KICK some ASS!

Rob Liefeld
January 2010

Rob Liefeld was one of the forefathers of the 1990s comics revolution — co-creating Cable *and* Deadpool, *and transforming* New Mutants *into* X-Force *before helping found Image Comics with his original property* Youngblood. *In 2007, Liefeld returned to Marvel to pencil the* Onslaught Reborn *miniseries.*

ONE

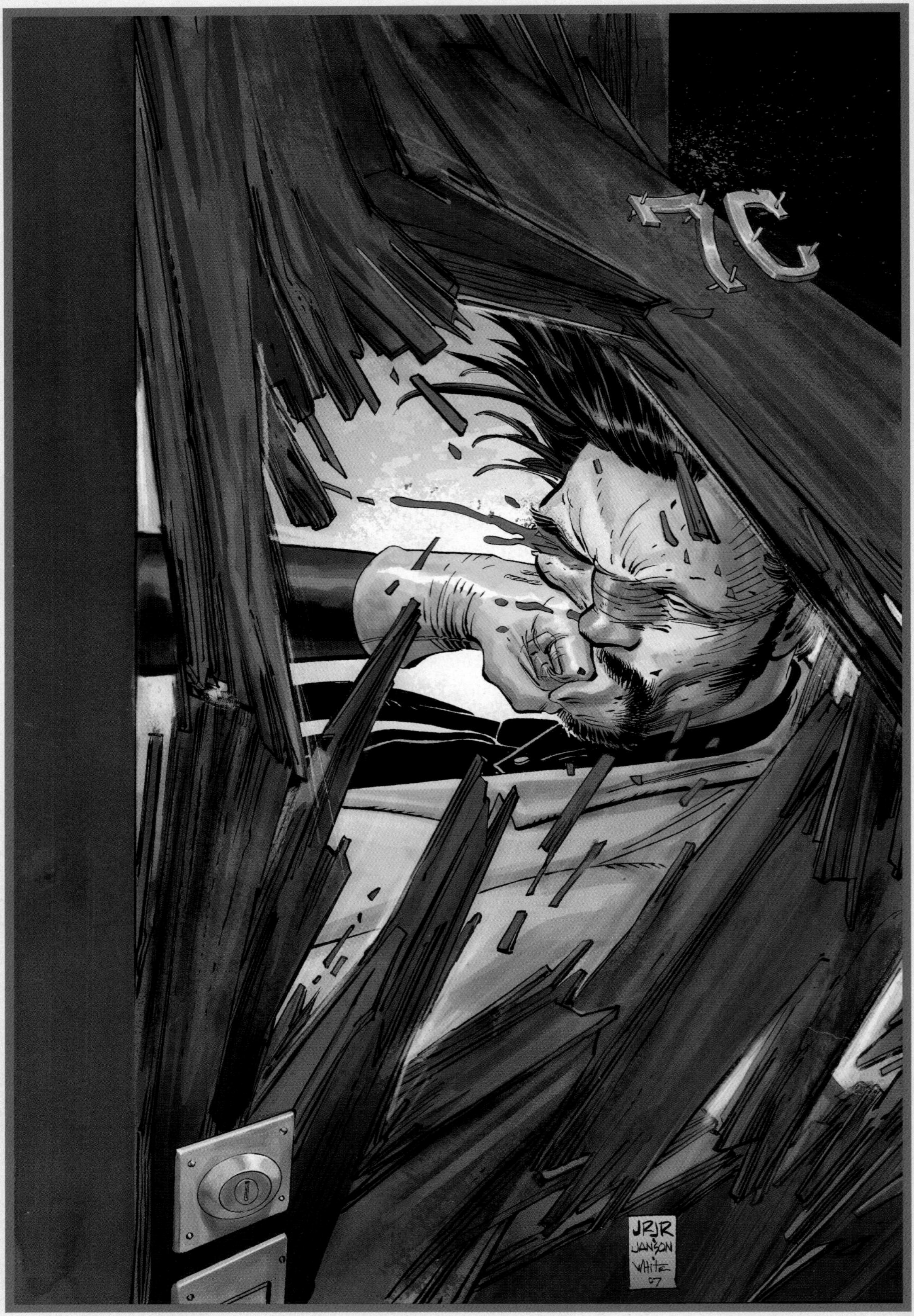
7C
JRJR
JANSON
WHITE
07

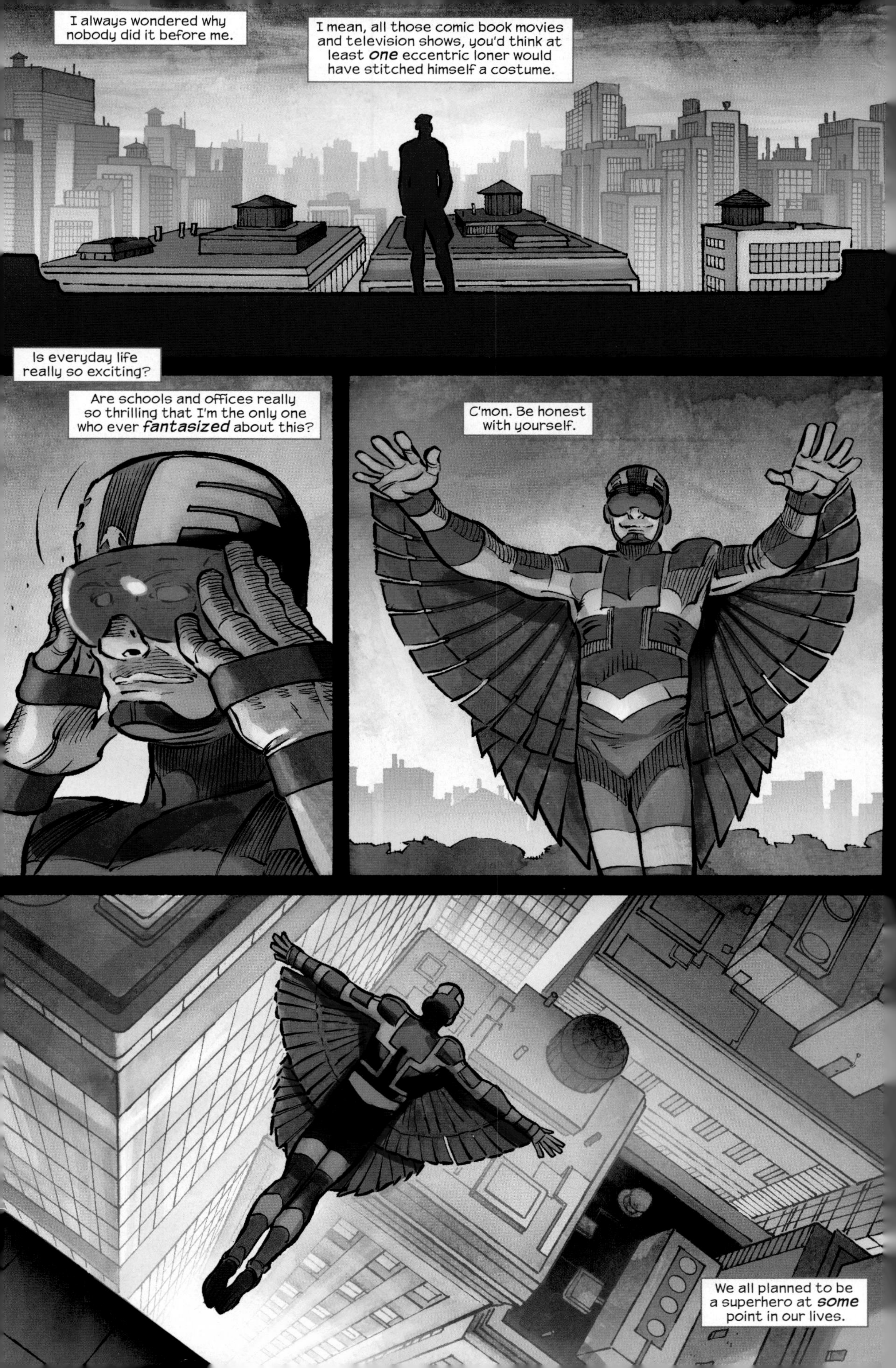

I always wondered why nobody did it before me.
I mean, all those comic book movies and television shows, you'd think at least *one* eccentric loner would have stitched himself a costume.
Is everyday life really so exciting?
Are schools and offices really so thrilling that I'm the only one who ever *fantasized* about this?
C'mon. Be honest with yourself.
We all planned to be a superhero at *some* point in our lives.

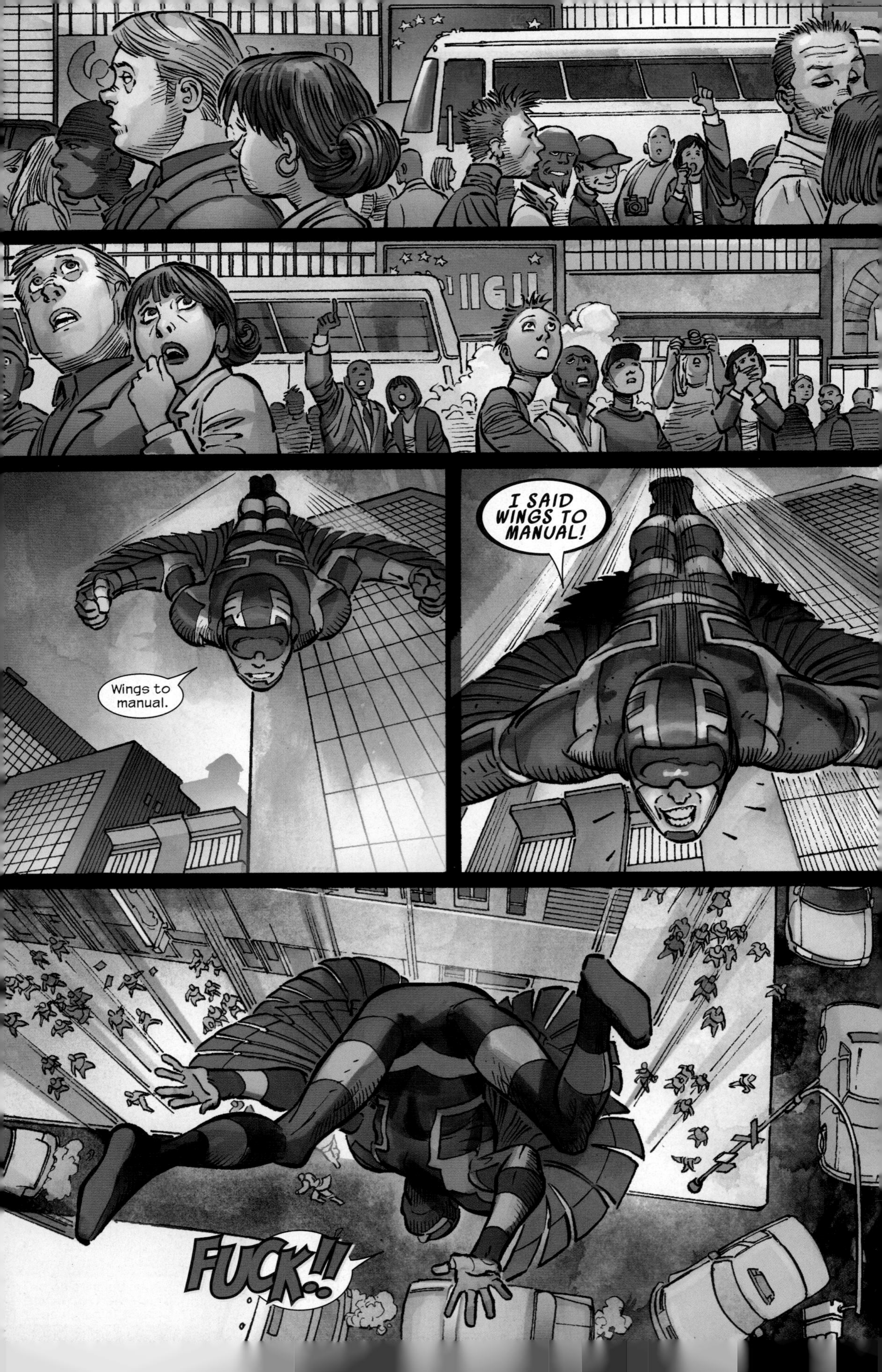
Wings to manual.
I SAID WINGS TO MANUAL!
FUCK!!

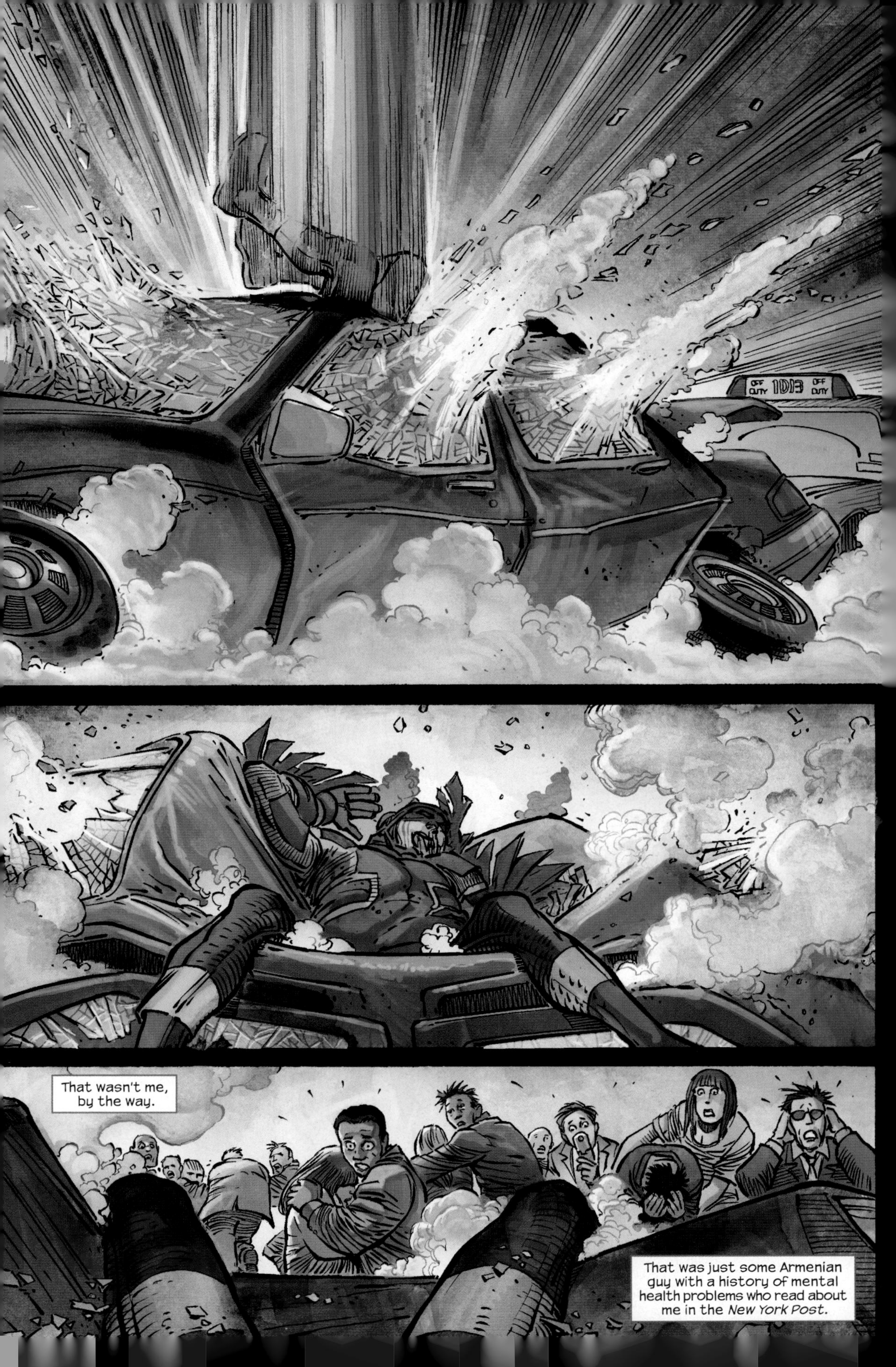
OFF DUTY
1D13
OFF DUTY
That wasn't me, by the way.
That was just some Armenian guy with a history of mental health problems who read about me in the *New York Post*.

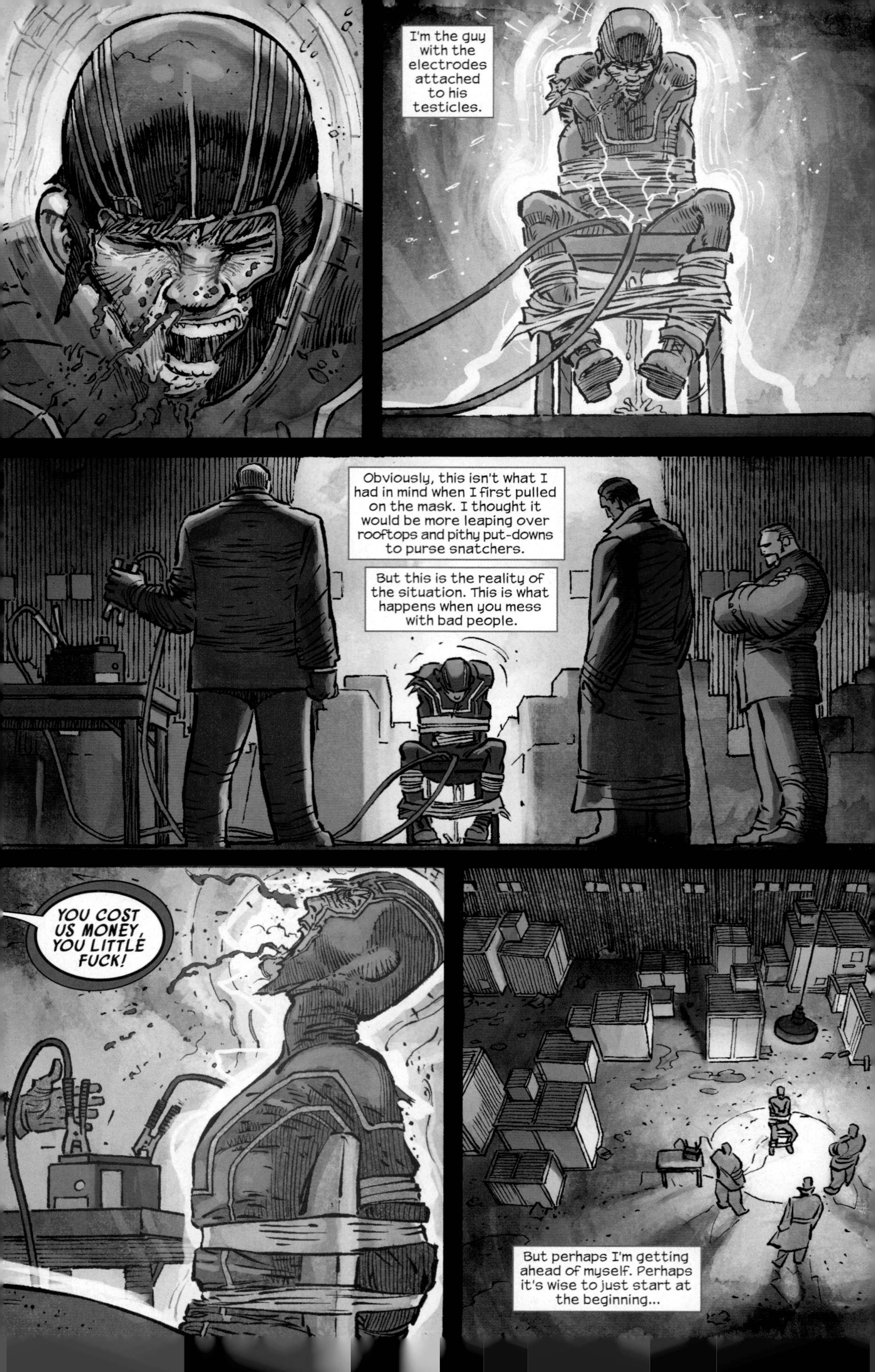

I'm the guy with the electrodes attached to his testicles.
Obviously, this isn't what I had in mind when I first pulled on the mask. I thought it would be more leaping over rooftops and pithy put-downs to purse snatchers.
But this is the reality of the situation. This is what happens when you mess with bad people.
YOU COST US MONEY, YOU LITTLE FUCK!
But perhaps I'm getting ahead of myself. Perhaps it's wise to just start at the beginning...

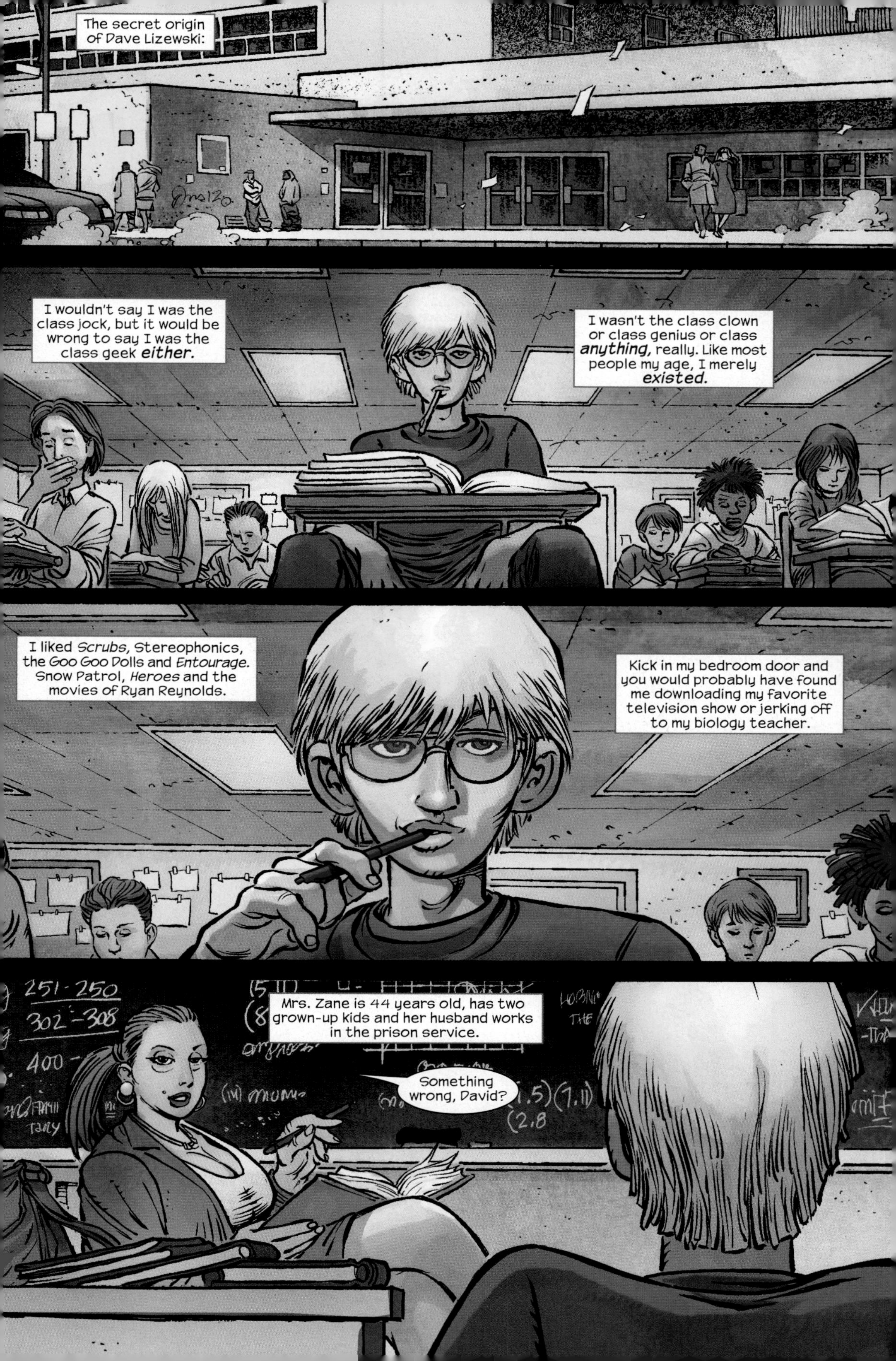
The secret origin of Dave Lizewski:
I wouldn't say I was the class jock, but it would be wrong to say I was the class geek *either.*
I wasn't the class clown or class genius or class *anything,* really. Like most people my age, I merely *existed.*
I liked *Scrubs,* Stereophonics, the *Goo Goo Dolls* and *Entourage.* Snow Patrol, *Heroes* and the movies of Ryan Reynolds.
Kick in my bedroom door and you would probably have found me downloading my favorite television show or jerking off to my biology teacher.
Mrs. Zane is 44 years old, has two grown-up kids and her husband works in the prison service.
Something wrong, David?

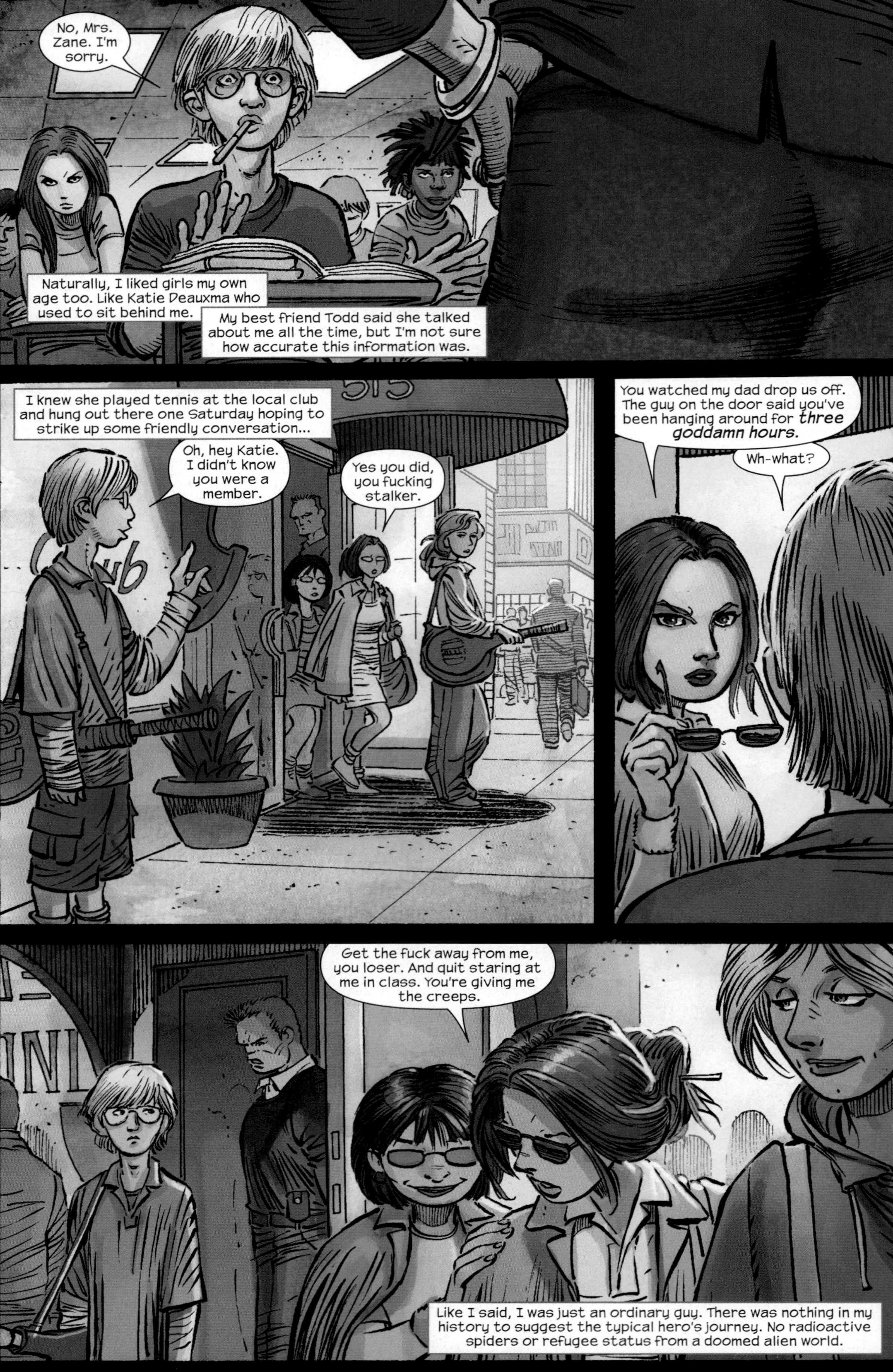
No, Mrs. Zane. I'm sorry.
Naturally, I liked girls my own age too. Like Katie Deauxma who used to sit behind me.
My best friend Todd said she talked about me all the time, but I'm not sure how accurate this information was.
I knew she played tennis at the local club and hung out there one Saturday hoping to strike up some friendly conversation...
Oh, hey Katie. I didn't know you were a member.
Yes you did, you fucking stalker.
You watched my dad drop us off. The guy on the door said you've been hanging around for *three goddamn hours.*
Wh-what?
Get the fuck away from me, you loser. And quit staring at me in class. You're giving me the creeps.
Like I said, I was just an ordinary guy. There was nothing in my history to suggest the typical hero's journey. No radioactive spiders or refugee status from a doomed alien world.

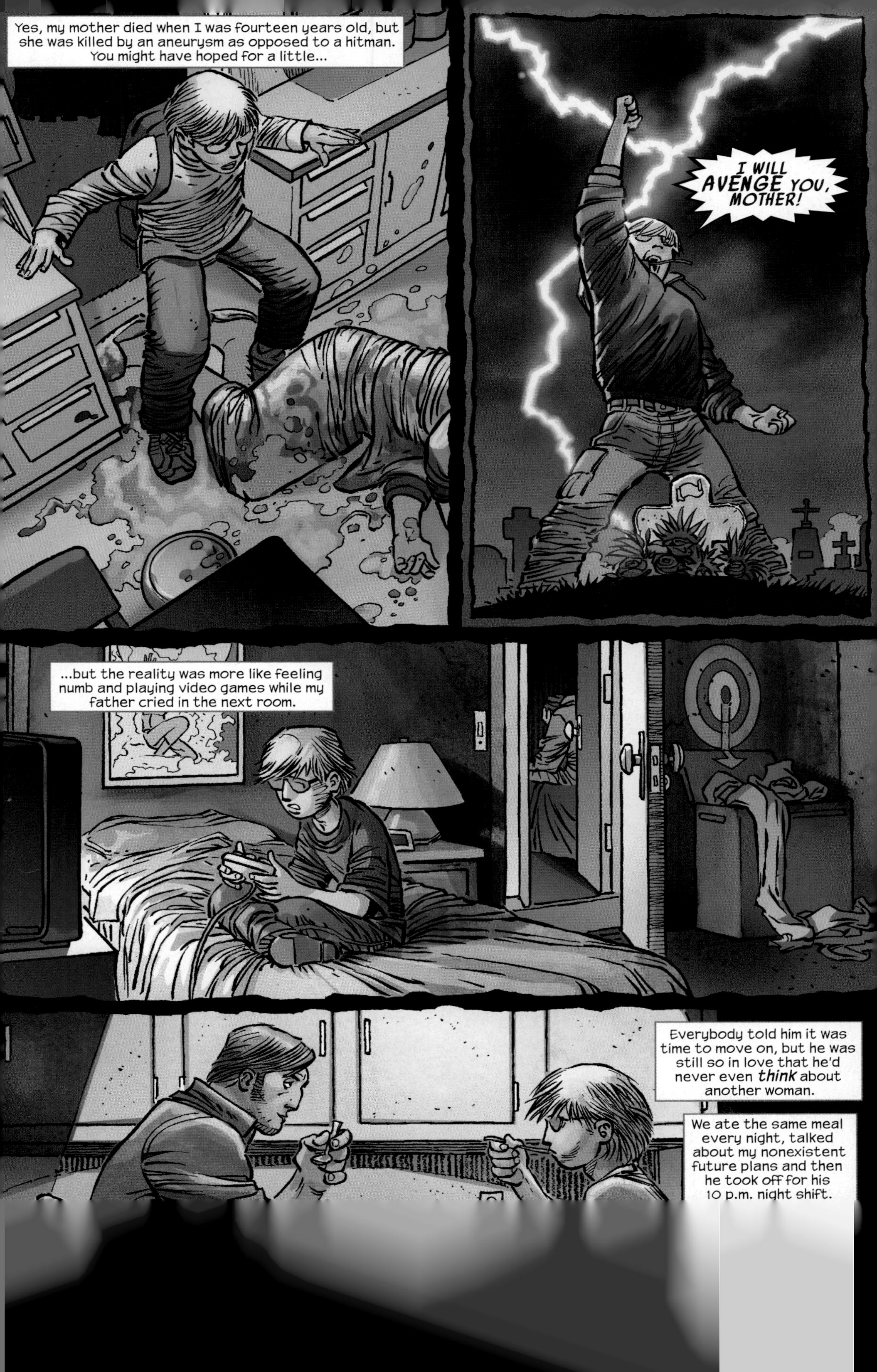
Yes, my mother died when I was fourteen years old, but she was killed by an aneurysm as opposed to a hitman. You might have hoped for a little...
I WILL AVENGE YOU, MOTHER!
...but the reality was more like feeling numb and playing video games while my father cried in the next room.
Everybody told him it was time to move on, but he was still so in love that he'd never even think about another woman.
We ate the same meal every night, talked about my nonexistent future plans and then he took off for his 10 p.m. night shift.

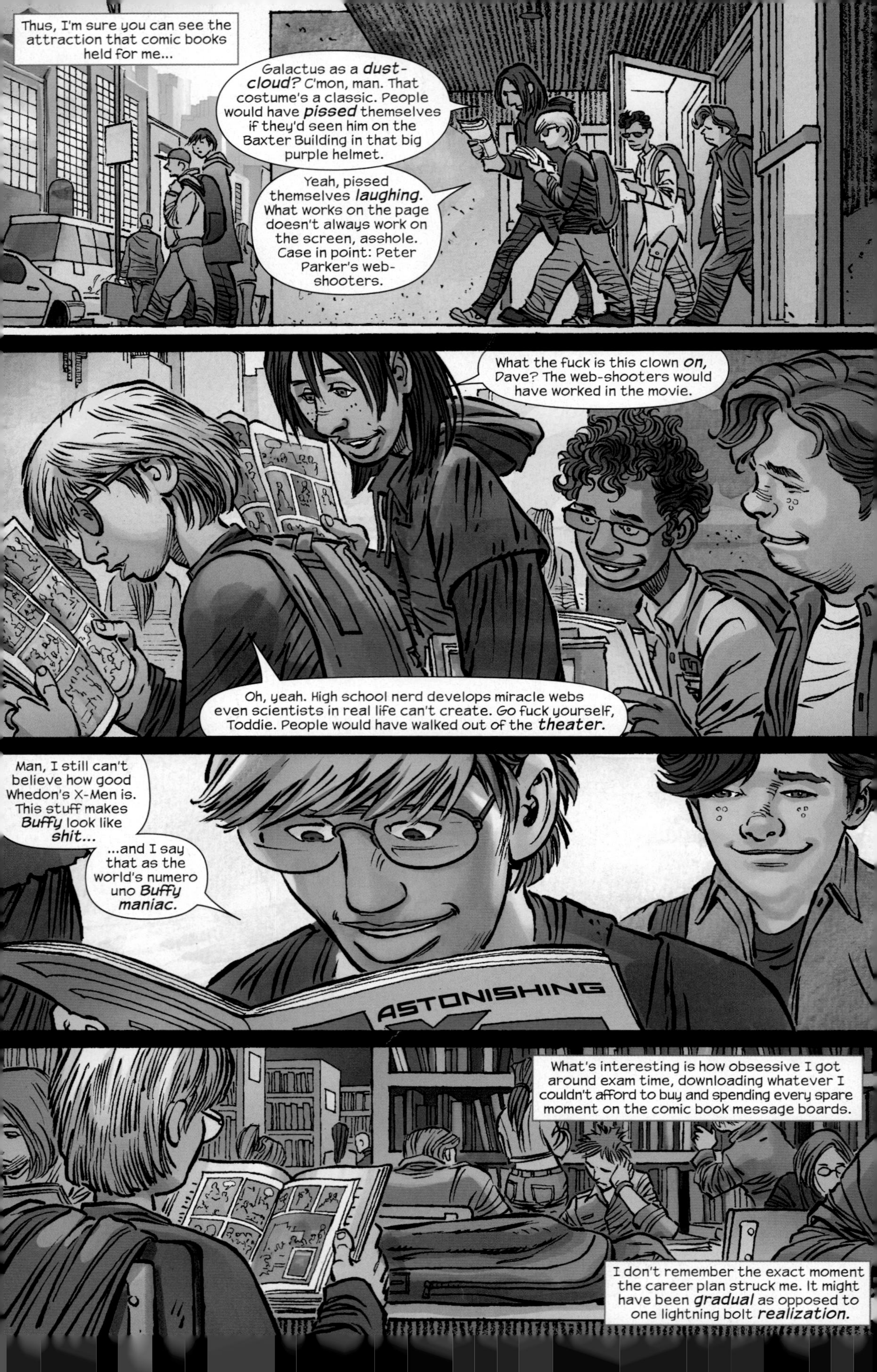

Thus, I'm sure you can see the attraction that comic books held for me...
Galactus as a dust-cloud? C'mon, man. That costume's a classic. People would have pissed themselves if they'd seen him on the Baxter Building in that big purple helmet.
Yeah, pissed themselves laughing. What works on the page doesn't always work on the screen, asshole. Case in point: Peter Parker's web-shooters.
What the fuck is this clown on, Dave? The web-shooters would have worked in the movie.
Oh, yeah. High school nerd develops miracle webs even scientists in real life can't create. Go fuck yourself, Toddie. People would have walked out of the theater.
Man, I still can't believe how good Whedon's X-Men is. This stuff makes Buffy look like shit...
...and I say that as the world's numero uno Buffy maniac.
ASTONISHING
What's interesting is how obsessive I got around exam time, downloading whatever I couldn't afford to buy and spending every spare moment on the comic book message boards.
I don't remember the exact moment the career plan struck me. It might have been gradual as opposed to one lightning bolt realization.

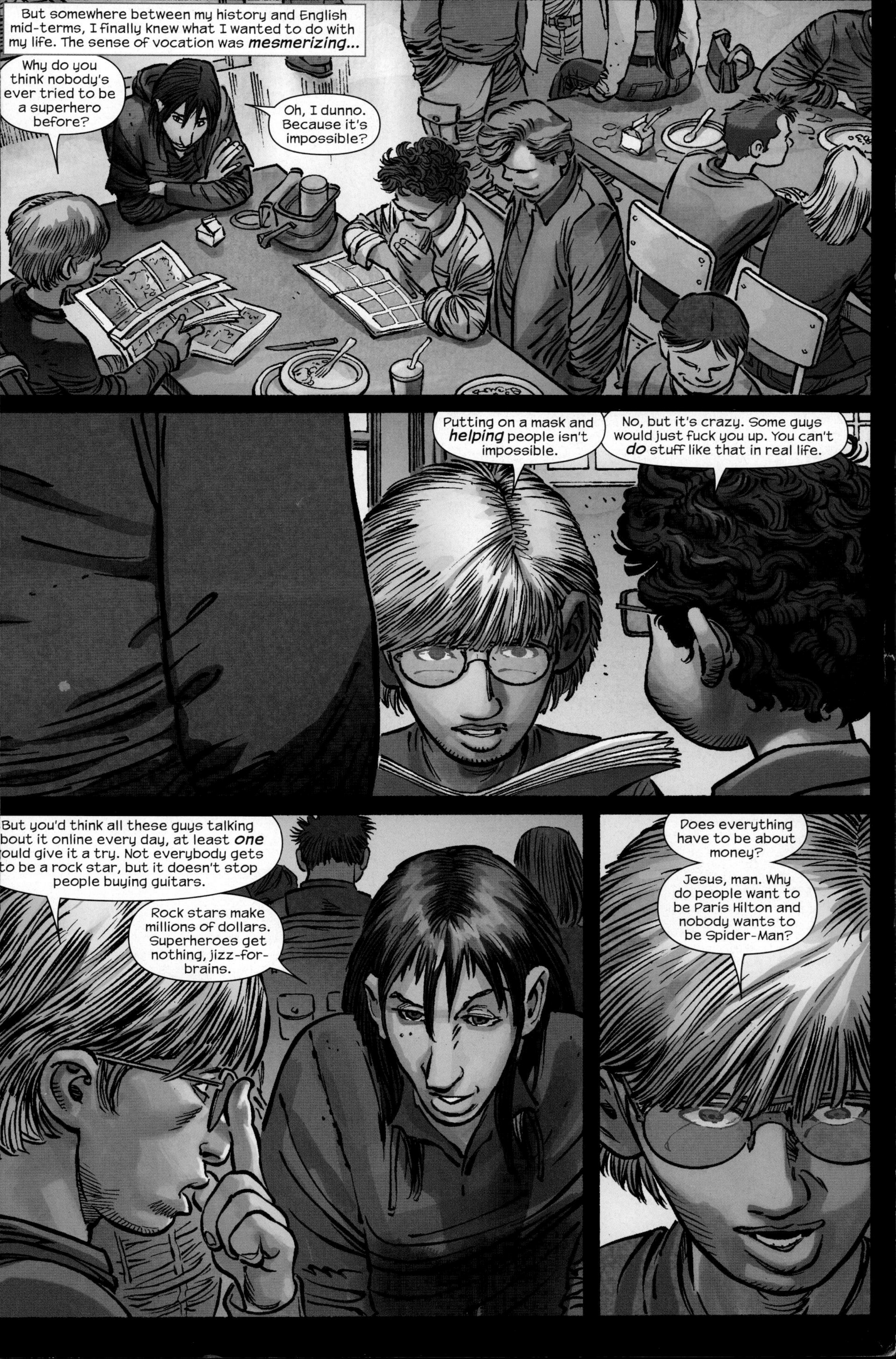
But somewhere between my history and English mid-terms, I finally knew what I wanted to do with my life. The sense of vocation was *mesmerizing...*
Why do you think nobody's ever tried to be a superhero before?
Oh, I dunno. Because it's impossible?
Putting on a mask and *helping* people isn't impossible.
No, but it's crazy. Some guys would just fuck you up. You can't *do* stuff like that in real life.
But you'd think all these guys talking bout it online every day, at least *one* ould give it a try. Not everybody gets to be a rock star, but it doesn't stop people buying guitars.
Rock stars make millions of dollars. Superheroes get nothing, jizz-for-brains.
Does everything have to be about money?
Jesus, man. Why do people want to be Paris Hilton and nobody wants to be Spider-Man?

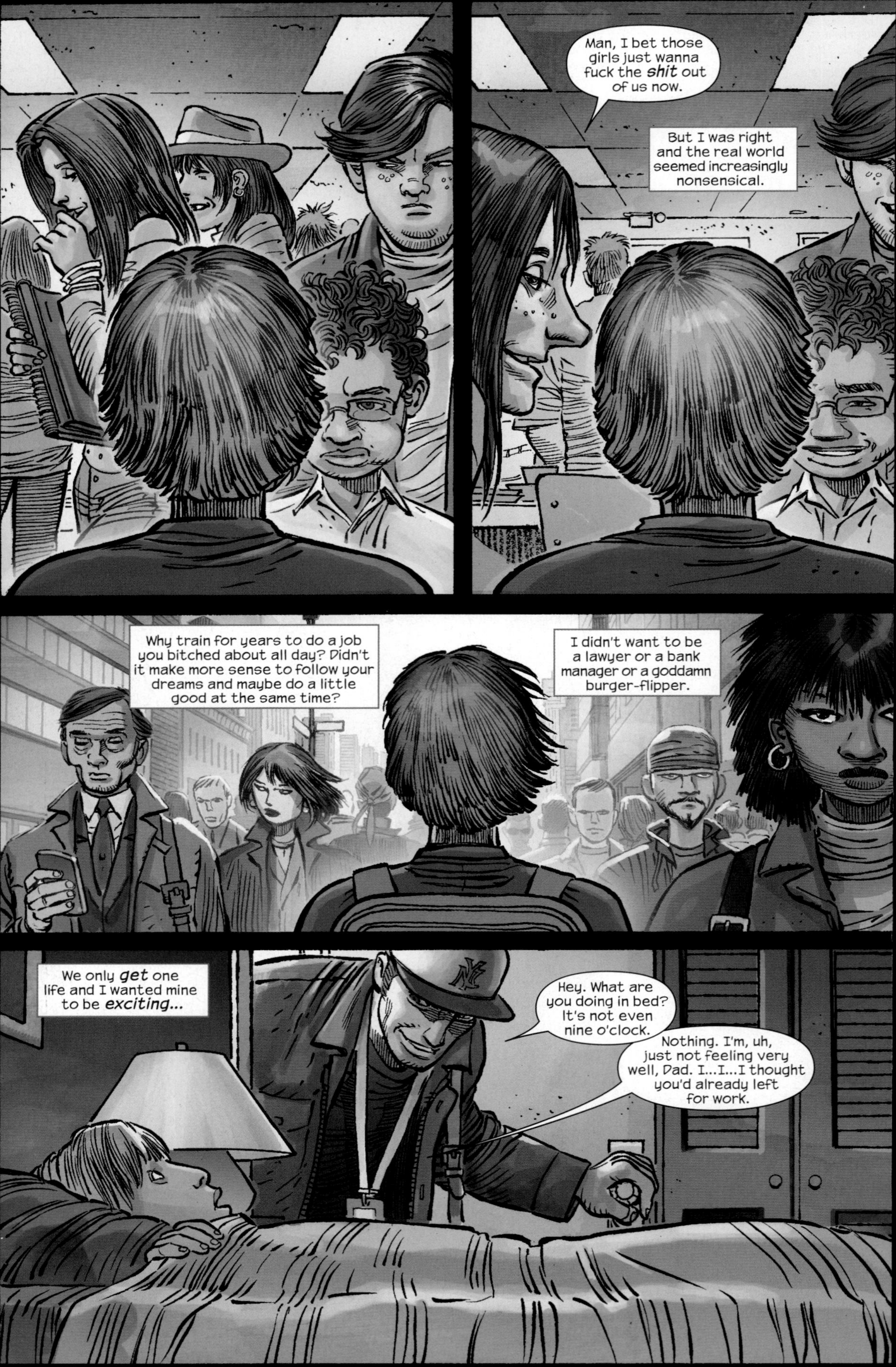
Man, I bet those girls just wanna fuck the *shit* out of us now.
But I was right and the real world seemed increasingly nonsensical.
Why train for years to do a job you bitched about all day? Didn't it make more sense to follow your dreams and maybe do a little good at the same time?
I didn't want to be a lawyer or a bank manager or a goddamn burger-flipper.
We only *get* one life and I wanted mine to be *exciting...*
Hey. What are you doing in bed? It's not even nine o'clock.
Nothing. I'm, uh, just not feeling very well, Dad. I...I...I thought you'd already left for work.
NY

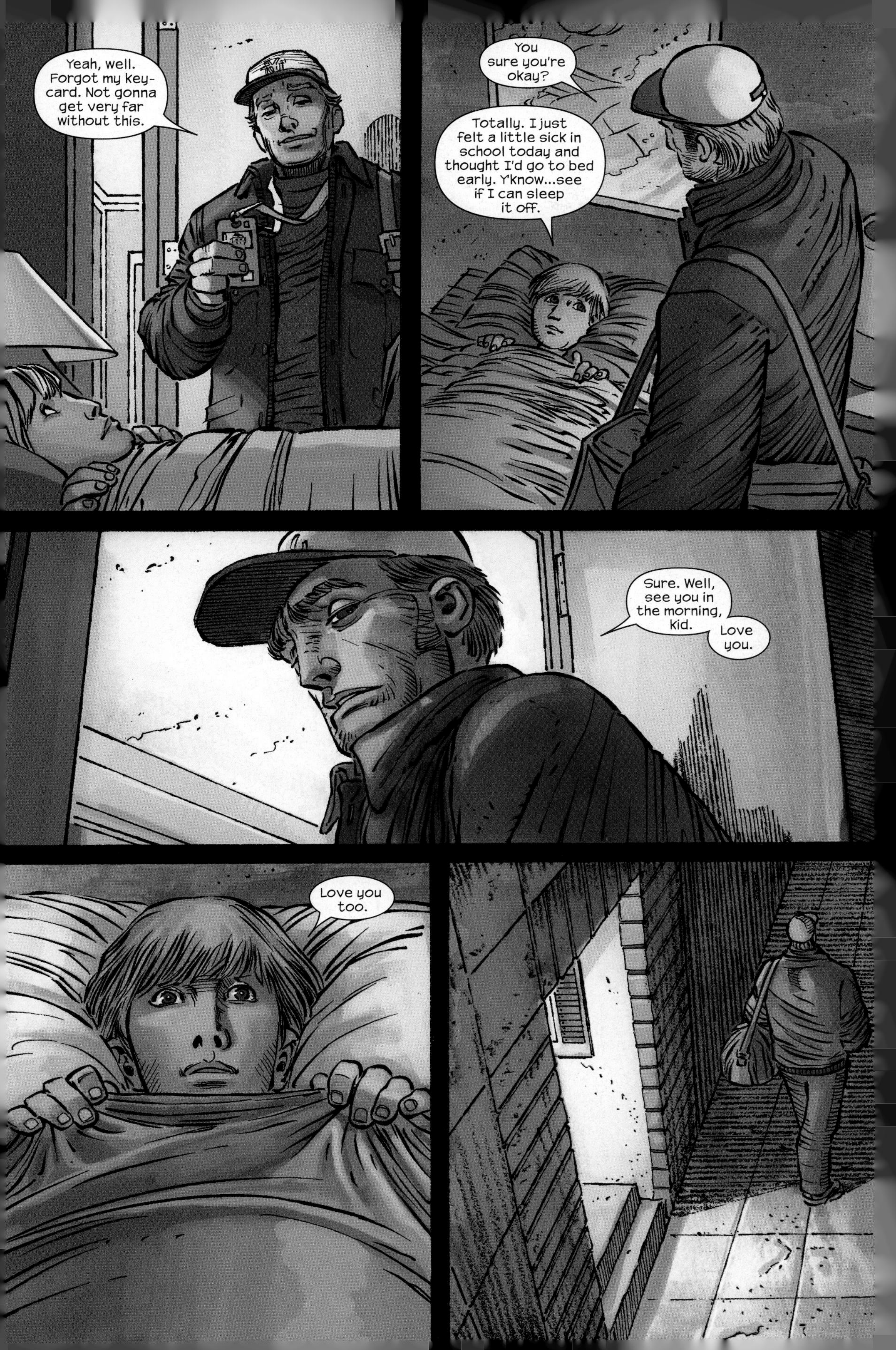

Yeah, well. Forgot my key-card. Not gonna get very far without this.
You sure you're okay?
Totally. I just felt a little sick in school today and thought I'd go to bed early. Y'know...see if I can sleep it off.
Sure. Well, see you in the morning, kid.
Love you.
Love you too.

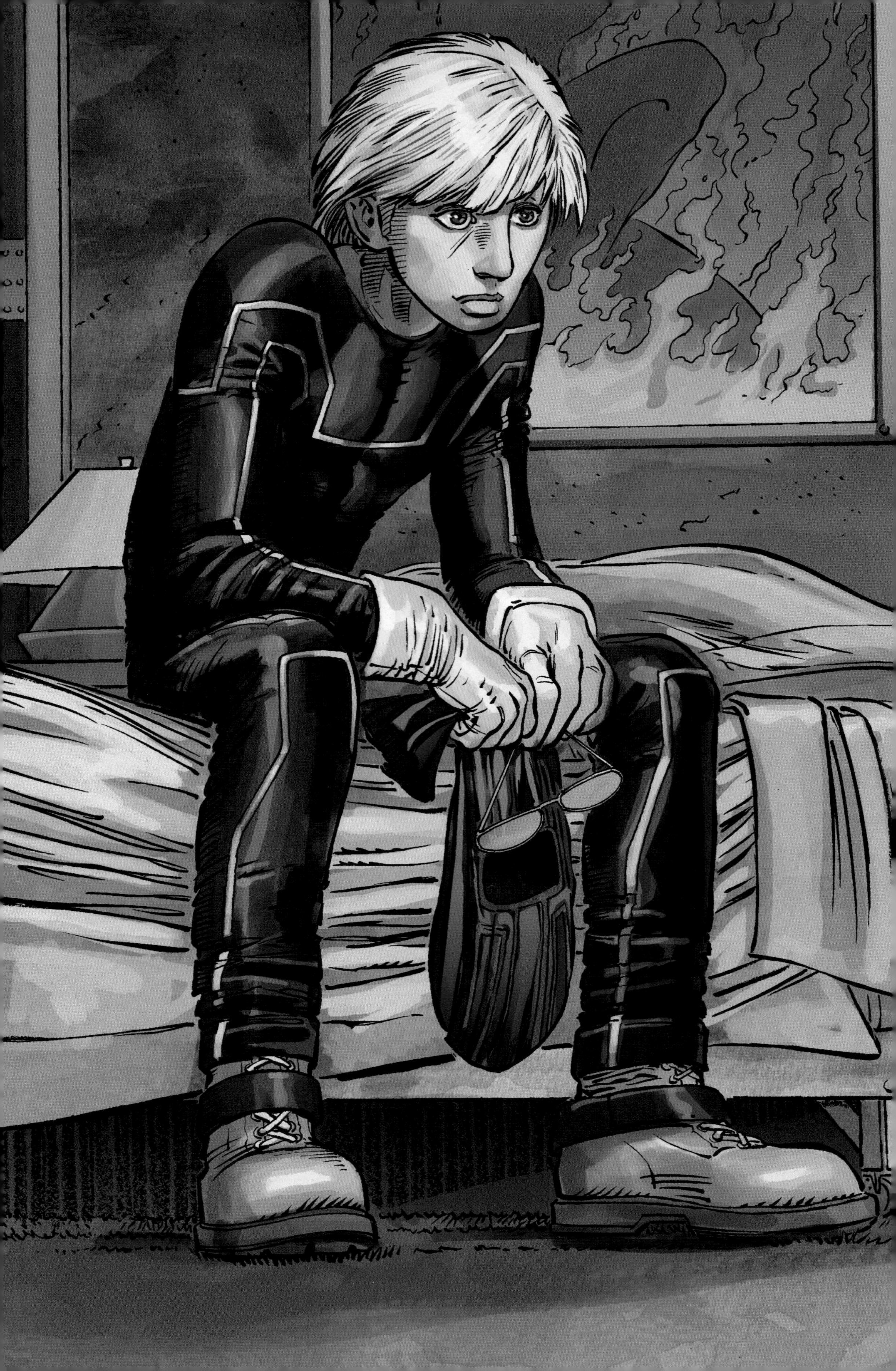

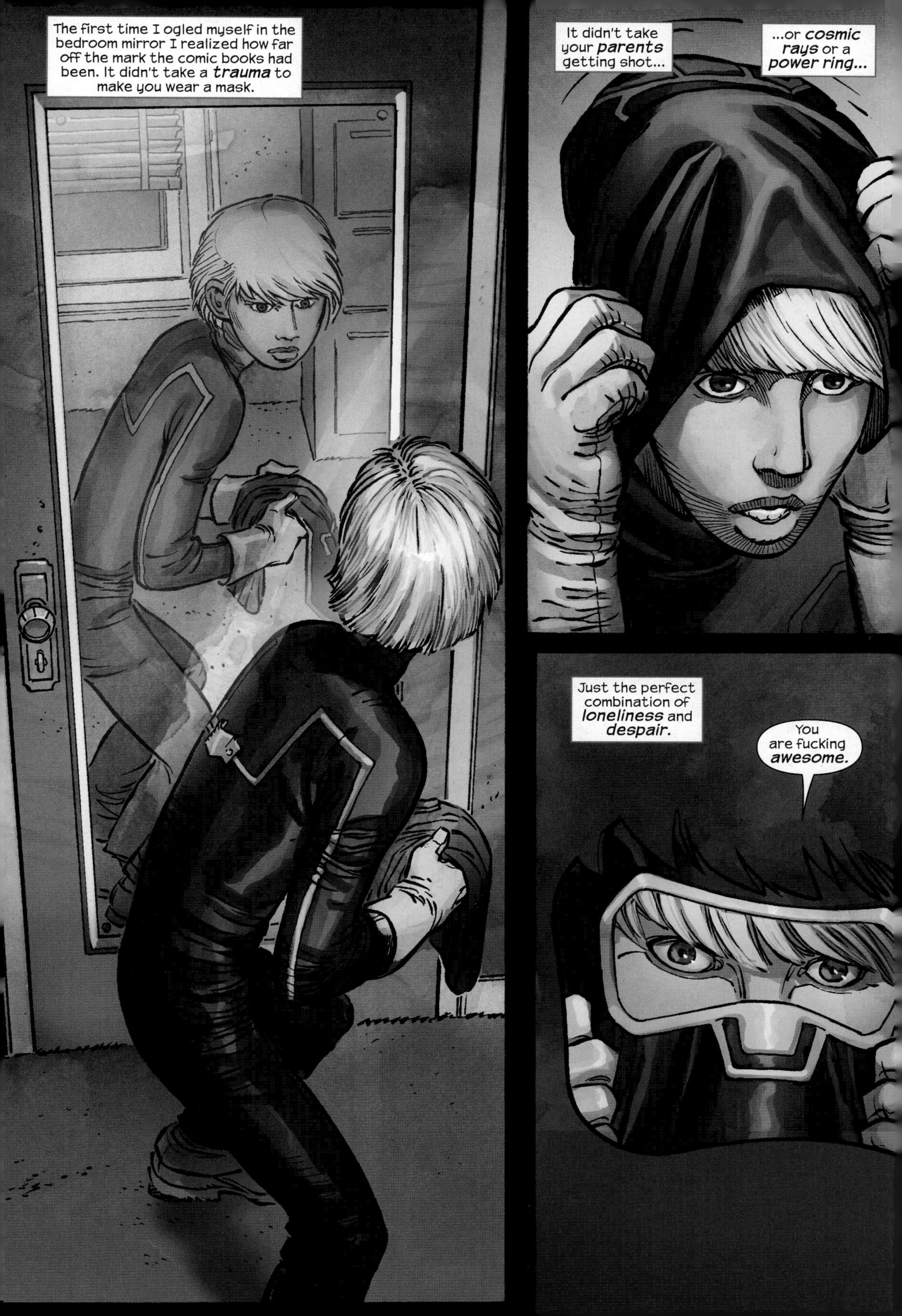
The first time I ogled myself in the bedroom mirror I realized how far off the mark the comic books had been. It didn't take a *trauma* to make you wear a mask.
It didn't take your *parents* getting shot...
...or *cosmic rays* or a *power ring*...
Just the perfect combination of *loneliness* and *despair*.
You are fucking *awesome*.

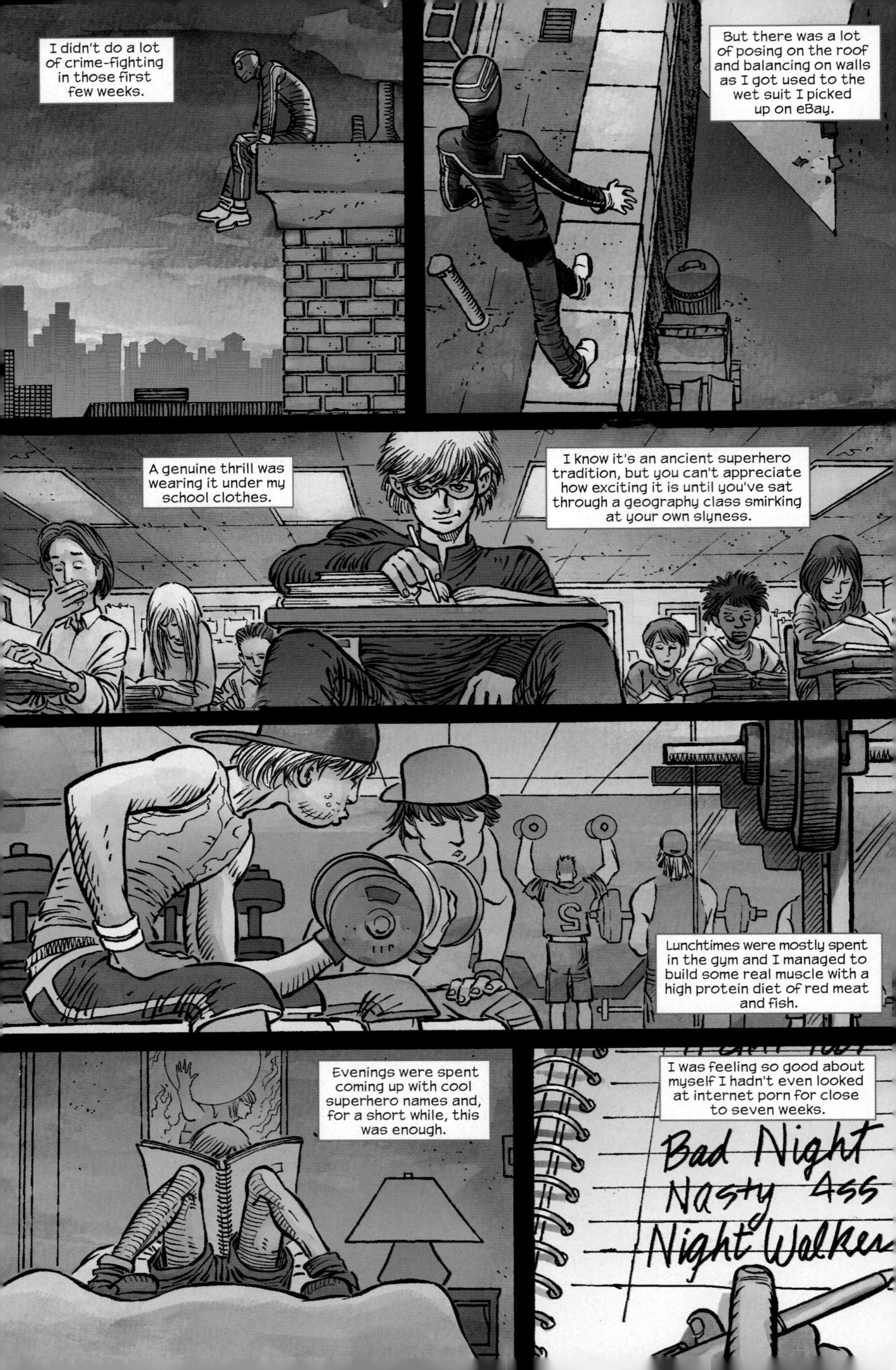

I didn't do a lot of crime-fighting in those first few weeks.
But there was a lot of posing on the roof and balancing on walls as I got used to the wet suit I picked up on eBay.
A genuine thrill was wearing it under my school clothes.
I know it's an ancient superhero tradition, but you can't appreciate how exciting it is until you've sat through a geography class smirking at your own slyness.
Lunchtimes were mostly spent in the gym and I managed to build some real muscle with a high protein diet of red meat and fish.
Evenings were spent coming up with cool superhero names and, for a short while, this was enough.
I was feeling so good about myself I hadn't even looked at internet porn for close to seven weeks.
Bad Night
Nasty Ass
Night Walker

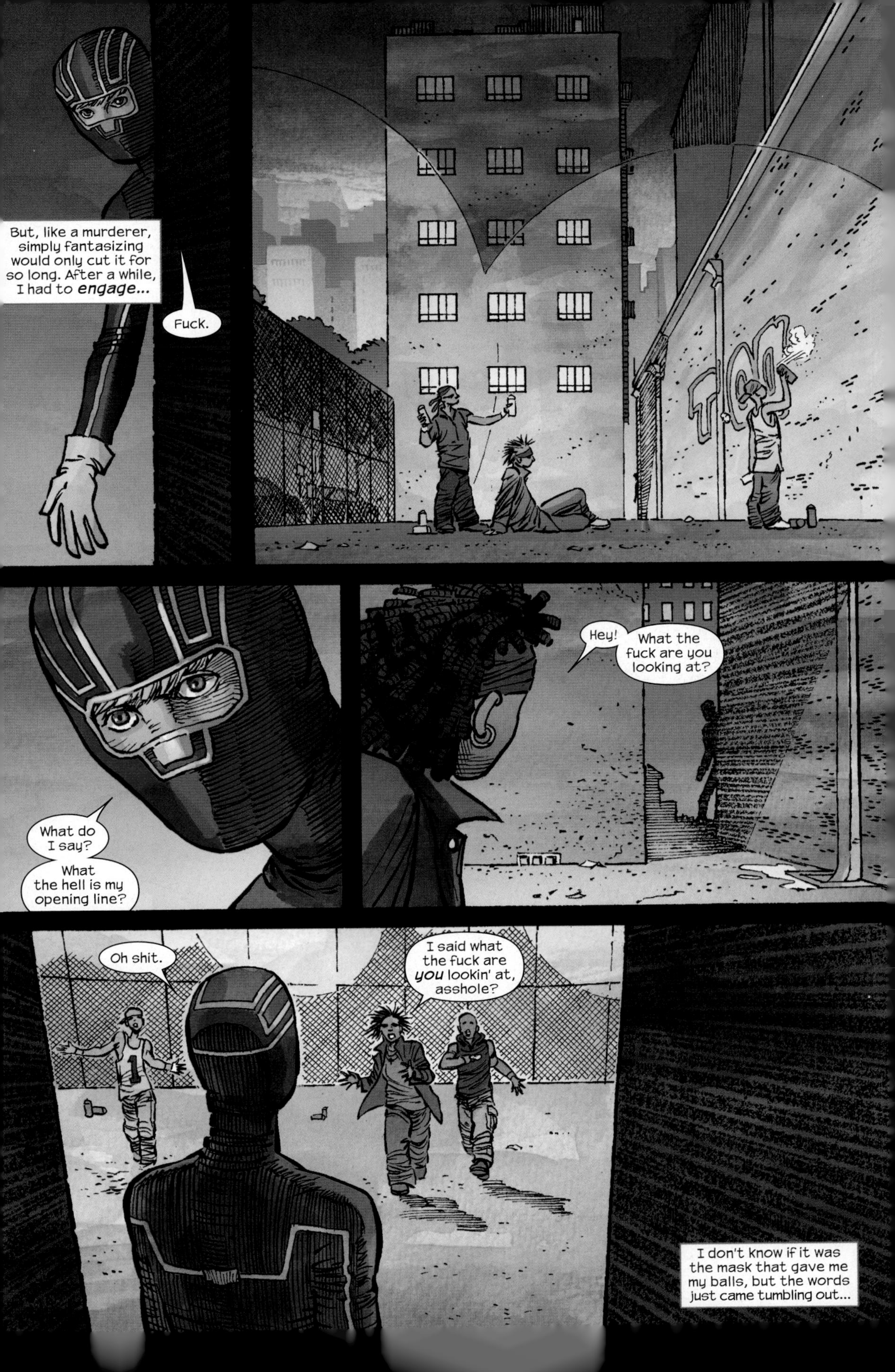

But, like a murderer, simply fantasizing would only cut it for so long. After a while, I had to *engage*...
Fuck.
What do I say?
What the hell is my opening line?
Hey!
What the fuck are you looking at?
Oh shit.
I said what the fuck are *you* lookin' at, asshole?
I don't know if it was the mask that gave me my balls, but the words just came tumbling out...

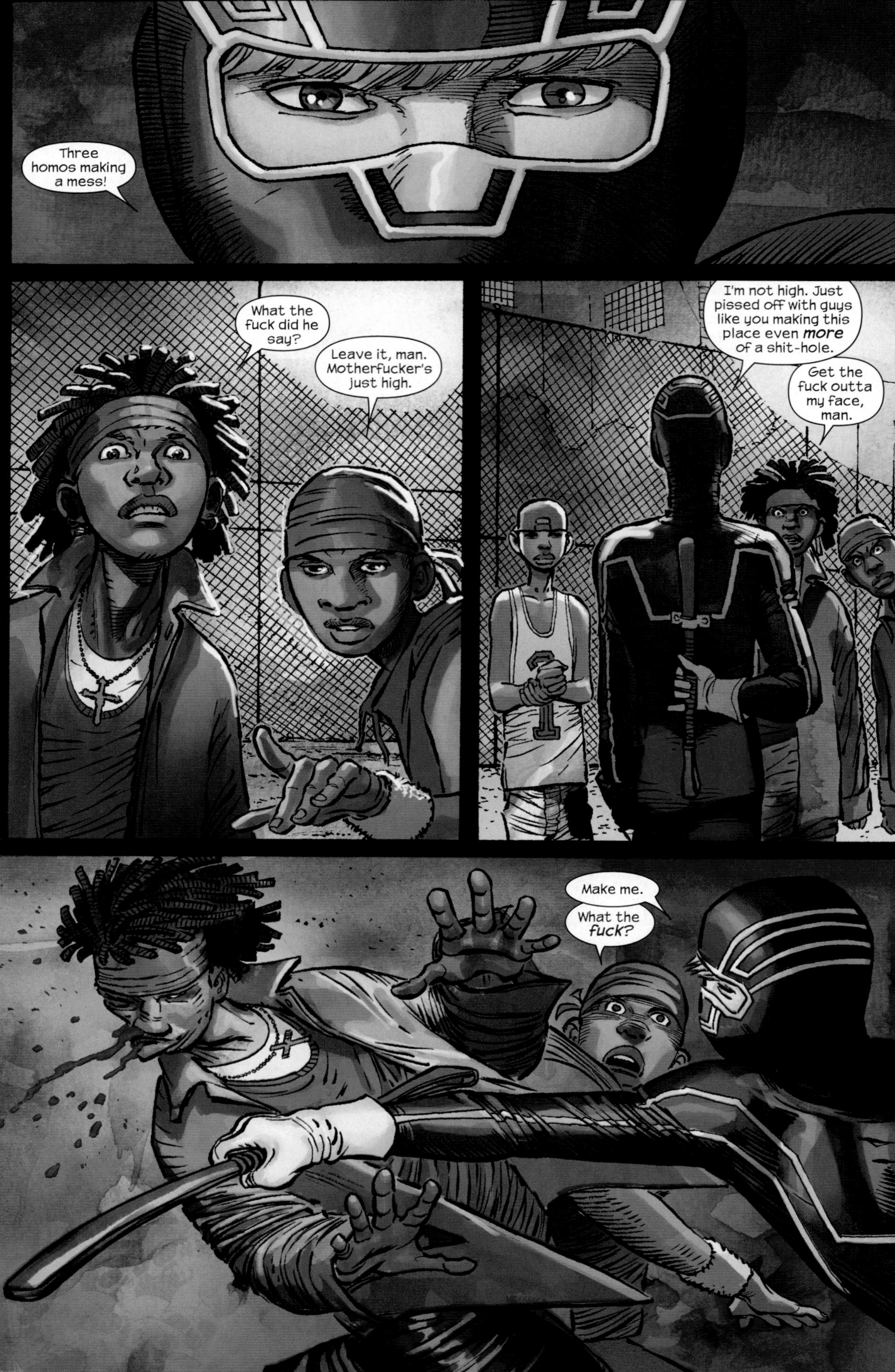
Three homos making a mess!
What the fuck did he say?
Leave it, man. Motherfucker's just high.
I'm not high. Just pissed off with guys like you making this place even *more* of a shit-hole.
Get the fuck outta my face, man.
Make me.
What the *fuck?*

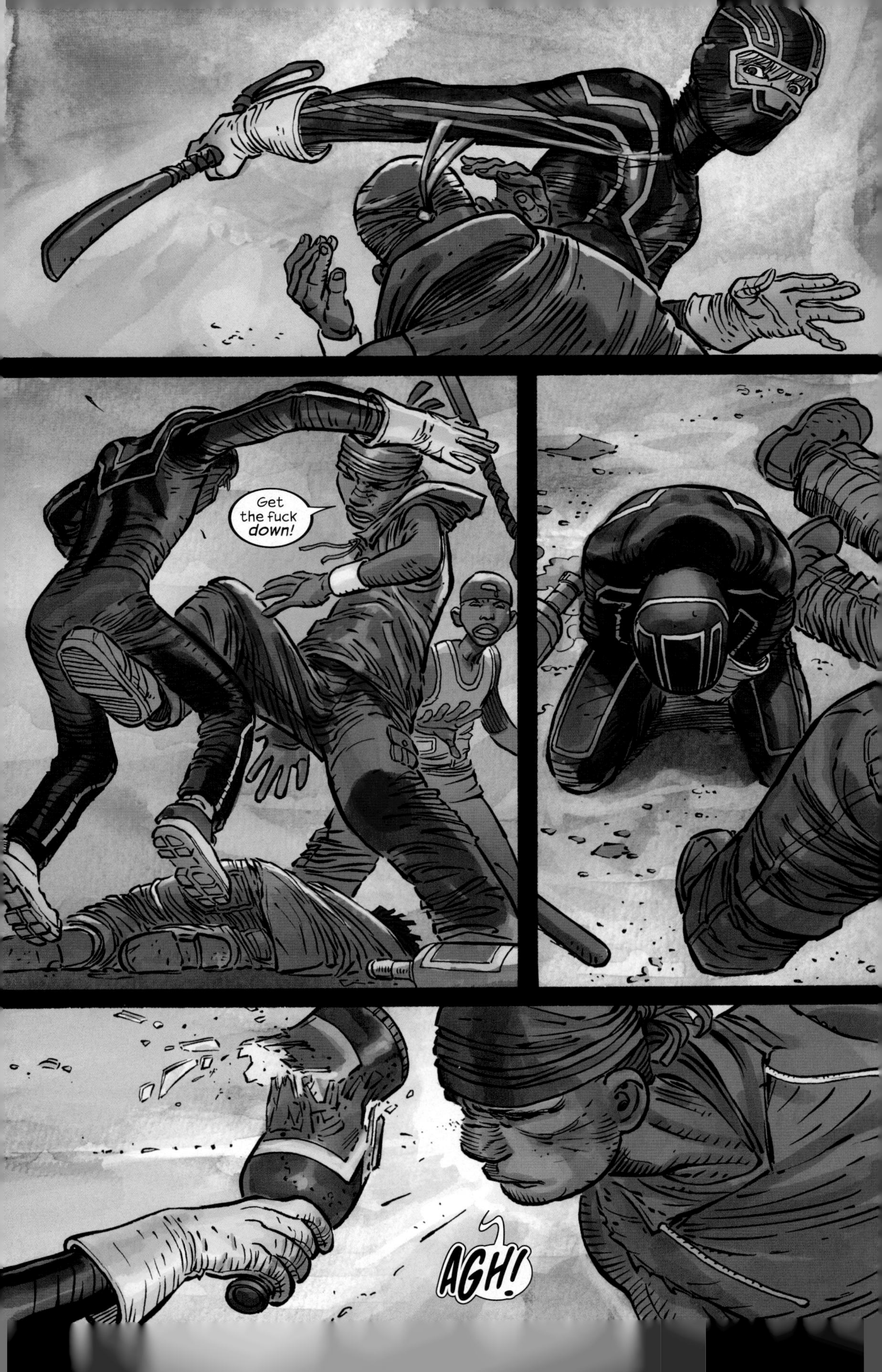

Get the fuck down!
AGH!

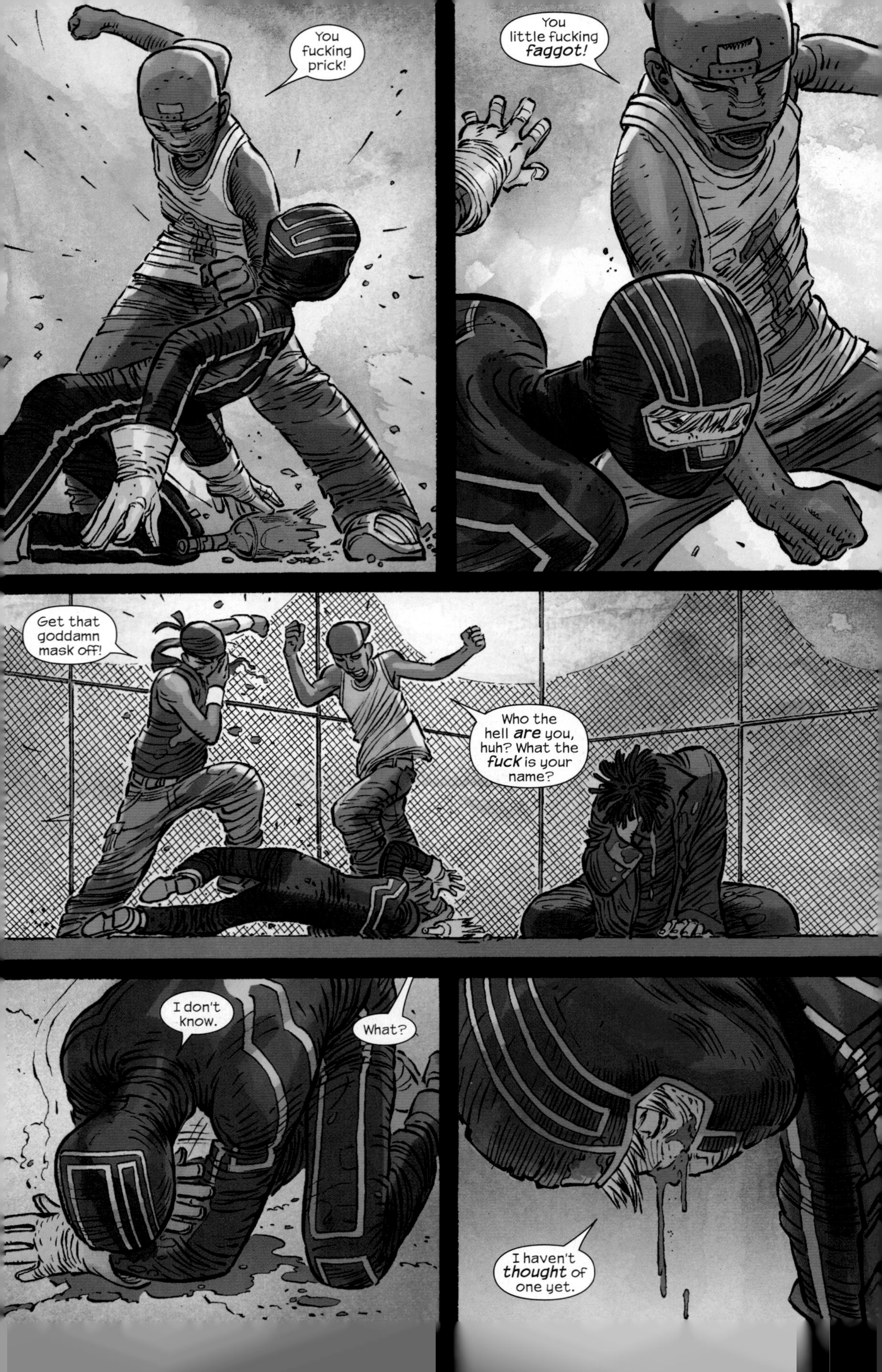
You fucking prick!
You little fucking *faggot!*
Get that goddamn mask off!
Who the hell *are* you, huh? What the *fuck* is your name?
I don't know.
What?
I haven't *thought* of one yet.

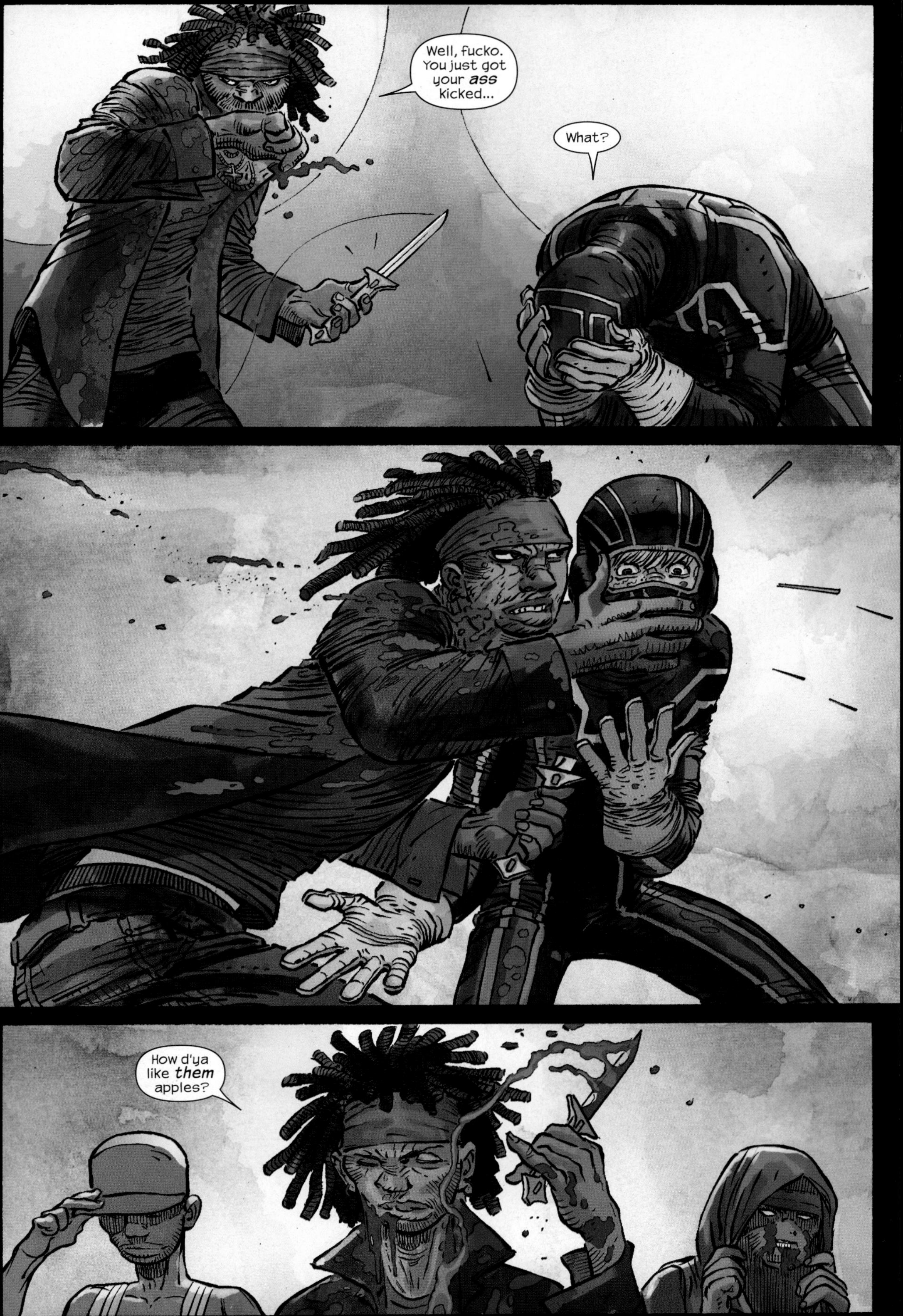
Well, fucko. You just got your *ass* kicked...
What?
How d'ya like *them* apples?

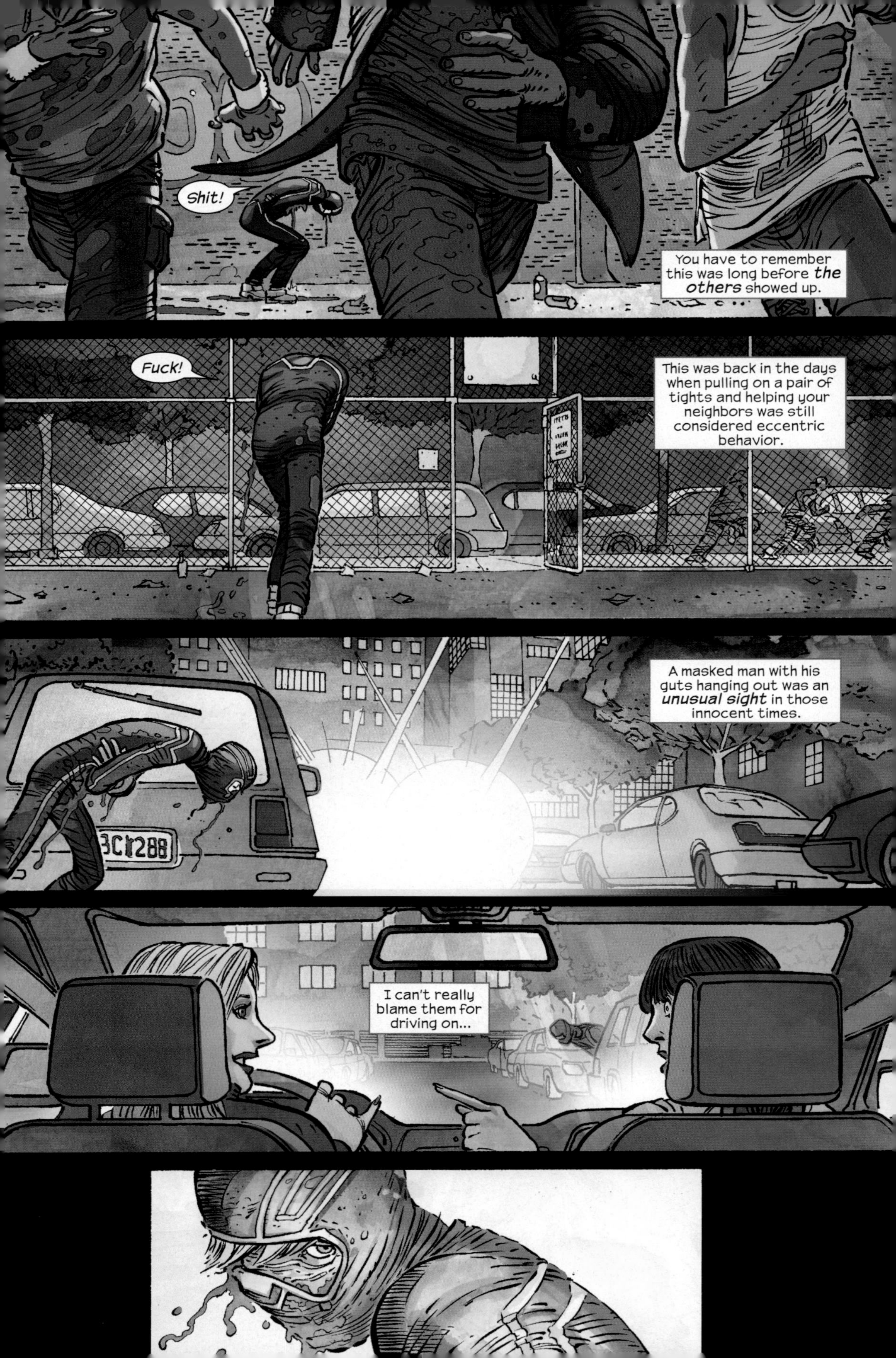
Shit!
You have to remember this was long before *the others* showed up.
Fuck!
This was back in the days when pulling on a pair of tights and helping your neighbors was still considered eccentric behavior.
A masked man with his guts hanging out was an *unusual sight* in those innocent times.
I can't really blame them for driving on...

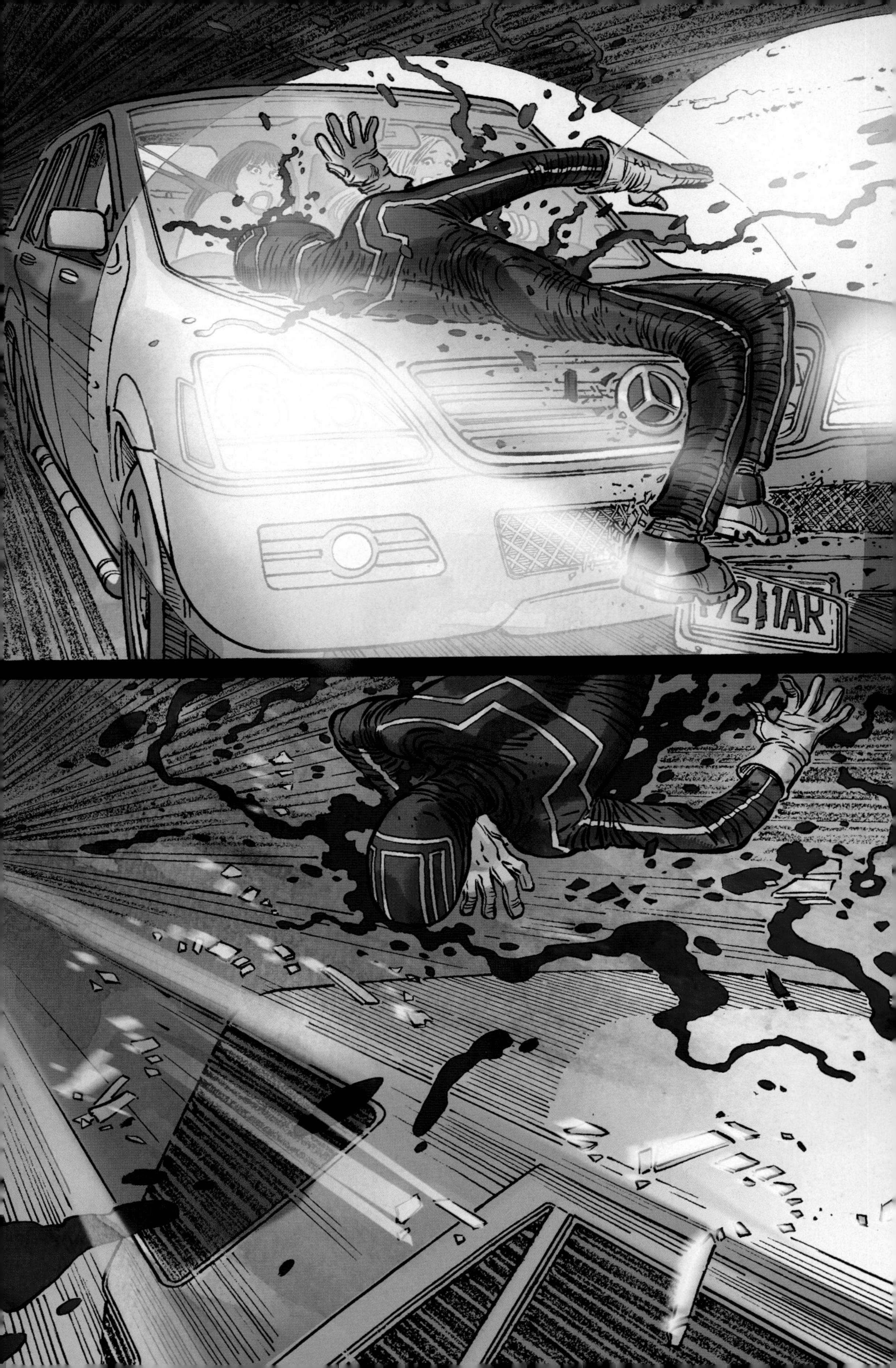

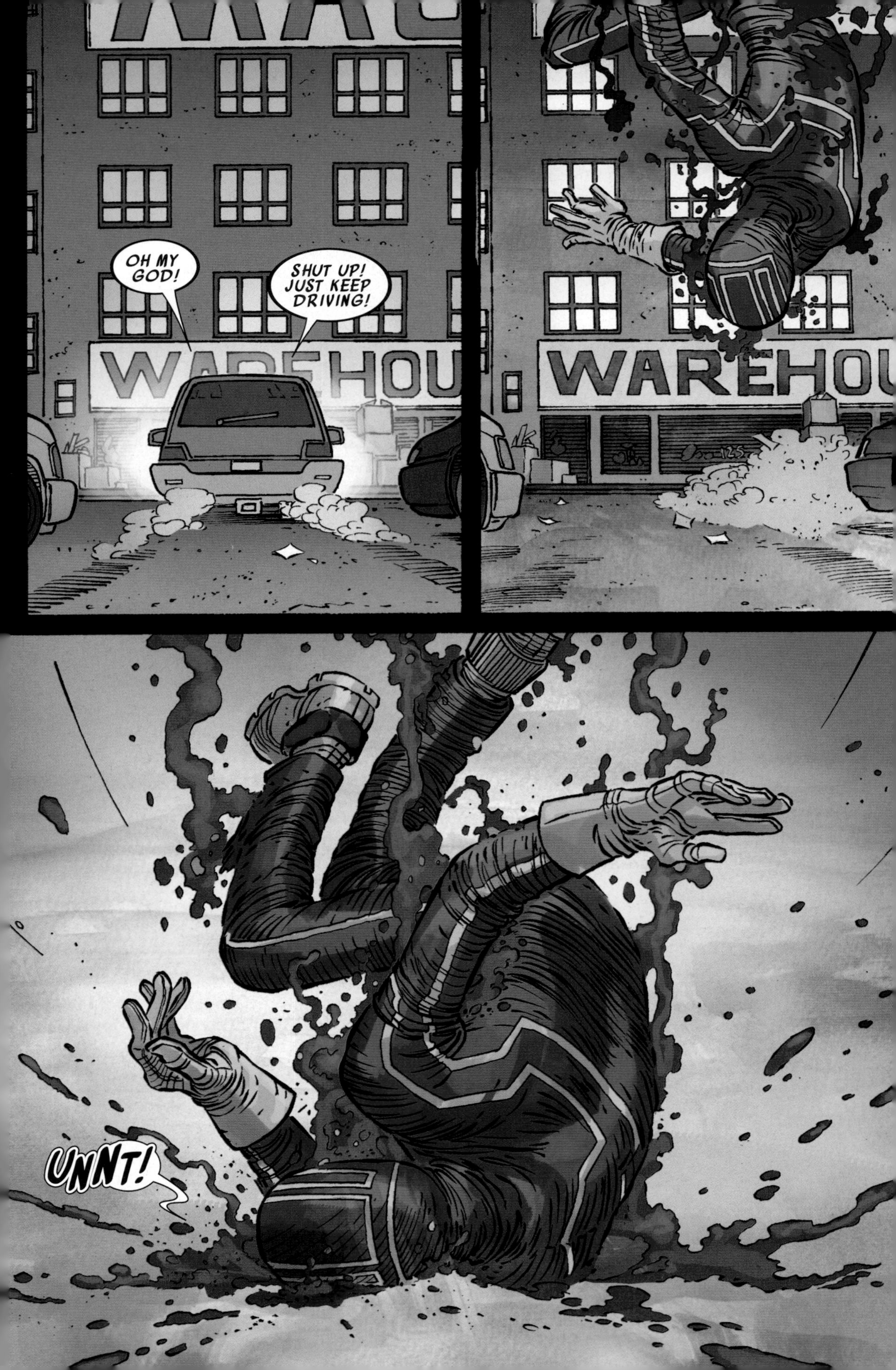
OH MY GOD!
SHUT UP! JUST KEEP DRIVING!
WAREHOU
WAREHOU
UNNT!

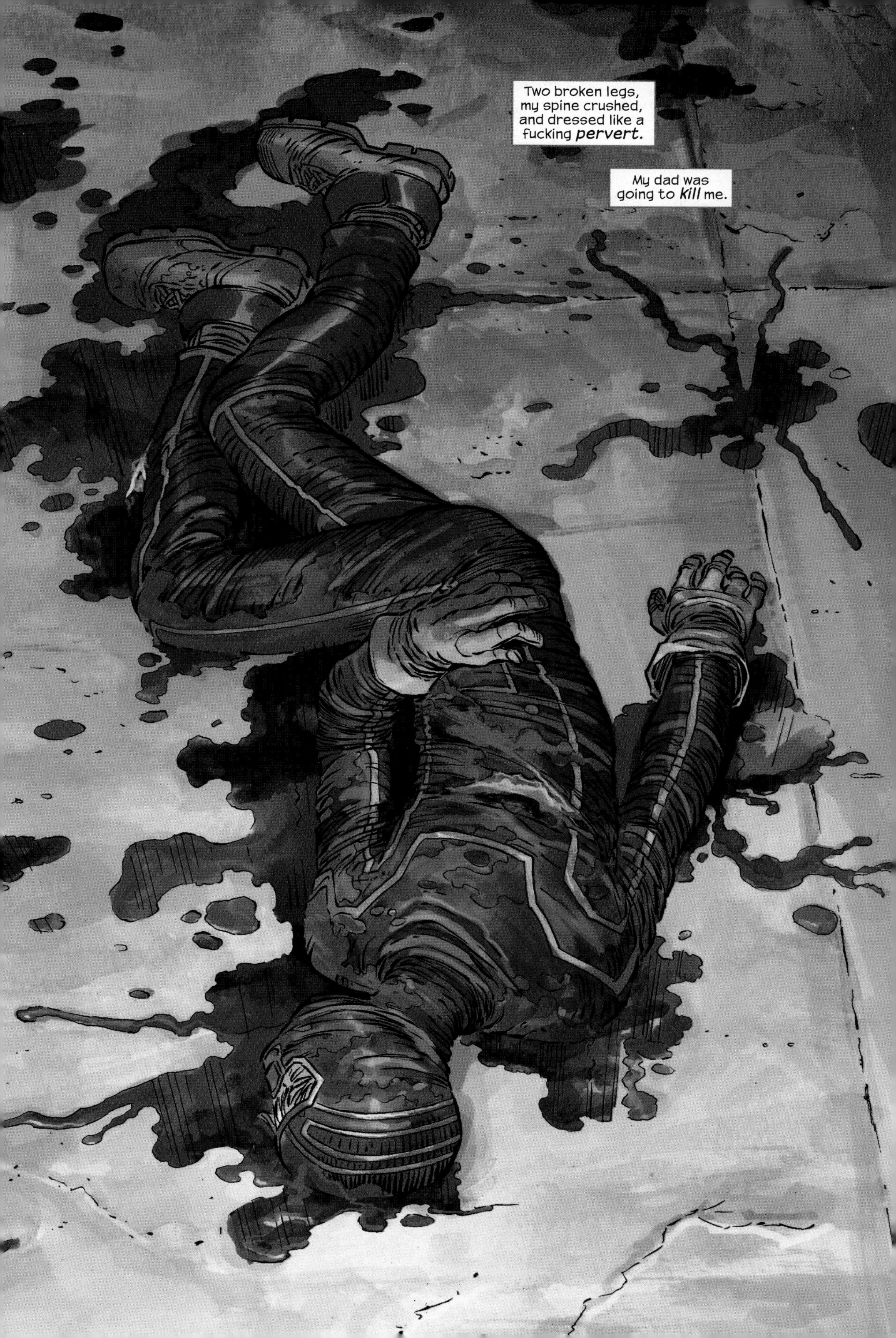
Two broken legs, my spine crushed, and dressed like a fucking *pervert.*
My dad was going to *kill* me.

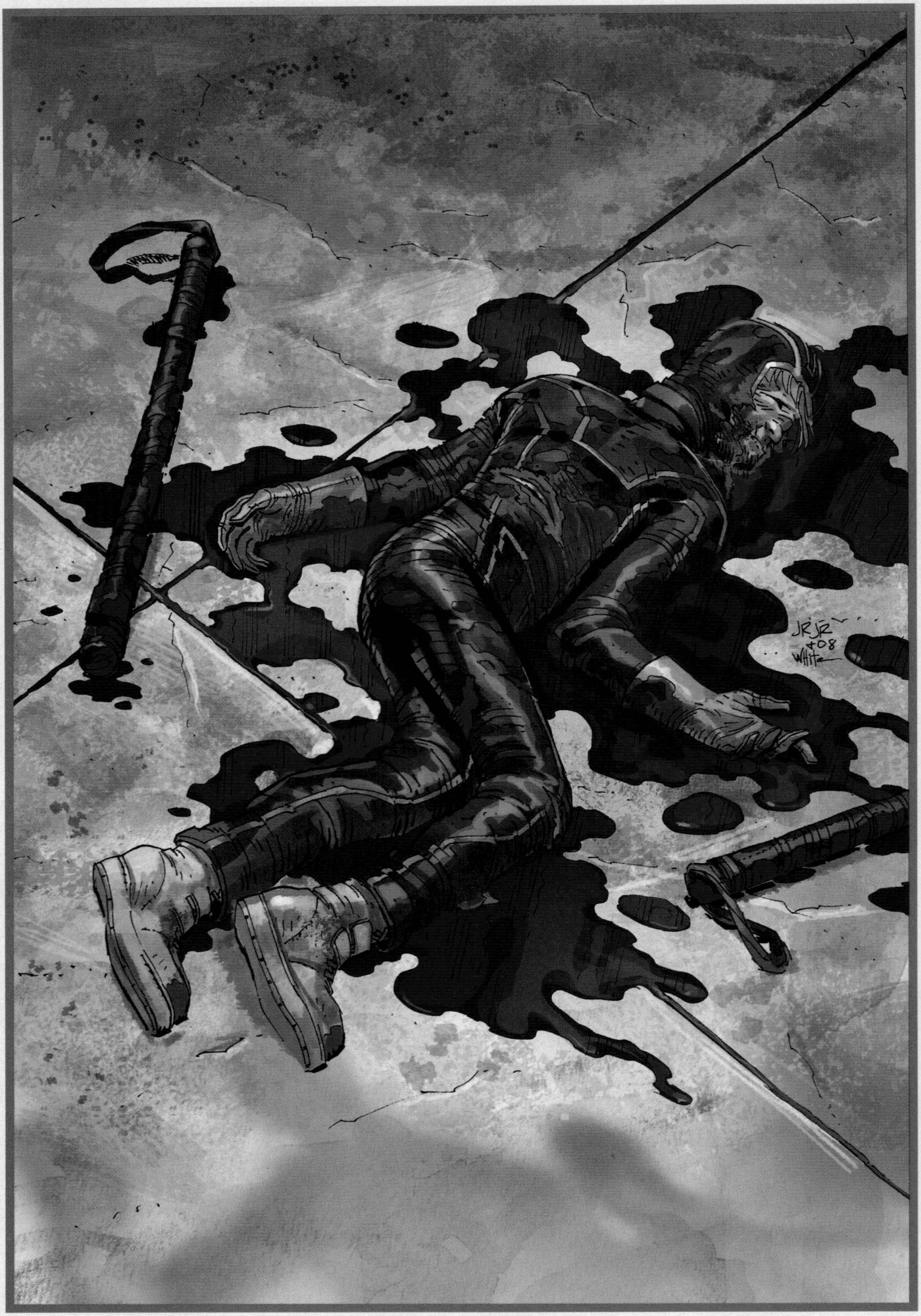

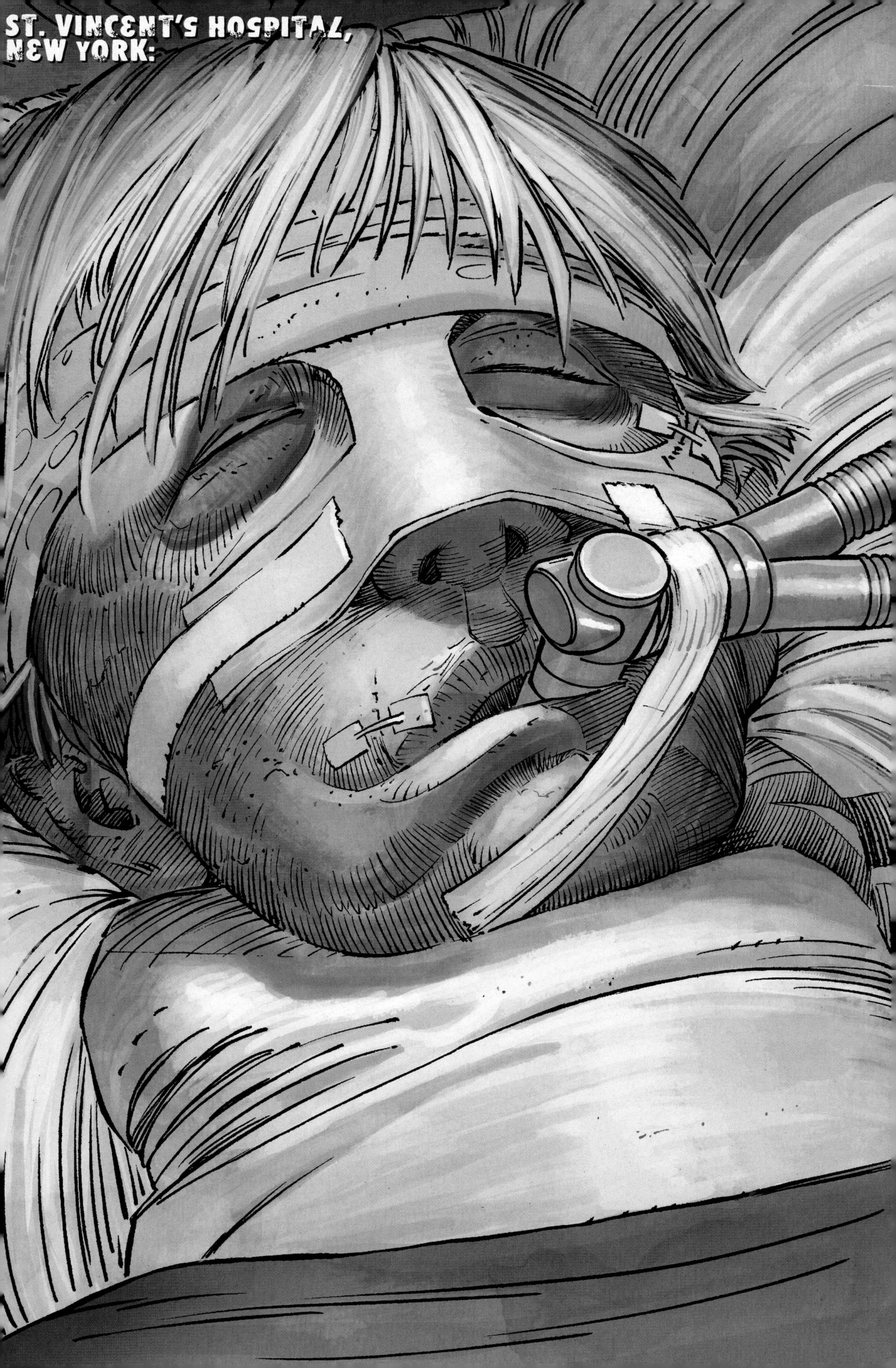
ST. VINCENT'S HOSPITAL, NEW YORK:

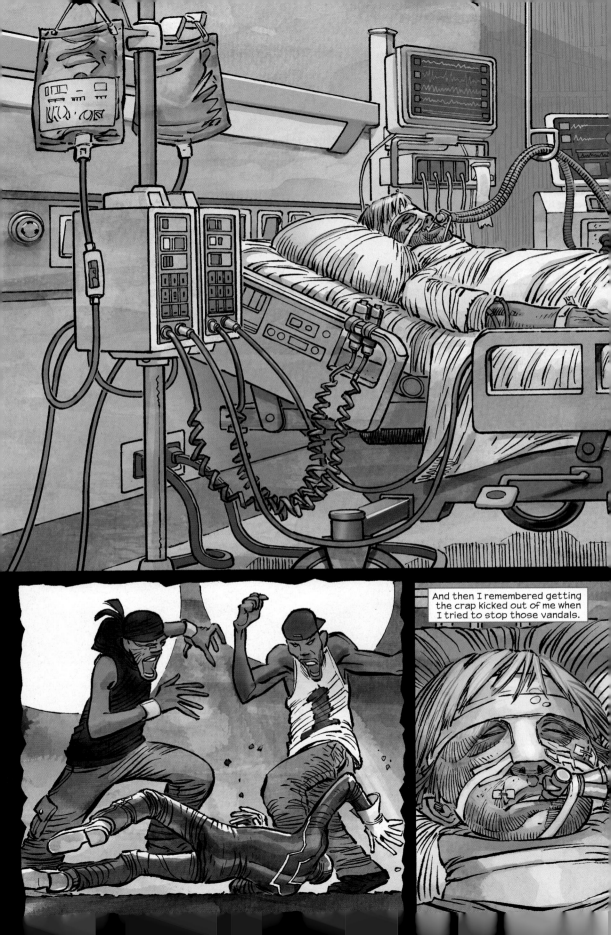

And then I remembered getting the crap kicked out of me when I tried to stop those vandals.

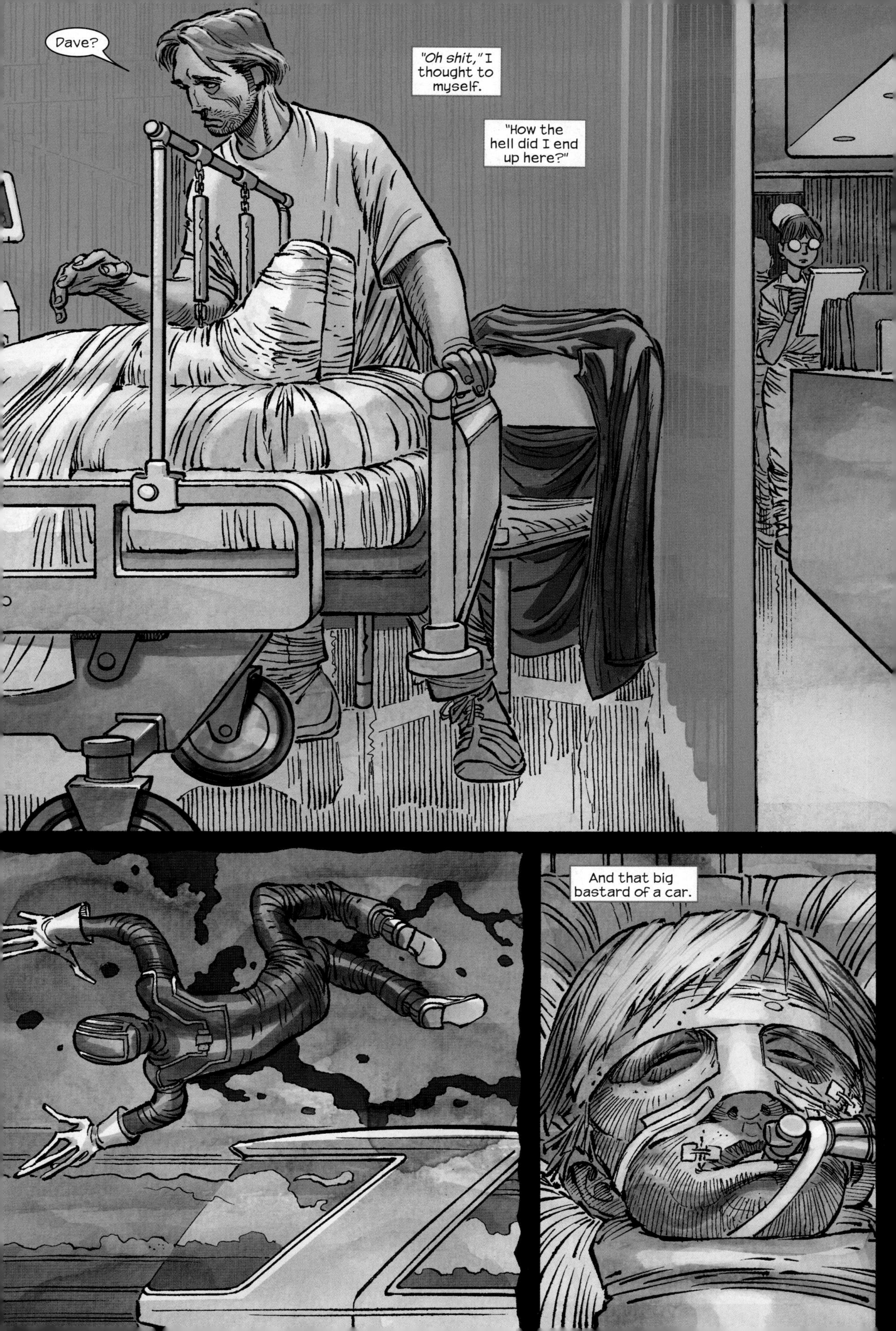

Dave?
"Oh shit," I thought to myself.
"How the hell did I end up here?"
And that big bastard of a car.

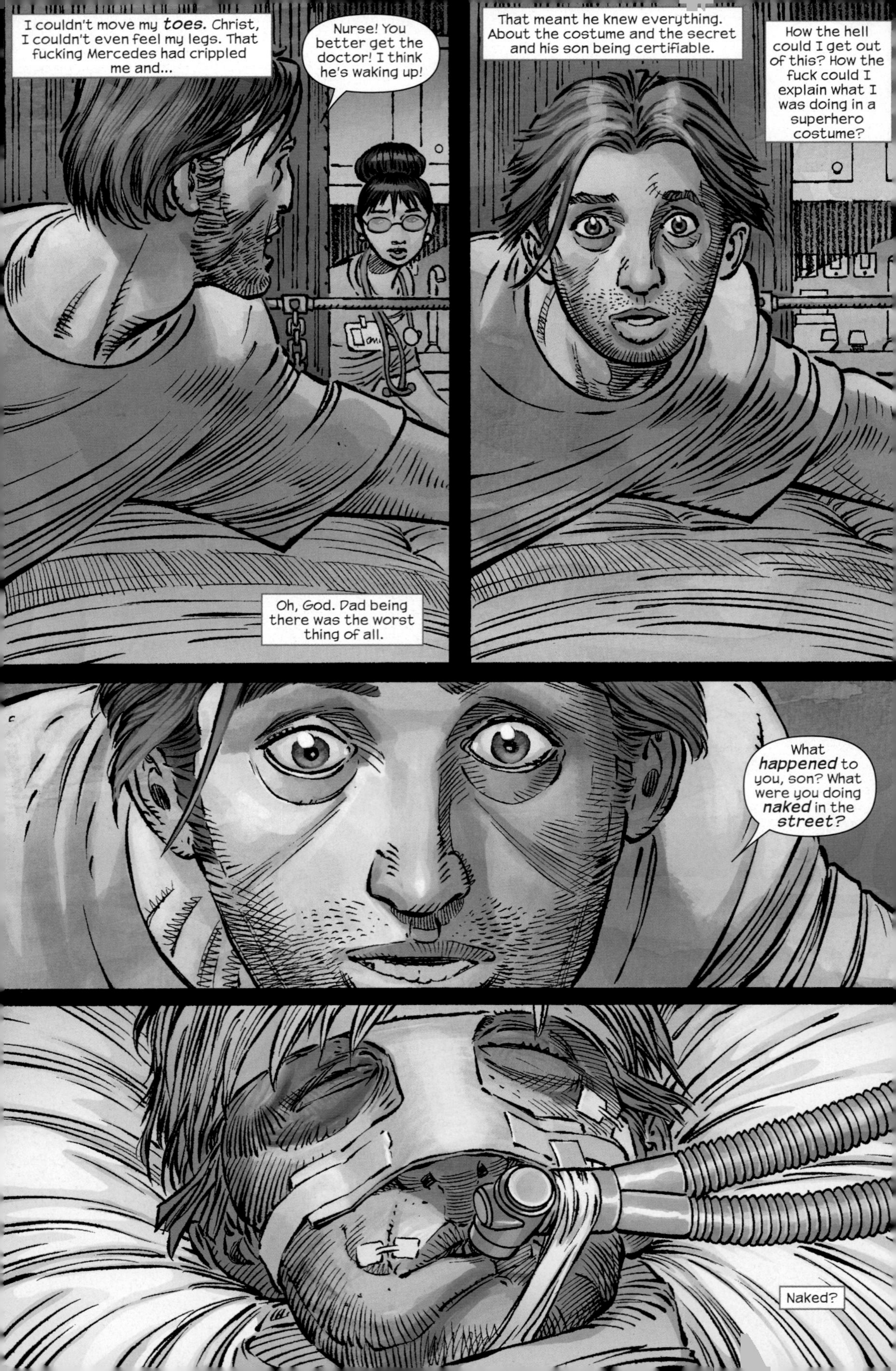
I couldn't move my **toes.** Christ, I couldn't even feel my legs. That fucking Mercedes had crippled me and...
Nurse! You better get the doctor! I think he's waking up!
Oh, God. Dad being there was the worst thing of all.
That meant he knew everything. About the costume and the secret and his son being certifiable.
How the hell could I get out of this? How the fuck could I explain what I was doing in a superhero costume?
What **happened** to you, son? What were you doing **naked** in the **street?**
Naked?

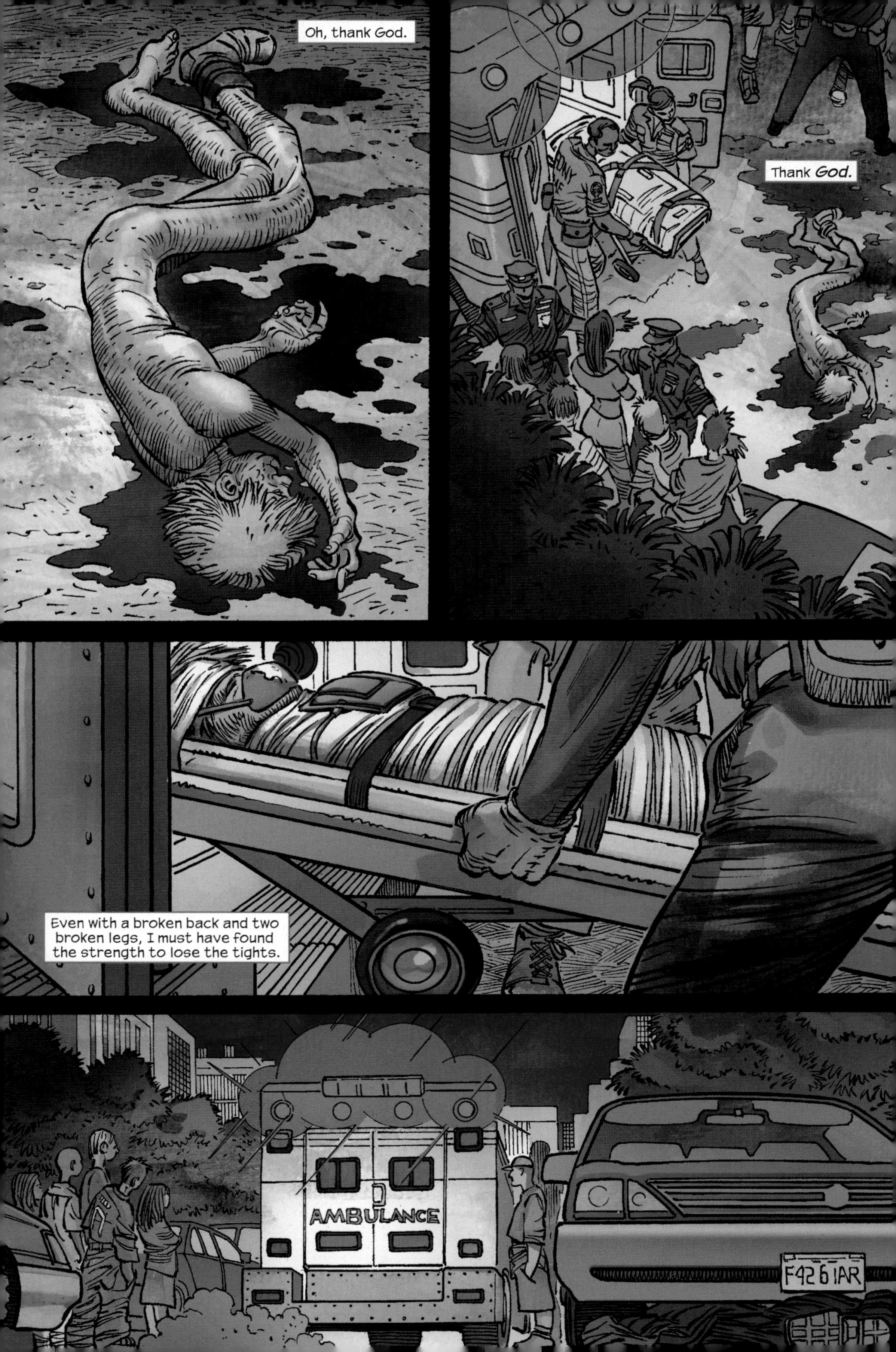
Oh, thank God.
Thank God.
Even with a broken back and two broken legs, I must have found the strength to lose the tights.
AMBULANCE
F426IAR

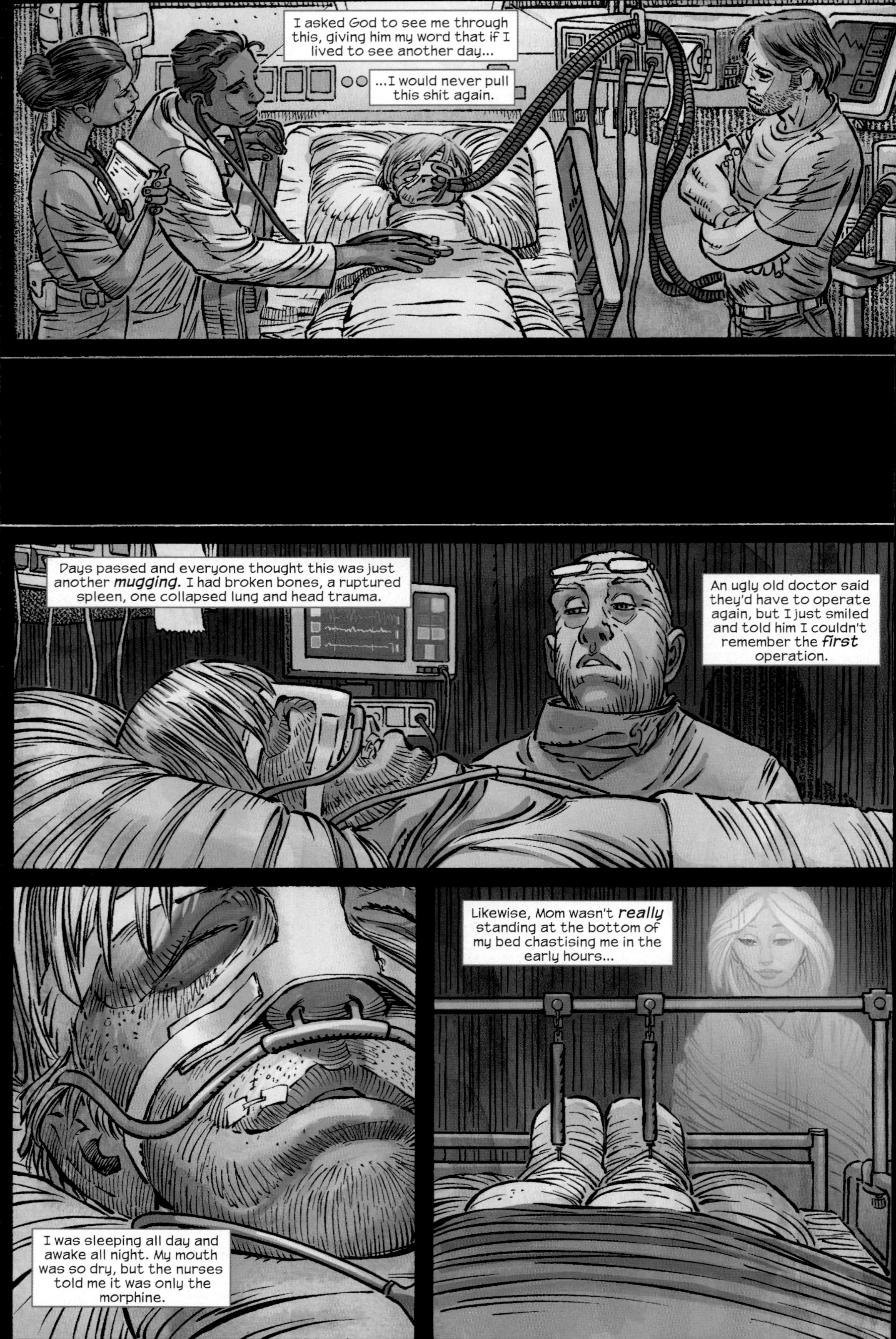
I asked God to see me through this, giving him my word that if I lived to see another day...
...I would never pull this shit again.
Days passed and everyone thought this was just another **mugging.** I had broken bones, a ruptured spleen, one collapsed lung and head trauma.
An ugly old doctor said they'd have to operate again, but I just smiled and told him I couldn't remember the ***first*** operation.
I was sleeping all day and awake all night. My mouth was so dry, but the nurses told me it was only the morphine.
Likewise, Mom wasn't ***really*** standing at the bottom of my bed chastising me in the early hours...

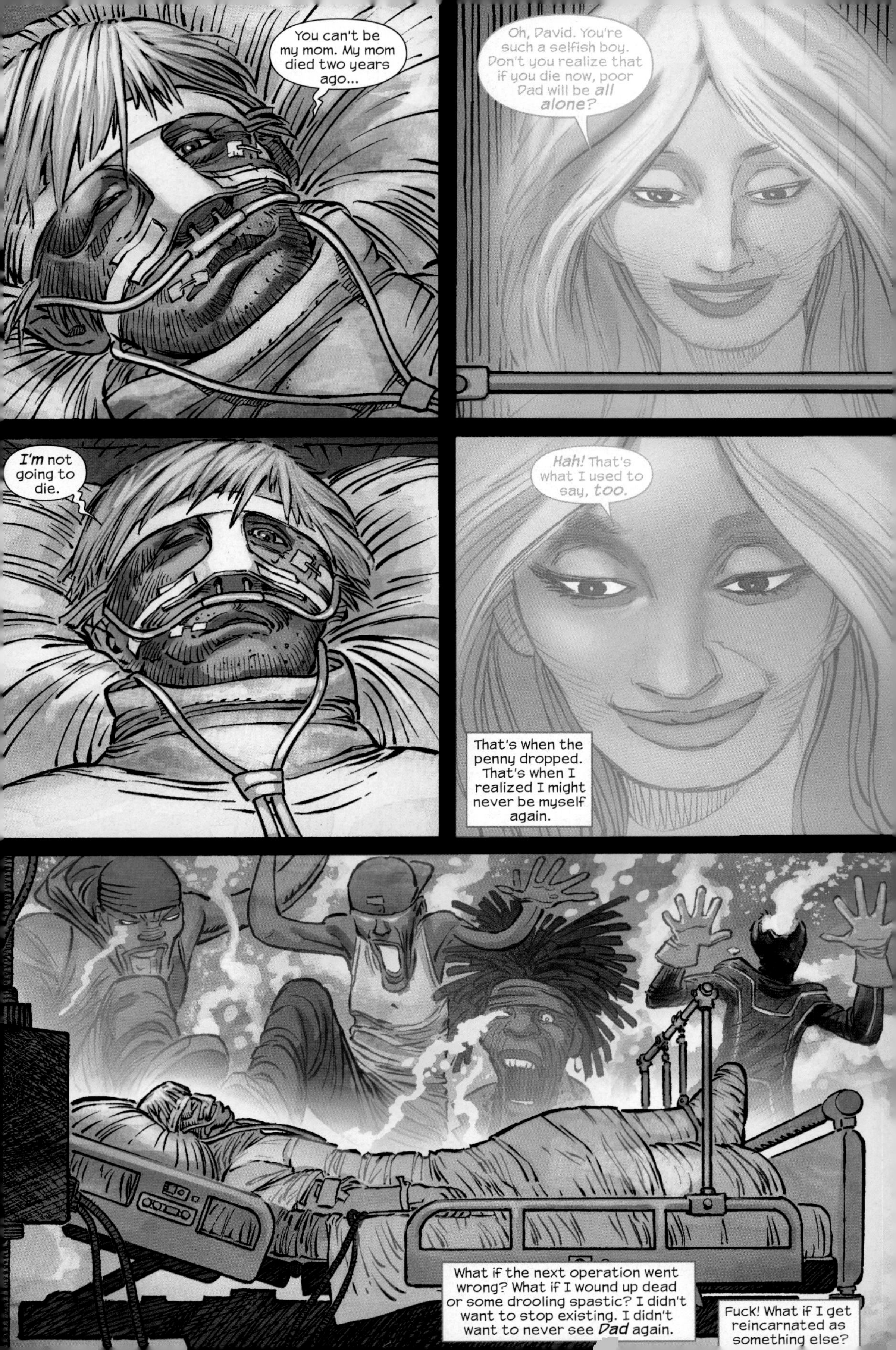
You can't be my mom. My mom died two years ago...
Oh, David. You're such a selfish boy. Don't you realize that if you die now, poor Dad will be *all alone?*
I'm not going to die.
Hah! That's what I used to say, *too.*
That's when the penny dropped. That's when I realized I might never be myself again.
What if the next operation went wrong? What if I wound up dead or some drooling spastic? I didn't want to stop existing. I didn't want to never see *Dad* again.
Fuck! What if I get reincarnated as something else?

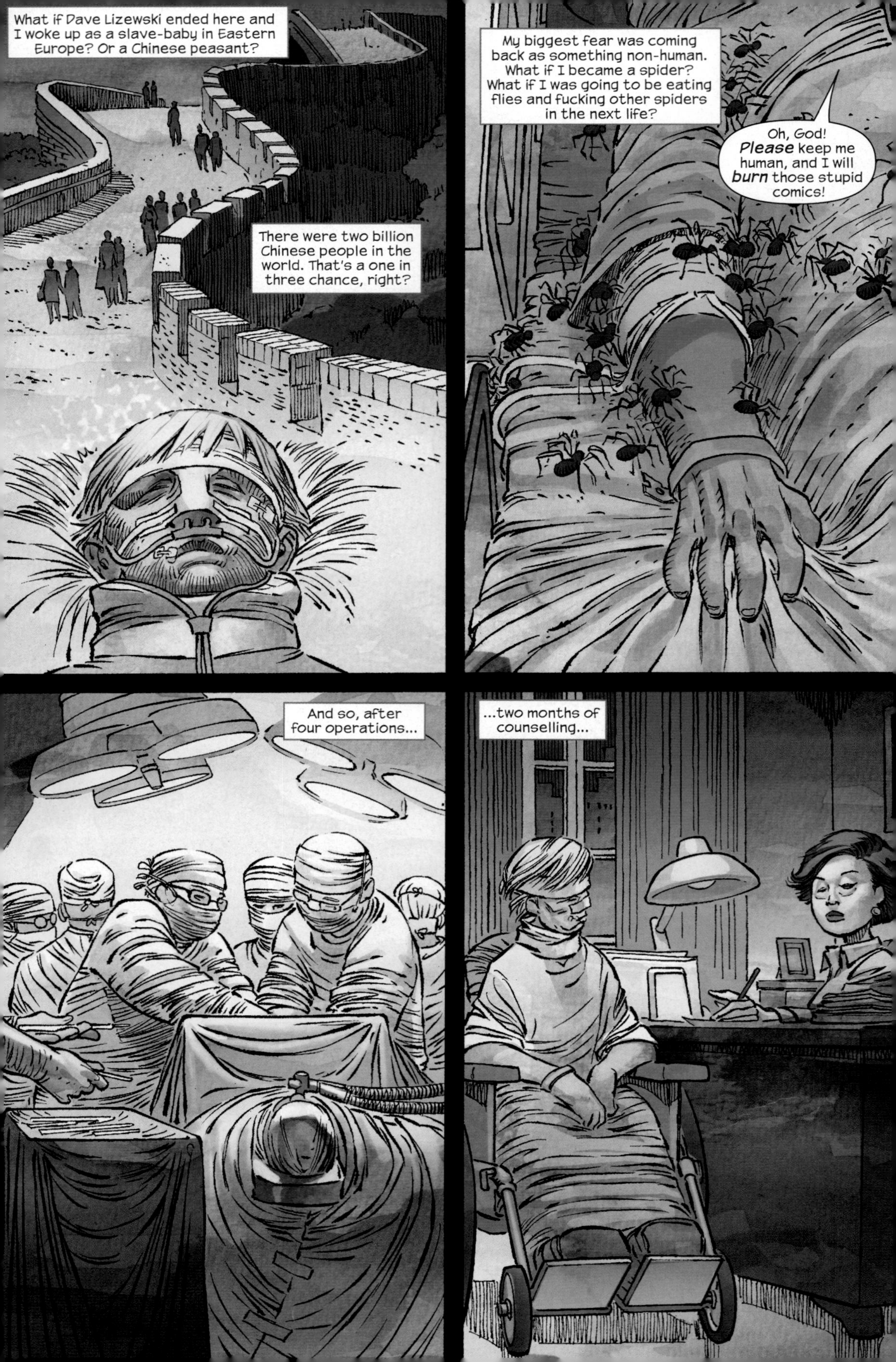
What if Dave Lizewski ended here and I woke up as a slave-baby in Eastern Europe? Or a Chinese peasant?
There were two billion Chinese people in the world. That's a one in three chance, right?
My biggest fear was coming back as something non-human. What if I became a spider? What if I was going to be eating flies and fucking other spiders in the next life?
Oh, God! *Please* keep me human, and I will *burn* those stupid comics!
And so, after four operations...
...two months of counselling...

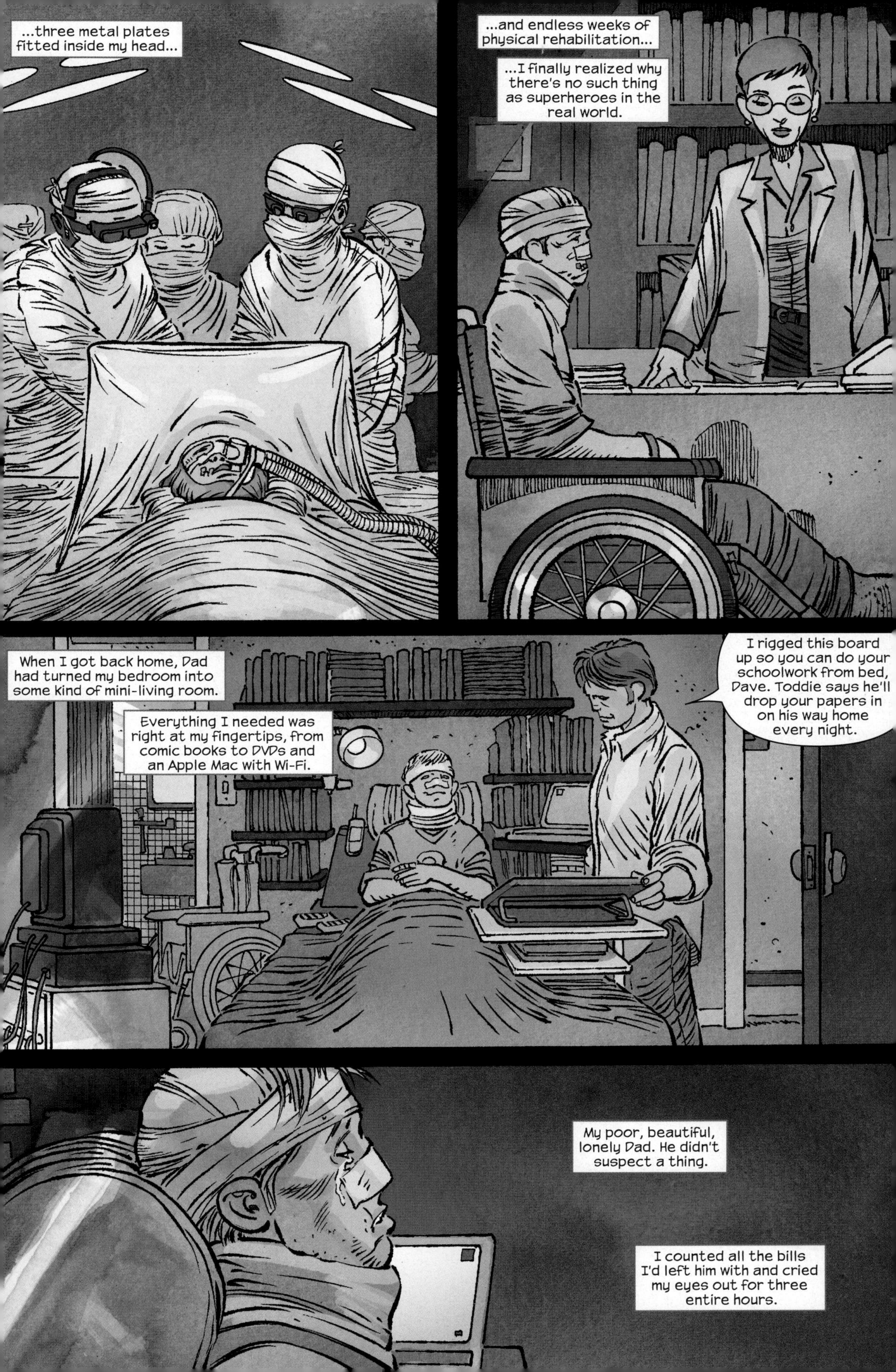
...three metal plates fitted inside my head...
...and endless weeks of physical rehabilitation...
...I finally realized why there's no such thing as superheroes in the real world.
When I got back home, Dad had turned my bedroom into some kind of mini-living room.
Everything I needed was right at my fingertips, from comic books to DVDs and an Apple Mac with Wi-Fi.
I rigged this board up so you can do your schoolwork from bed, Dave. Toddie says he'll drop your papers in on his way home every night.
My poor, beautiful, lonely Dad. He didn't suspect a thing.
I counted all the bills I'd left him with and cried my eyes out for three entire hours.

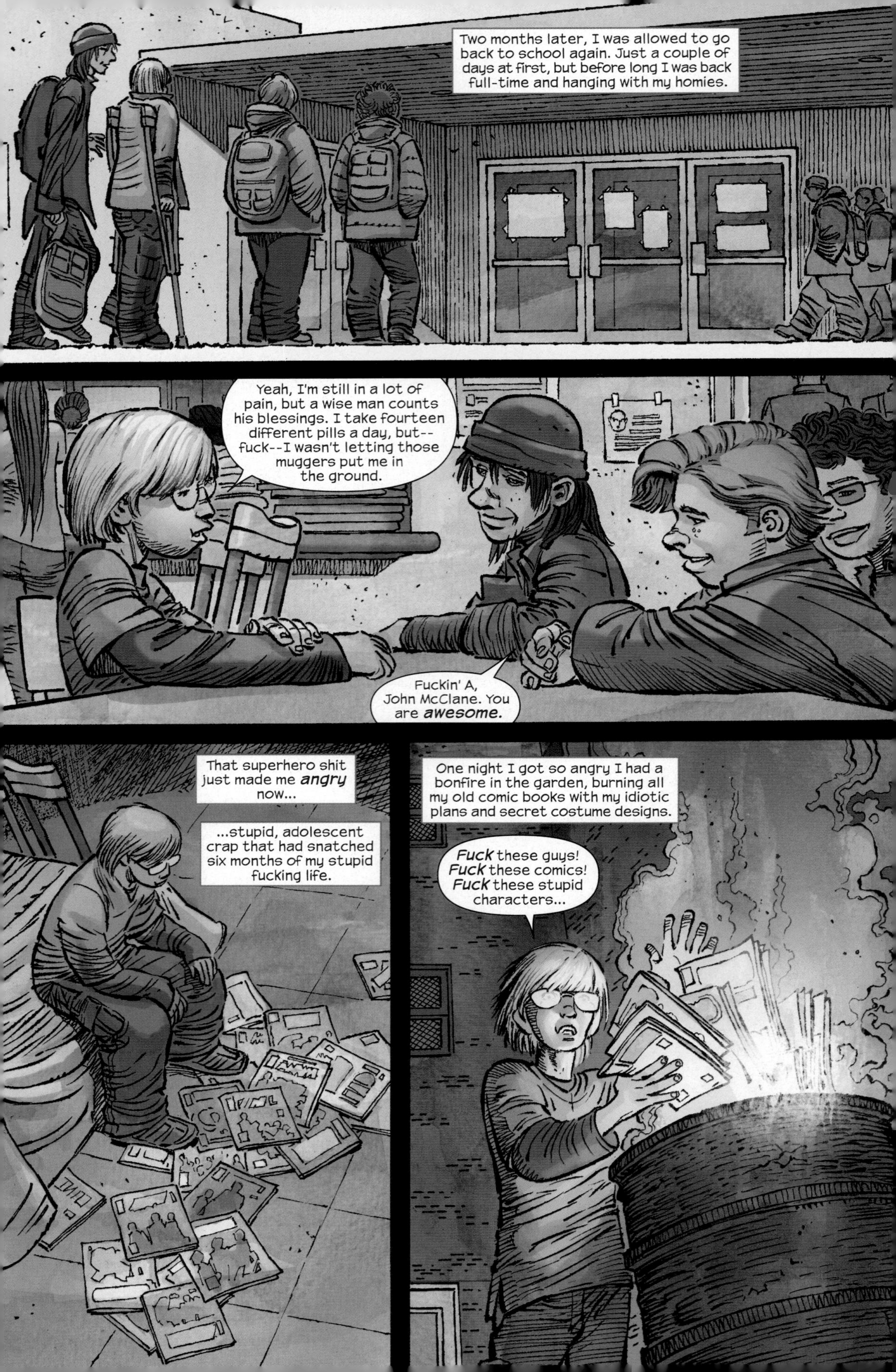

Two months later, I was allowed to go back to school again. Just a couple of days at first, but before long I was back full-time and hanging with my homies.
Yeah, I'm still in a lot of pain, but a wise man counts his blessings. I take fourteen different pills a day, but--fuck--I wasn't letting those muggers put me in the ground.
Fuckin' A, John McClane. You are *awesome.*
That superhero shit just made me *angry* now...
...stupid, adolescent crap that had snatched six months of my stupid fucking life.
One night I got so angry I had a bonfire in the garden, burning all my old comic books with my idiotic plans and secret costume designs.
Fuck these guys! *Fuck* these comics! *Fuck* these stupid characters...

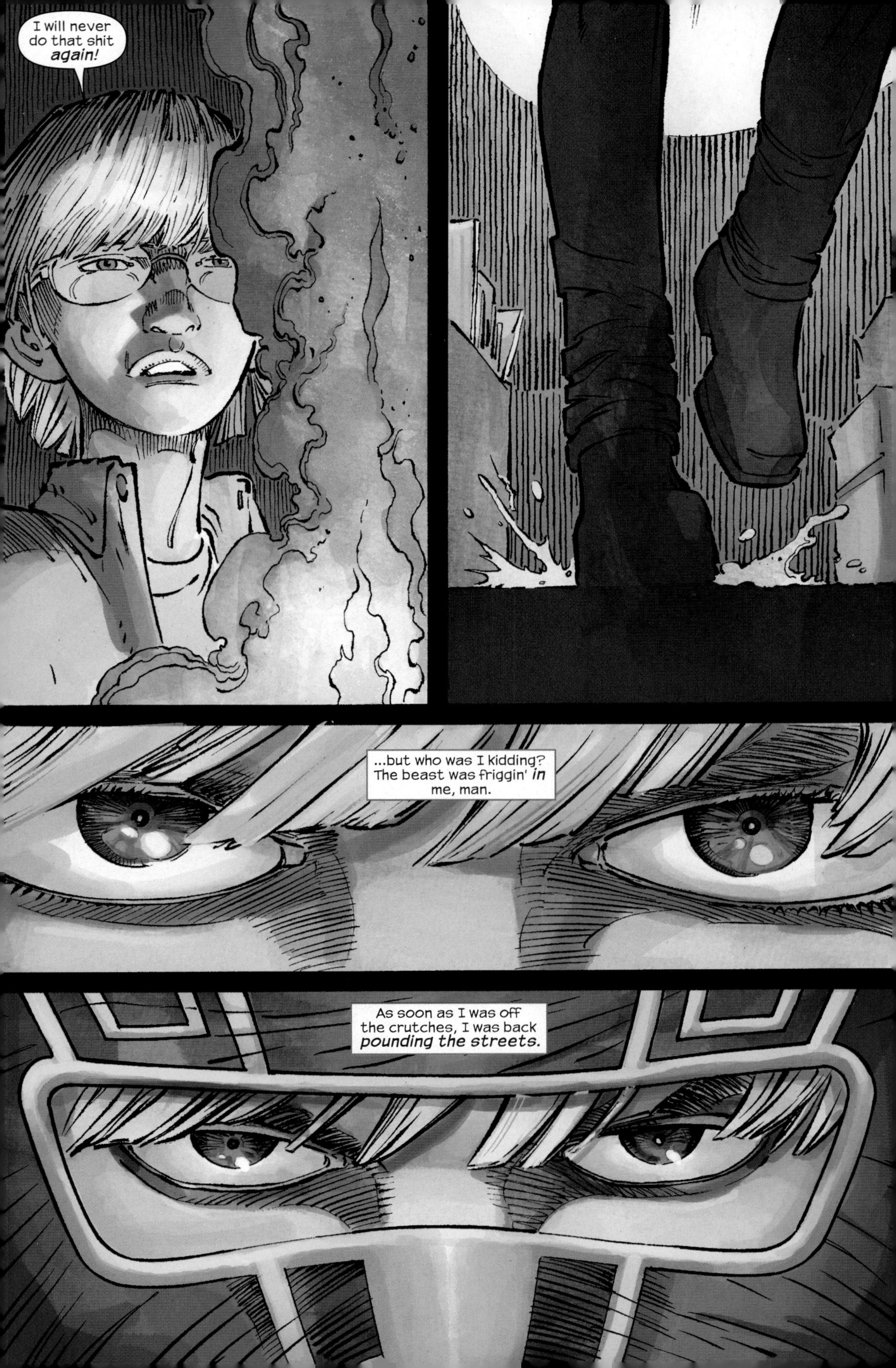
I will never do that shit *again!*
...but who was I kidding? The beast was friggin' *in* me, man.
As soon as I was off the crutches, I was back *pounding the streets.*

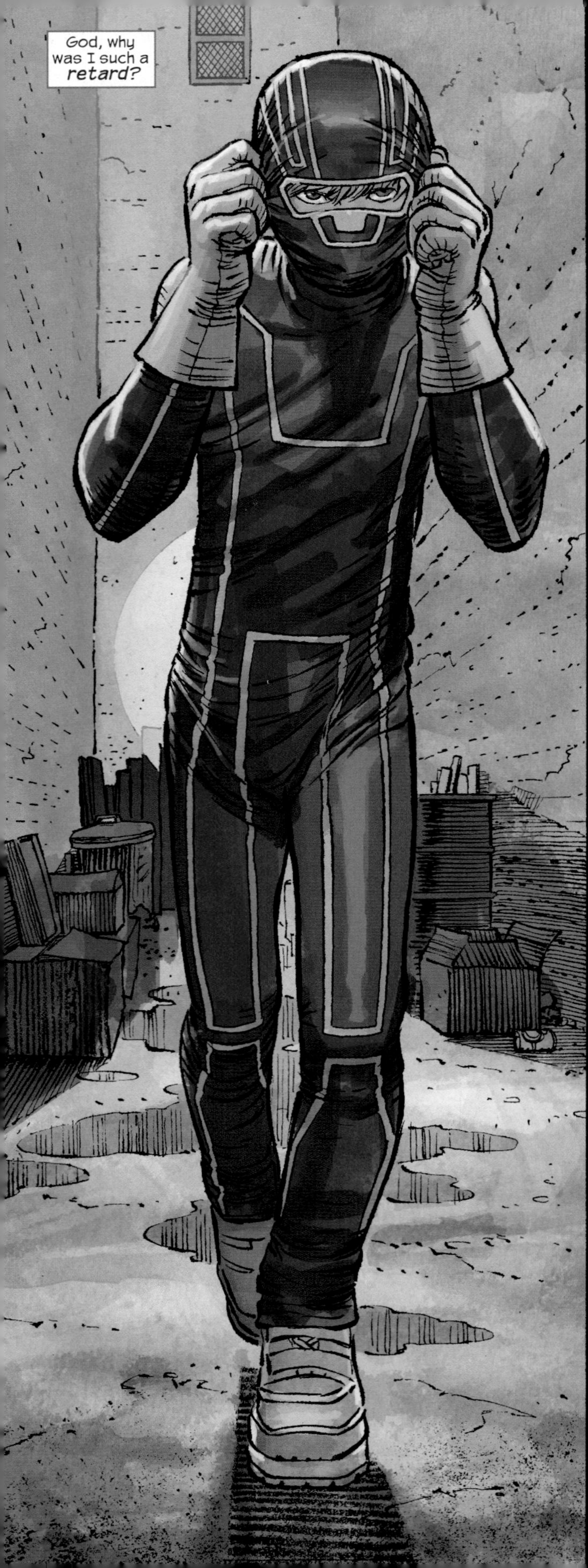
God, why was I such a *retard?*

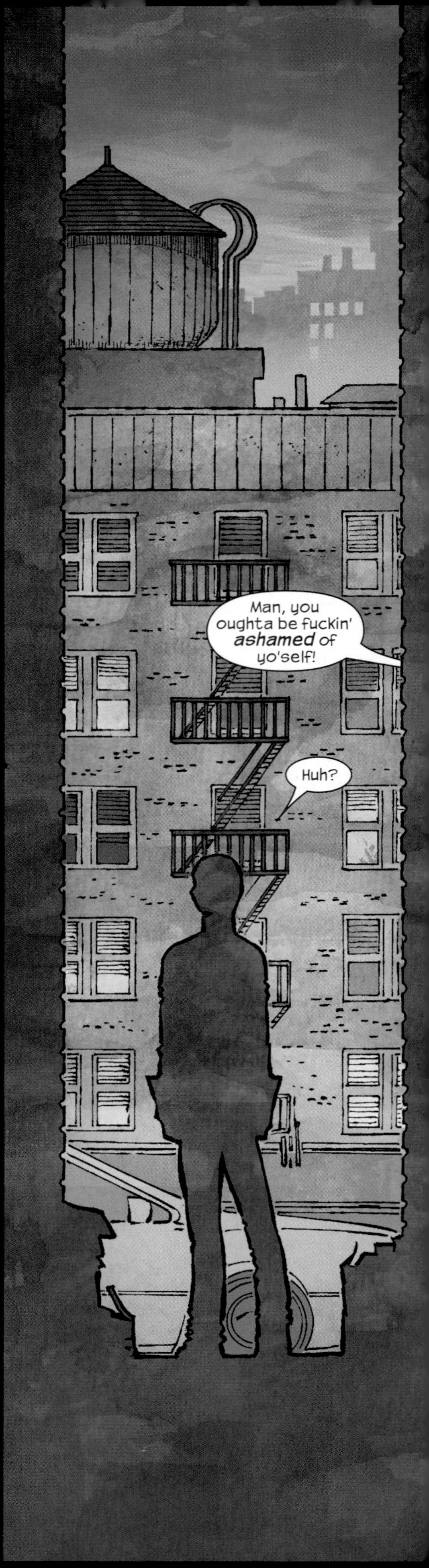
Man, you oughta be fuckin' ***ashamed*** of yo'self!
Huh?

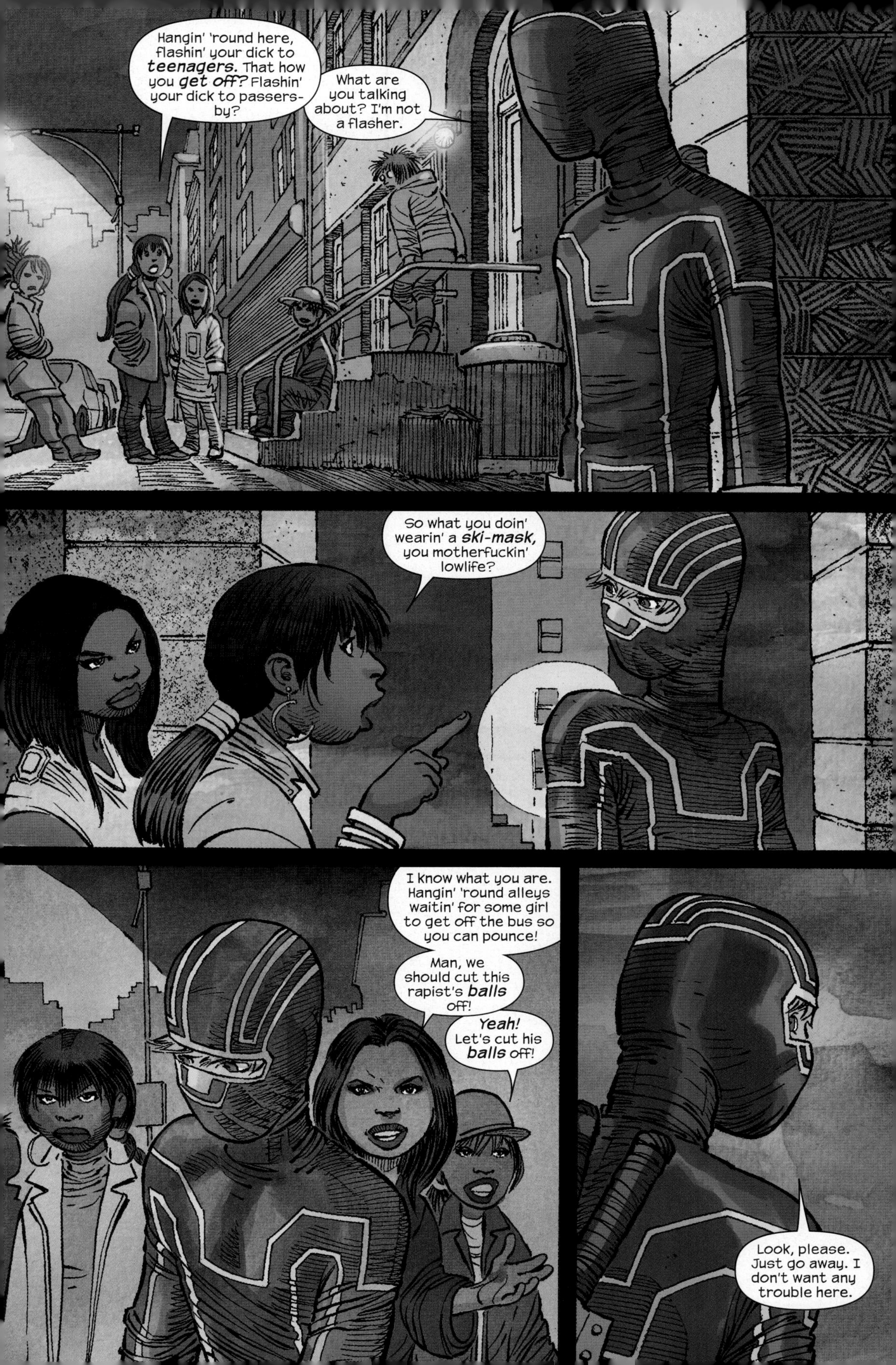
Hangin' 'round here, flashin' your dick to teenagers. That how you get off? Flashin' your dick to passers-by?
What are you talking about? I'm not a flasher.
So what you doin' wearin' a ski-mask, you motherfuckin' lowlife?
I know what you are. Hangin' 'round alleys waitin' for some girl to get off the bus so you can pounce!
Man, we should cut this rapist's balls off!
Yeah! Let's cut his balls off!
Look, please. Just go away. I don't want any trouble here.

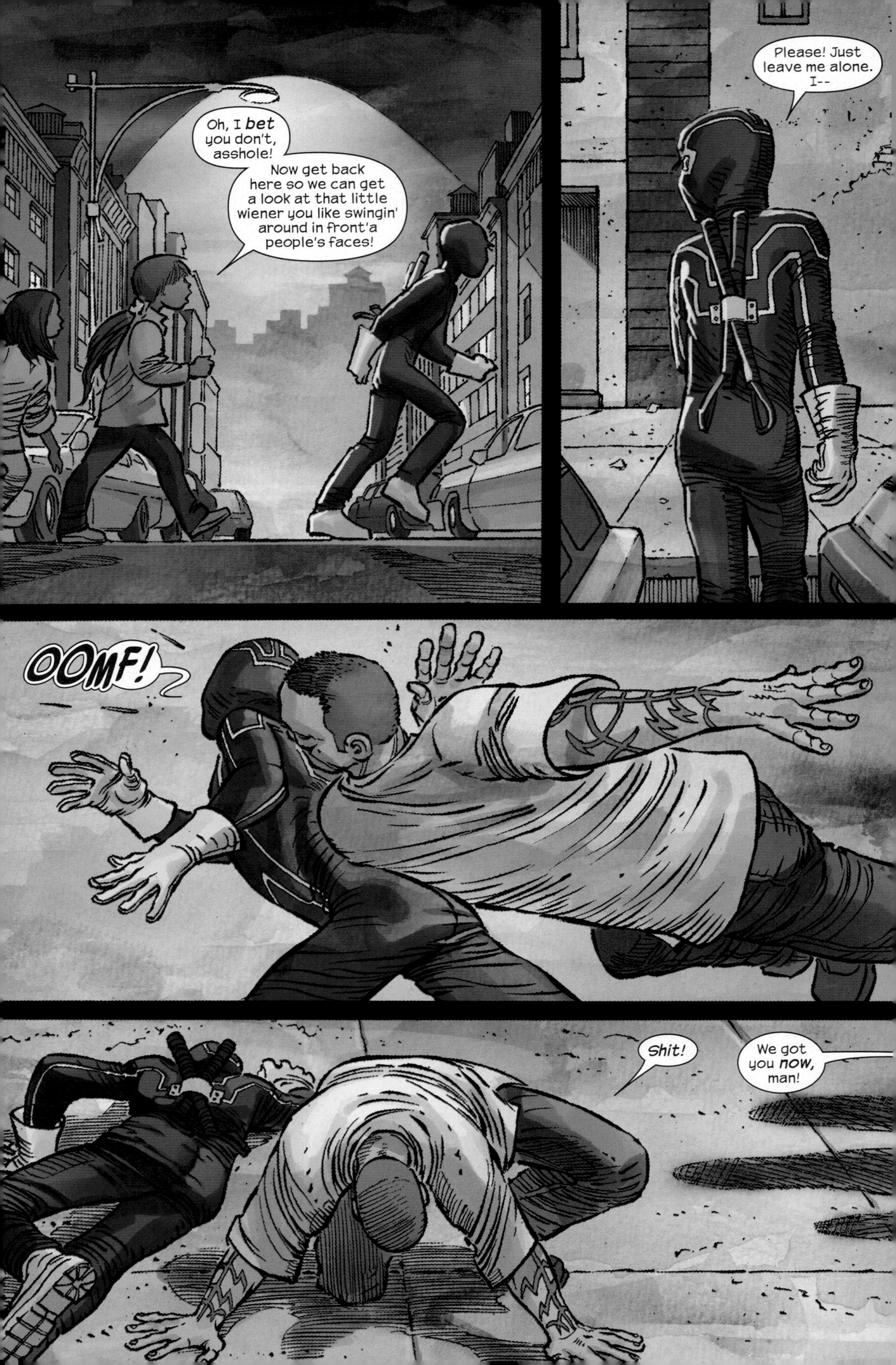
Oh, I bet you don't, asshole!
Now get back here so we can get a look at that little wiener you like swingin' around in front'a people's faces!
Please! Just leave me alone. I--
OOMF!
Shit!
We got you now, man!

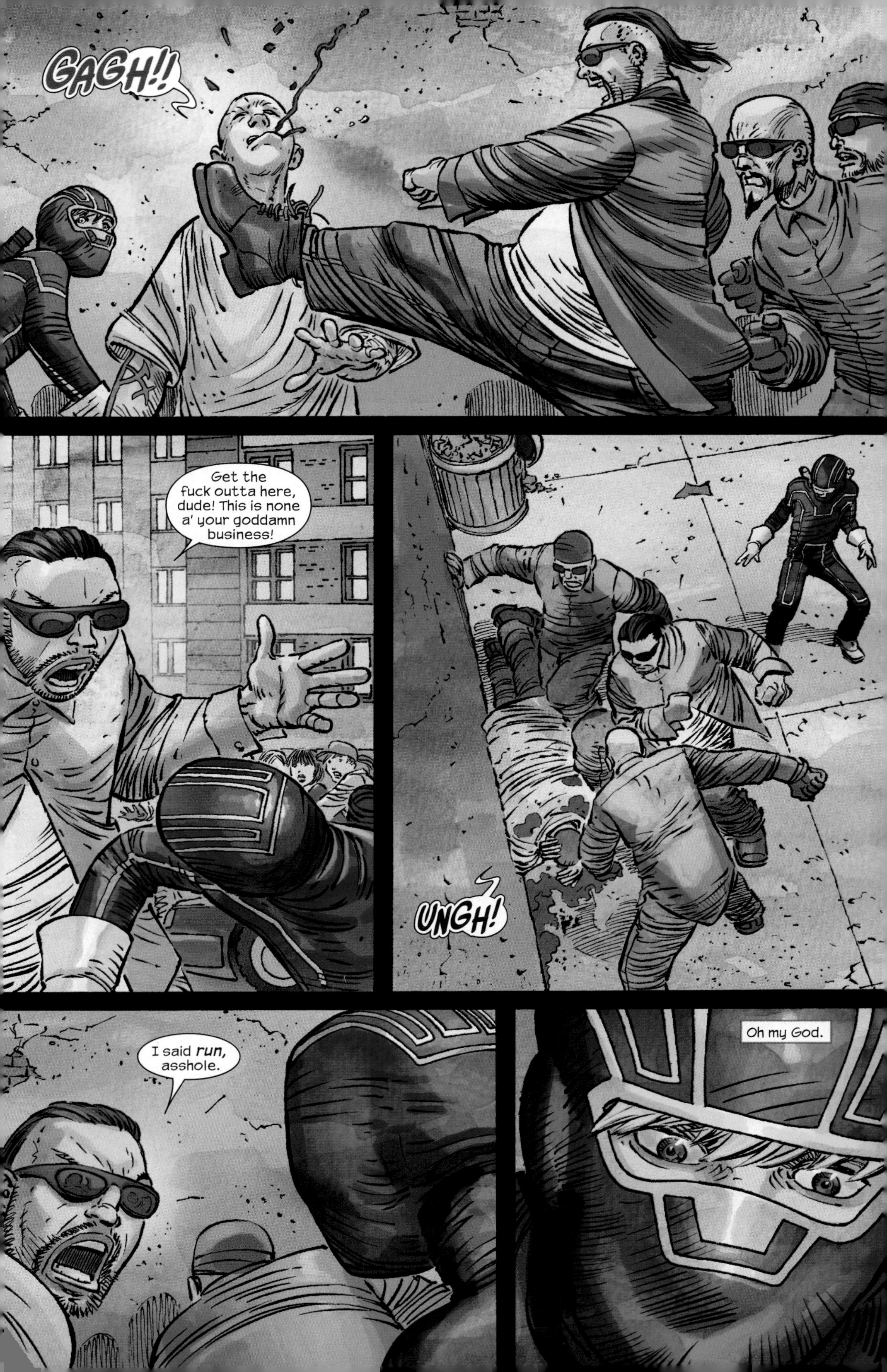
GAGH!!
Get the fuck outta here, dude! This is none a' your goddamn business!
UNGH!
I said *run*, asshole.
Oh my God.

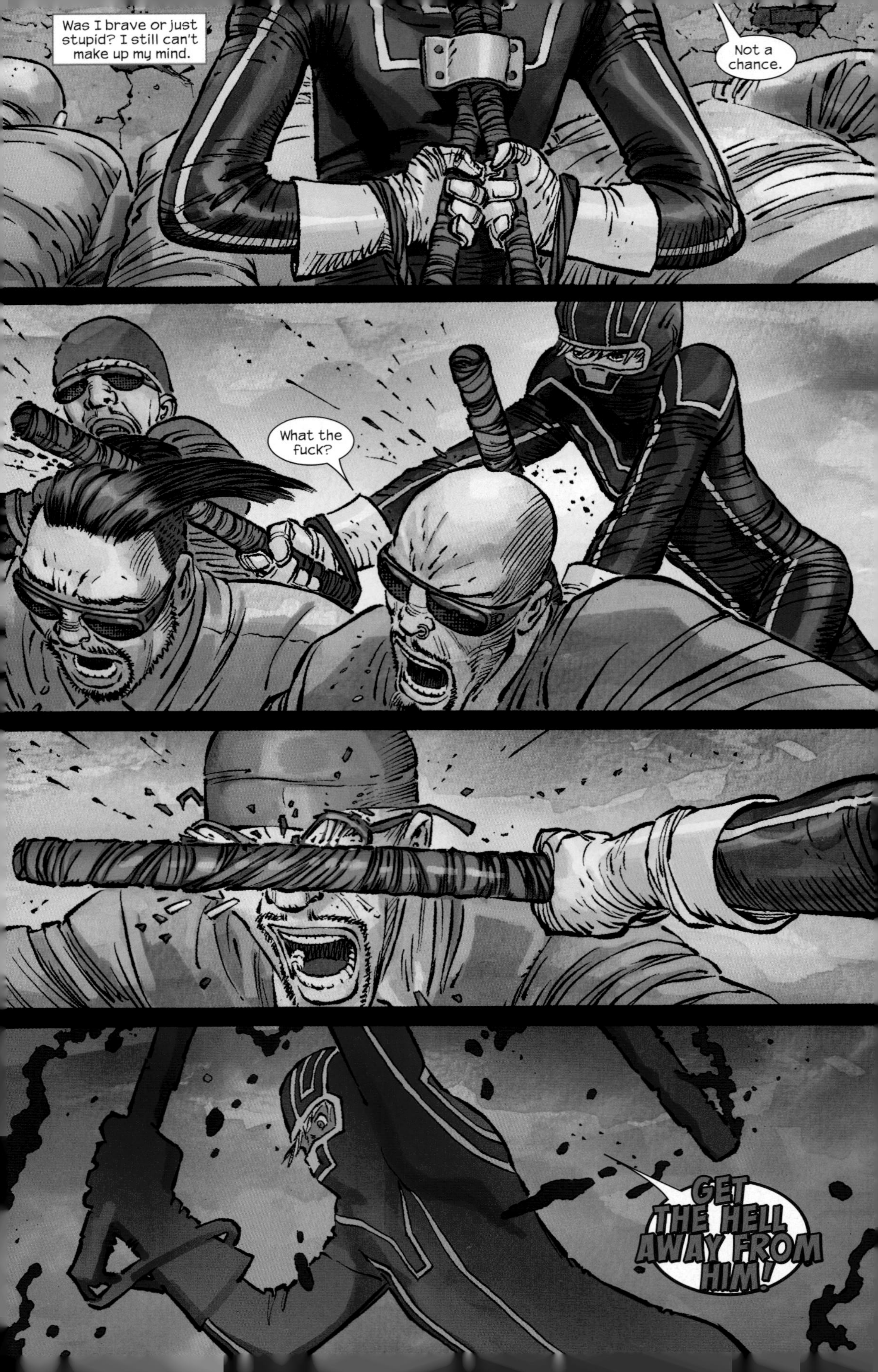
Was I brave or just stupid? I still can't make up my mind.
Not a chance.
What the fuck?
GET THE HELL AWAY FROM HIM!

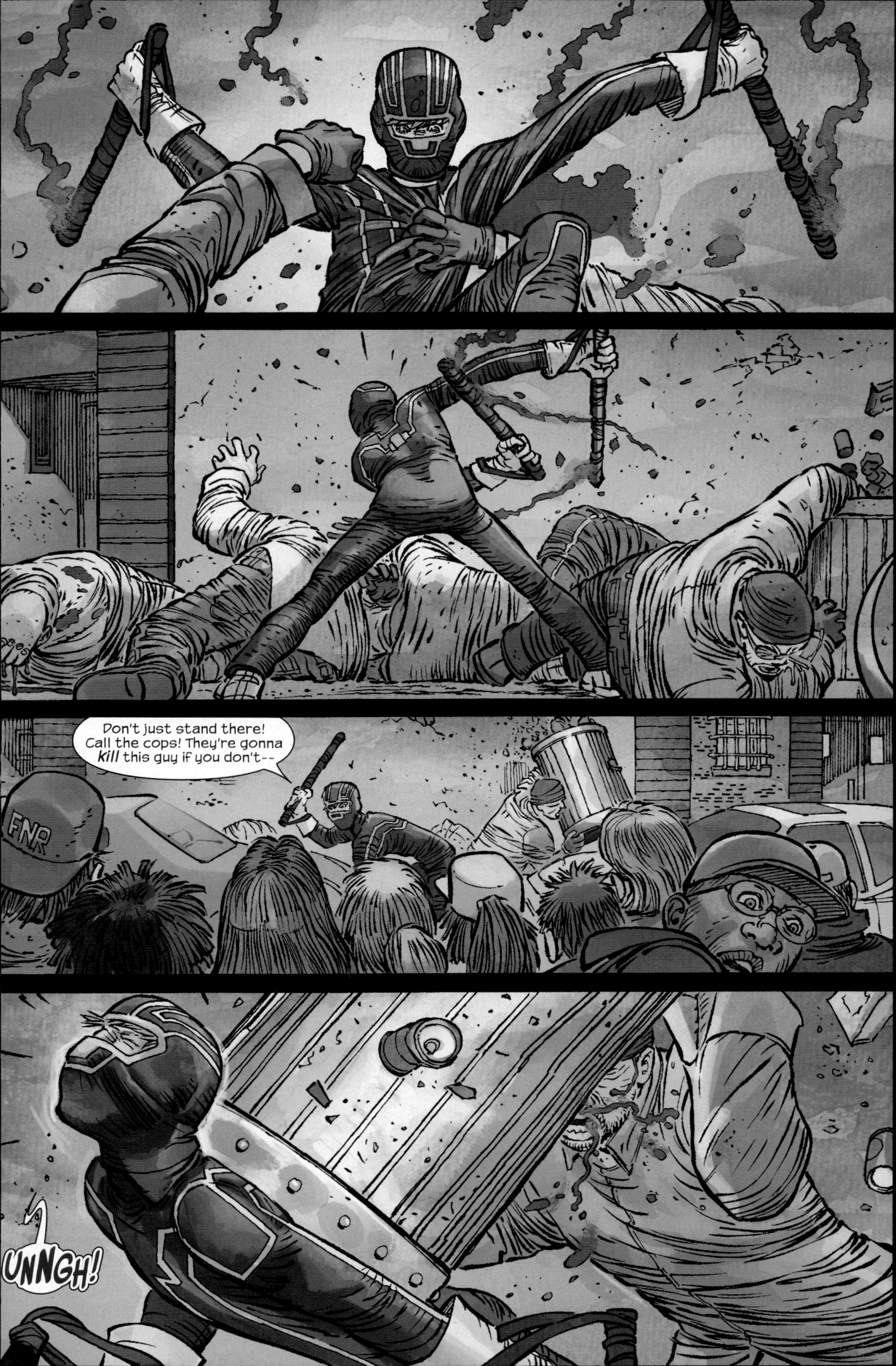
Don't just stand there! Call the cops! They're gonna *kill* this guy if you don't--
FNR
UNNGH!

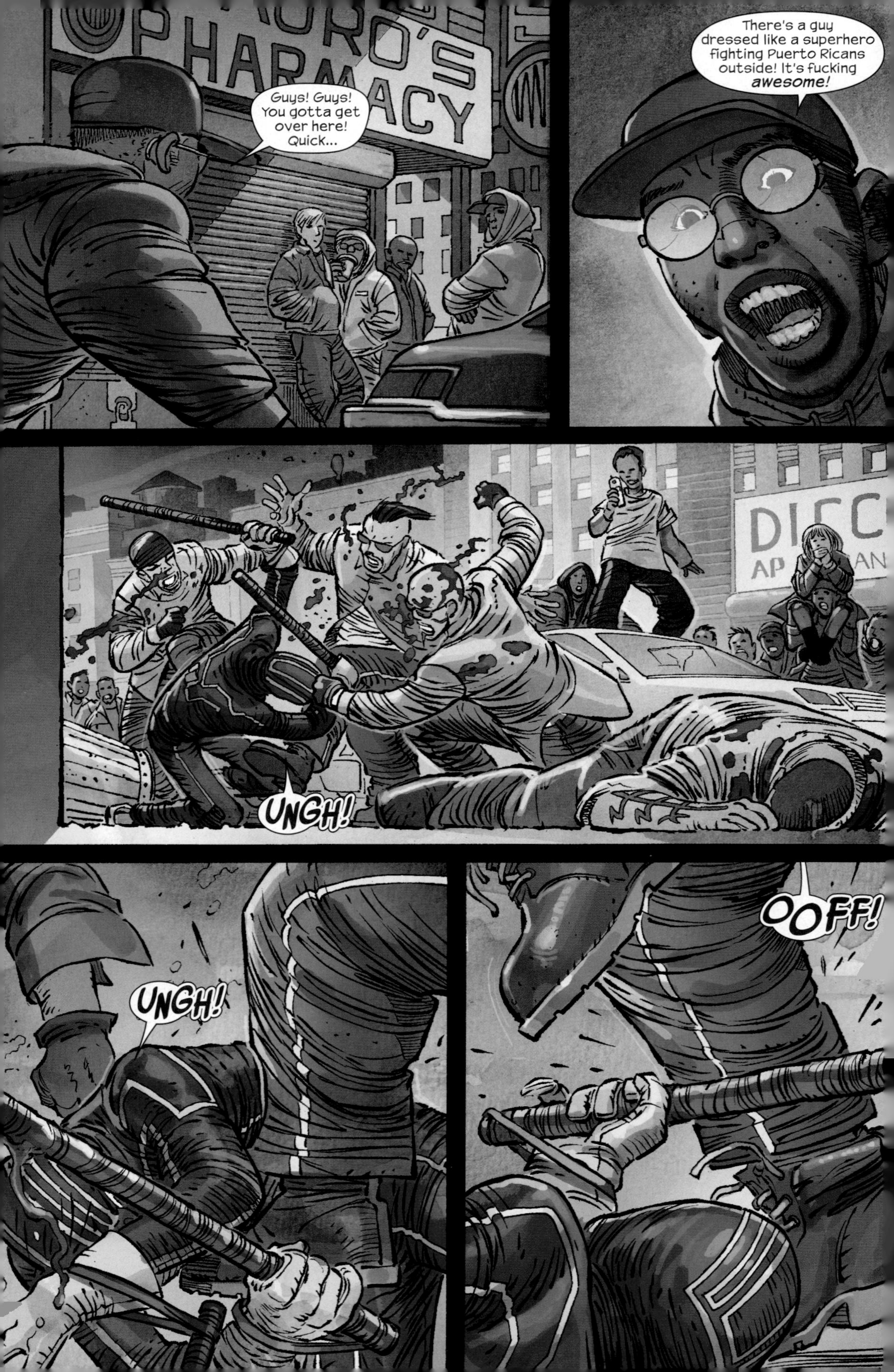
PHARMACY
Guys! Guys! You gotta get over here! Quick...
There's a guy dressed like a superhero fighting Puerto Ricans outside! It's fucking ***awesome!***
UNGH!
UNGH!
OOFF!

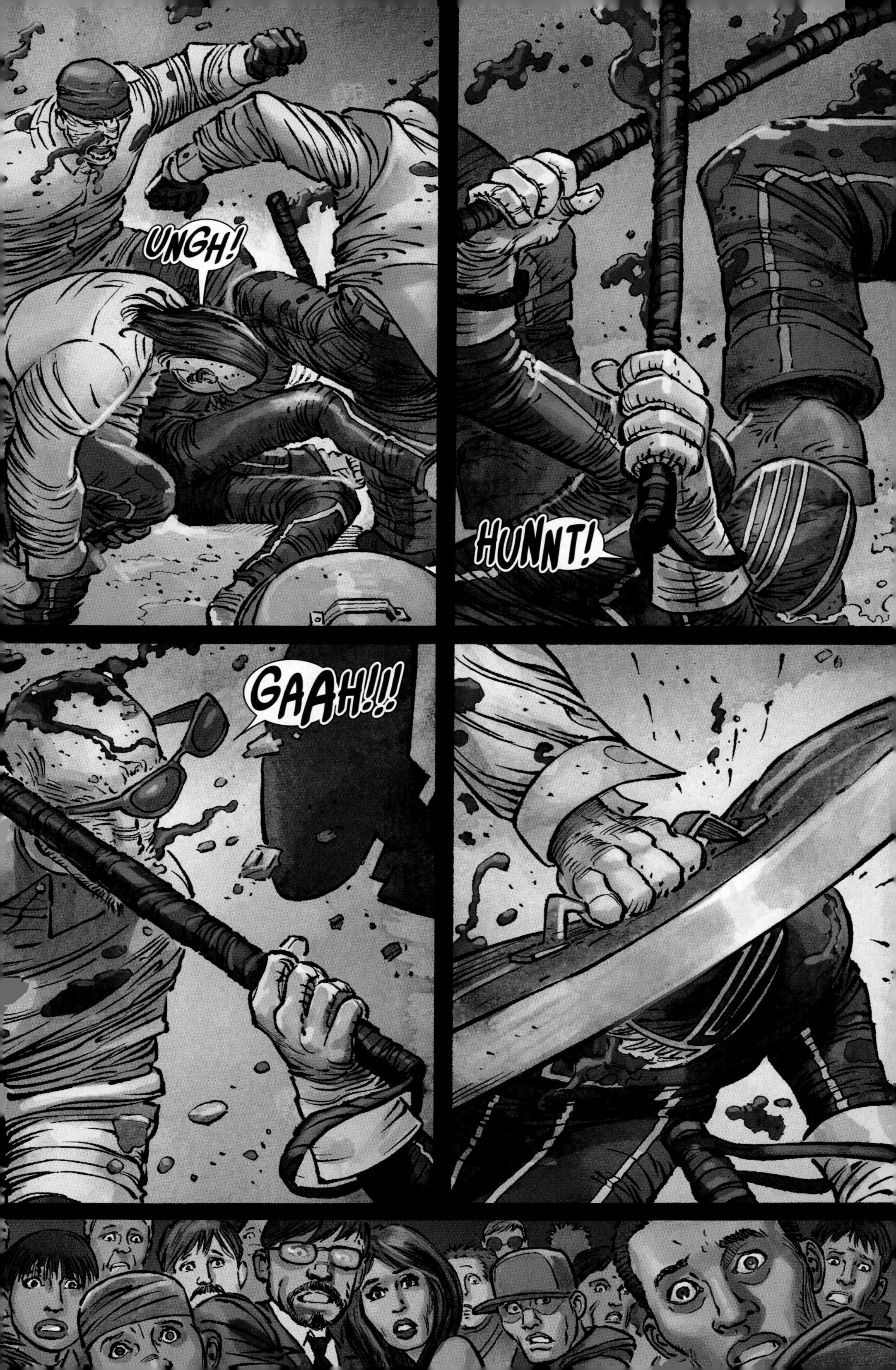
UNGH!
HUNNT!
GAAH!!!

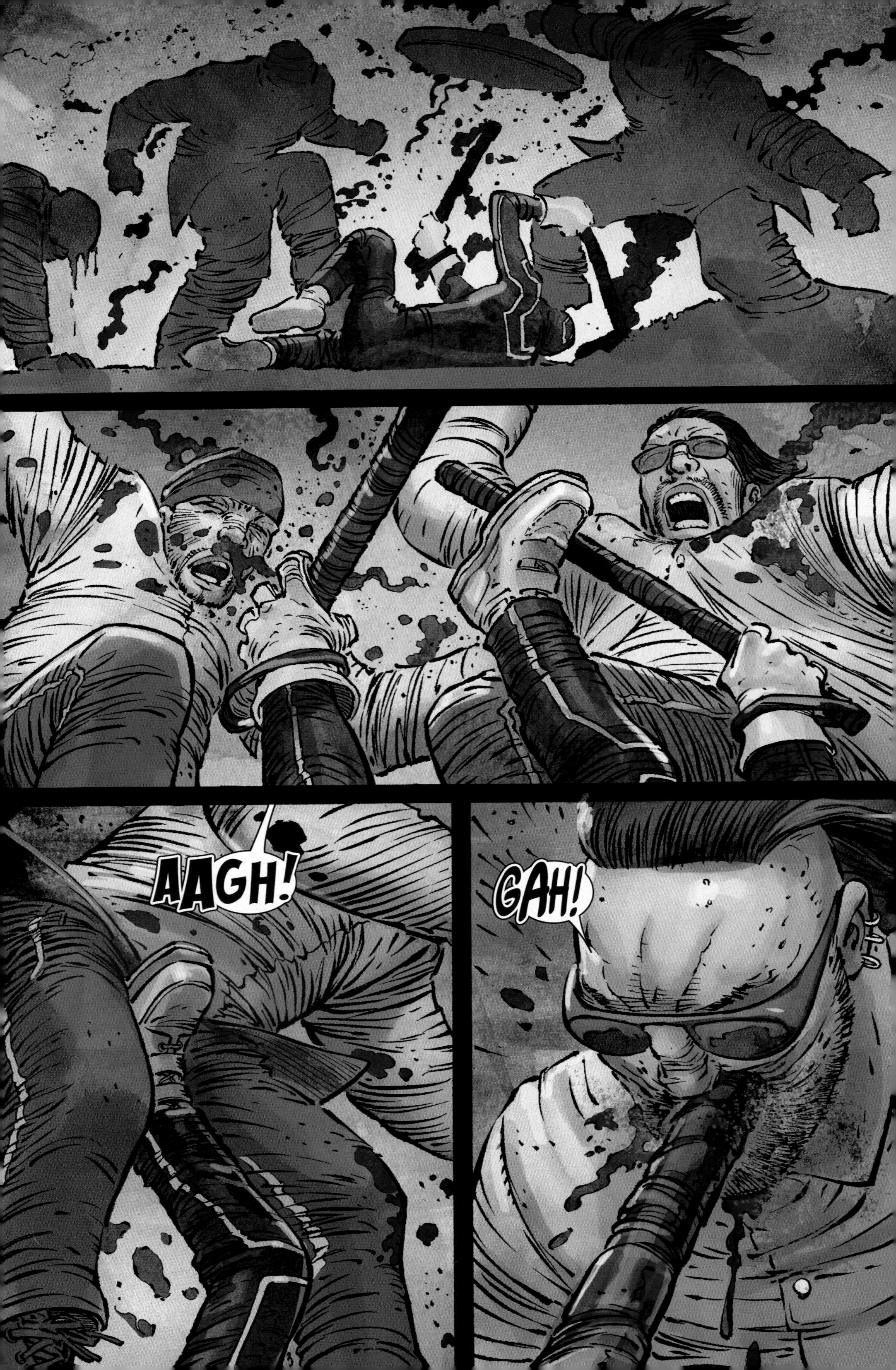
AAGH!
GAH!

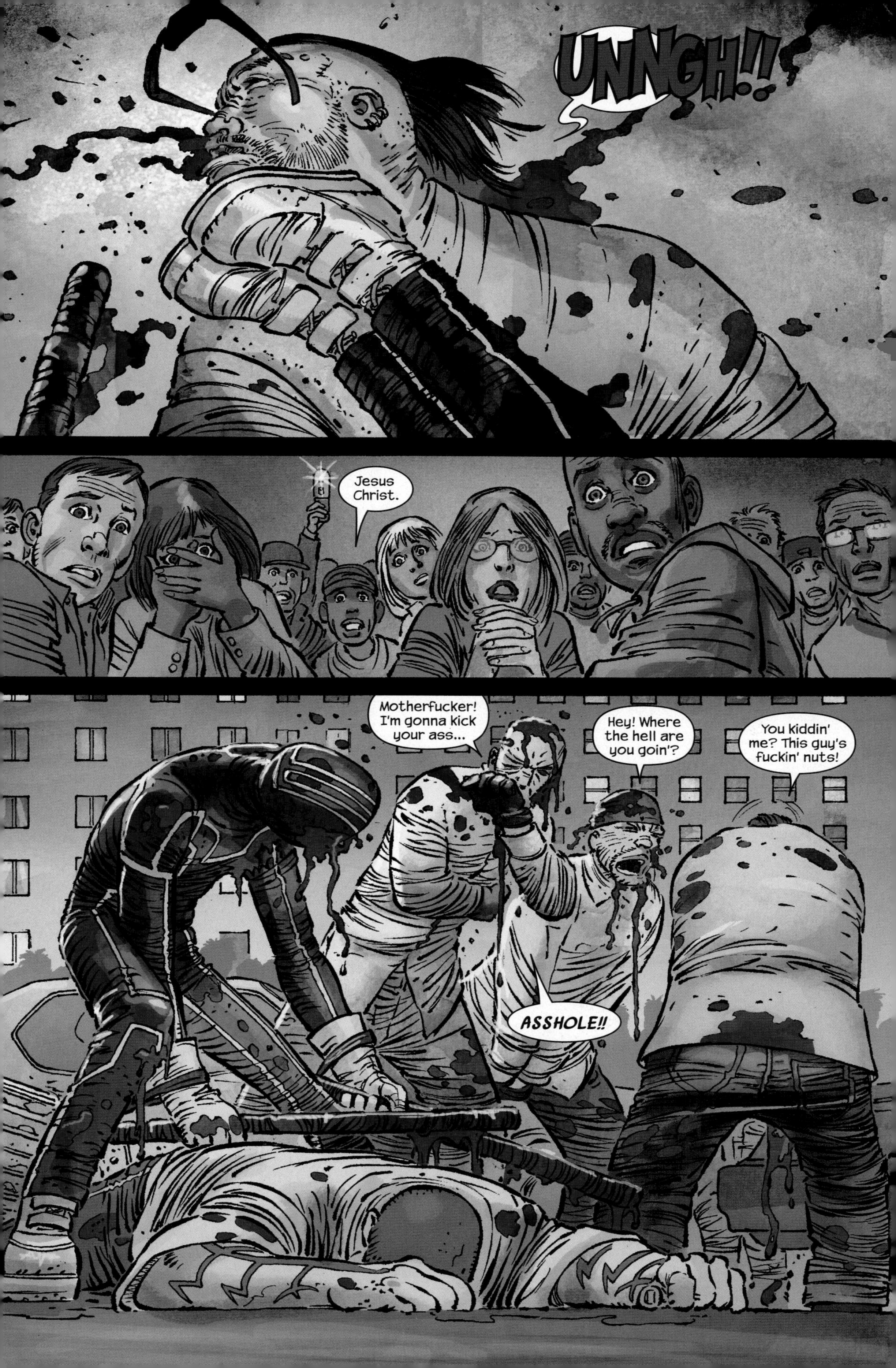
UNNGH!!
Jesus Christ.
Motherfucker! I'm gonna kick your ass...
Hey! Where the hell are you goin'?
You kiddin' me? This guy's fuckin' nuts!
ASSHOLE!!

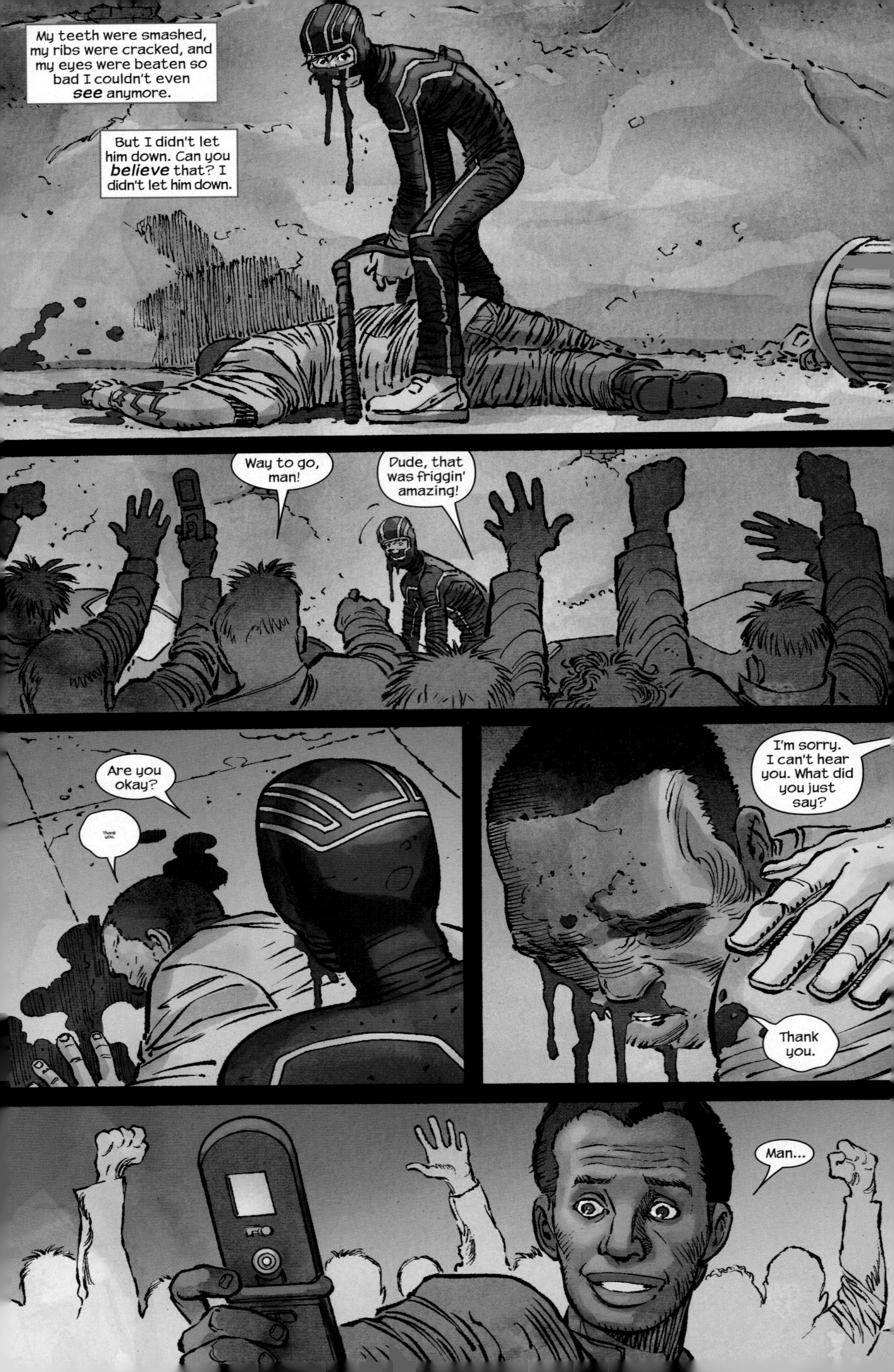
My teeth were smashed, my ribs were cracked, and my eyes were beaten so bad I couldn't even *see* anymore.
But I didn't let him down. Can you *believe* that? I didn't let him down.
Way to go, man!
Dude, that was friggin' amazing!
Are you okay?
Thank you.
I'm sorry. I can't hear you. What did you just say?
Thank you.
Man...

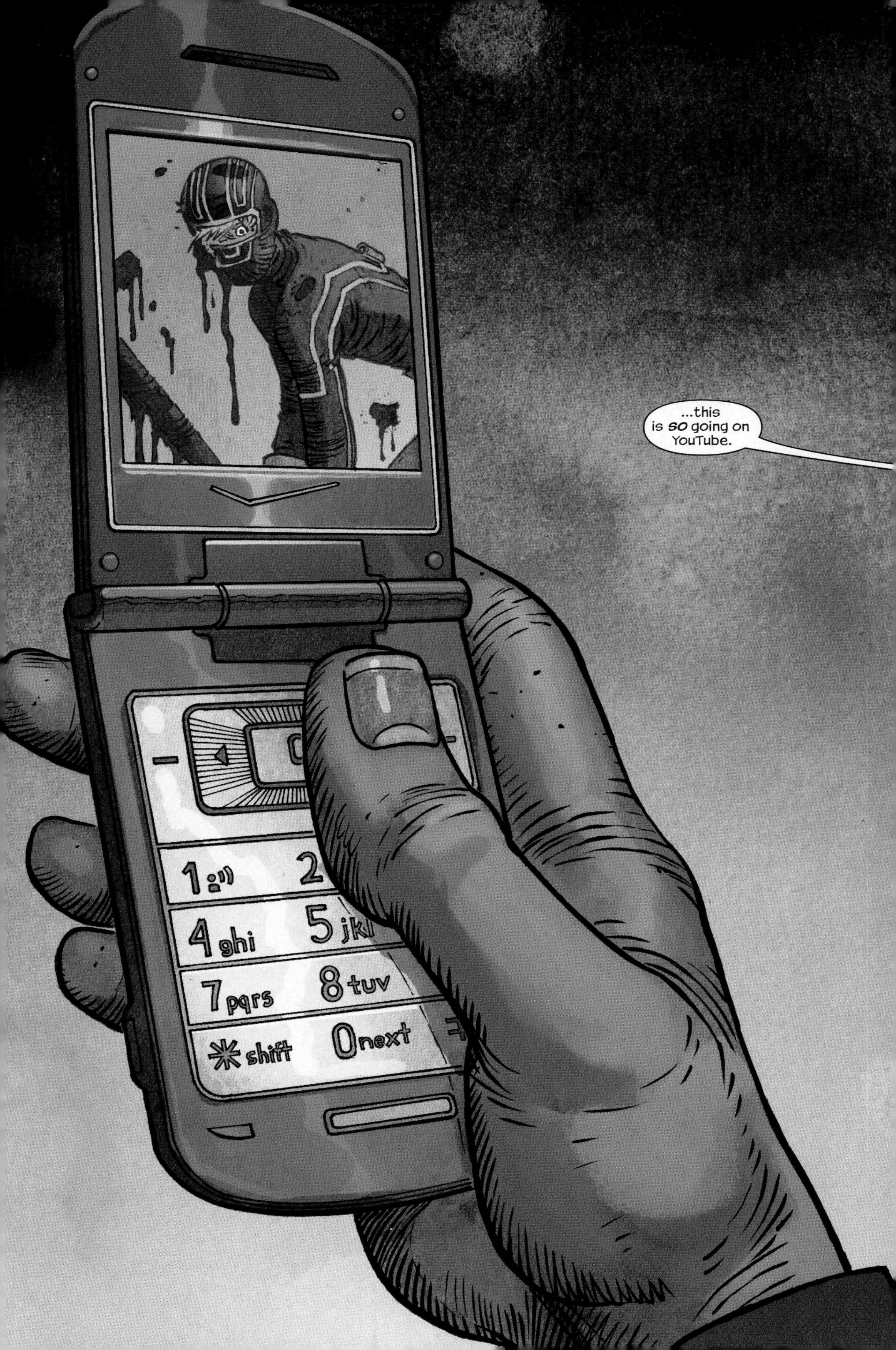
...this is SO going on YouTube.

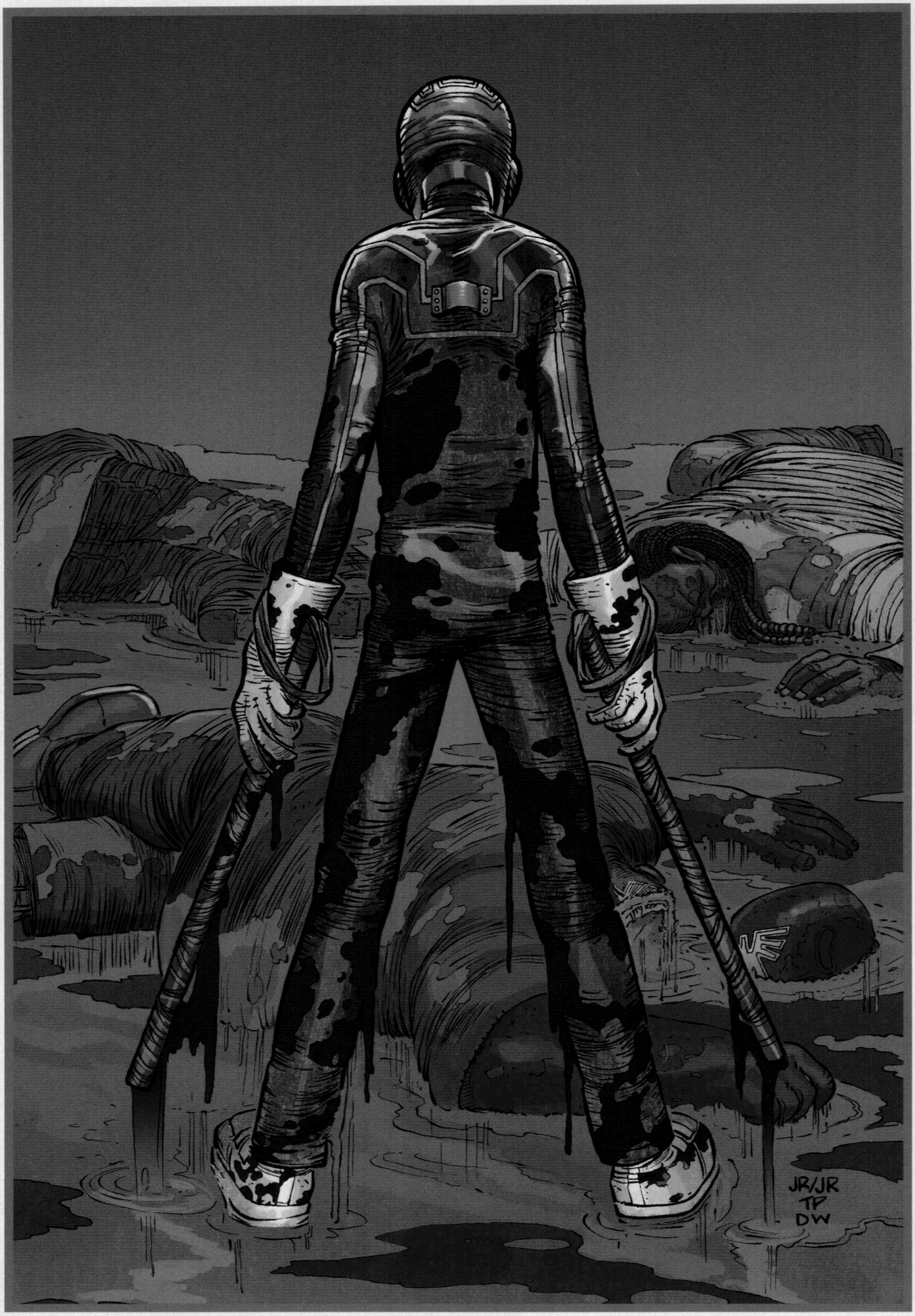
JR/JR
TP
DW

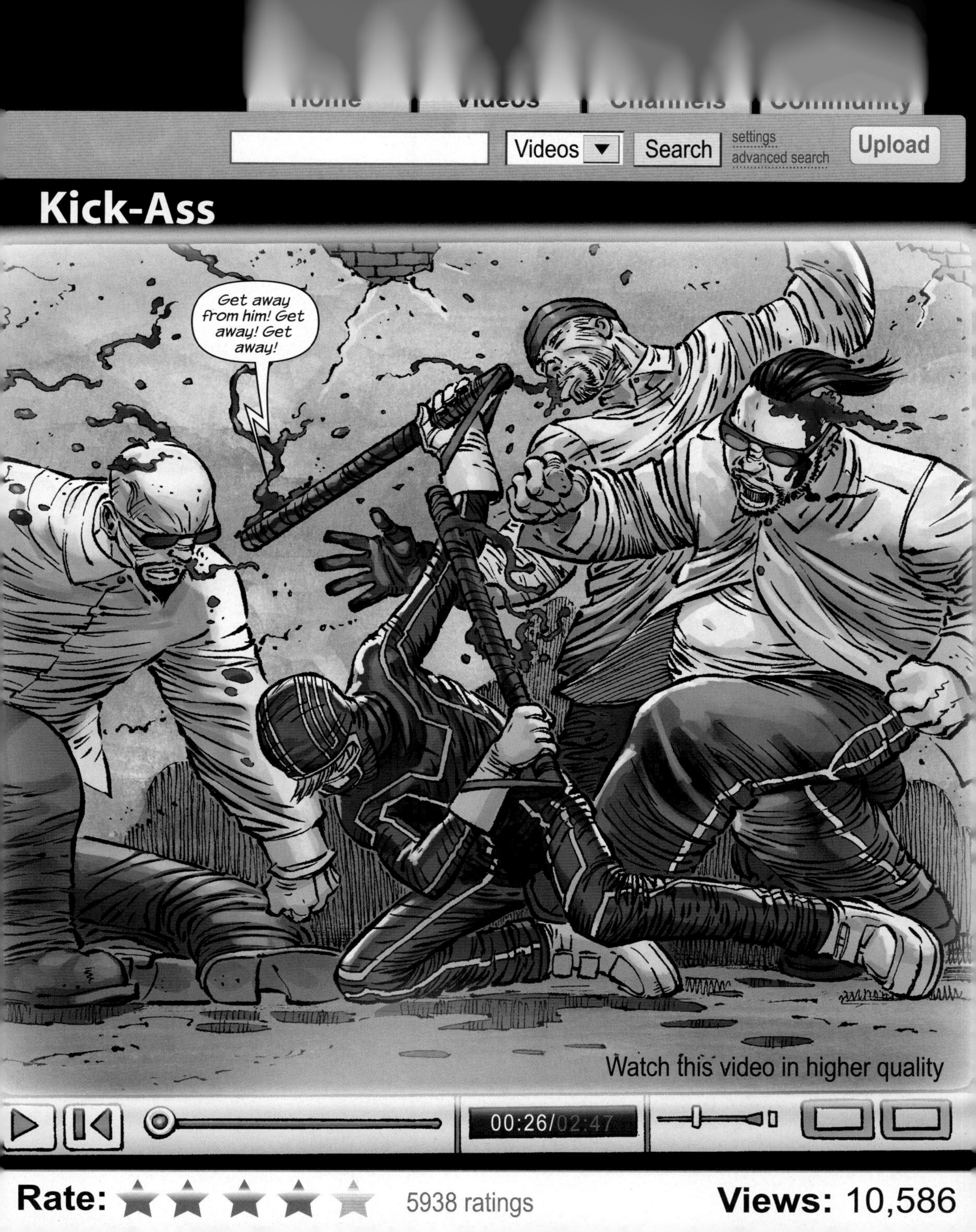
Videos
Search
settings
advanced search
Upload
Kick-Ass
Get away from him! Get away! Get away!
Watch this video in higher quality
00:26/02:47
Rate:
5938 ratings
Views: 10,586

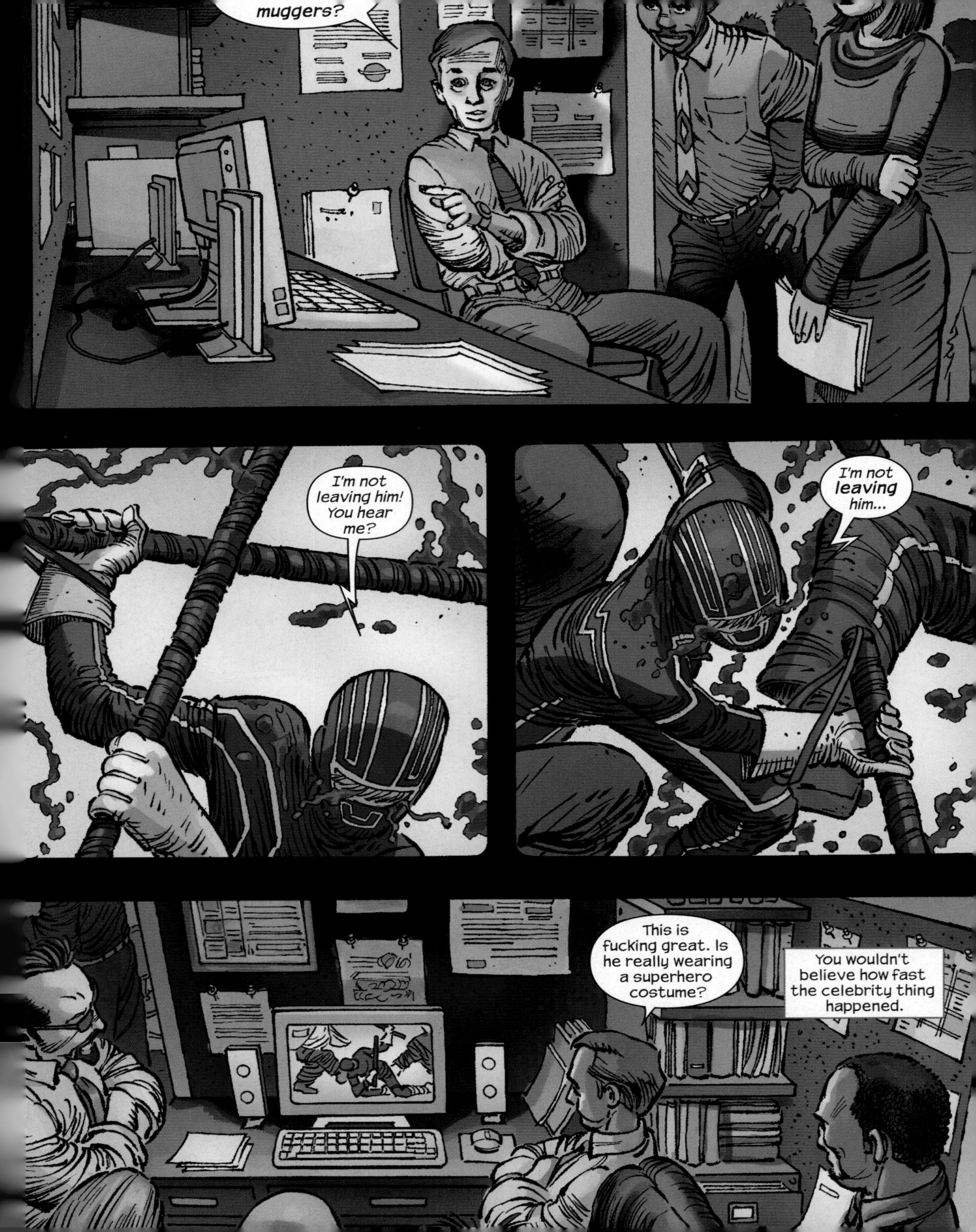
muggers?
I'm not leaving him! You hear me?
I'm not leaving him...
This is fucking great. Is he really wearing a superhero costume?
You wouldn't believe how fast the celebrity thing happened.

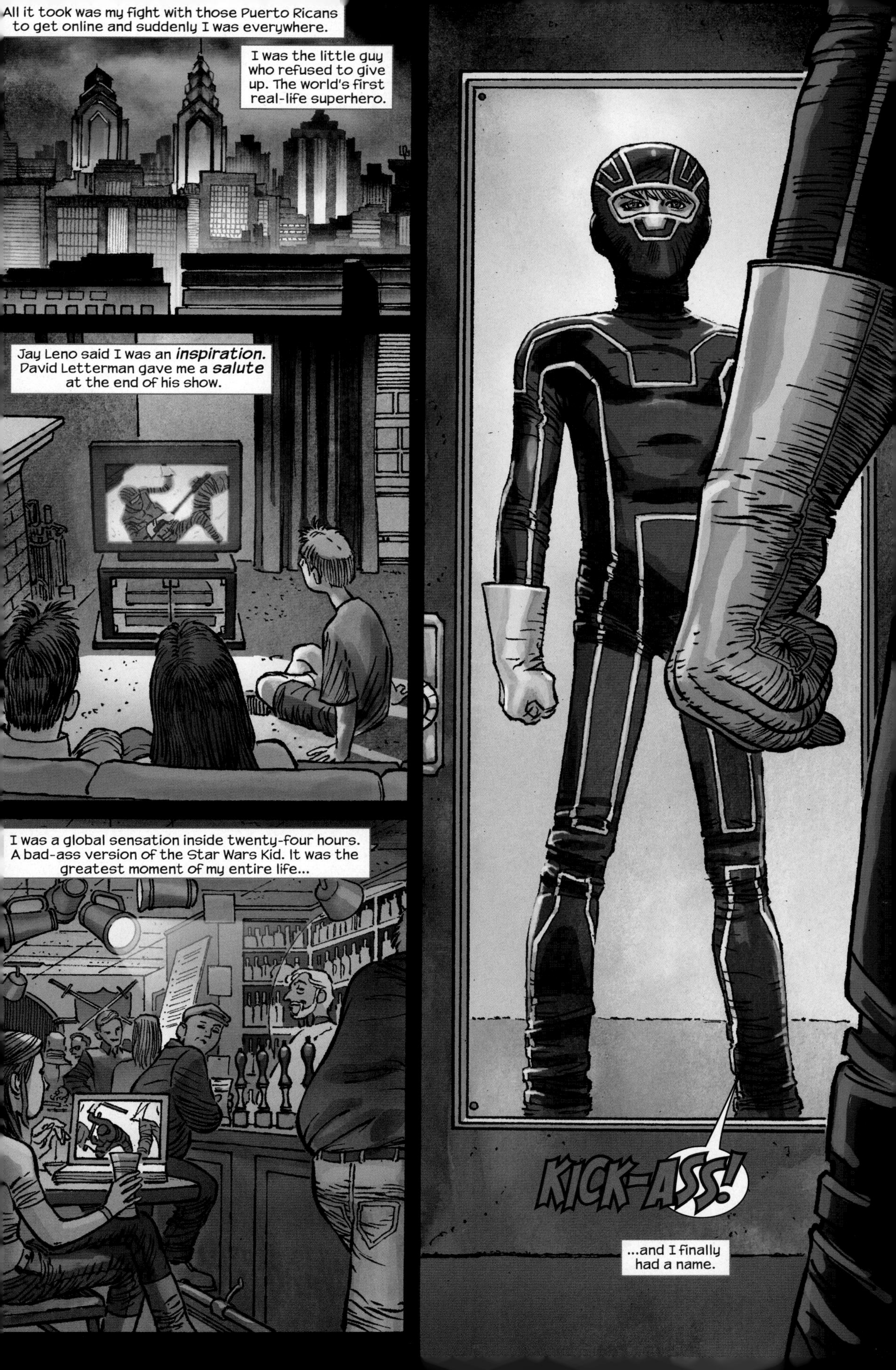
All it took was my fight with those Puerto Ricans to get online and suddenly I was everywhere.
I was the little guy who refused to give up. The world's first real-life superhero.
Jay Leno said I was an *inspiration.* David Letterman gave me a *salute* at the end of his show.
I was a global sensation inside twenty-four hours. A bad-ass version of the Star Wars Kid. It was the greatest moment of my entire life...
KICK-ASS!
...and I finally had a name.

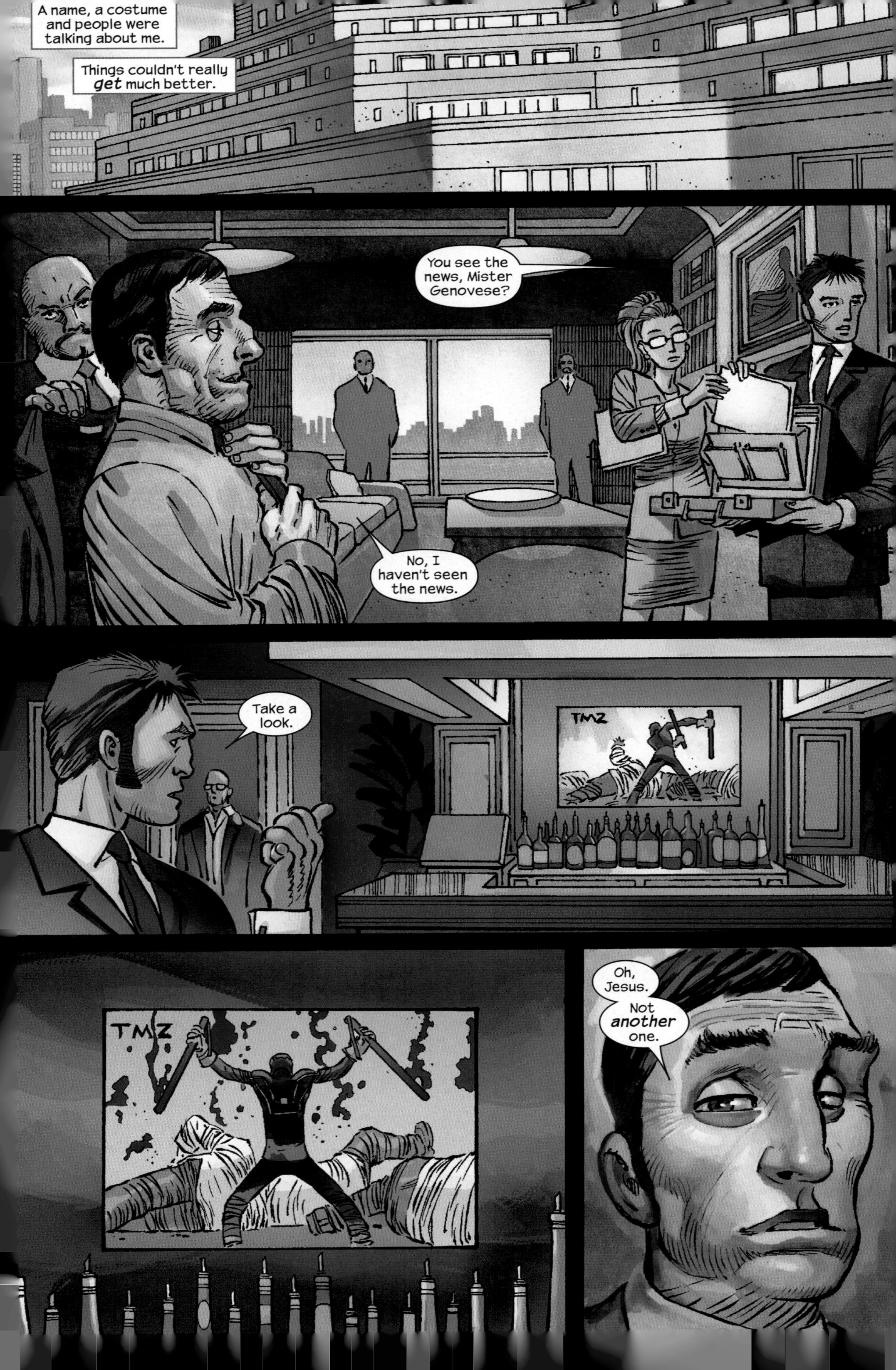
A name, a costume and people were talking about me.
Things couldn't really *get* much better.
You see the news, Mister Genovese?
No, I haven't seen the news.
Take a look.
TMZ
TMZ
Oh, Jesus.
Not *another* one.

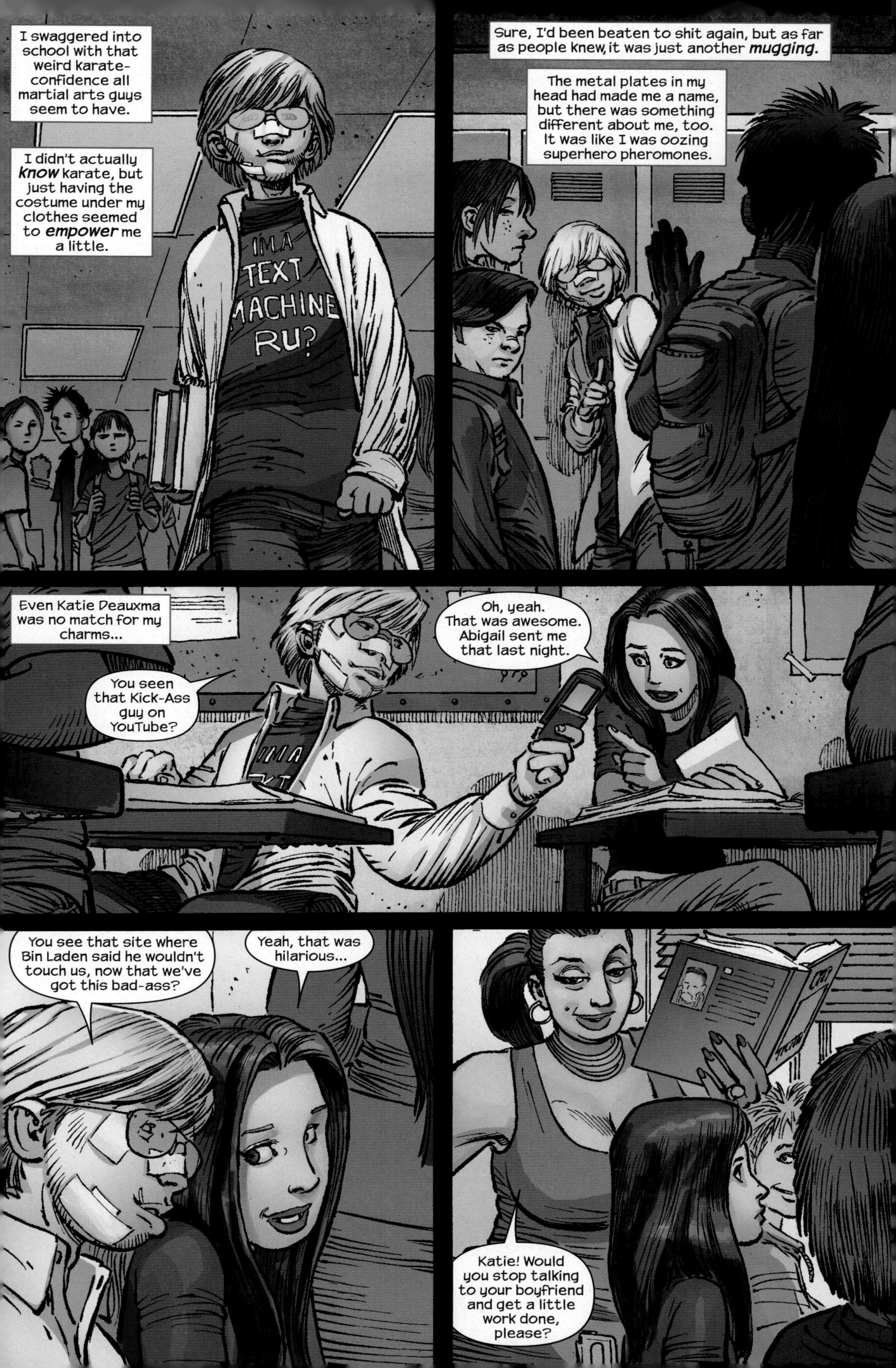

I swaggered into school with that weird karate-confidence all martial arts guys seem to have.
I didn't actually *know* karate, but just having the costume under my clothes seemed to *empower* me a little.
IM A TEXT MACHINE RU?
Sure, I'd been beaten to shit again, but as far as people knew, it was just another *mugging.*
The metal plates in my head had made me a name, but there was something different about me, too. It was like I was oozing superhero pheromones.
Even Katie Deauxma was no match for my charms...
You seen that Kick-Ass guy on YouTube?
Oh, yeah. That was awesome. Abigail sent me that last night.
You see that site where Bin Laden said he wouldn't touch us, now that we've got this bad-ass?
Yeah, that was hilarious...
Katie! Would you stop talking to your boyfriend and get a little work done, please?

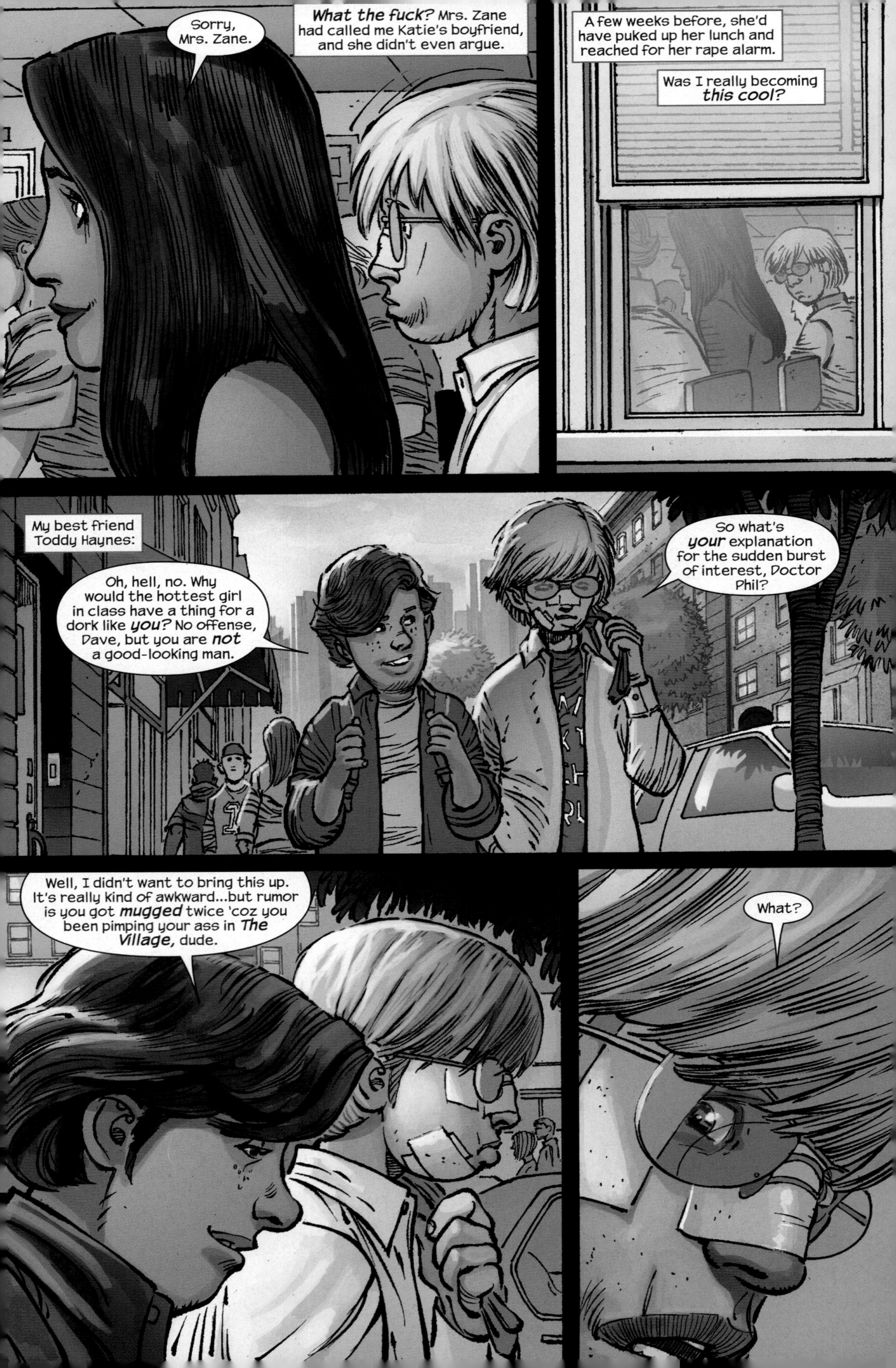
Sorry, Mrs. Zane.
What the fuck? Mrs. Zane had called me Katie's boyfriend, and she didn't even argue.
A few weeks before, she'd have puked up her lunch and reached for her rape alarm.
Was I really becoming this cool?
My best friend Toddy Haynes:
Oh, hell, no. Why would the hottest girl in class have a thing for a dork like you? No offense, Dave, but you are not a good-looking man.
So what's your explanation for the sudden burst of interest, Doctor Phil?
Well, I didn't want to bring this up. It's really kind of awkward...but rumor is you got mugged twice 'coz you been pimping your ass in The Village, dude.
What?

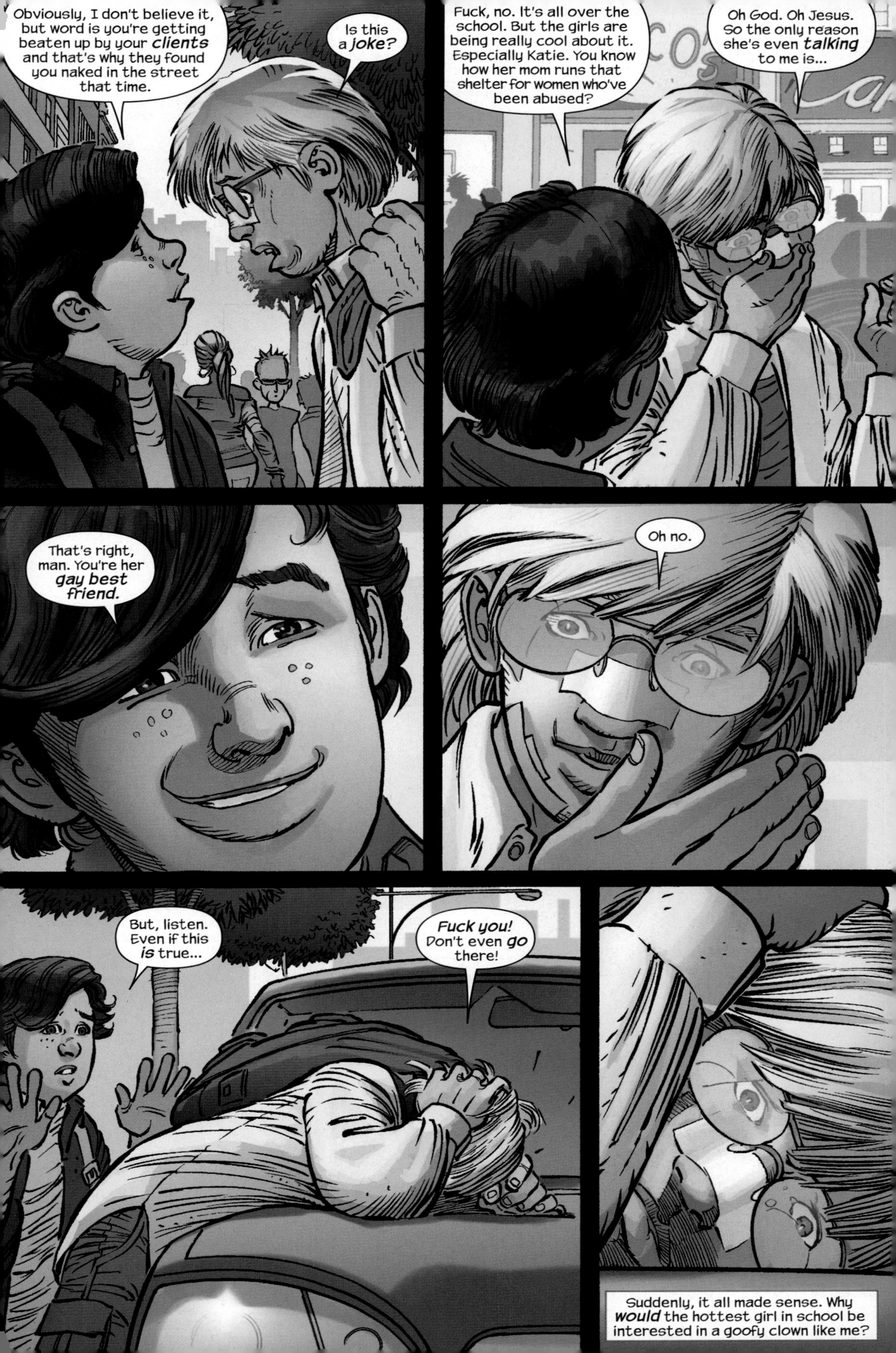

Obviously, I don't believe it, but word is you're getting beaten up by your clients and that's why they found you naked in the street that time.
Is this a joke?
Fuck, no. It's all over the school. But the girls are being really cool about it. Especially Katie. You know how her mom runs that shelter for women who've been abused?
Oh God. Oh Jesus. So the only reason she's even talking to me is...
That's right, man. You're her gay best friend.
Oh no.
But, listen. Even if this is true...
Fuck you! Don't even go there!
Suddenly, it all made sense. Why would the hottest girl in school be interested in a goofy clown like me?

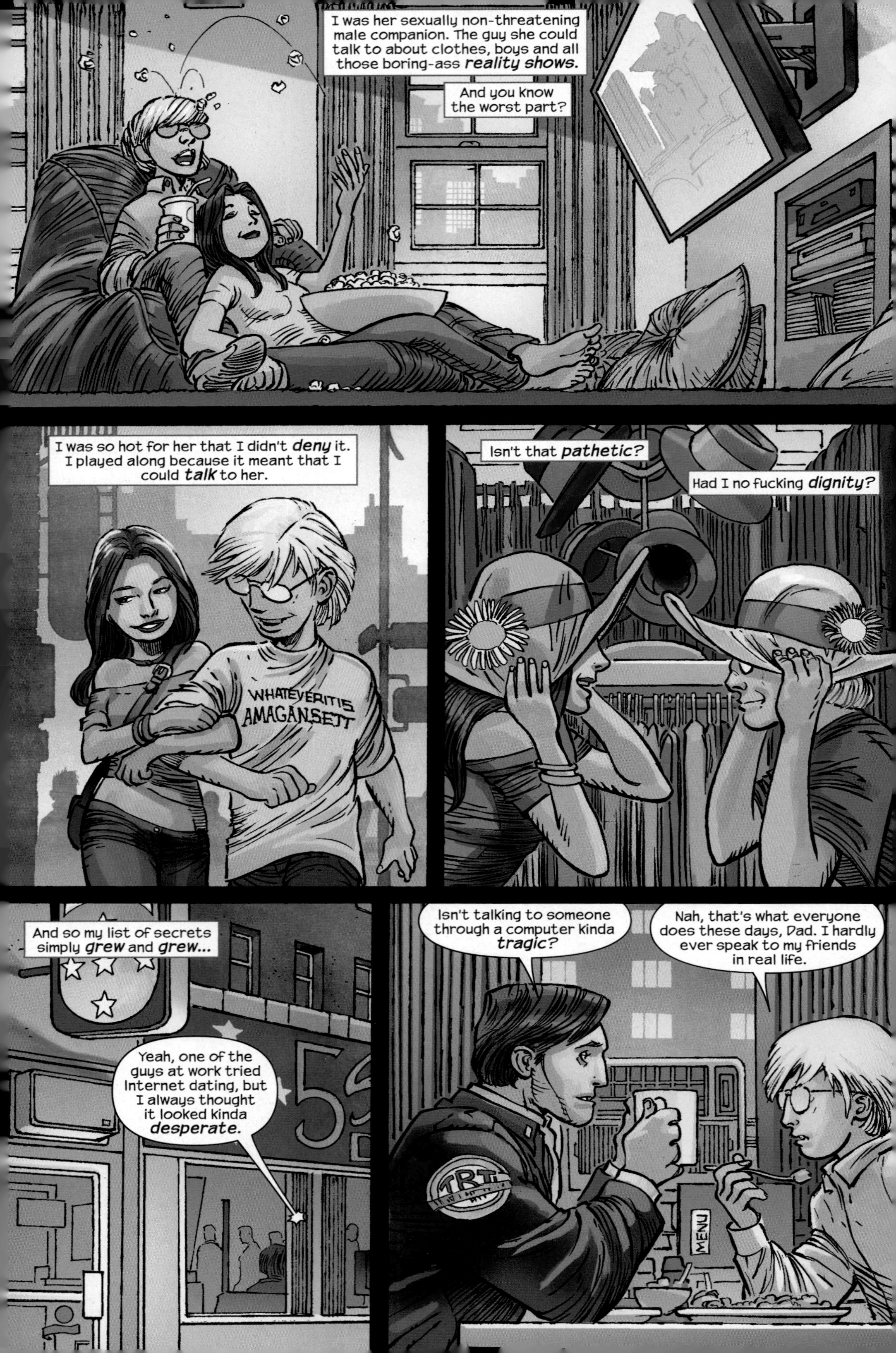
I was her sexually non-threatening male companion. The guy she could talk to about clothes, boys and all those boring-ass *reality shows.*
And you know the worst part?
I was so hot for her that I didn't *deny* it. I played along because it meant that I could *talk* to her.
WHATEVER IT IS AMAGANSETT
Isn't that *pathetic?*
Had I no fucking *dignity?*
And so my list of secrets simply *grew* and *grew*...
Yeah, one of the guys at work tried Internet dating, but I always thought it looked kinda *desperate.*
Isn't talking to someone through a computer kinda *tragic?*
Nah, that's what everyone does these days, Dad. I hardly ever speak to my friends in real life.
MENU

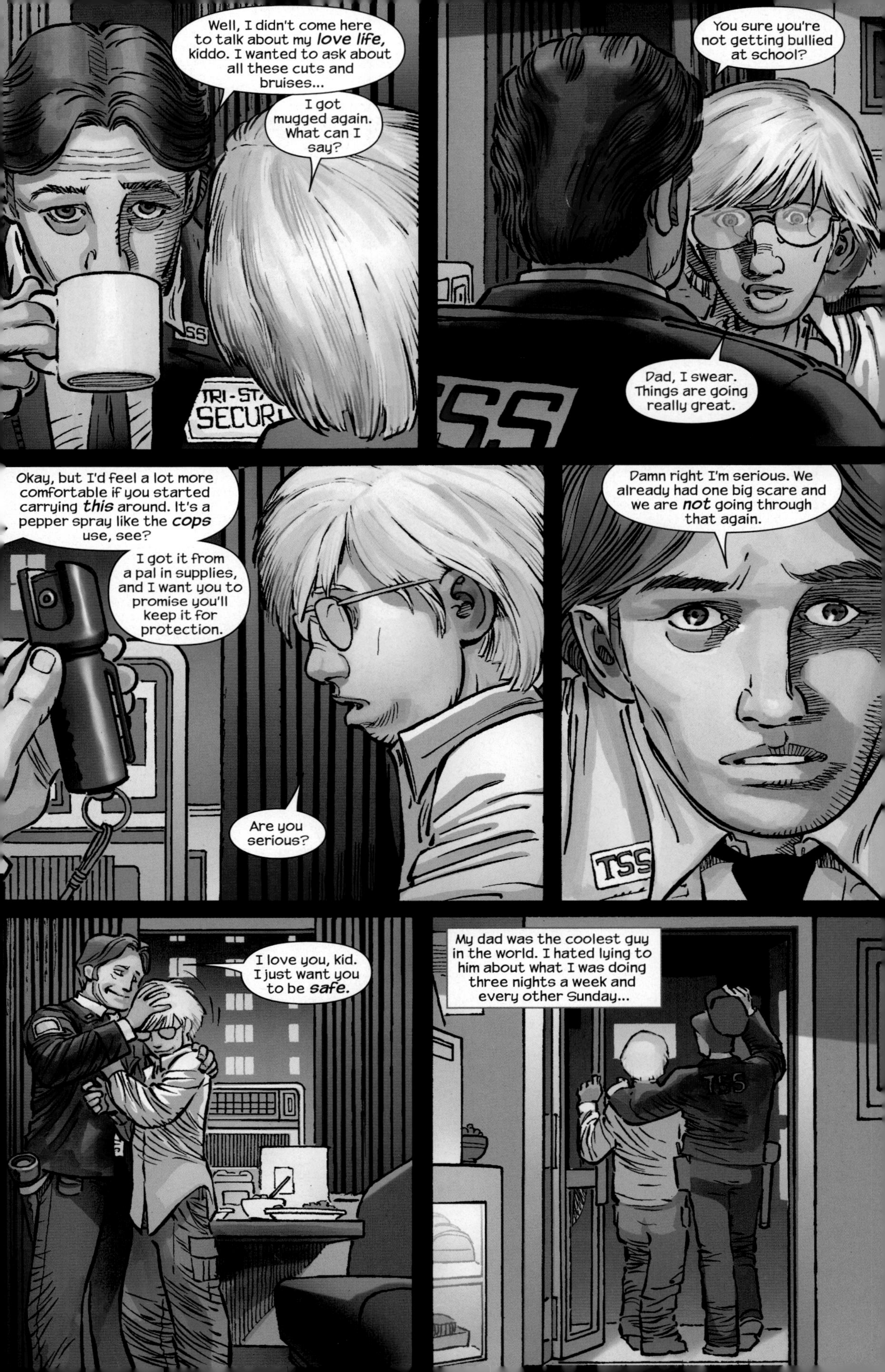
Well, I didn't come here to talk about my *love life,* kiddo. I wanted to ask about all these cuts and bruises...
I got mugged again. What can I say?
TRI-ST
SECUR
TSS
You sure you're not getting bullied at school?
Dad, I swear. Things are going really great.
TSS
Okay, but I'd feel a lot more comfortable if you started carrying ***this*** around. It's a pepper spray like the ***cops*** use, see?
I got it from a pal in supplies, and I want you to promise you'll keep it for protection.
Are you serious?
Damn right I'm serious. We already had one big scare and we are ***not*** going through that again.
TSS
I love you, kid. I just want you to be ***safe.***
My dad was the coolest guy in the world. I hated lying to him about what I was doing three nights a week and every other Sunday...
TSS

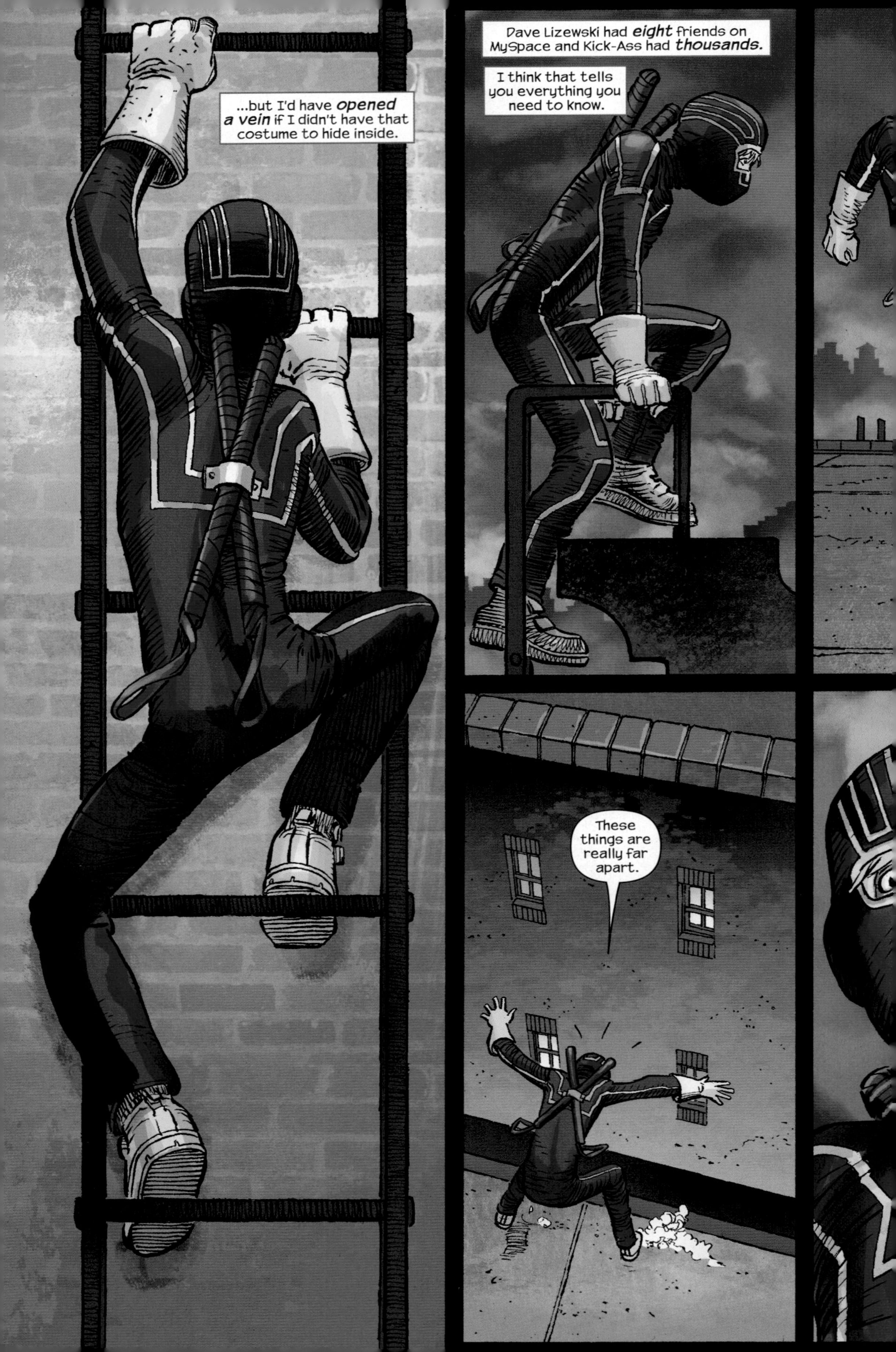
...but I'd have opened a vein if I didn't have that costume to hide inside.
Dave Lizewski had eight friends on MySpace and Kick-Ass had thousands.
I think that tells you everything you need to know.
These things are really far apart.

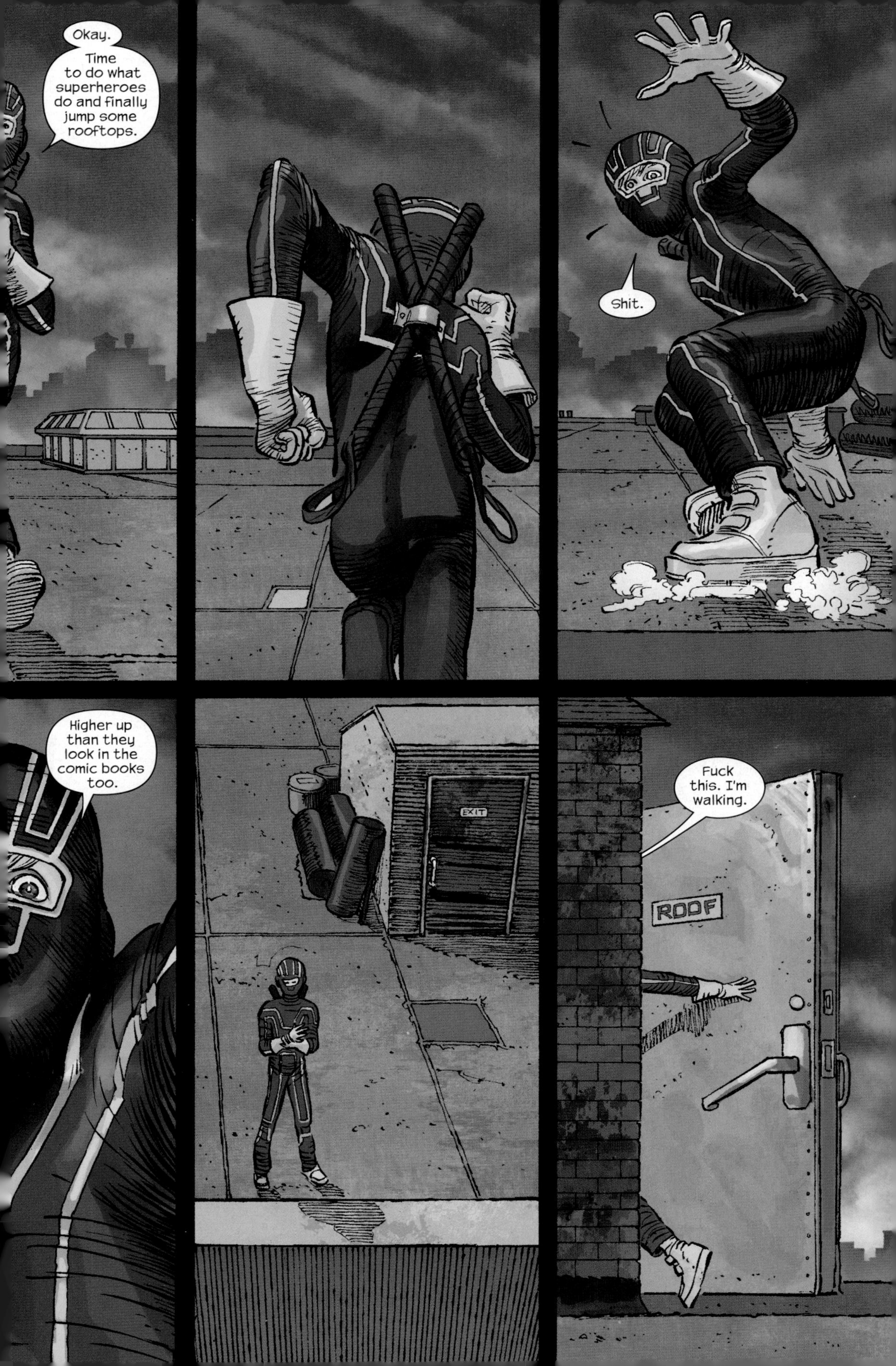
Okay.
Time to do what superheroes do and finally jump some rooftops.
Shit.
Higher up than they look in the comic books too.
EXIT
Fuck this. I'm walking.
ROOF

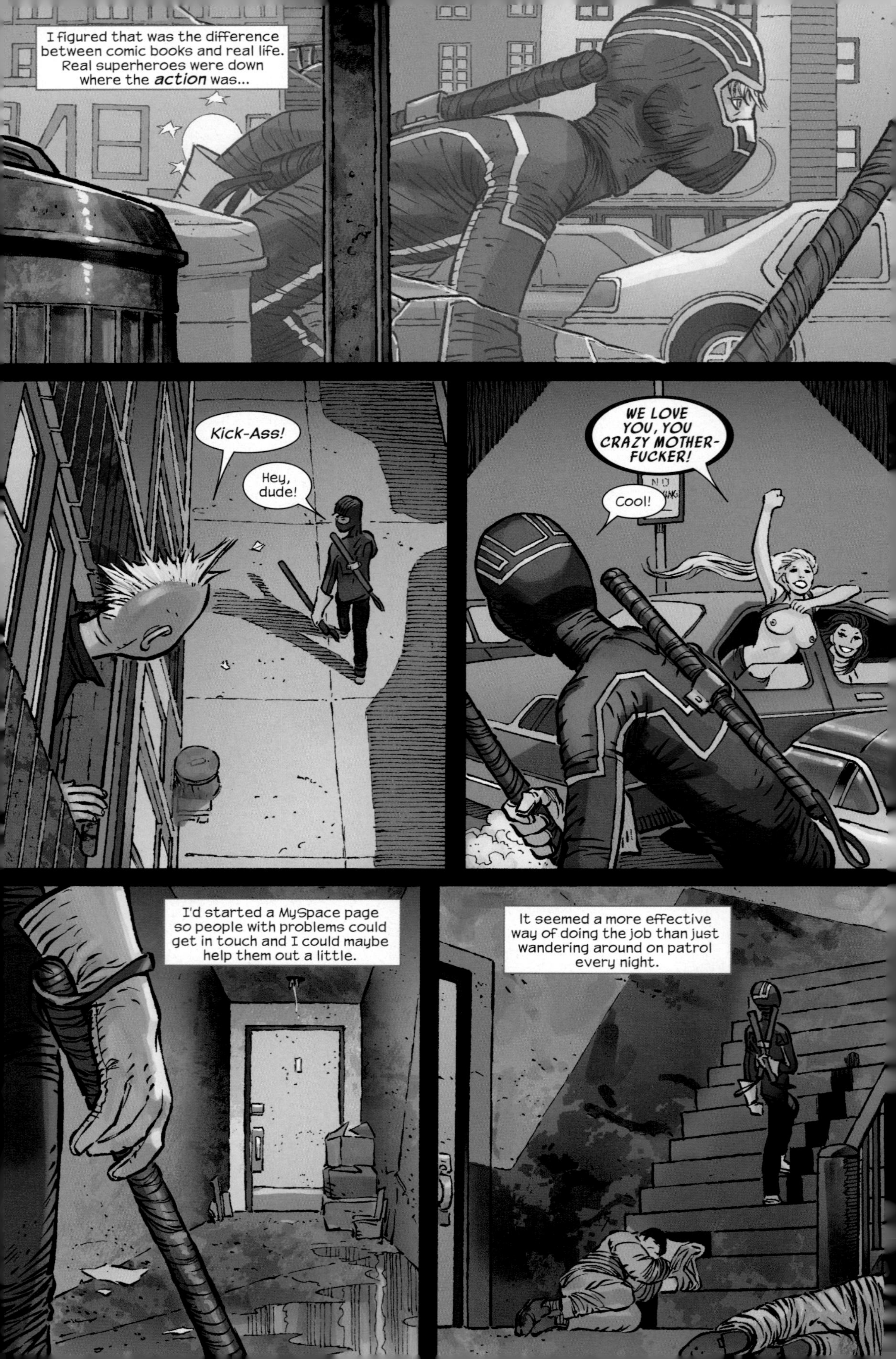

I figured that was the difference between comic books and real life. Real superheroes were down where the *action* was...
Kick-Ass!
Hey, dude!
WE LOVE YOU, YOU CRAZY MOTHER-FUCKER!
Cool!
I'd started a MySpace page so people with problems could get in touch and I could maybe help them out a little.
It seemed a more effective way of doing the job than just wandering around on patrol every night.

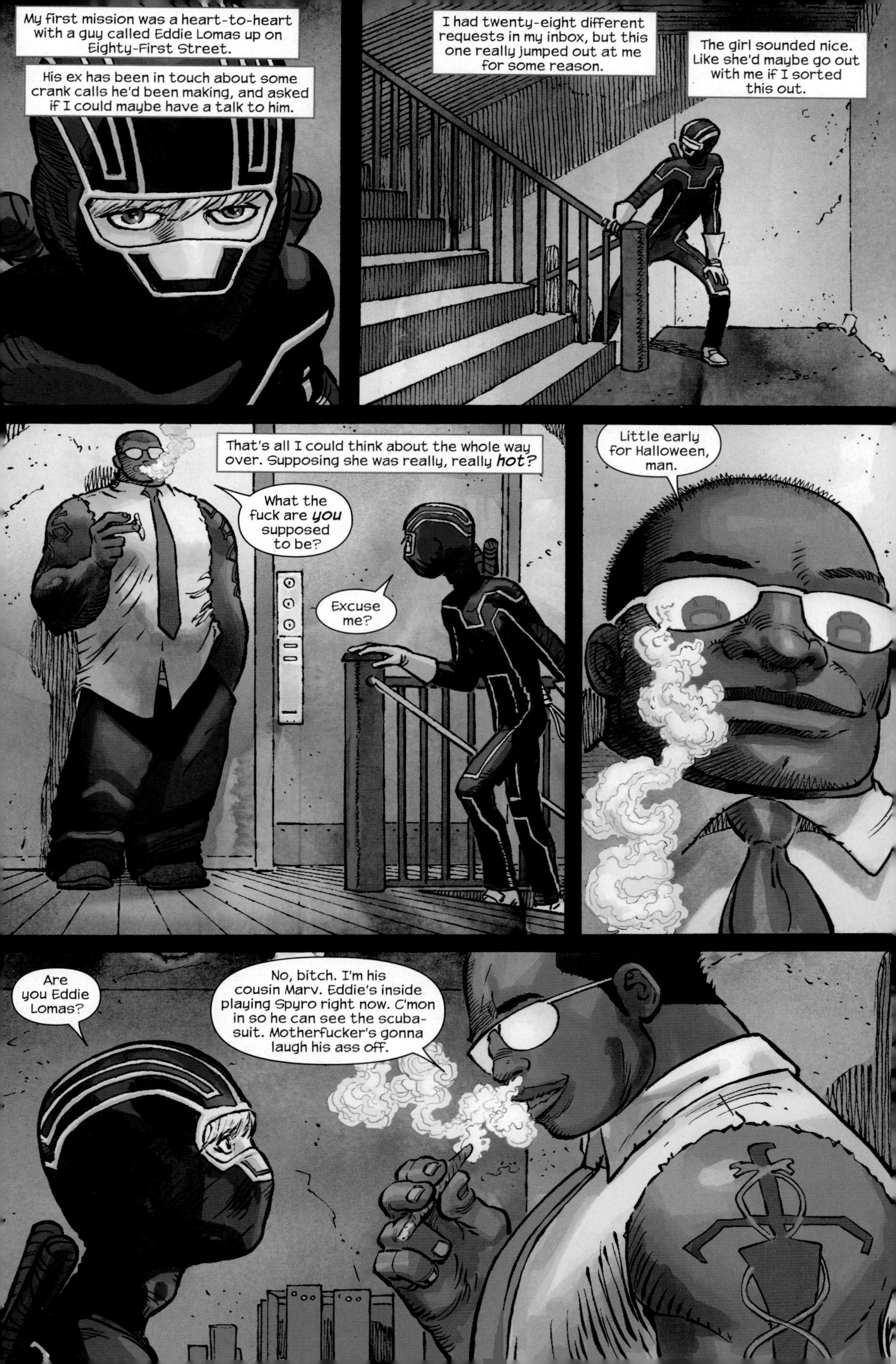
My first mission was a heart-to-heart with a guy called Eddie Lomas up on Eighty-First Street.
His ex has been in touch about some crank calls he'd been making, and asked if I could maybe have a talk to him.
I had twenty-eight different requests in my inbox, but this one really jumped out at me for some reason.
The girl sounded nice. Like she'd maybe go out with me if I sorted this out.
That's all I could think about the whole way over. Supposing she was really, really *hot?*
What the fuck are *you* supposed to be?
Excuse me?
Little early for Halloween, man.
Are you Eddie Lomas?
No, bitch. I'm his cousin Marv. Eddie's inside playing Spyro right now. C'mon in so he can see the scuba-suit. Motherfucker's gonna laugh his ass off.

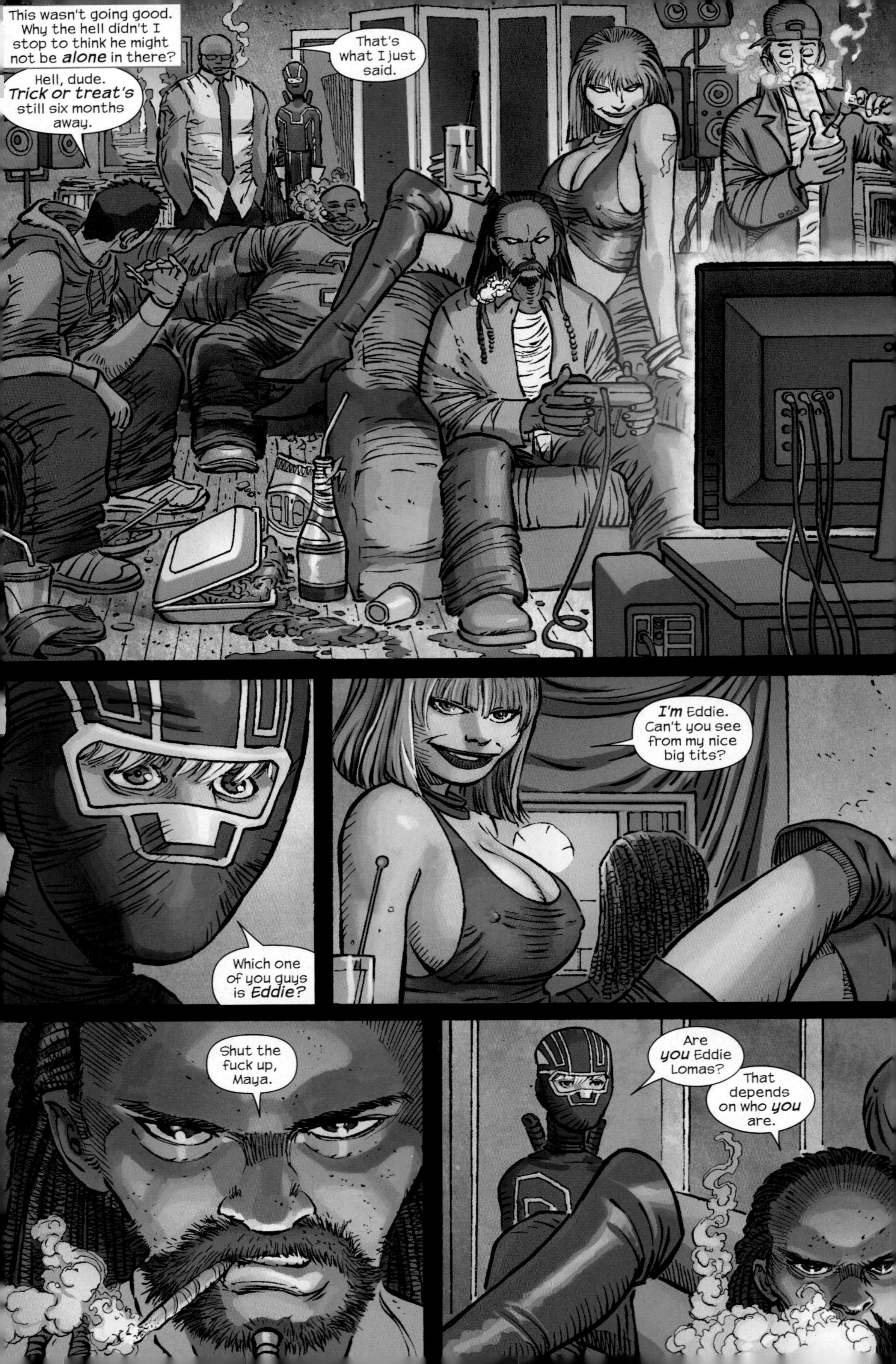
This wasn't going good. Why the hell didn't I stop to think he might not be *alone* in there?
That's what I just said.
Hell, dude. *Trick or treat's* still six months away.
Which one of you guys is *Eddie*?
I'm Eddie. Can't you see from my nice big tits?
Shut the fuck up, Maya.
Are *you* Eddie Lomas?
That depends on who *you* are.

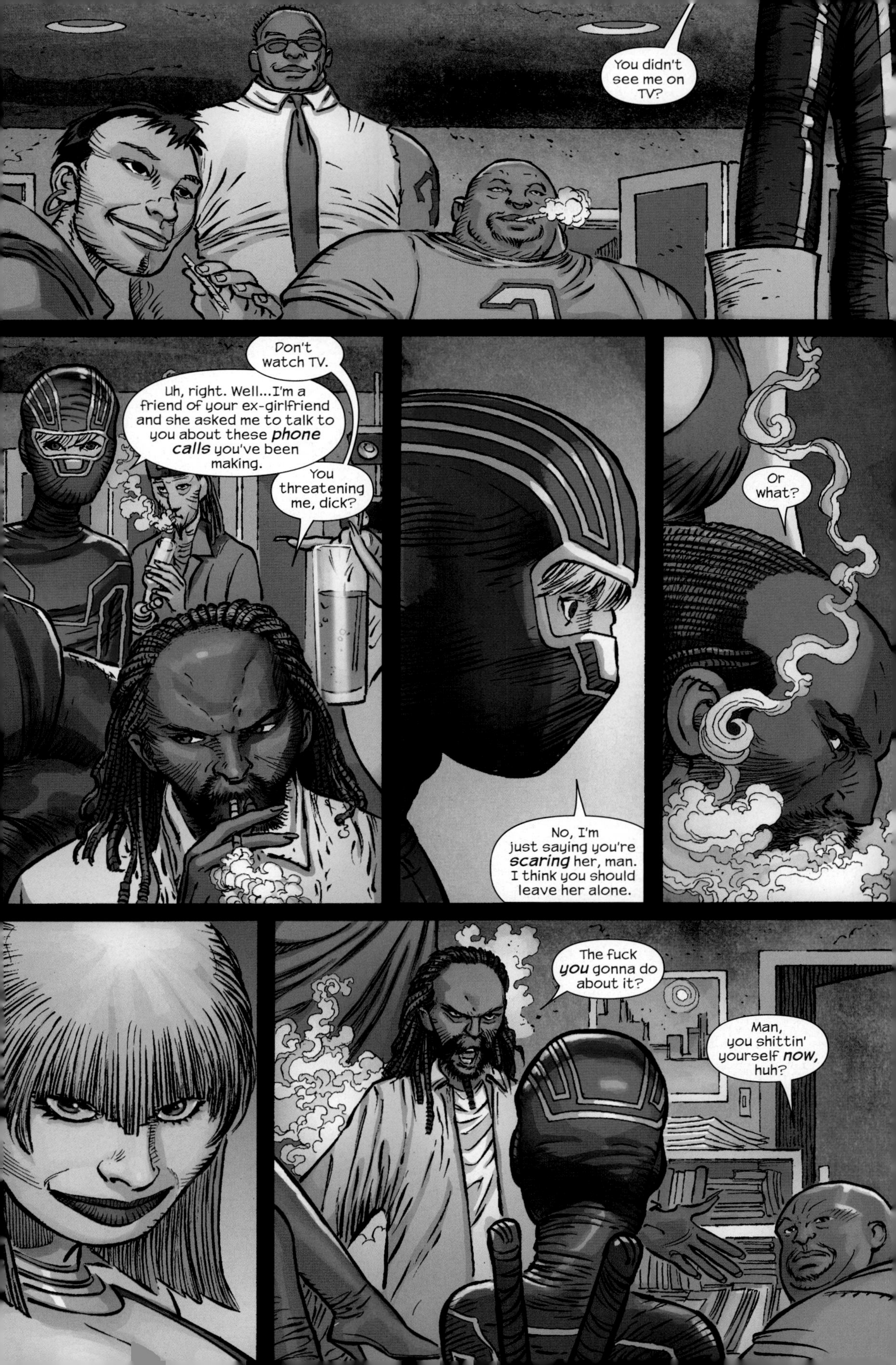
You didn't see me on TV?
Don't watch TV.
Uh, right. Well...I'm a friend of your ex-girlfriend and she asked me to talk to you about these *phone calls* you've been making.
You threatening me, dick?
No, I'm just saying you're *scaring* her, man. I think you should leave her alone.
Or what?
The fuck *you* gonna do about it?
Man, you shittin' yourself *now,* huh?

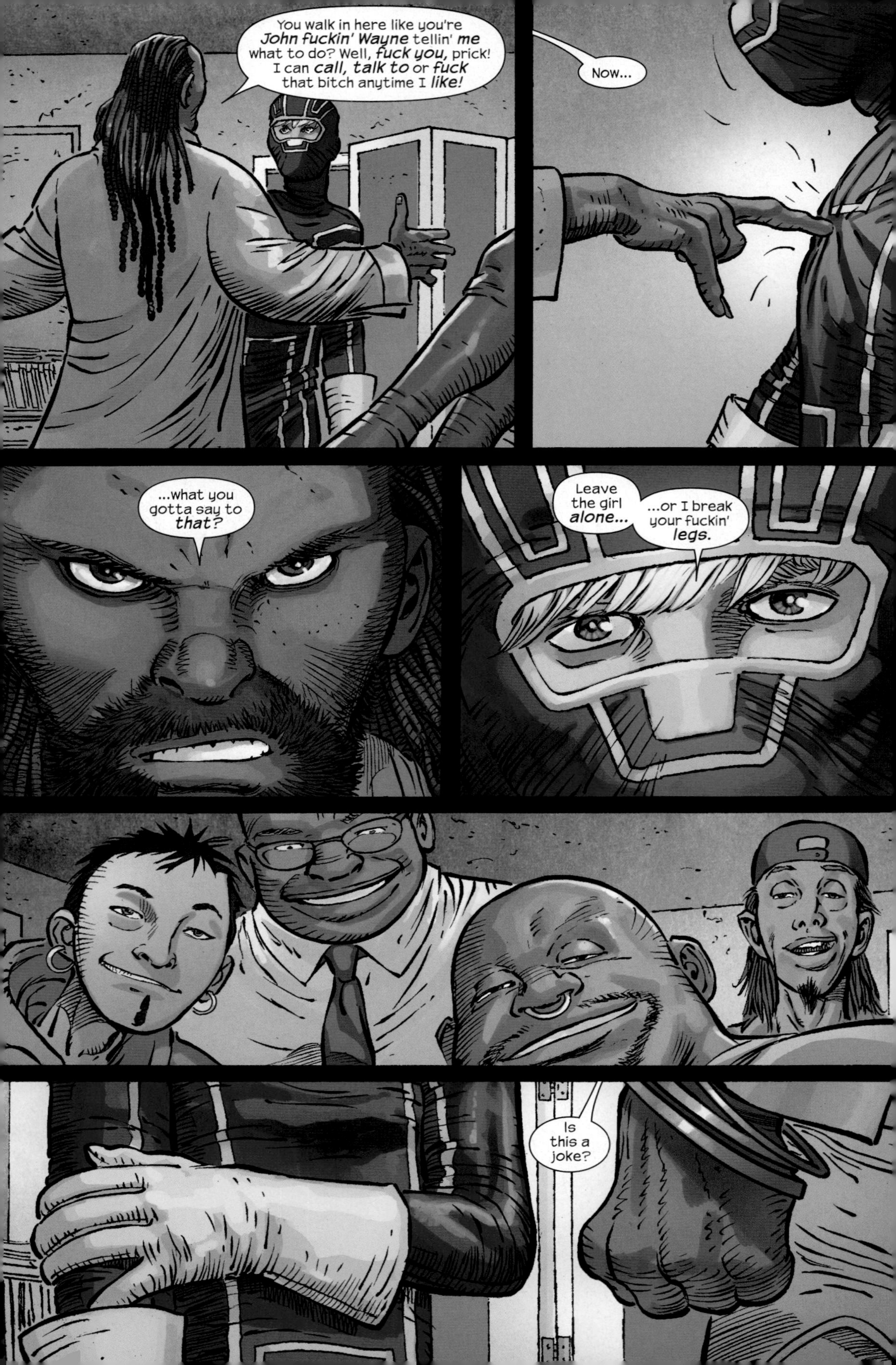
You walk in here like you're John fuckin' Wayne tellin' me what to do? Well, fuck you, prick! I can call, talk to or fuck that bitch anytime I like!
Now...
...what you gotta say to that?
Leave the girl alone...
...or I break your fuckin' legs.
Is this a joke?

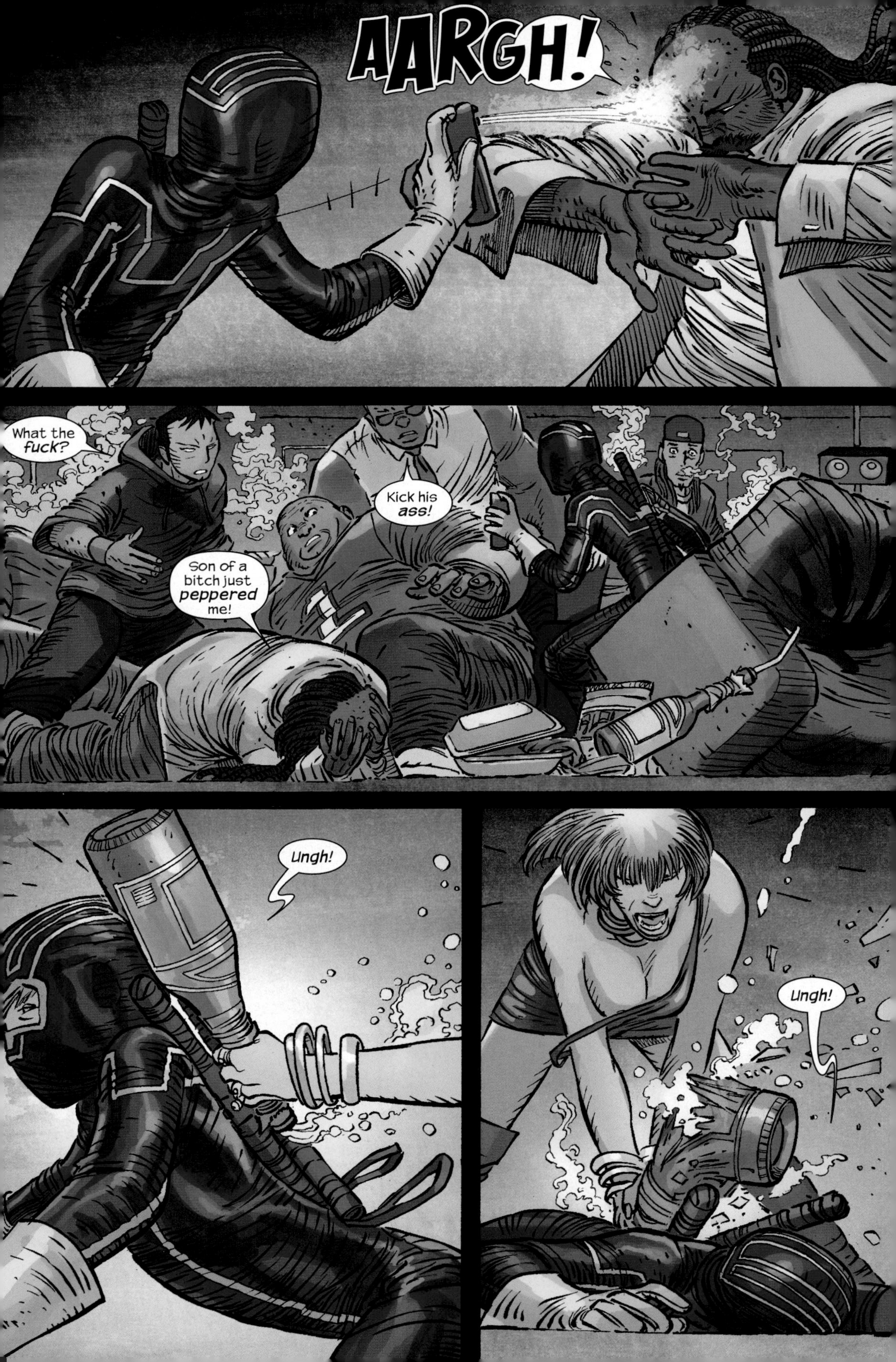
AARGH!
What the *fuck?*
Kick his *ass!*
Son of a bitch just *peppered* me!
Ungh!
Ungh!

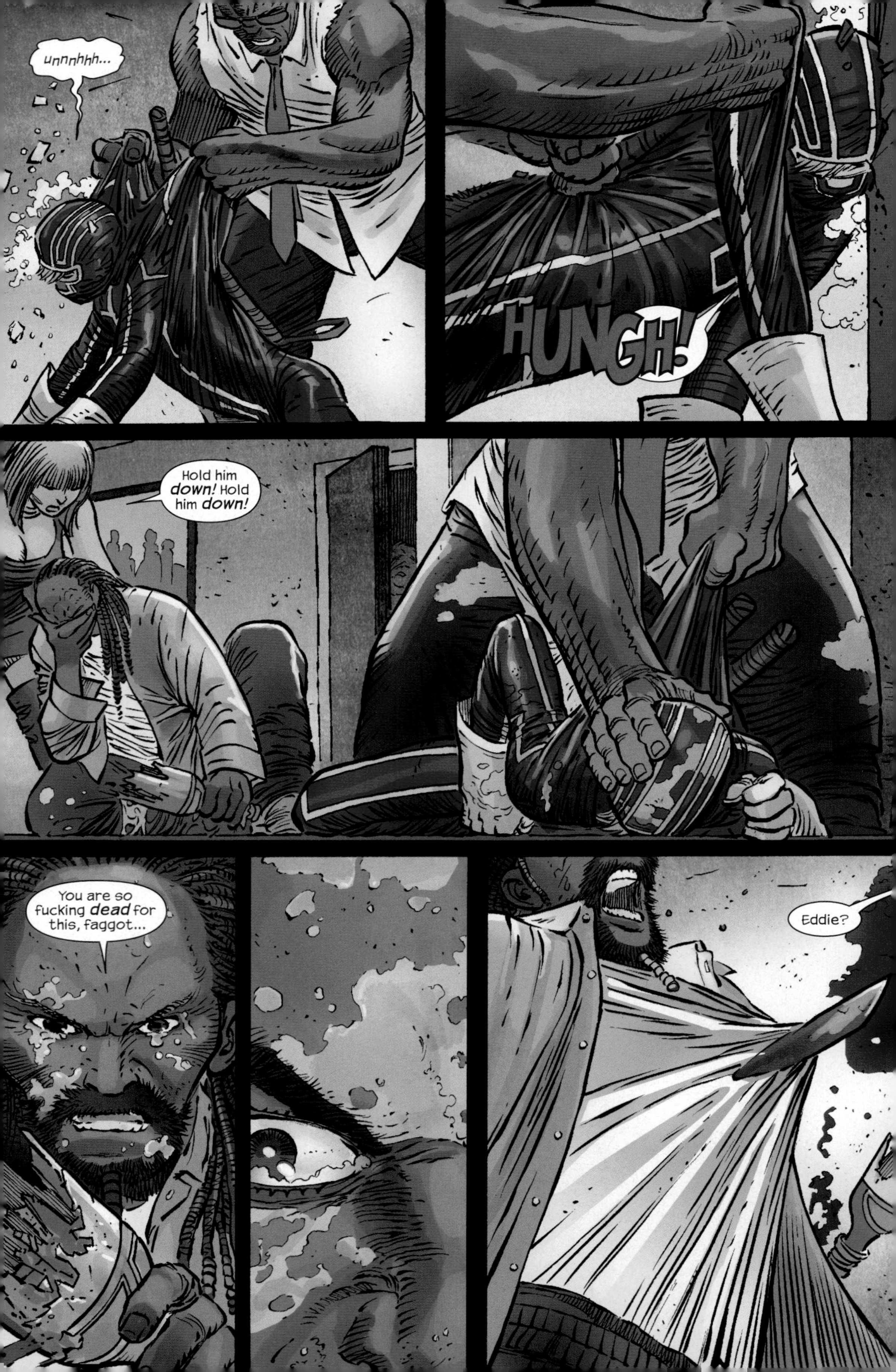
unnnhhh...
HUNGH!
Hold him *down!* Hold him *down!*
You are so fucking *dead* for this, faggot...
Eddie?

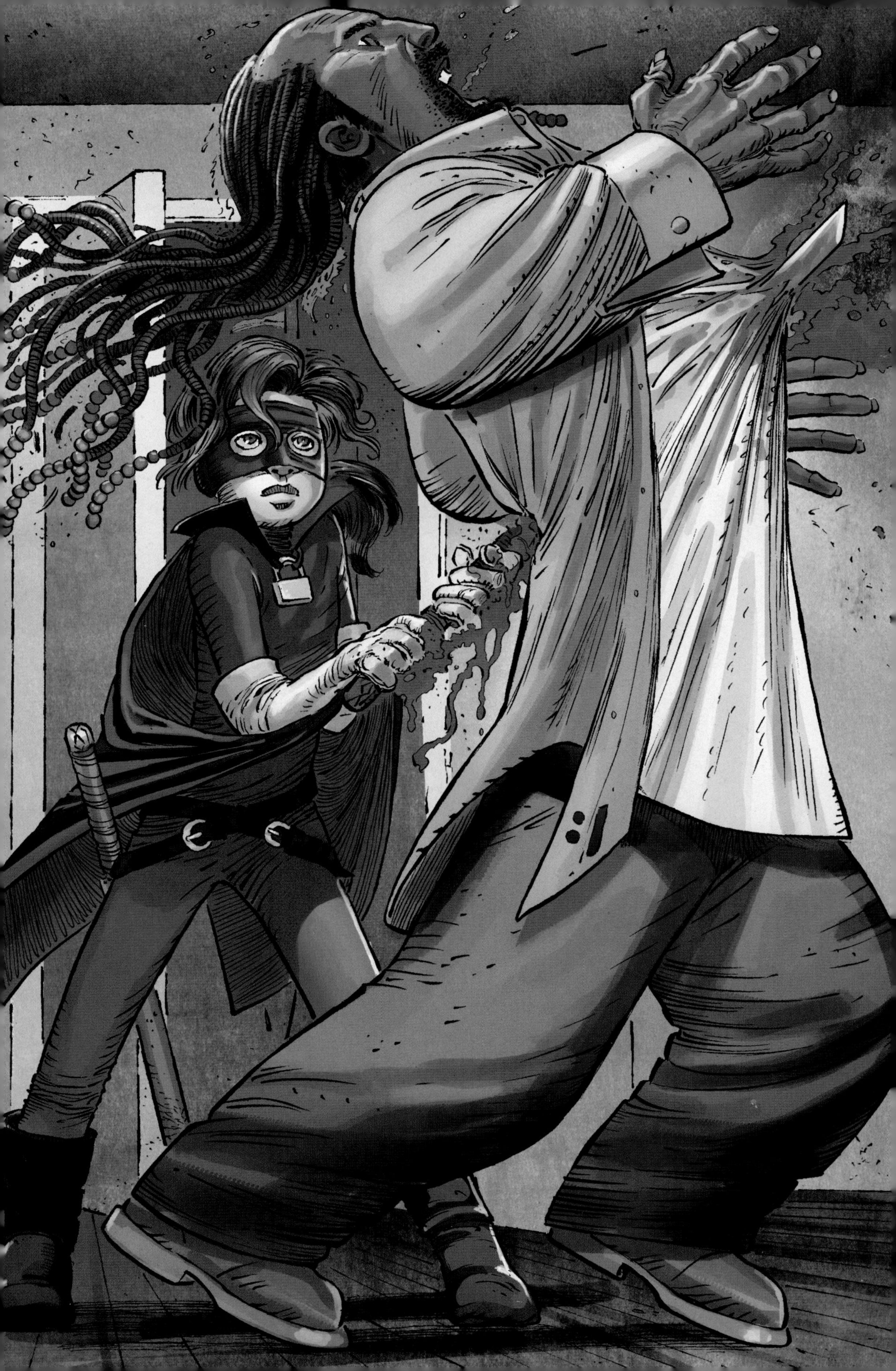

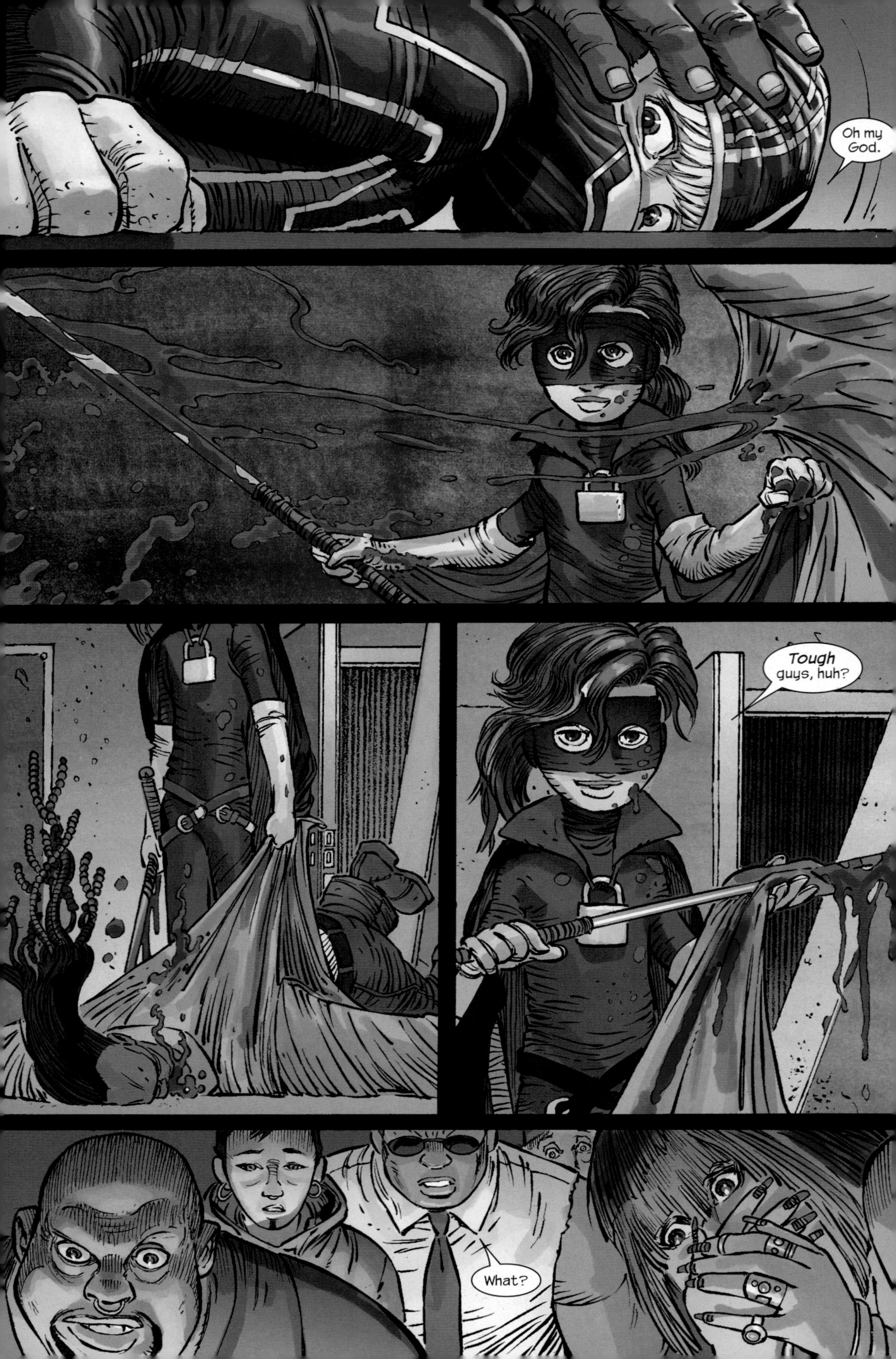
Oh my God.
Tough guys, huh?
What?

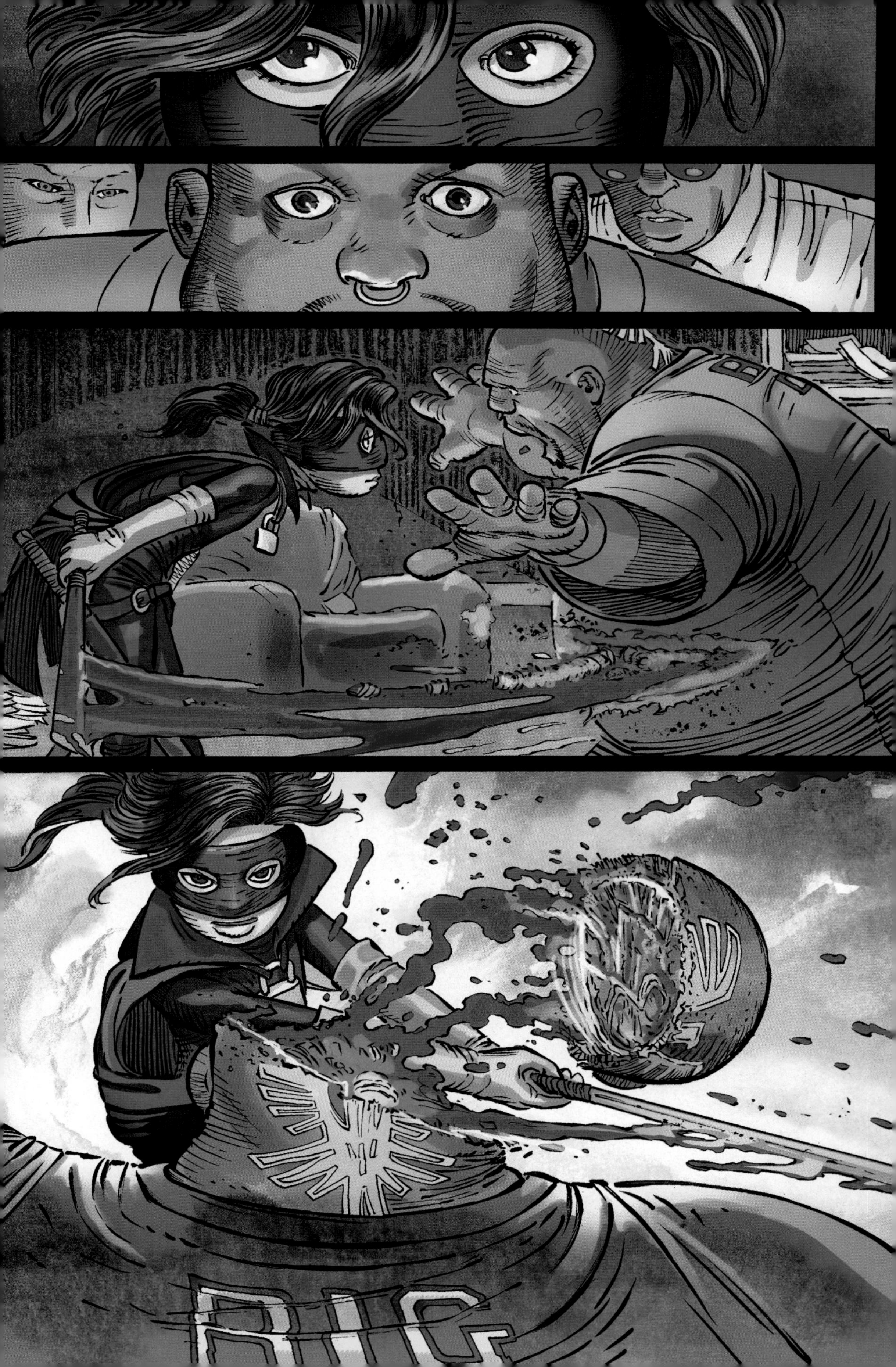

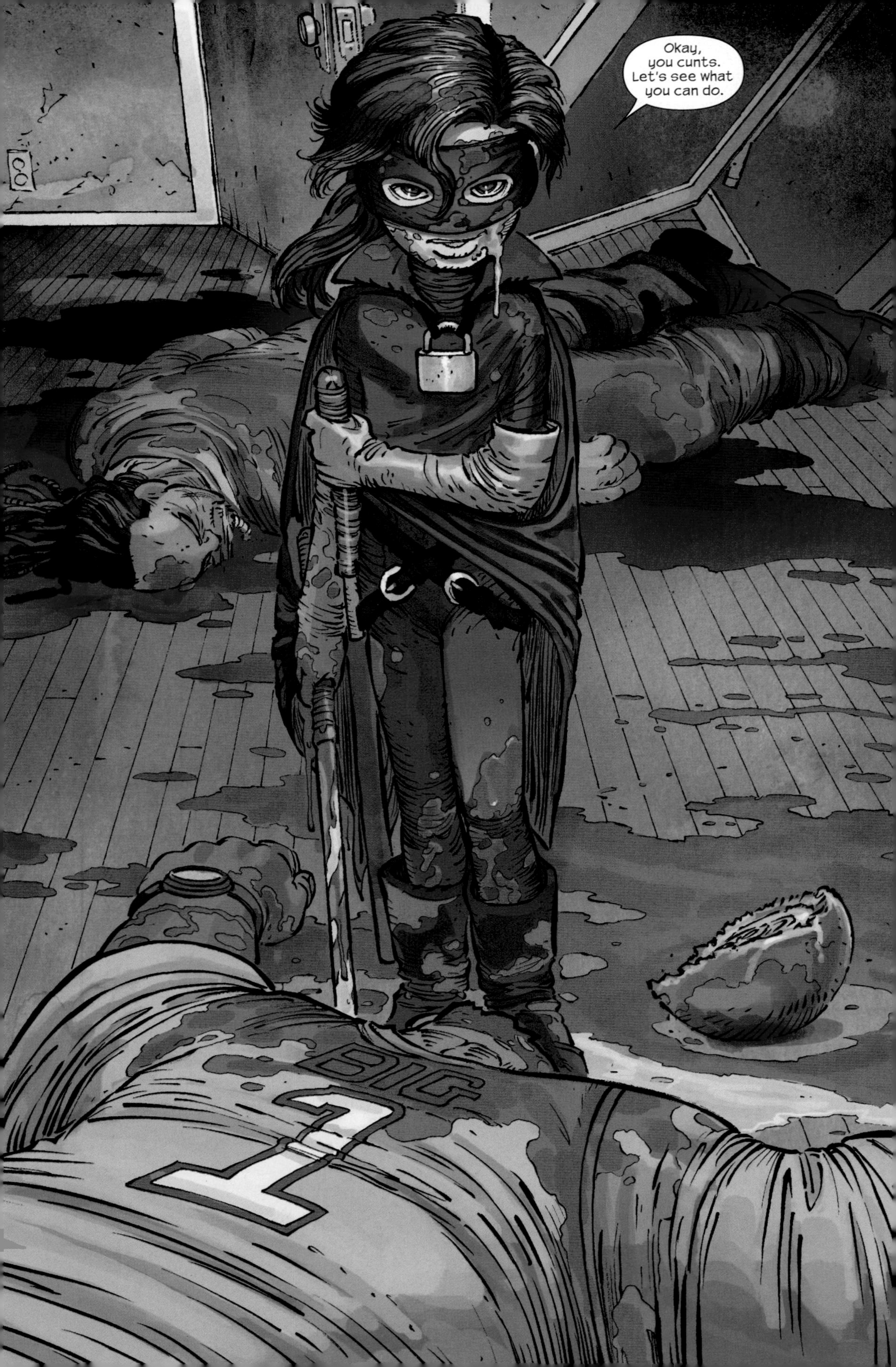
Okay, you cunts. Let's see what you can do.
BIG

FOUR

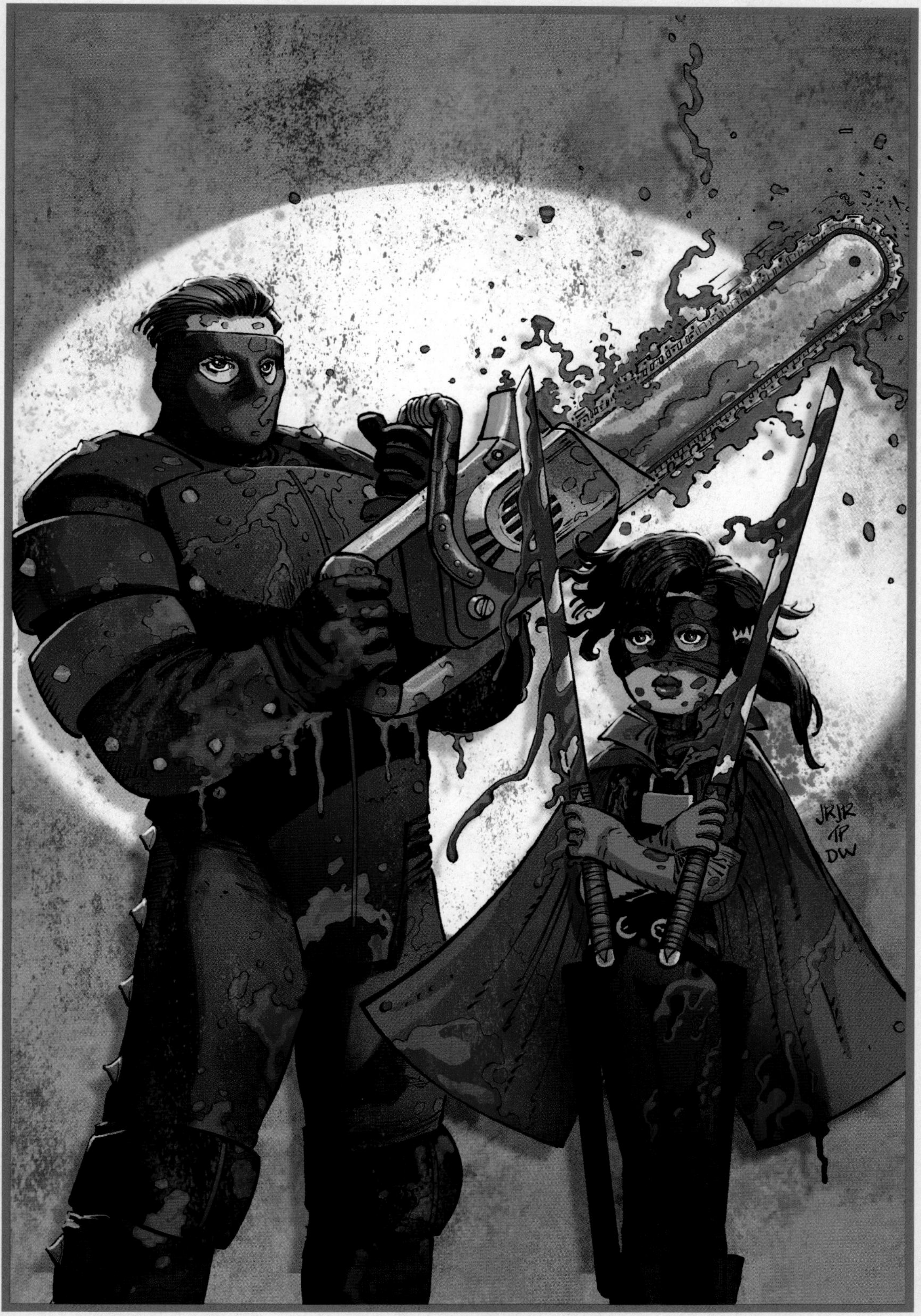
JRJR
TP
DW

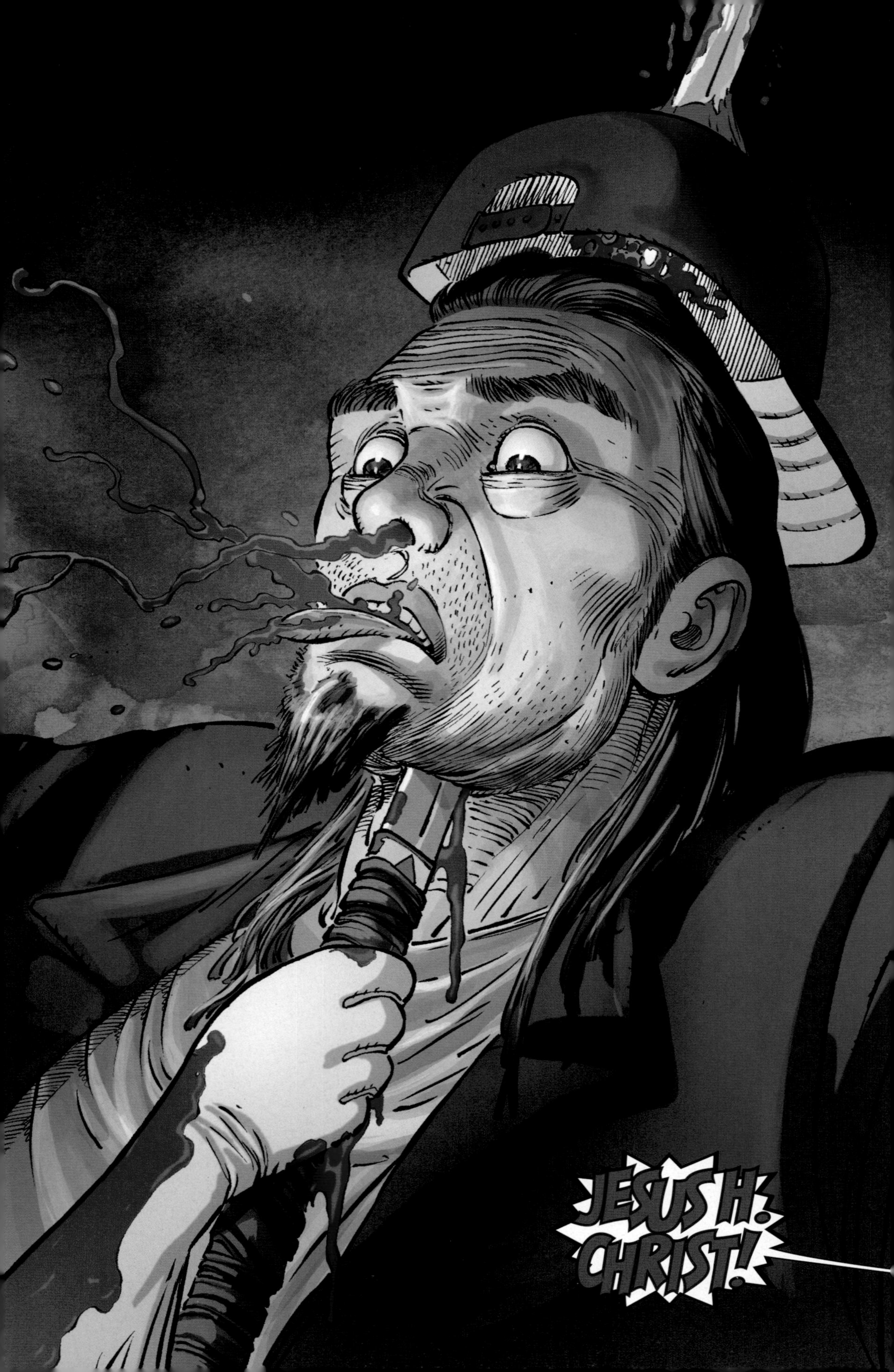
JESUS H. CHRIST!

She was like John Rambo meets Polly Pocket.

Dakota Fanning crossed with Death Wish 4.

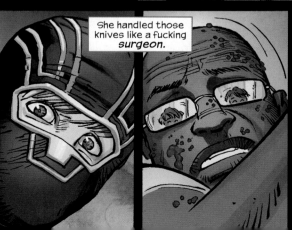

She handled those knives like a fucking *surgeon.*

I still can't believe she was only *ten...*

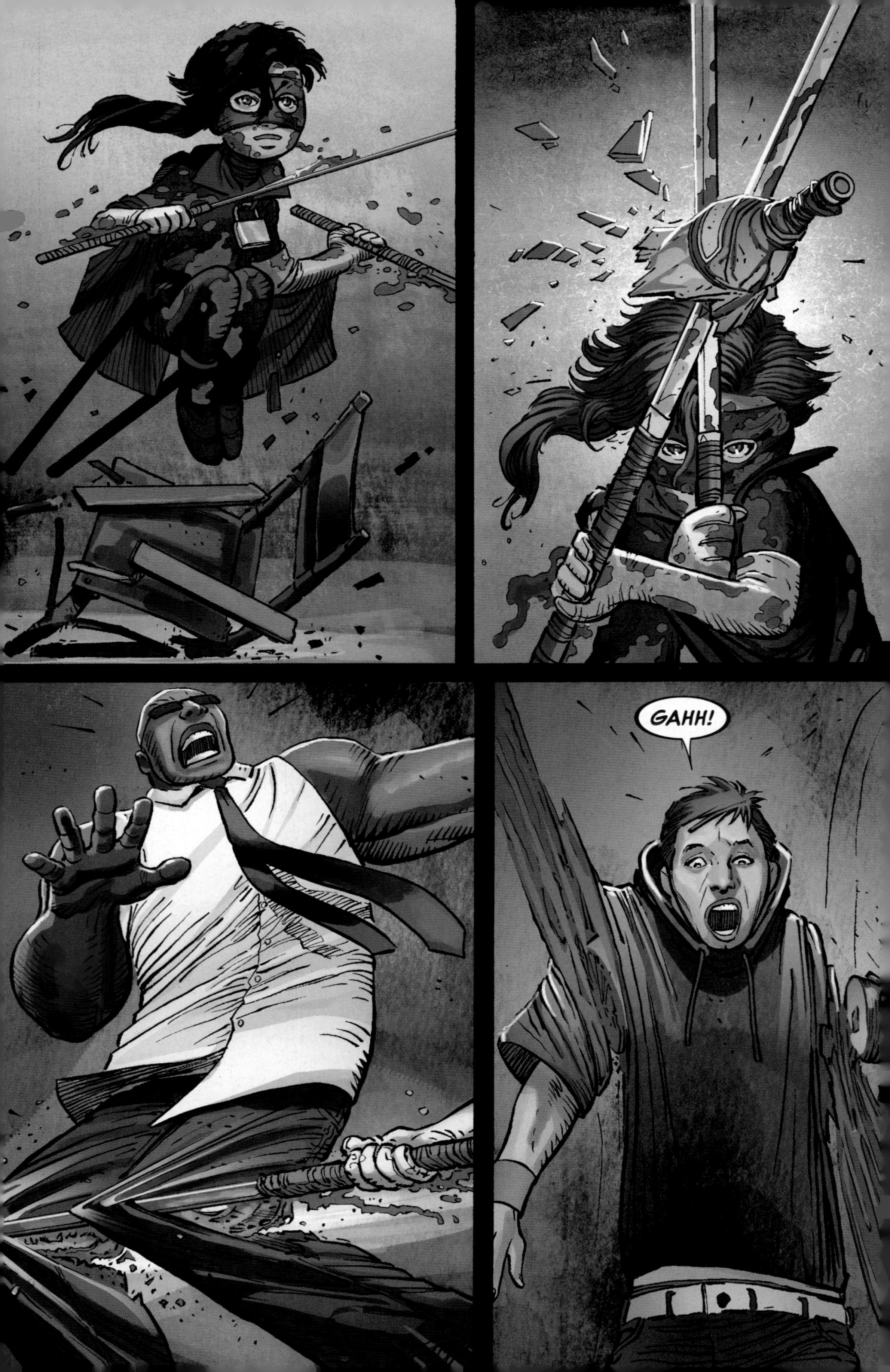
GAHH!

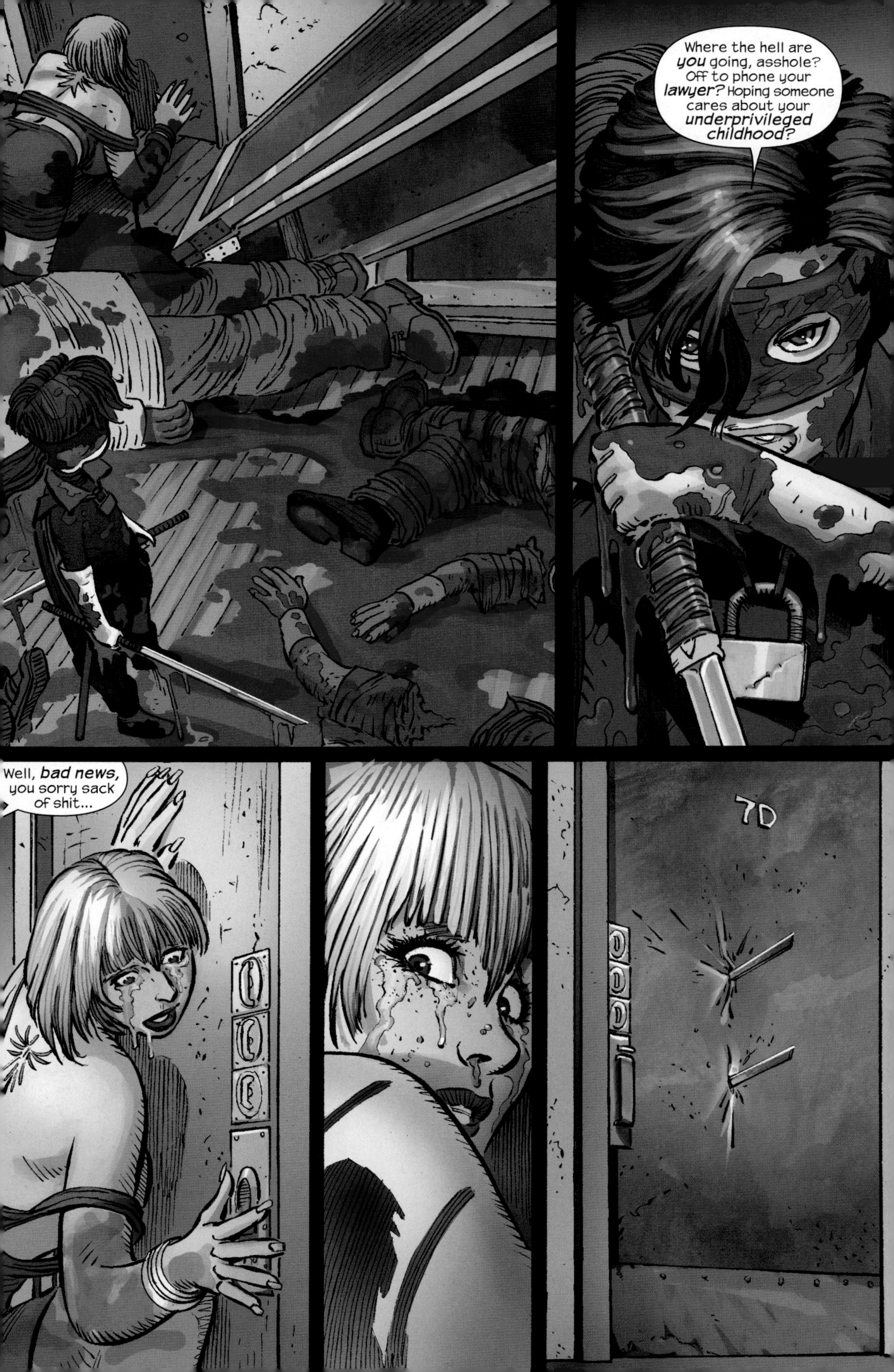
Where the hell are *you* going, asshole? Off to phone your *lawyer?* Hoping someone cares about your *underprivileged childhood?*
Well, *bad news,* you sorry sack of shit...
7D

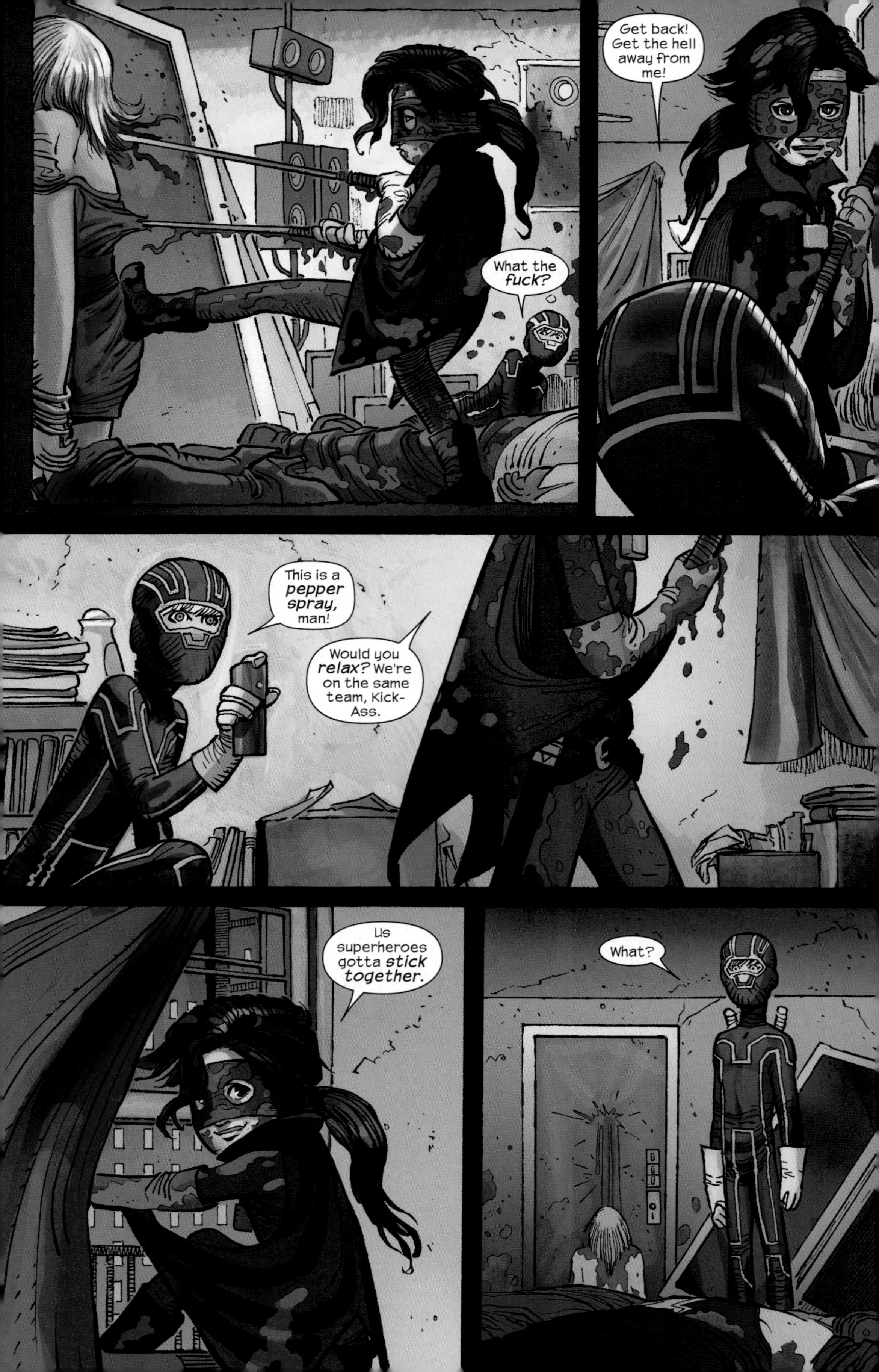
What the fuck?
Get back! Get the hell away from me!
This is a pepper spray, man!
Would you relax? We're on the same team, Kick-Ass.
Us superheroes gotta stick together.
What?

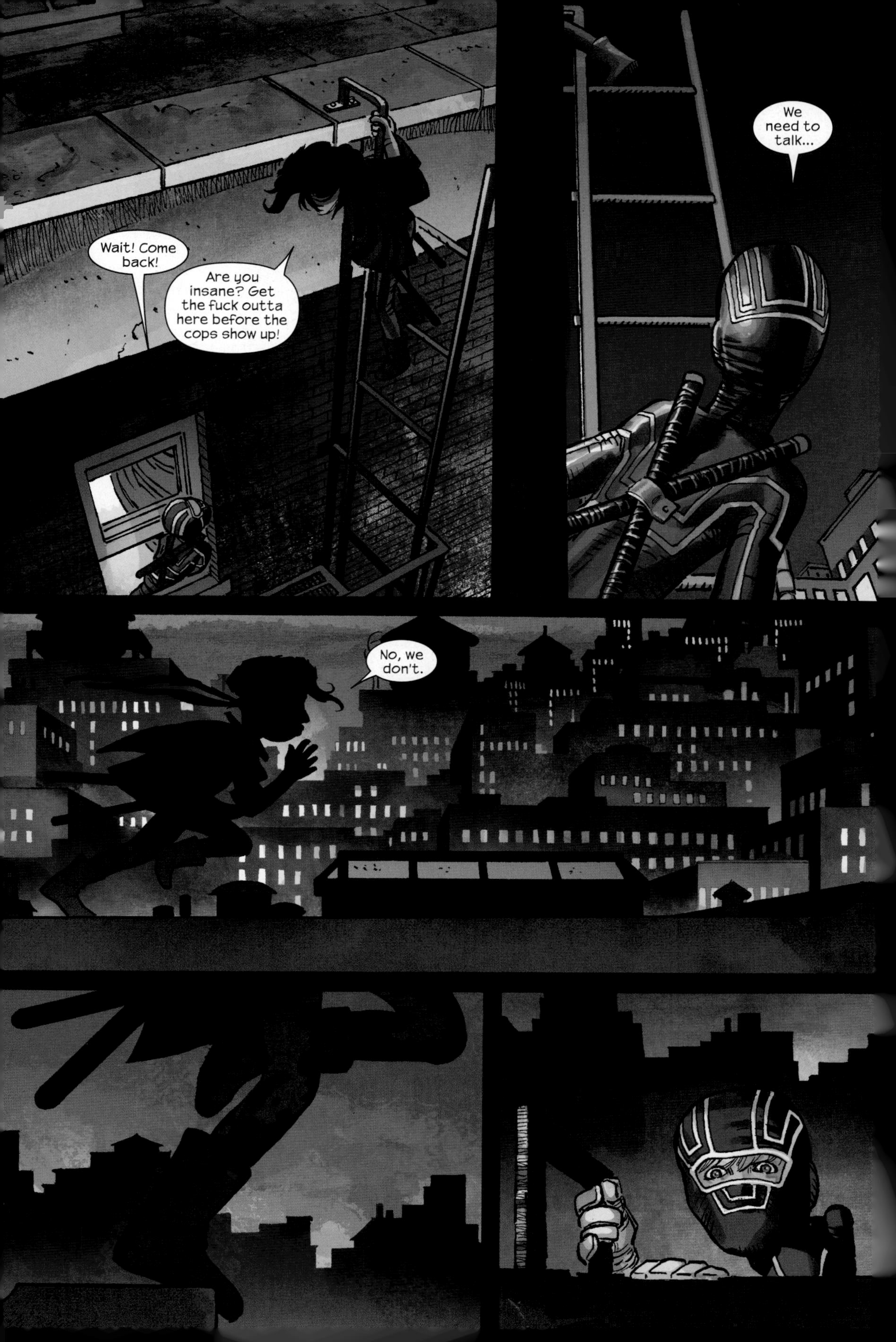
Wait! Come back!
Are you insane? Get the fuck outta here before the cops show up!
We need to talk...
No, we don't.

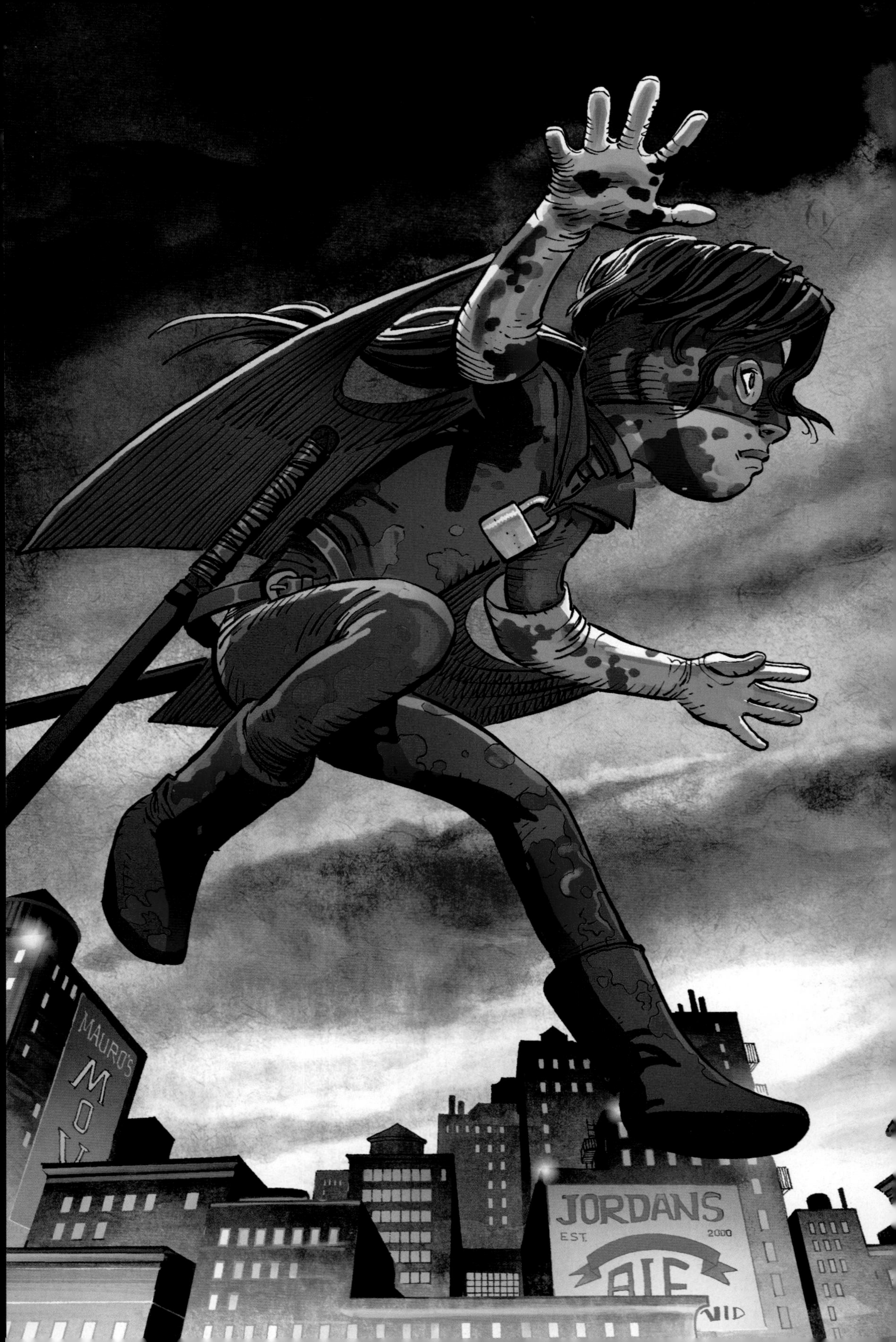
MAURO'S
JORDANS
EST. 2000

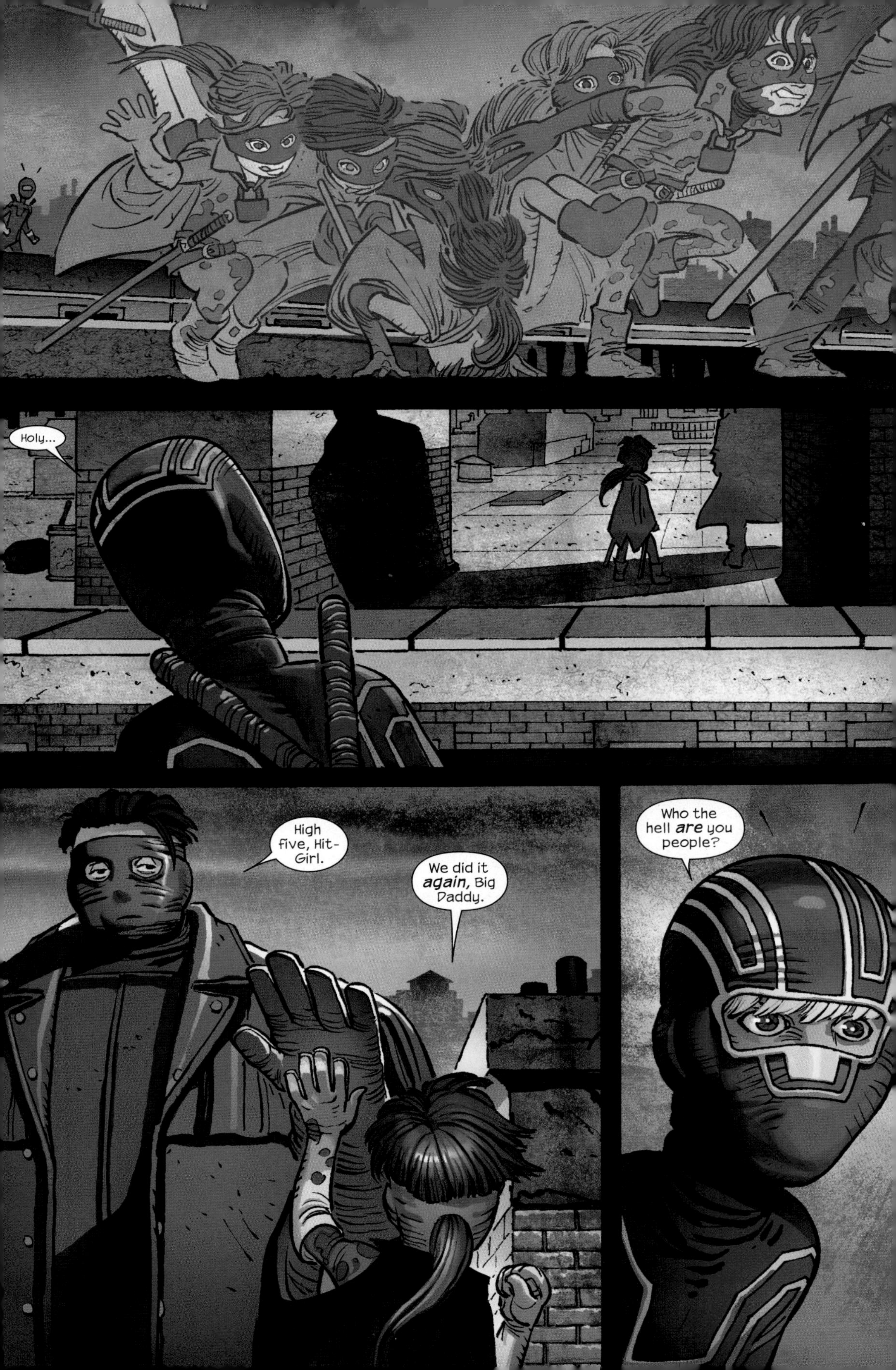
Holy...
High five, Hit-Girl.
We did it *again*, Big Daddy.
Who the hell *are* you people?

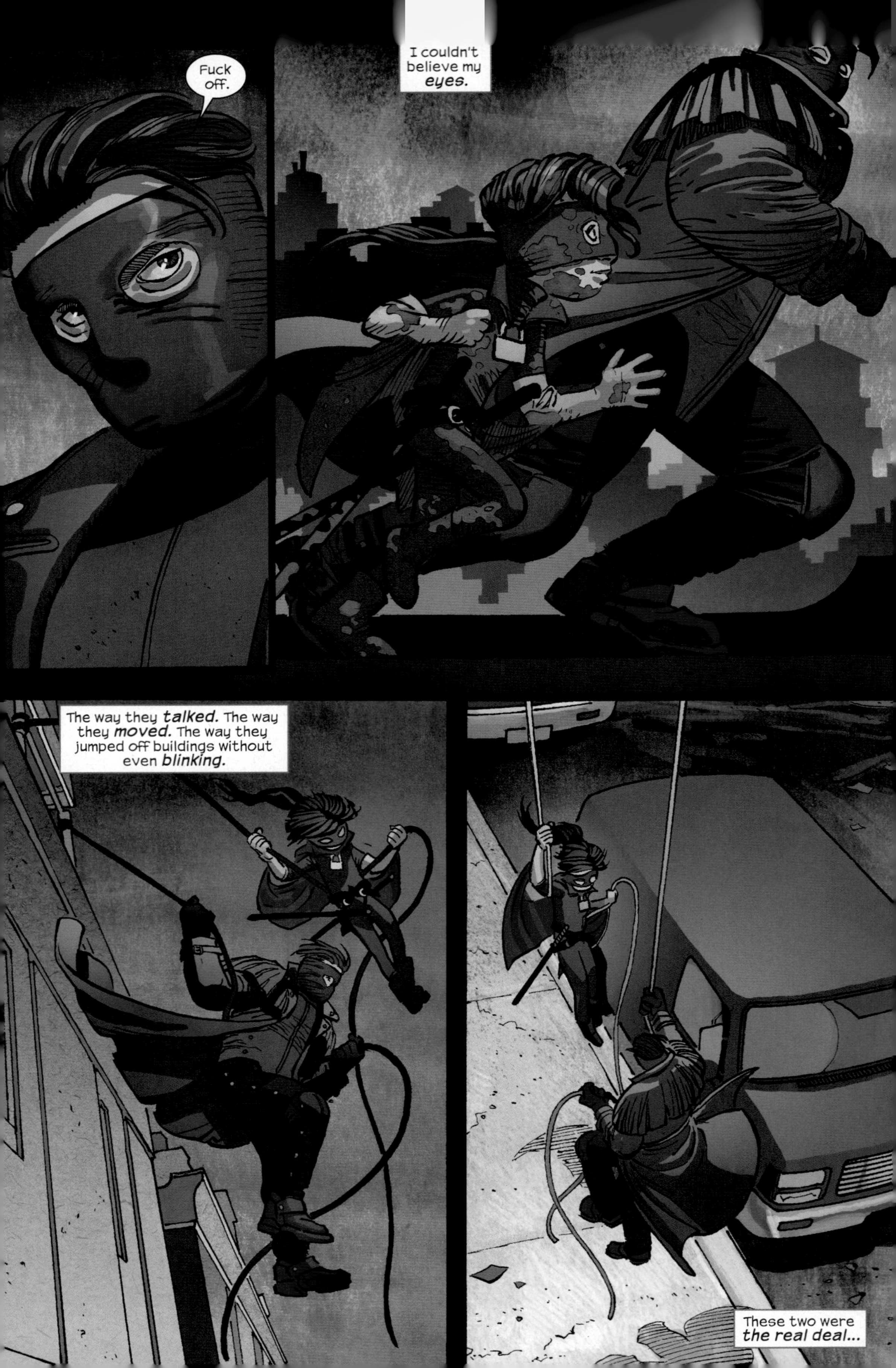
Fuck off.
I couldn't believe my *eyes.*
The way they *talked.* The way they *moved.* The way they jumped off buildings without even *blinking.*
These two were *the real deal...*

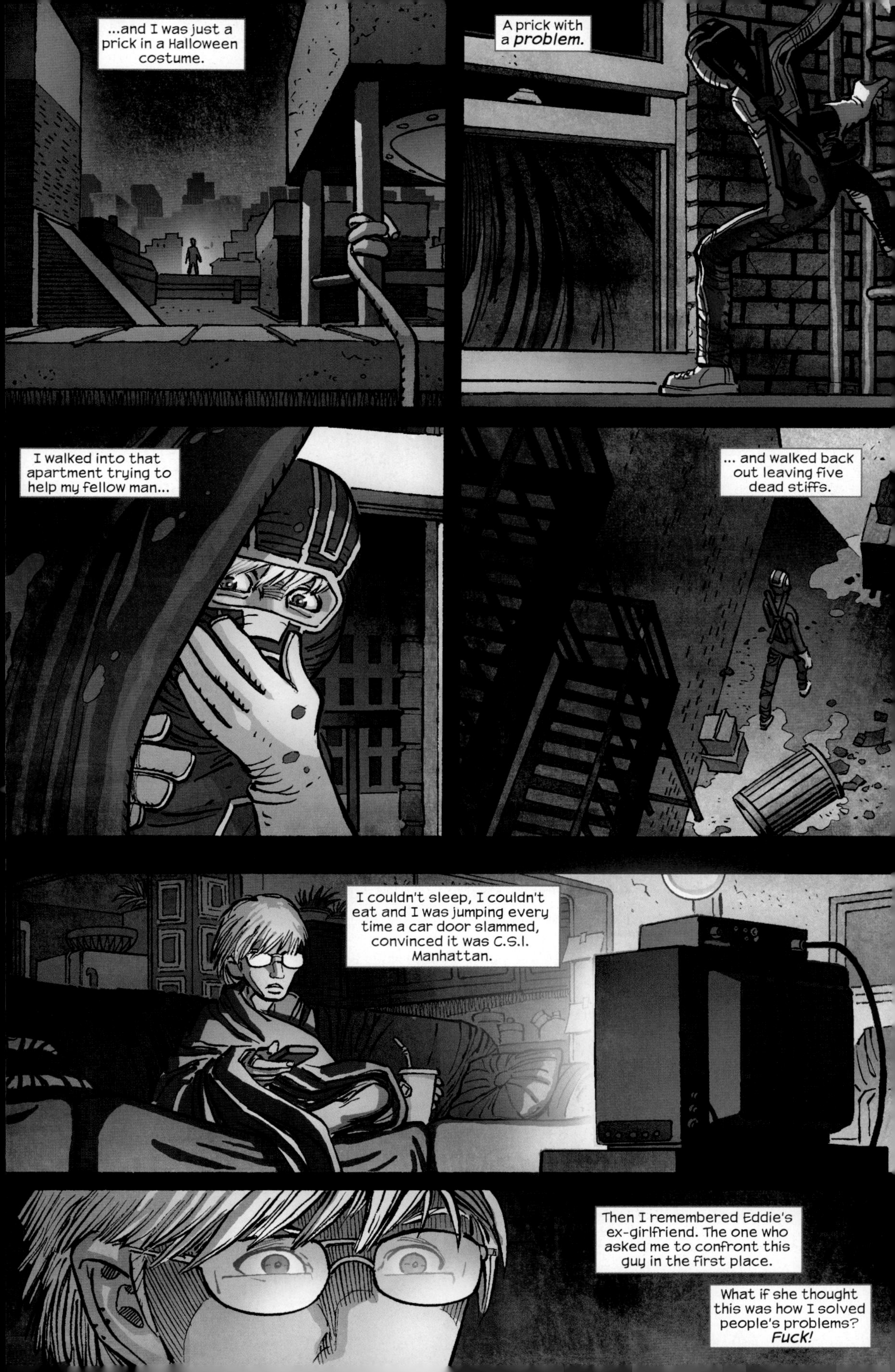

...and I was just a prick in a Halloween costume.
A prick with a *problem.*
I walked into that apartment trying to help my fellow man...
... and walked back out leaving five dead stiffs.
I couldn't sleep, I couldn't eat and I was jumping every time a car door slammed, convinced it was C.S.I. Manhattan.
Then I remembered Eddie's ex-girlfriend. The one who asked me to confront this guy in the first place.
What if she thought this was how I solved people's problems? ***Fuck!***

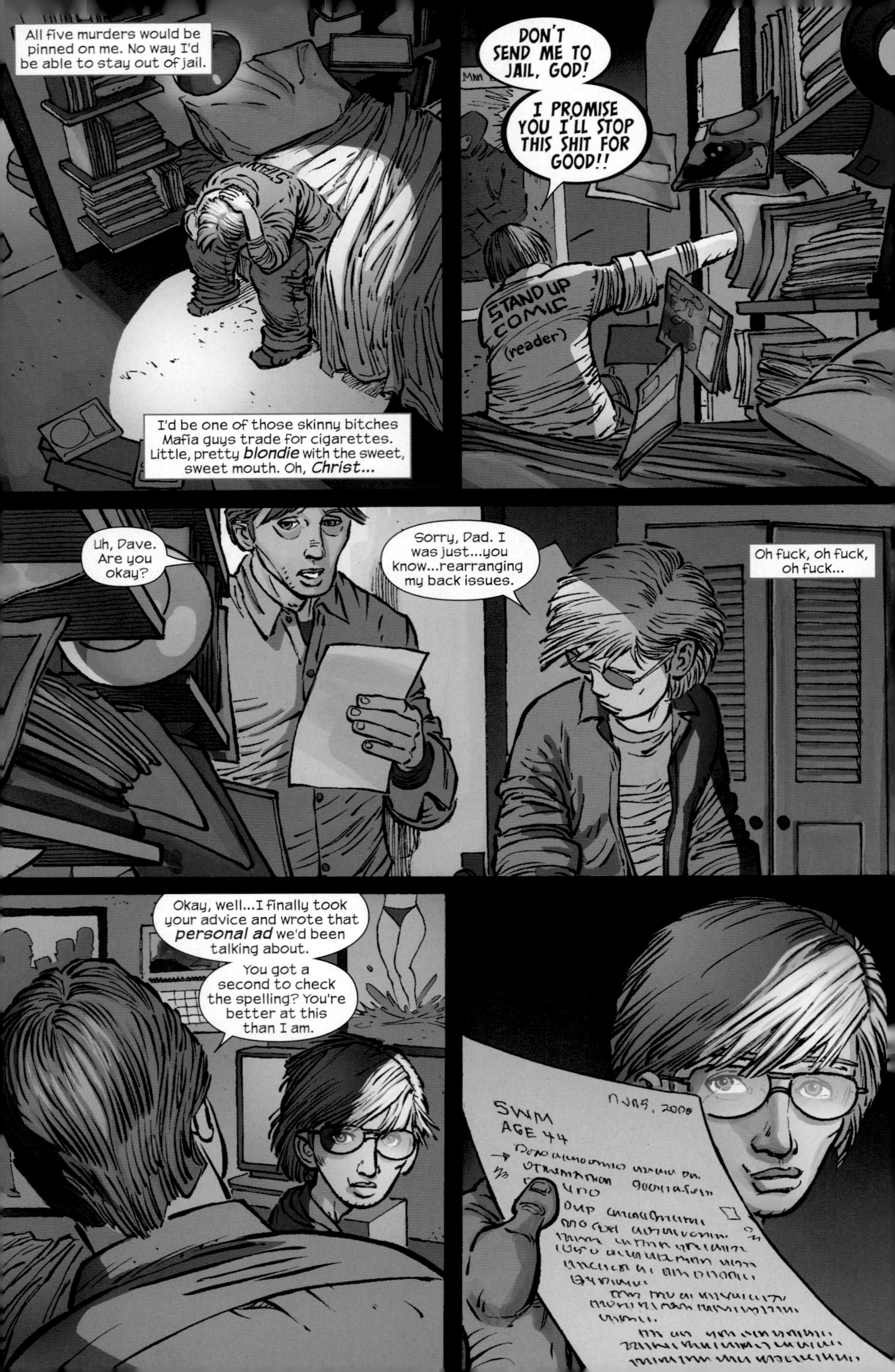
All five murders would be pinned on me. No way I'd be able to stay out of jail.
I'd be one of those skinny bitches Mafia guys trade for cigarettes. Little, pretty *blondie* with the sweet, sweet mouth. Oh, *Christ*...
DON'T SEND ME TO JAIL, GOD!
I PROMISE YOU I'LL STOP THIS SHIT FOR GOOD!!
STAND UP COMIC (reader)
Uh, Dave. Are you okay?
Sorry, Dad. I was just...you know...rearranging my back issues.
Oh fuck, oh fuck, oh fuck...
Okay, well...I finally took your advice and wrote that *personal ad* we'd been talking about.
You got a second to check the spelling? You're better at this than I am.
SWM
AGE 44

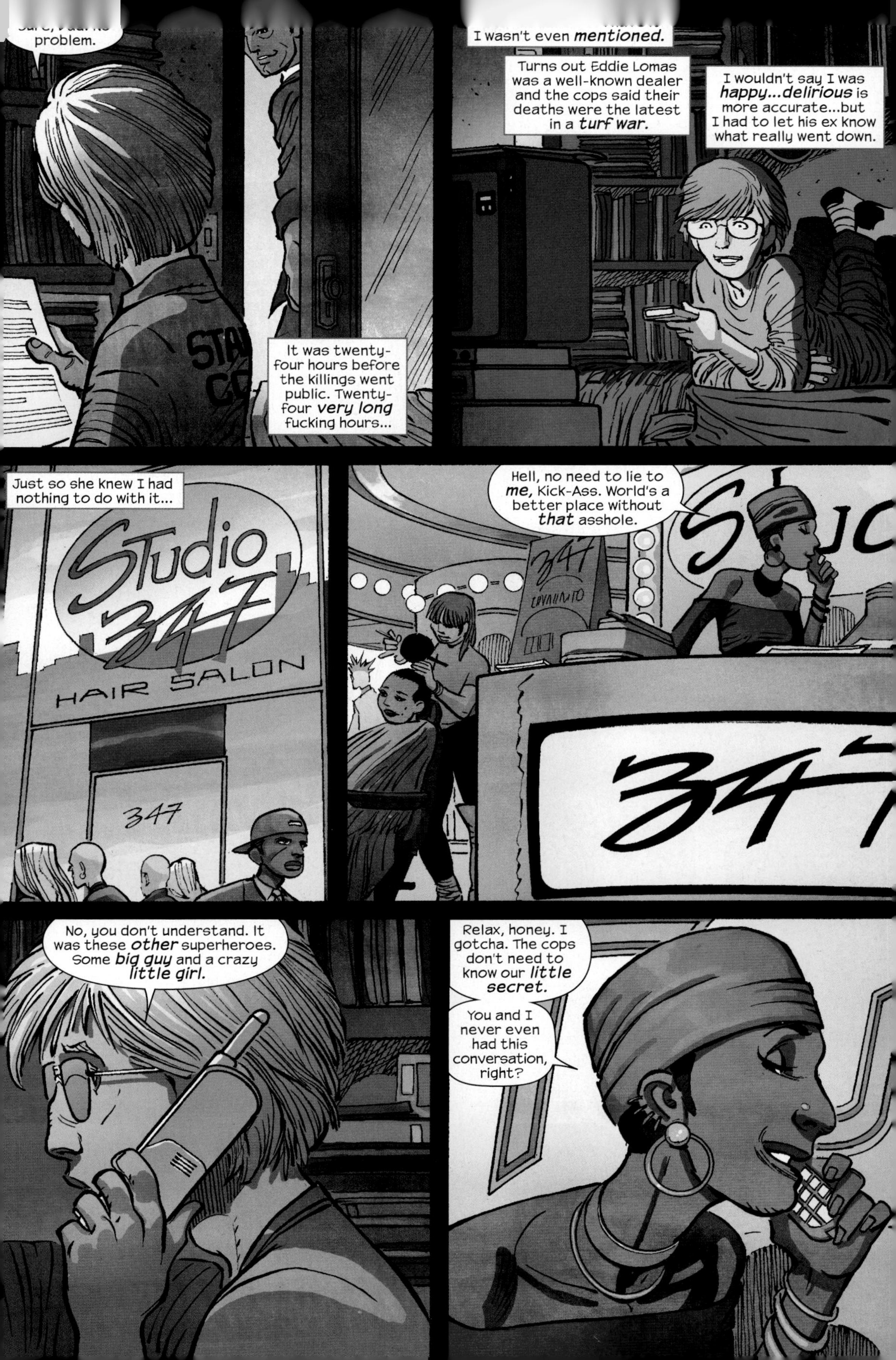
problem.
It was twenty-four hours before the killings went public. Twenty-four *very long* fucking hours...
I wasn't even *mentioned.*
Turns out Eddie Lomas was a well-known dealer and the cops said their deaths were the latest in a *turf war.*
I wouldn't say I was *happy...delirious* is more accurate...but I had to let his ex know what really went down.
Just so she knew I had nothing to do with it...
Studio 347
HAIR SALON
347
Hell, no need to lie to *me,* Kick-Ass. World's a better place without *that* asshole.
347
No, you don't understand. It was these *other* superheroes. Some *big guy* and a crazy *little girl.*
Relax, honey. I gotcha. The cops don't need to know our *little secret.*
You and I never even had this conversation, right?

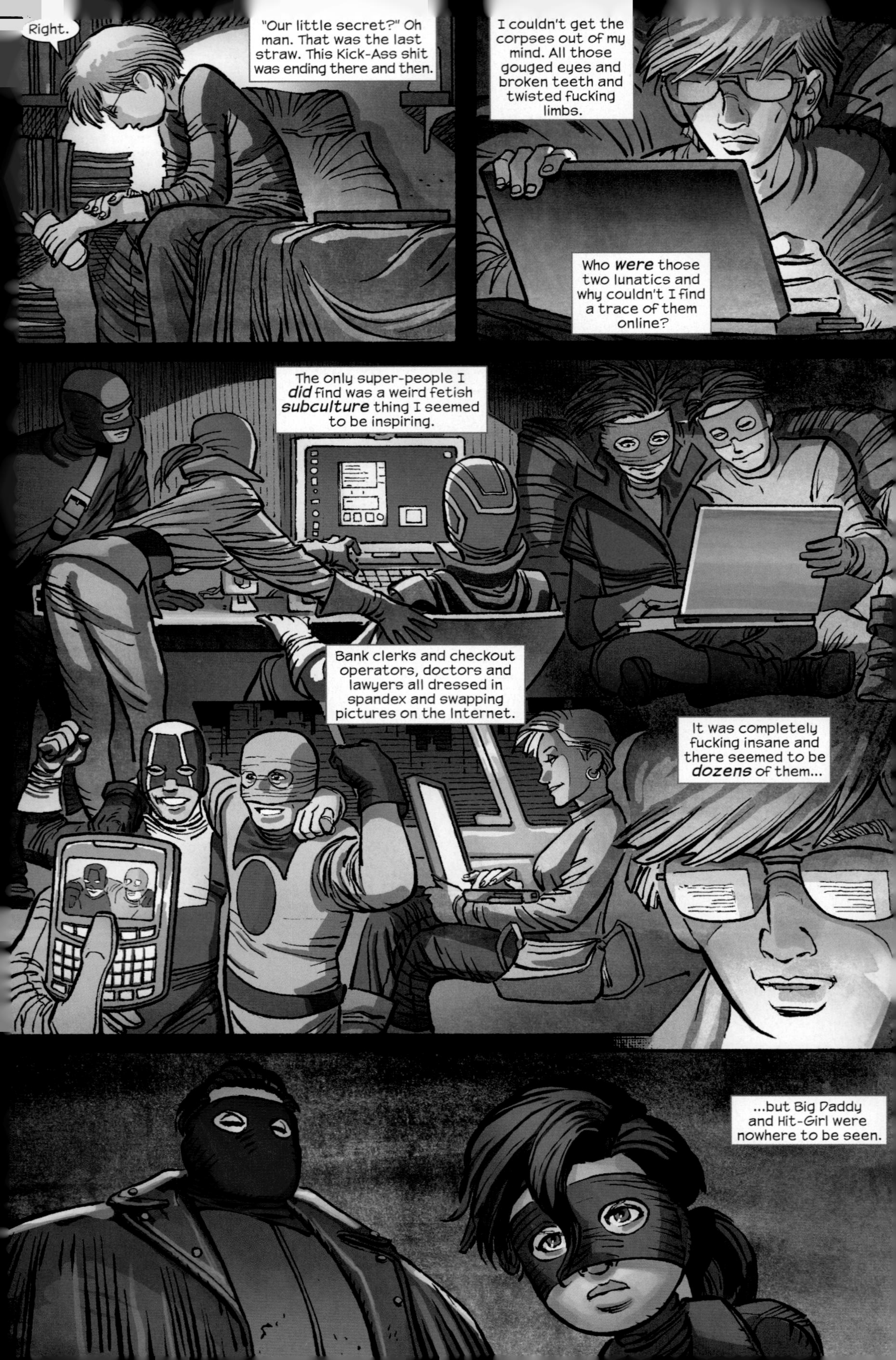
Right.
"Our little secret?" Oh man. That was the last straw. This Kick-Ass shit was ending there and then.
I couldn't get the corpses out of my mind. All those gouged eyes and broken teeth and twisted fucking limbs.
Who *were* those two lunatics and why couldn't I find a trace of them online?
The only super-people I *did* find was a weird fetish *subculture* thing I seemed to be inspiring.
Bank clerks and checkout operators, doctors and lawyers all dressed in spandex and swapping pictures on the Internet.
It was completely fucking insane and there seemed to be *dozens* of them...
...but Big Daddy and Hit-Girl were nowhere to be seen.

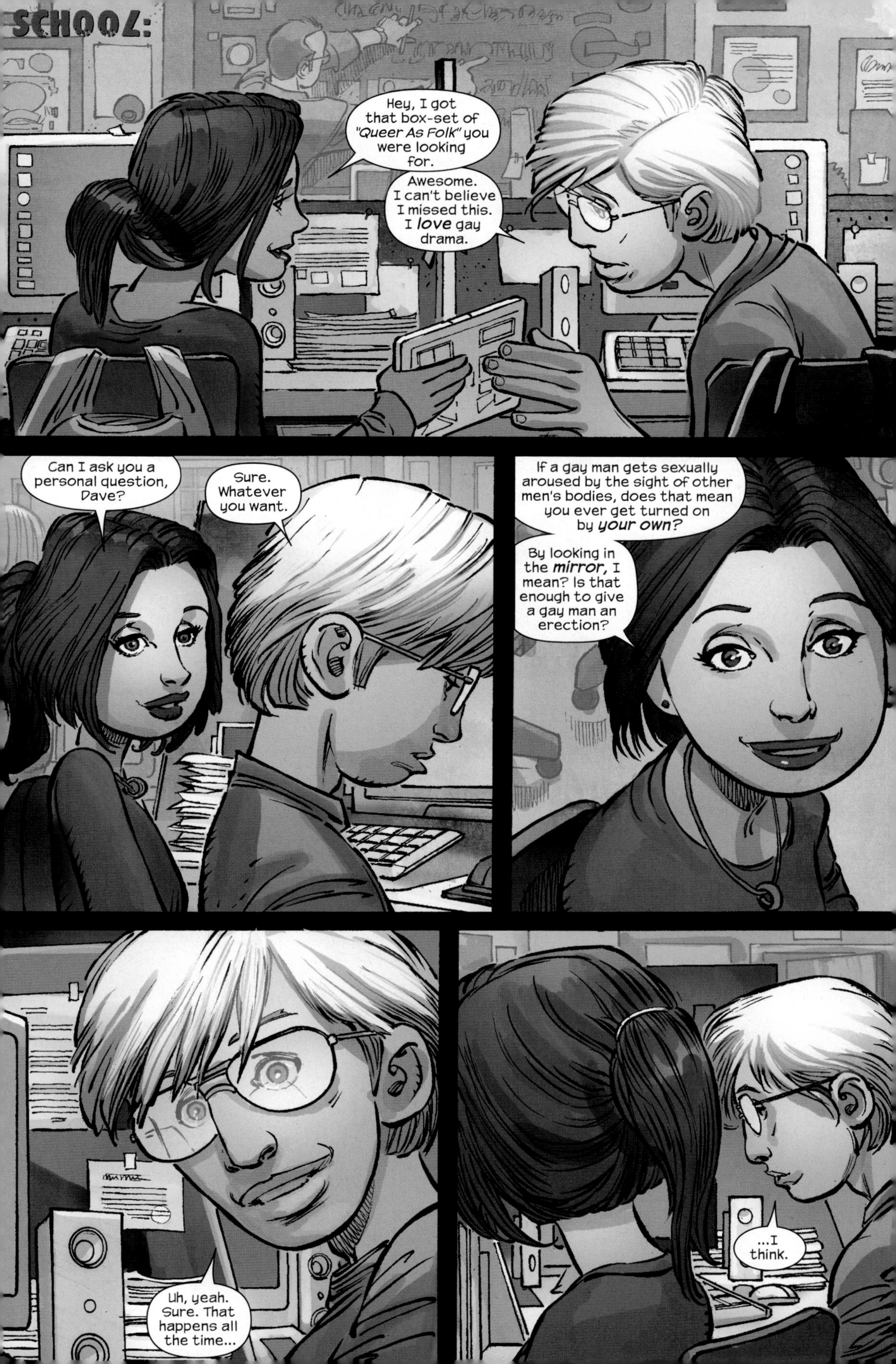
SCHOOL:
Hey, I got that box-set of "Queer As Folk" you were looking for.
Awesome. I can't believe I missed this. I love gay drama.
Can I ask you a personal question, Dave?
Sure. Whatever you want.
If a gay man gets sexually aroused by the sight of other men's bodies, does that mean you ever get turned on by your own?
By looking in the mirror, I mean? Is that enough to give a gay man an erection?
Uh, yeah. Sure. That happens all the time...
...I think.

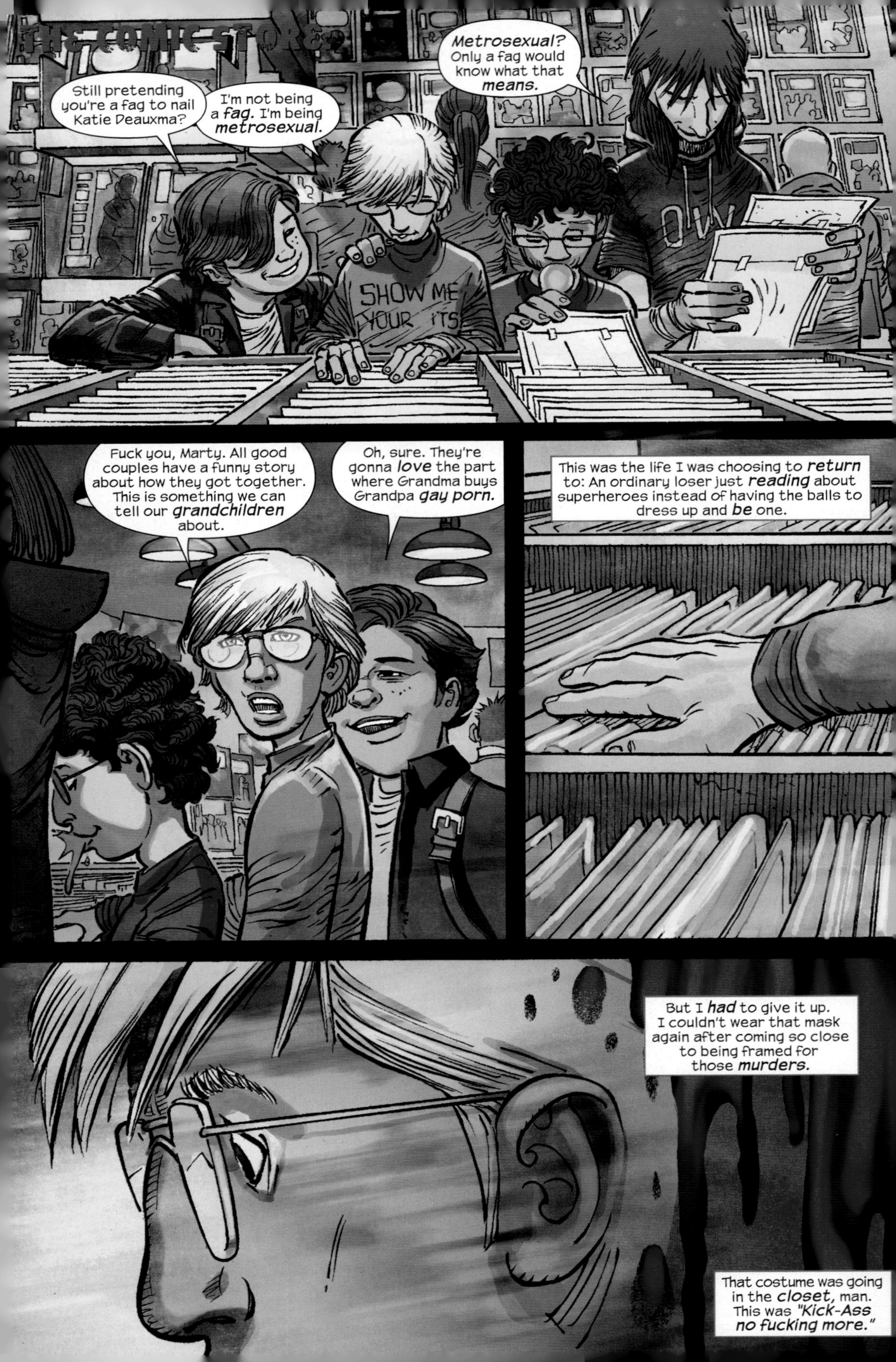
Still pretending you're a fag to nail Katie Deauxma?
I'm not being a fag. I'm being metrosexual.
Metrosexual? Only a fag would know what that means.
SHOW ME YOUR ITS
Fuck you, Marty. All good couples have a funny story about how they got together. This is something we can tell our grandchildren about.
Oh, sure. They're gonna love the part where Grandma buys Grandpa gay porn.
This was the life I was choosing to return to: An ordinary loser just reading about superheroes instead of having the balls to dress up and be one.
But I had to give it up. I couldn't wear that mask again after coming so close to being framed for those murders.
That costume was going in the closet, man. This was "Kick-Ass no fucking more."

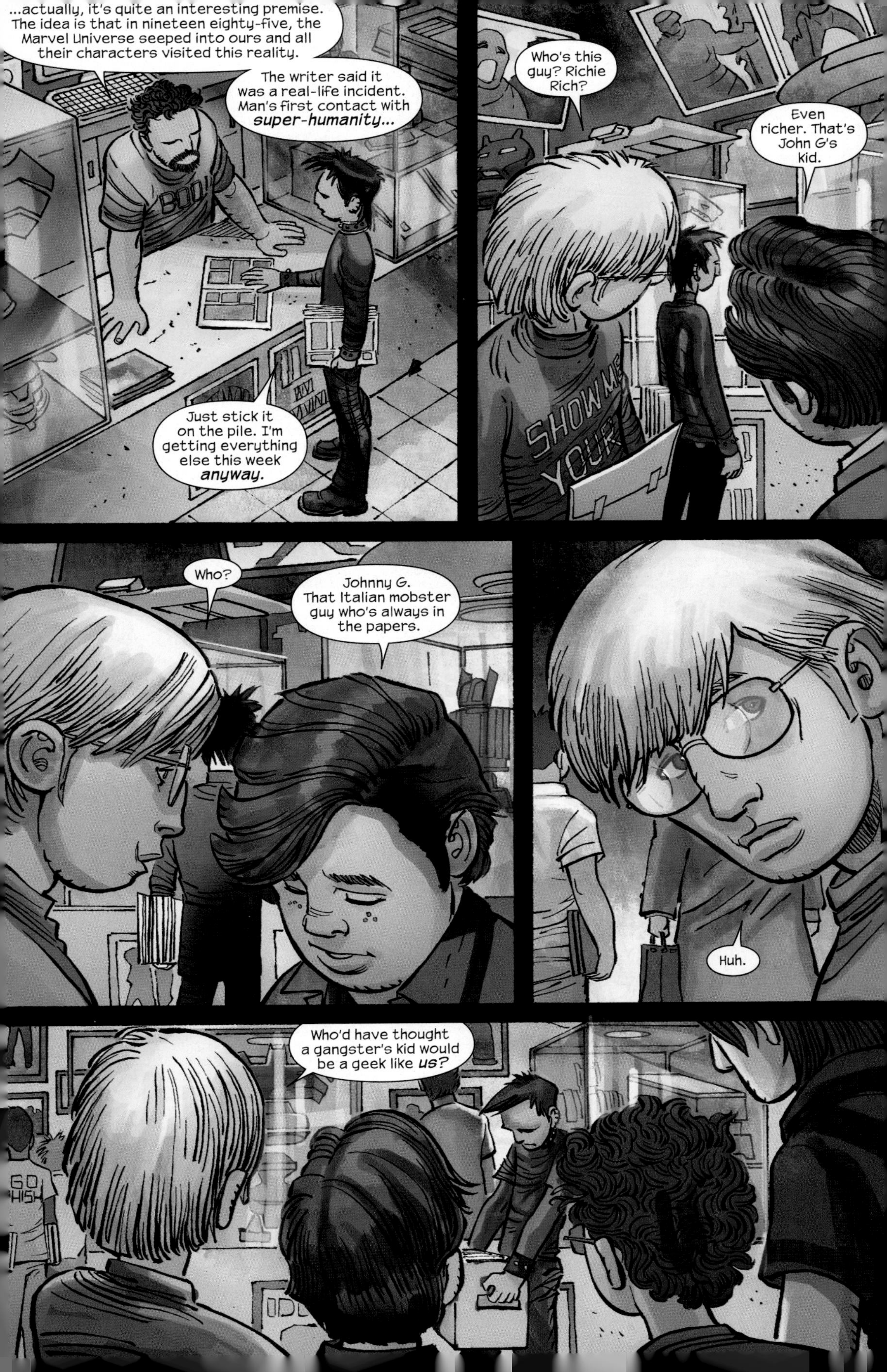
...actually, it's quite an interesting premise. The idea is that in nineteen eighty-five, the Marvel Universe seeped into ours and all their characters visited this reality.
The writer said it was a real-life incident. Man's first contact with *super-humanity...*
Just stick it on the pile. I'm getting everything else this week *anyway.*
Who's this guy? Richie Rich?
Even richer. That's John G's kid.
Who?
Johnny G. That Italian mobster guy who's always in the papers.
Huh.
Who'd have thought a gangster's kid would be a geek like *us?*

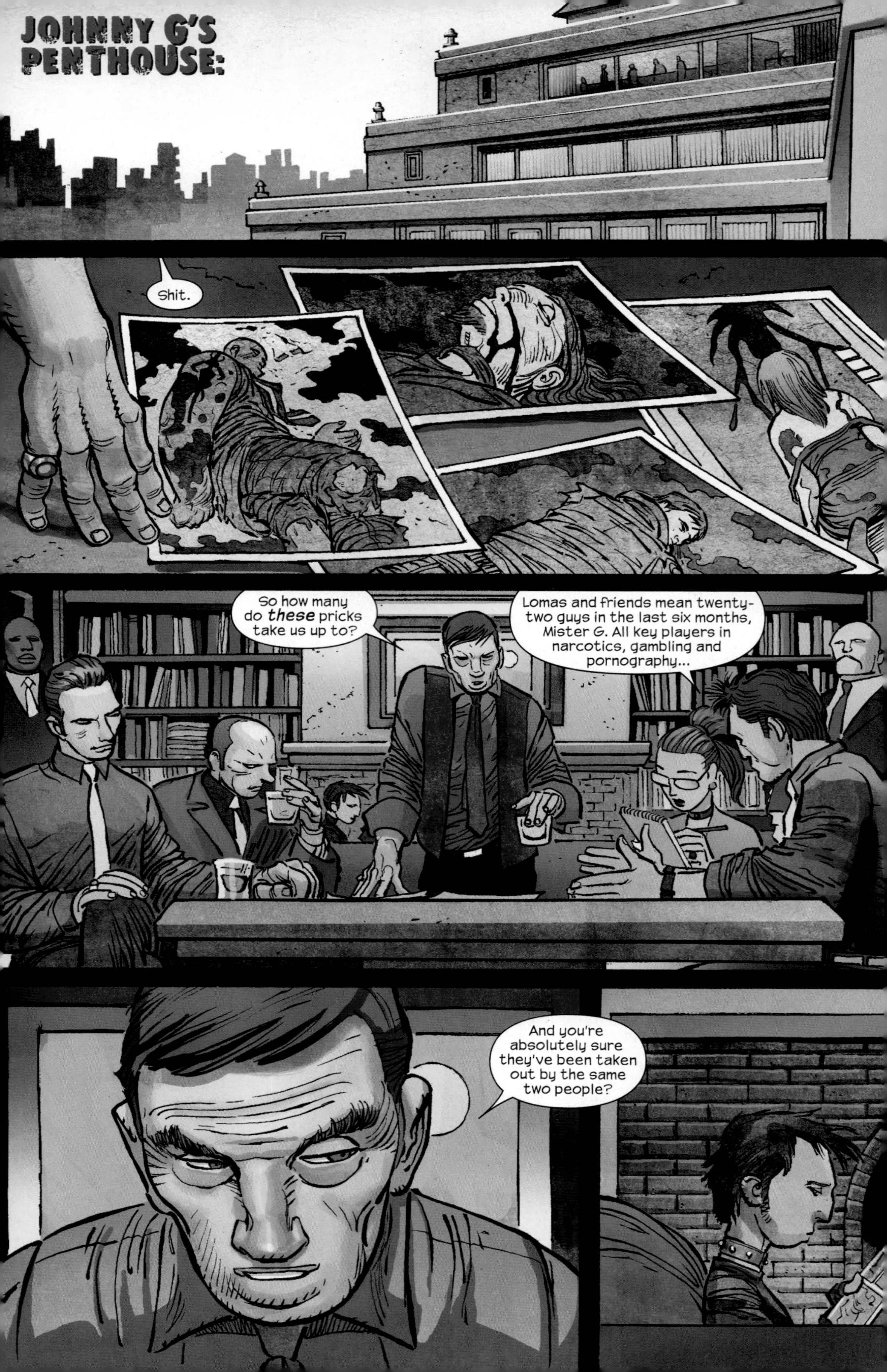
JOHNNY G'S PENTHOUSE:
Shit.
So how many do *these* pricks take us up to?
Lomas and friends mean twenty-two guys in the last six months, Mister G. All key players in narcotics, gambling and pornography...
And you're absolutely sure they've been taken out by the same two people?

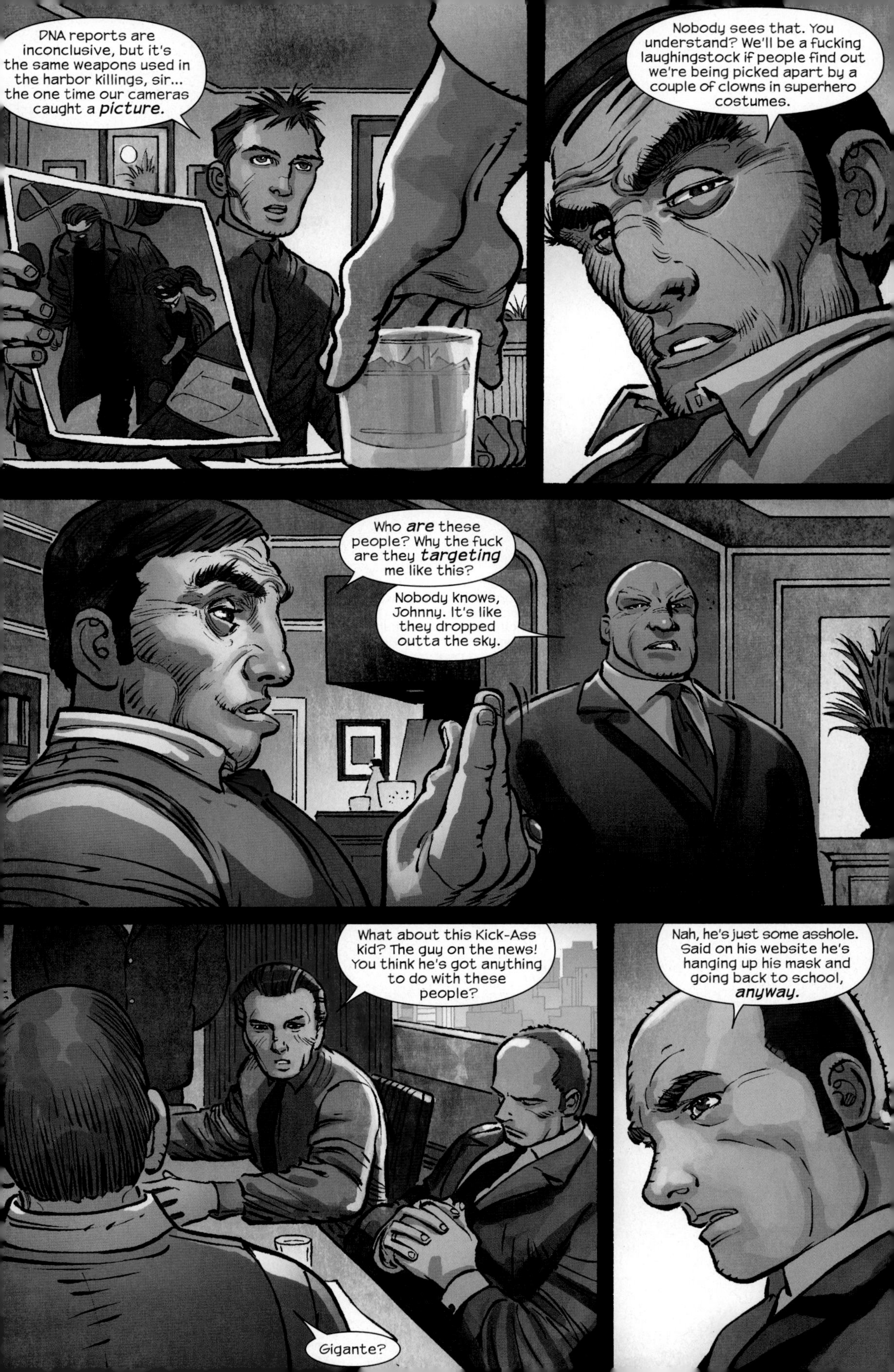
DNA reports are inconclusive, but it's the same weapons used in the harbor killings, sir... the one time our cameras caught a *picture.*
Nobody sees that. You understand? We'll be a fucking laughingstock if people find out we're being picked apart by a couple of clowns in superhero costumes.
Who *are* these people? Why the fuck are they *targeting* me like this?
Nobody knows, Johnny. It's like they dropped outta the sky.
What about this Kick-Ass kid? The guy on the news! You think he's got anything to do with these people?
Gigante?
Nah, he's just some asshole. Said on his website he's hanging up his mask and going back to school, *anyway.*

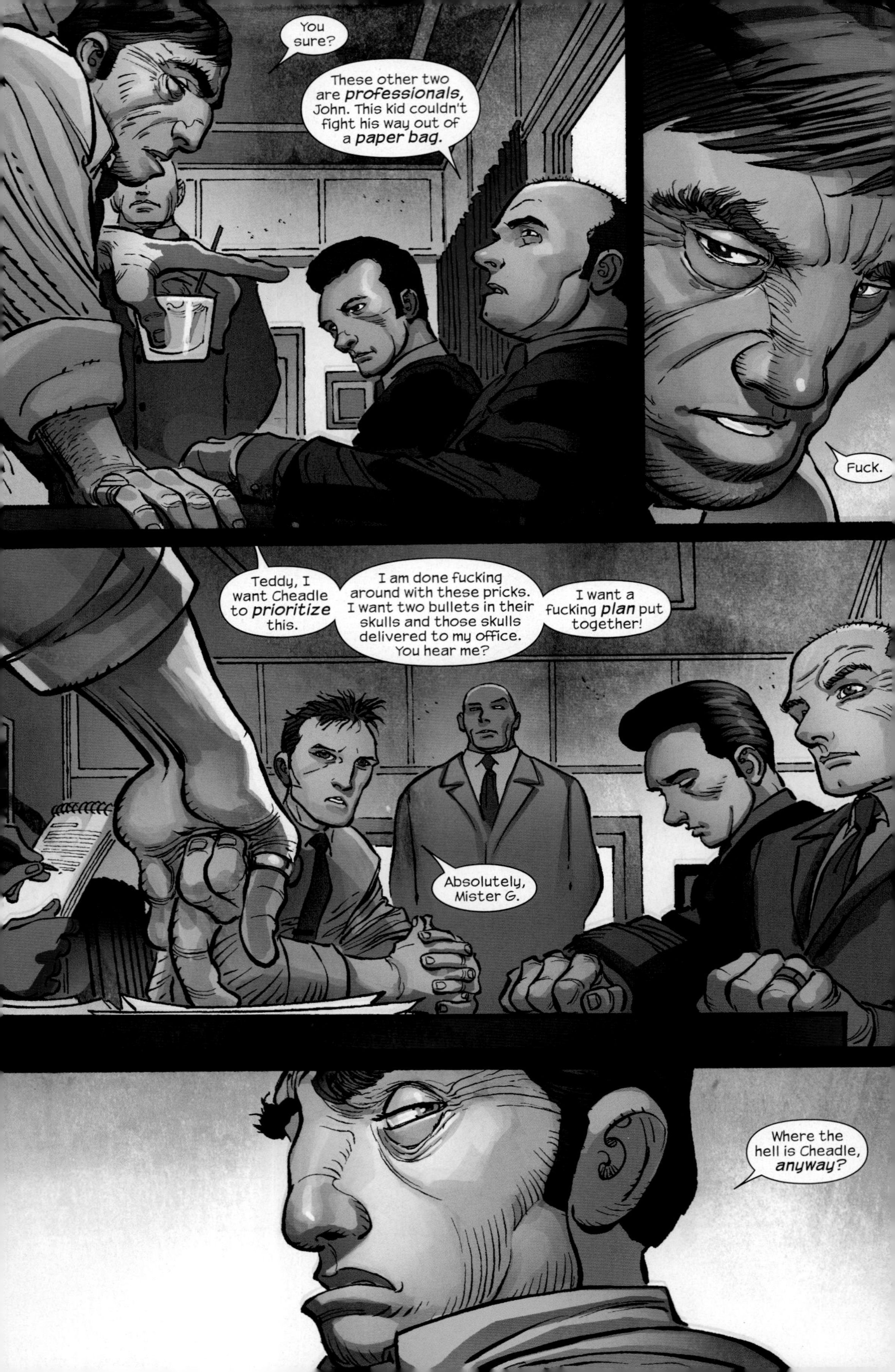
You sure?
These other two are *professionals*, John. This kid couldn't fight his way out of a *paper bag.*
Fuck.
Teddy, I want Cheadle to *prioritize* this.
I am done fucking around with these pricks. I want two bullets in their skulls and those skulls delivered to my office. You hear me?
I want a fucking *plan* put together!
Absolutely, Mister G.
Where the hell is Cheadle, *anyway*?

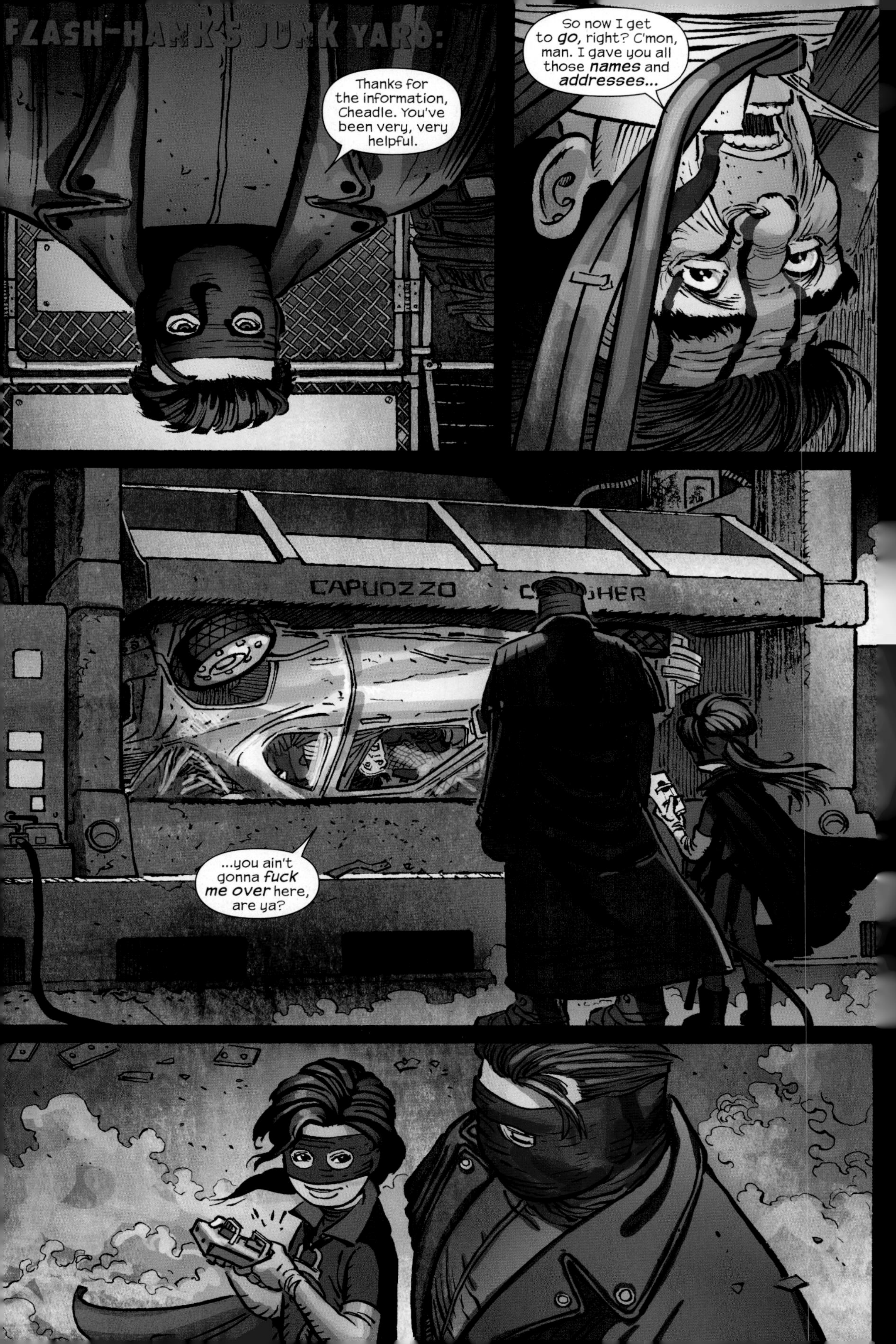
FLASH-HANK'S JUNK YARD:
Thanks for the information, Cheadle. You've been very, very helpful.
So now I get to *go,* right? C'mon, man. I gave you all those *names* and *addresses...*
CAPUOZZO
...you ain't gonna *fuck me over* here, are ya?

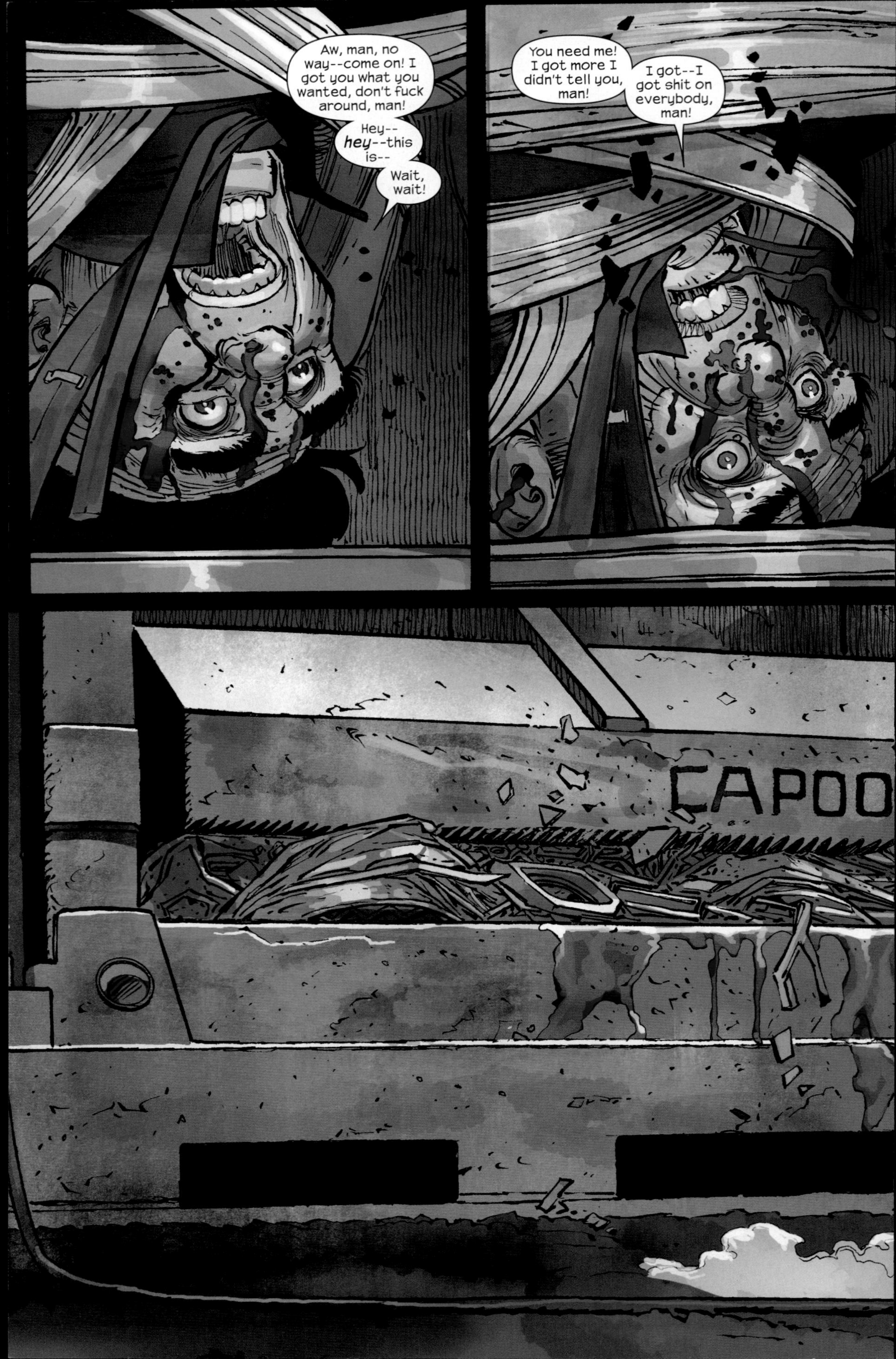

Aw, man, no way--come on! I got you what you wanted, don't fuck around, man!
Hey-- *hey*--this is--
Wait, wait!
You need me! I got more I didn't tell you, man!
I got--I got shit on everybody, man!
CAPOO

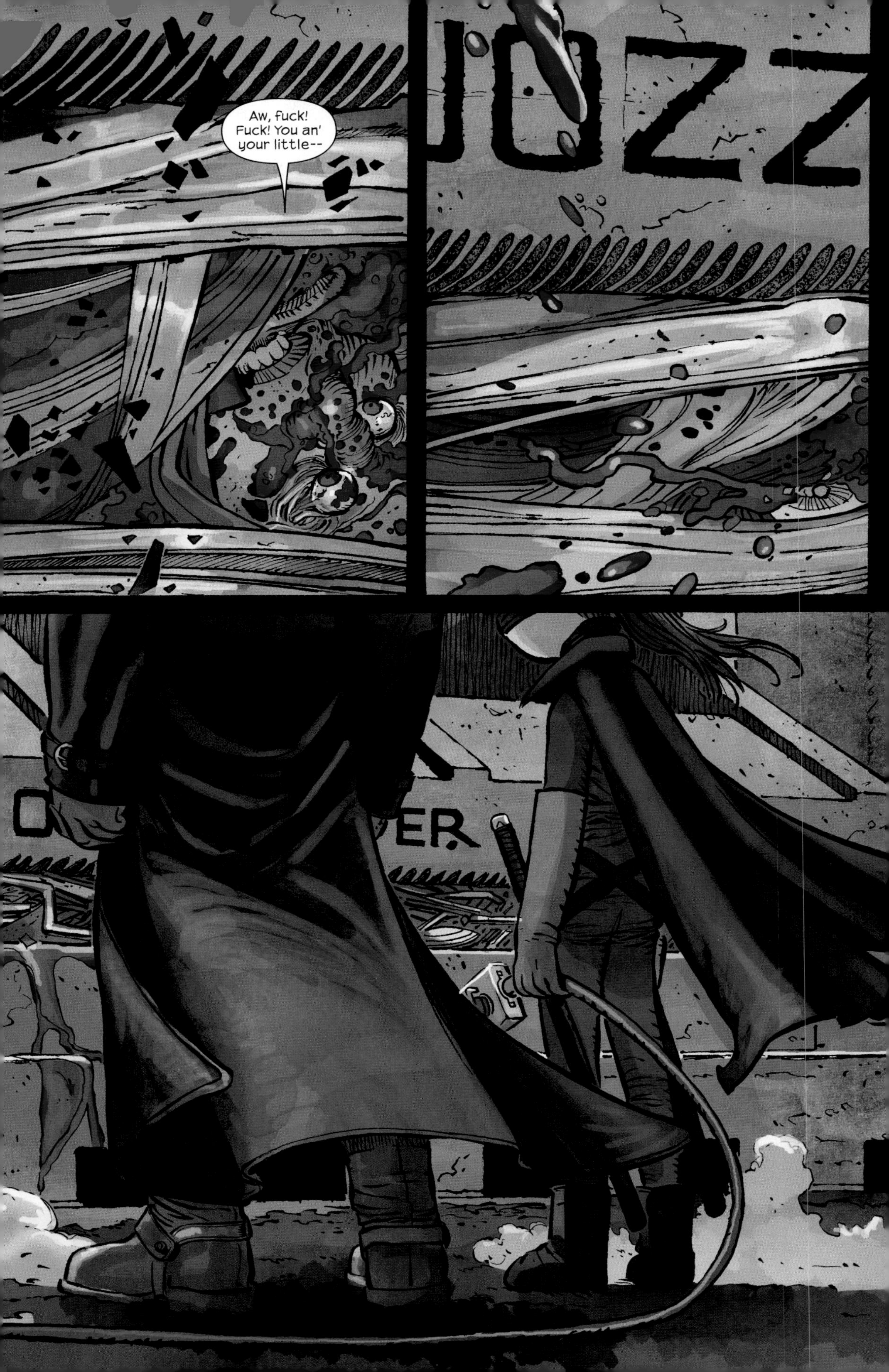
Aw, fuck! Fuck! You an' your little--

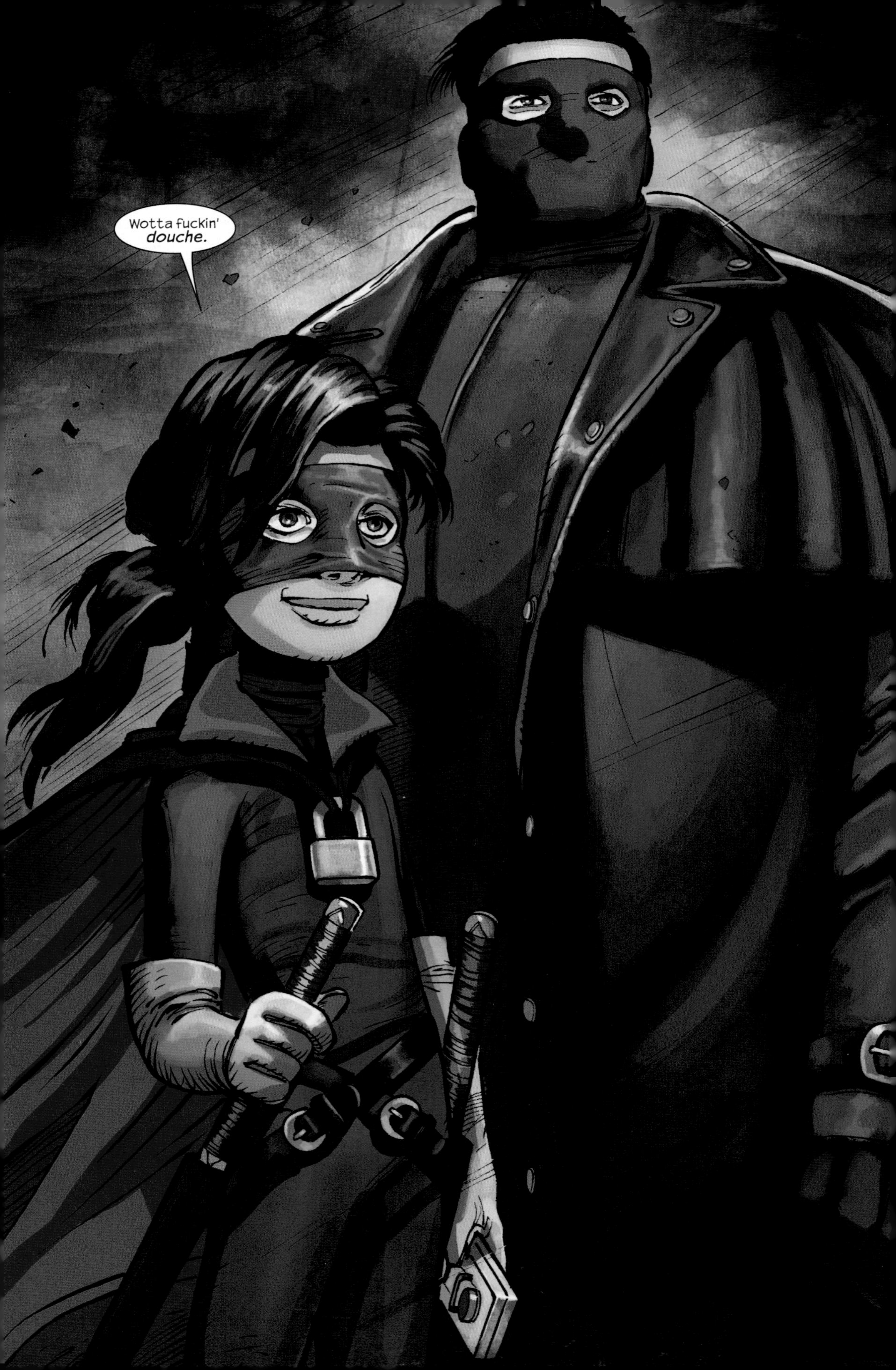
Wotta fuckin' *douche.*

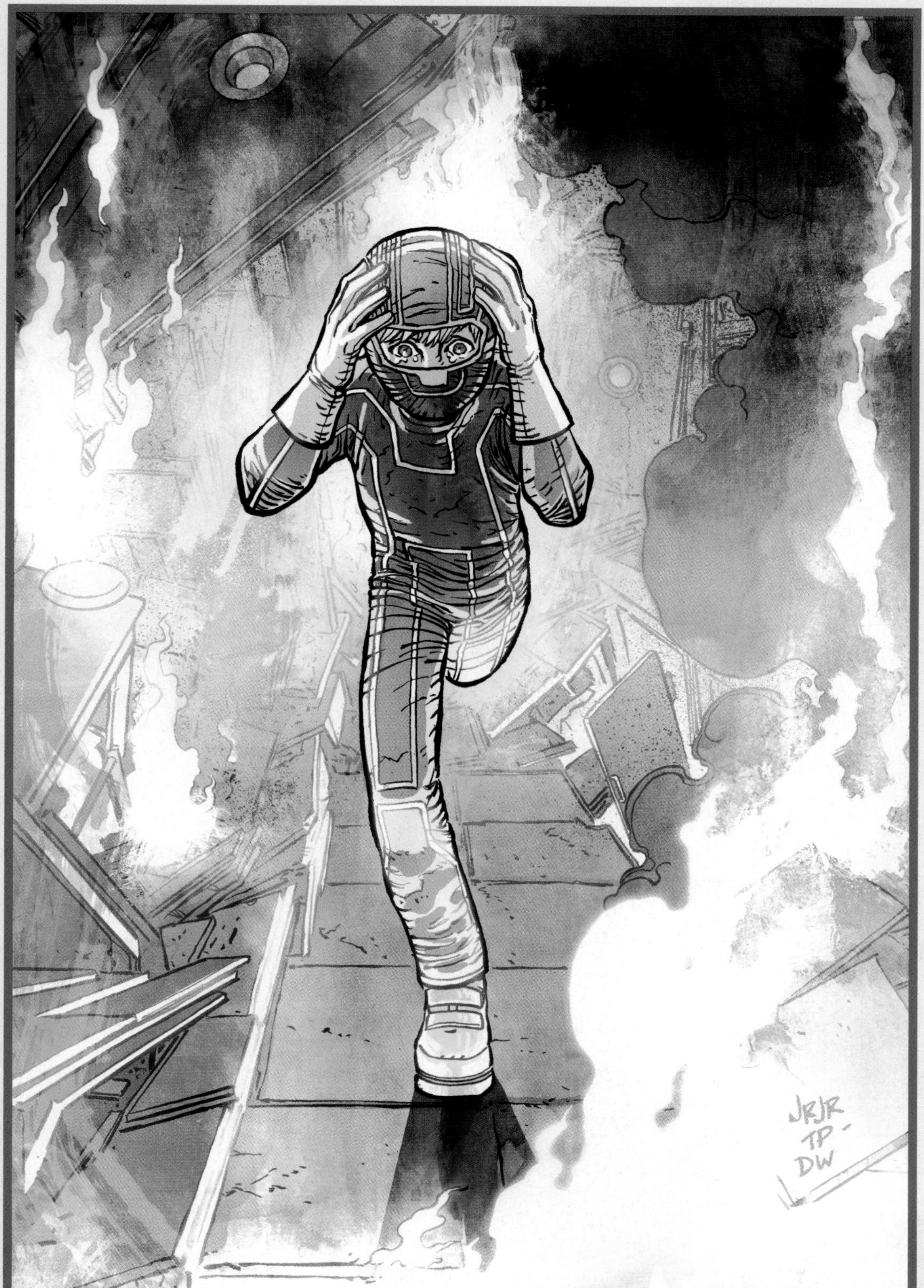
JRJR
TP
DW

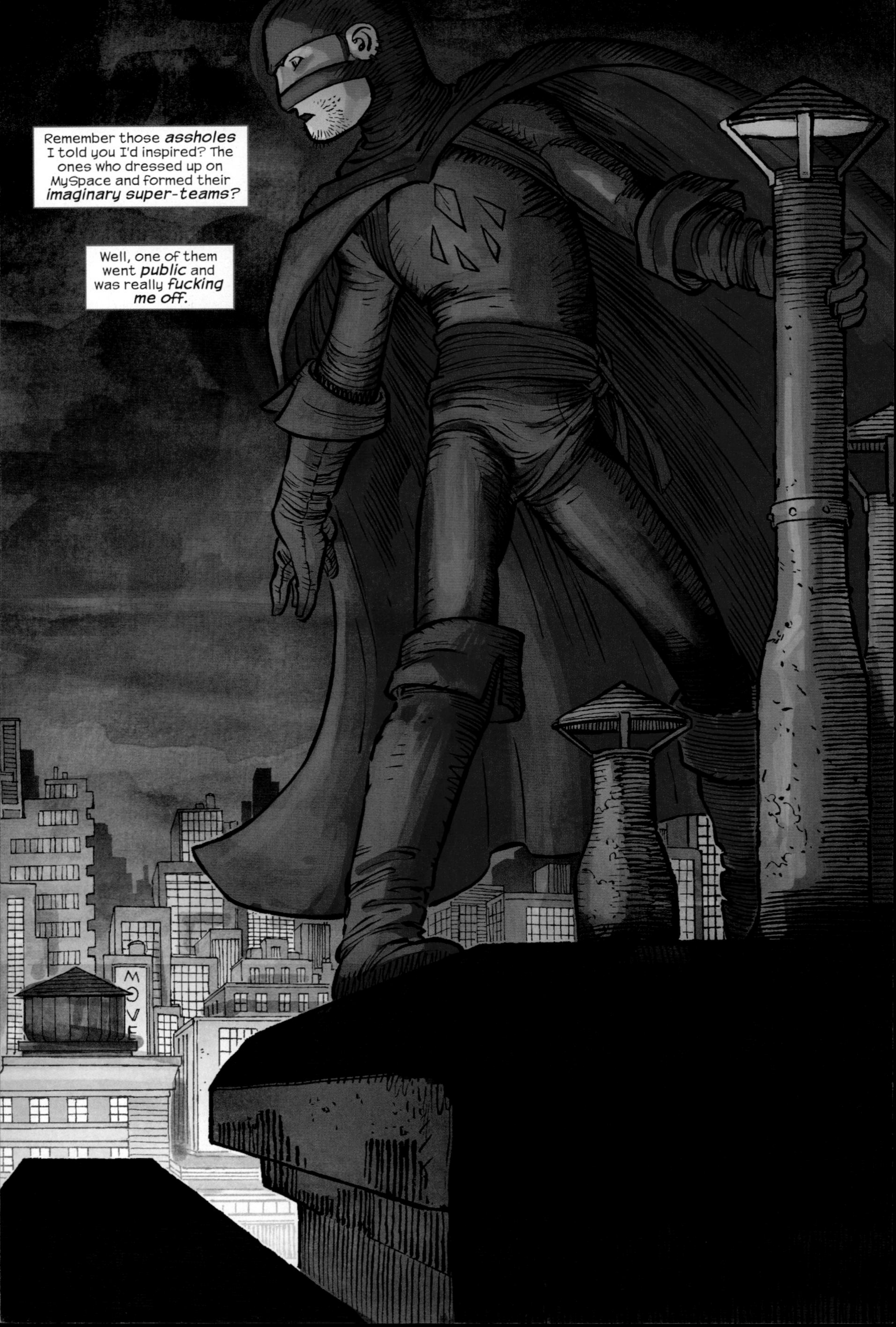
Remember those *assholes* I told you I'd inspired? The ones who dressed up on MySpace and formed their *imaginary super-teams?*
Well, one of them went *public* and was really *fucking me off*.
MOVE

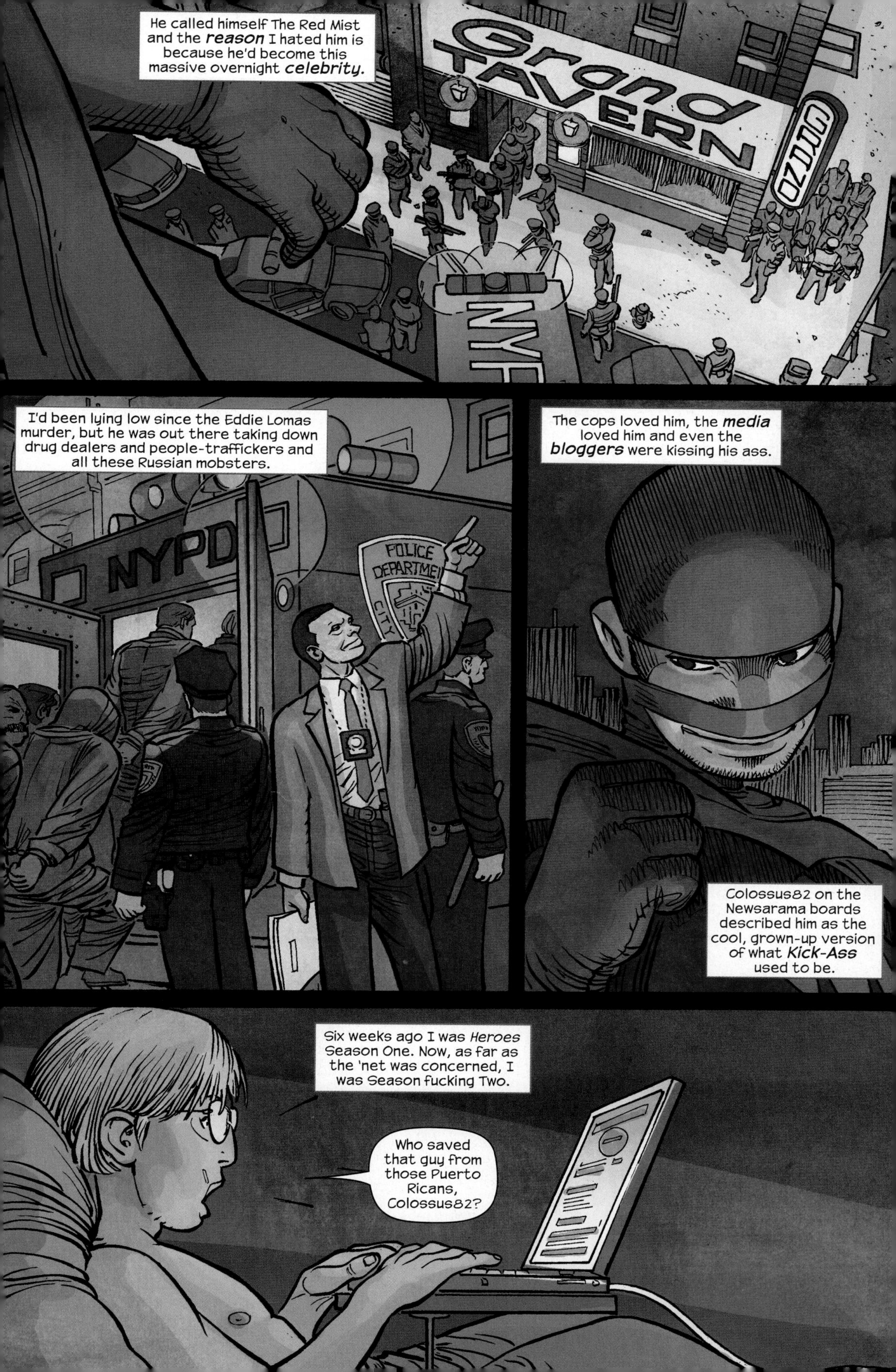
He called himself The Red Mist and the *reason* I hated him is because he'd become this massive overnight *celebrity*.
Grand TAVERN
GRAND
NYP
I'd been lying low since the Eddie Lomas murder, but he was out there taking down drug dealers and people-traffickers and all these Russian mobsters.
NYPD
POLICE DEPARTMENT
CITY
The cops loved him, the *media* loved him and even the *bloggers* were kissing his ass.
Colossus82 on the Newsarama boards described him as the cool, grown-up version of what *Kick-Ass* used to be.
Six weeks ago I was *Heroes* Season One. Now, as far as the 'net was concerned, I was Season fucking Two.
Who saved that guy from those Puerto Ricans, Colossus82?

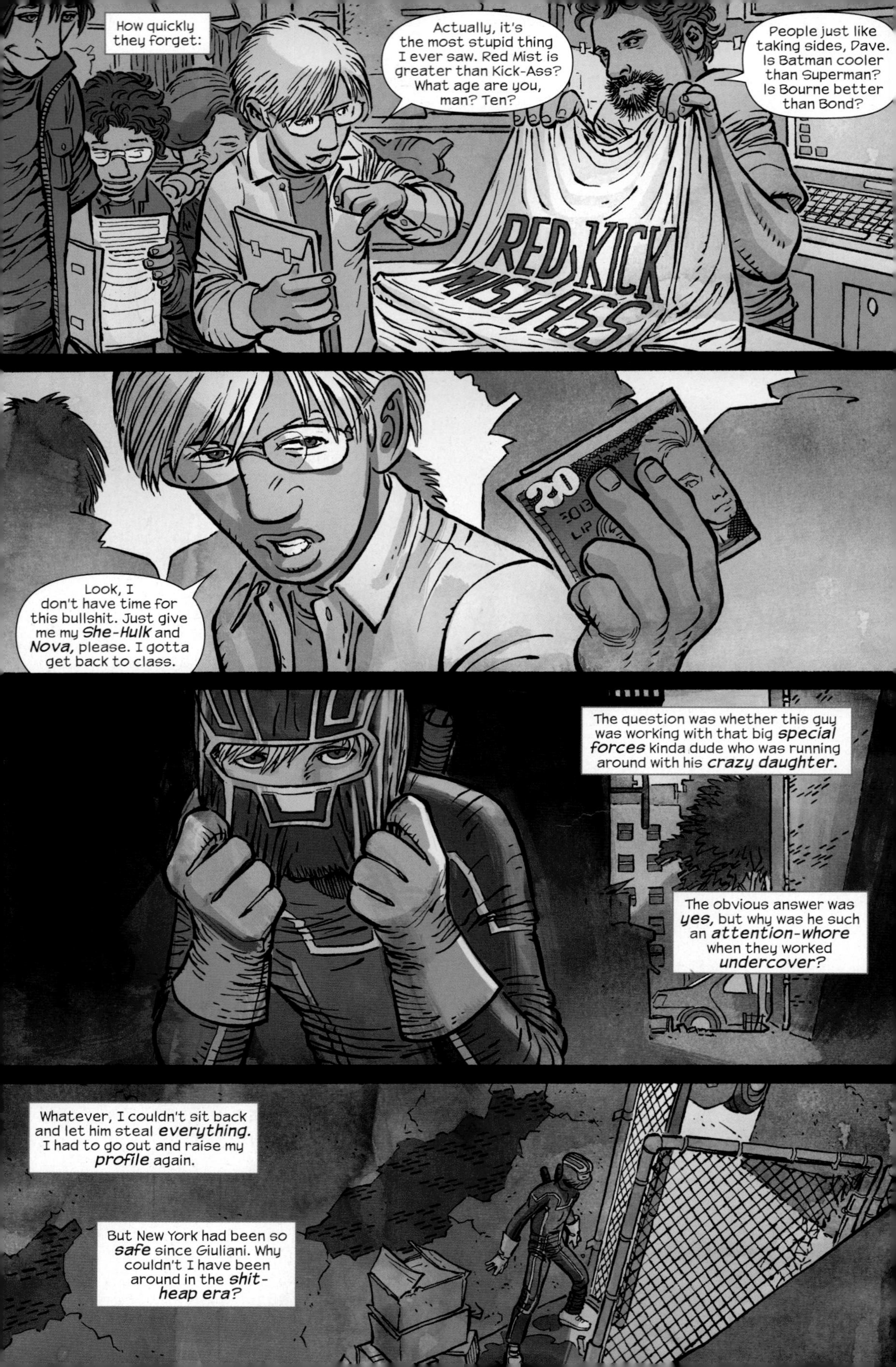
How quickly they forget:
Actually, it's the most stupid thing I ever saw. Red Mist is greater than Kick-Ass? What age are you, man? Ten?
People just like taking sides, Dave. Is Batman cooler than Superman? Is Bourne better than Bond?
RED KICK MIST ASS
Look, I don't have time for this bullshit. Just give me my *She-Hulk* and *Nova,* please. I gotta get back to class.
The question was whether this guy was working with that big *special forces* kinda dude who was running around with his *crazy daughter*.
The obvious answer was *yes,* but why was he such an *attention-whore* when they worked *undercover*?
Whatever, I couldn't sit back and let him steal *everything*. I had to go out and raise my *profile* again.
But New York had been so *safe* since Giuliani. Why couldn't I have been around in the *shit-heap era*?

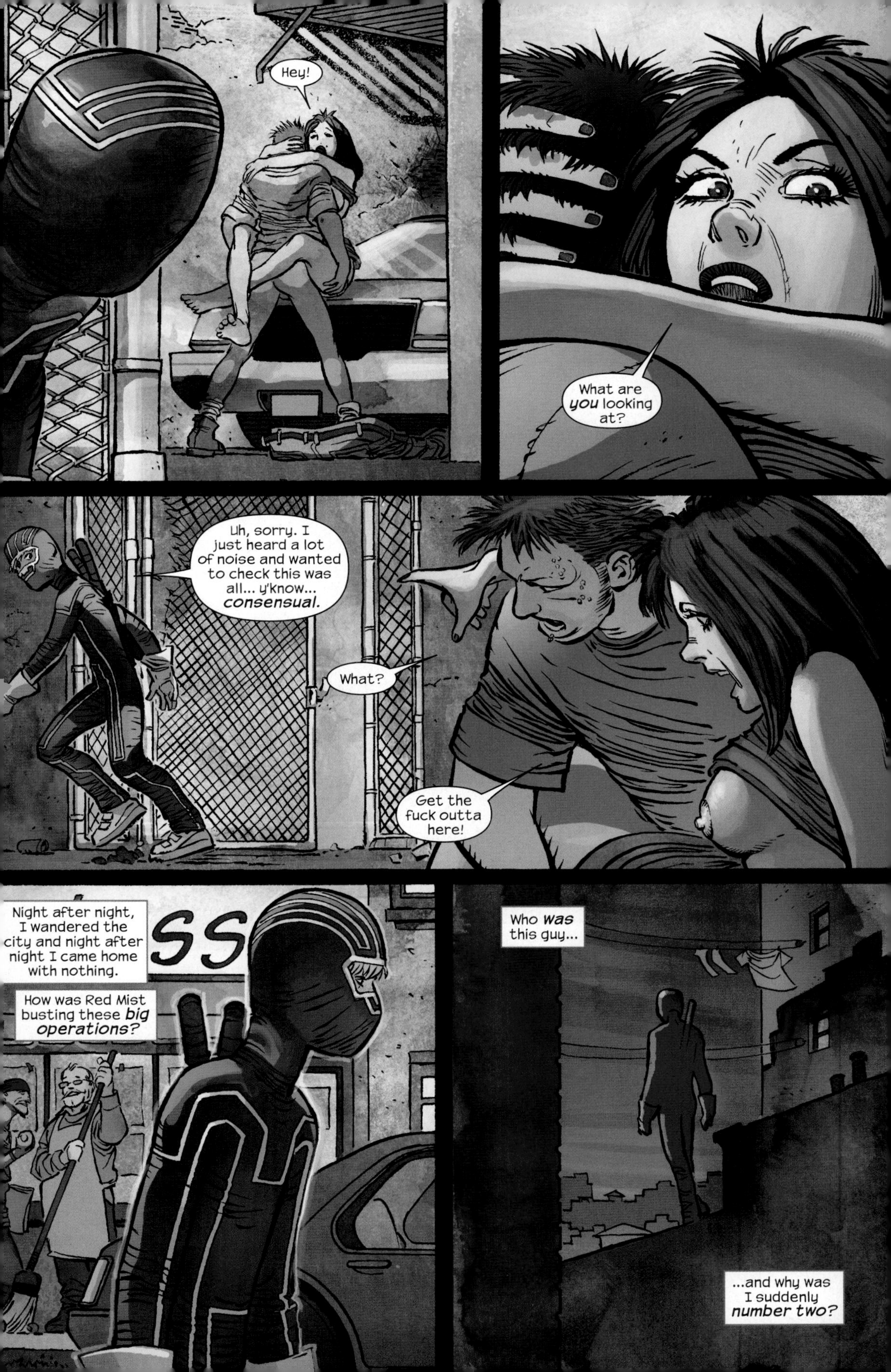

Hey!
What are *you* looking at?
Uh, sorry. I just heard a lot of noise and wanted to check this was all... y'know... ***consensual.***
What?
Get the fuck outta here!
Night after night, I wandered the city and night after night I came home with nothing.
How was Red Mist busting these ***big operations***?
Who ***was*** this guy...
...and why was I suddenly ***number two***?

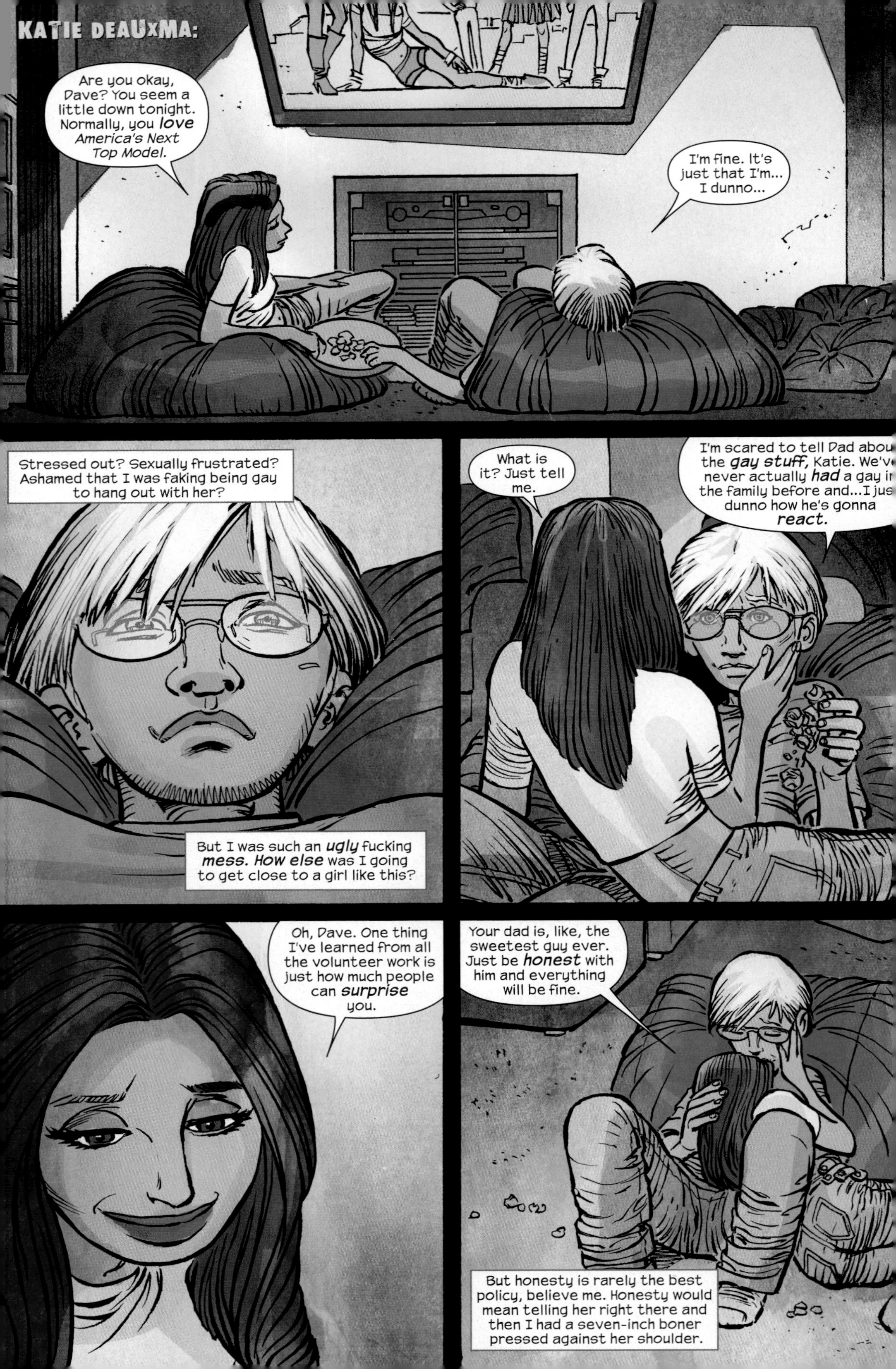
KATIE DEAUxMA:
Are you okay, Dave? You seem a little down tonight. Normally, you love America's Next Top Model.
I'm fine. It's just that I'm... I dunno...
Stressed out? Sexually frustrated? Ashamed that I was faking being gay to hang out with her?
But I was such an ugly fucking mess. How else was I going to get close to a girl like this?
What is it? Just tell me.
I'm scared to tell Dad about the gay stuff, Katie. We've never actually had a gay in the family before and...I just dunno how he's gonna react.
Oh, Dave. One thing I've learned from all the volunteer work is just how much people can surprise you.
Your dad is, like, the sweetest guy ever. Just be honest with him and everything will be fine.
But honesty is rarely the best policy, believe me. Honesty would mean telling her right there and then I had a seven-inch boner pressed against her shoulder.

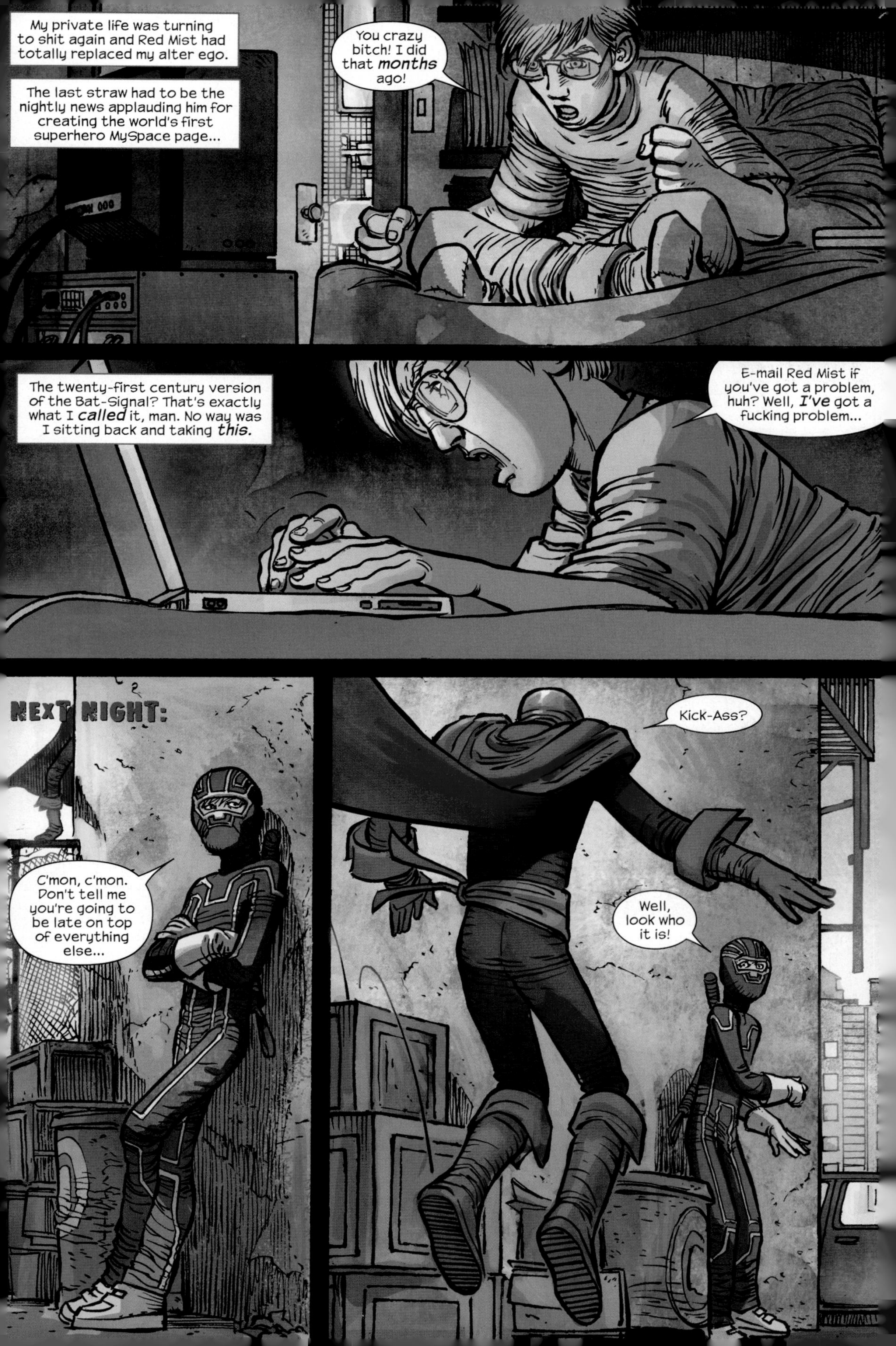
My private life was turning to shit again and Red Mist had totally replaced my alter ego.
The last straw had to be the nightly news applauding him for creating the world's first superhero MySpace page...
You crazy bitch! I did that *months* ago!
The twenty-first century version of the Bat-Signal? That's exactly what I *called* it, man. No way was I sitting back and taking *this.*
E-mail Red Mist if you've got a problem, huh? Well, *I've* got a fucking problem...
NEXT NIGHT:
C'mon, c'mon. Don't tell me you're going to be late on top of everything else...
Kick-Ass?
Well, look who it is!

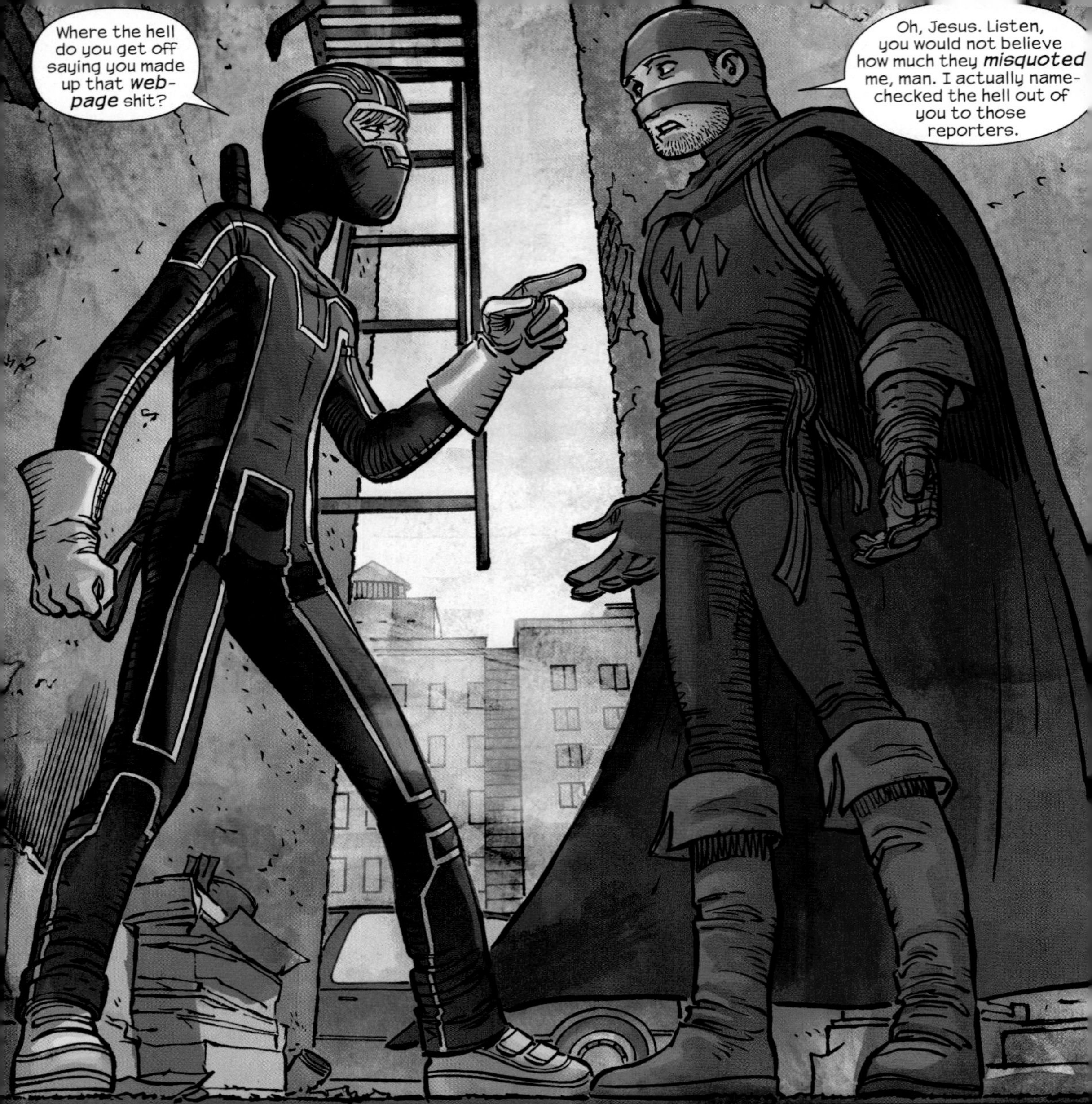
Where the hell do you get off saying you made up that *web-page* shit?
Oh, Jesus. Listen, you would not believe how much they *misquoted* me, man. I actually name-checked the hell out of you to those reporters.

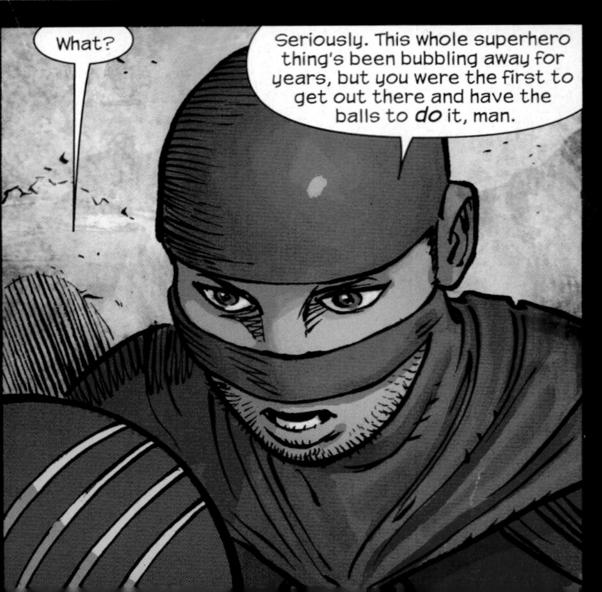
What?
Seriously. This whole superhero thing's been bubbling away for years, but you were the first to get out there and have the balls to *do* it, man.

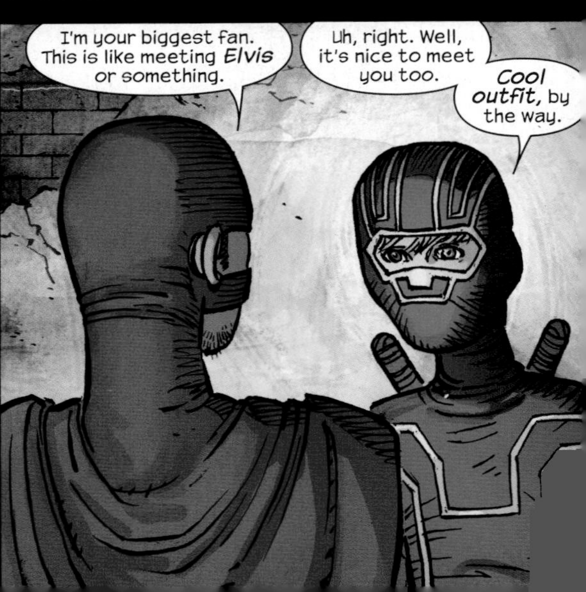
I'm your biggest fan. This is like meeting *Elvis* or something.
Uh, right. Well, it's nice to meet you too.
Cool outfit, by the way.

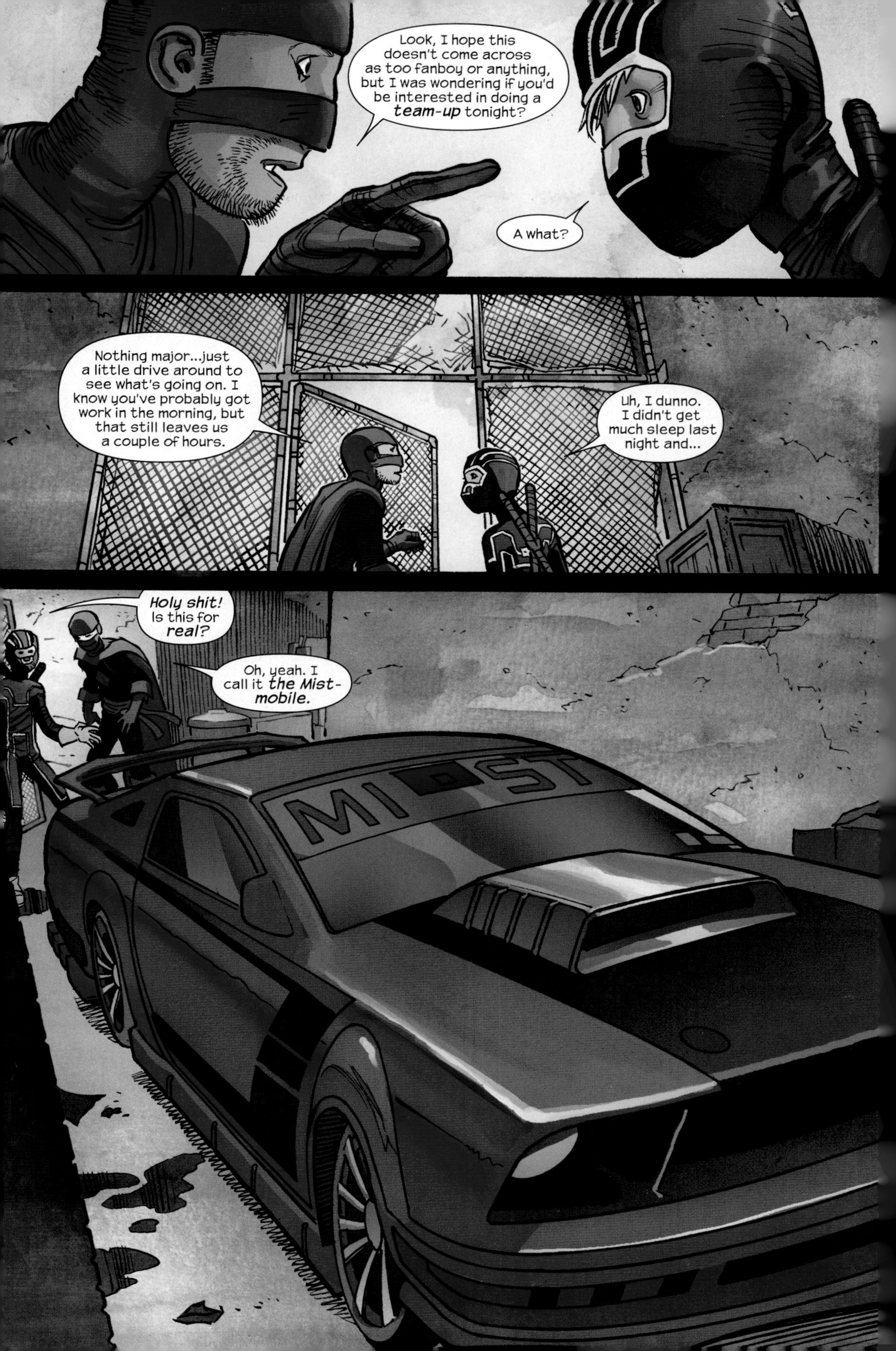
Look, I hope this doesn't come across as too fanboy or anything, but I was wondering if you'd be interested in doing a *team-up* tonight?
A what?
Nothing major...just a little drive around to see what's going on. I know you've probably got work in the morning, but that still leaves us a couple of hours.
Uh, I dunno. I didn't get much sleep last night and...
Holy shit! Is this for *real?*
Oh, yeah. I call it *the Mist-mobile.*
MIST

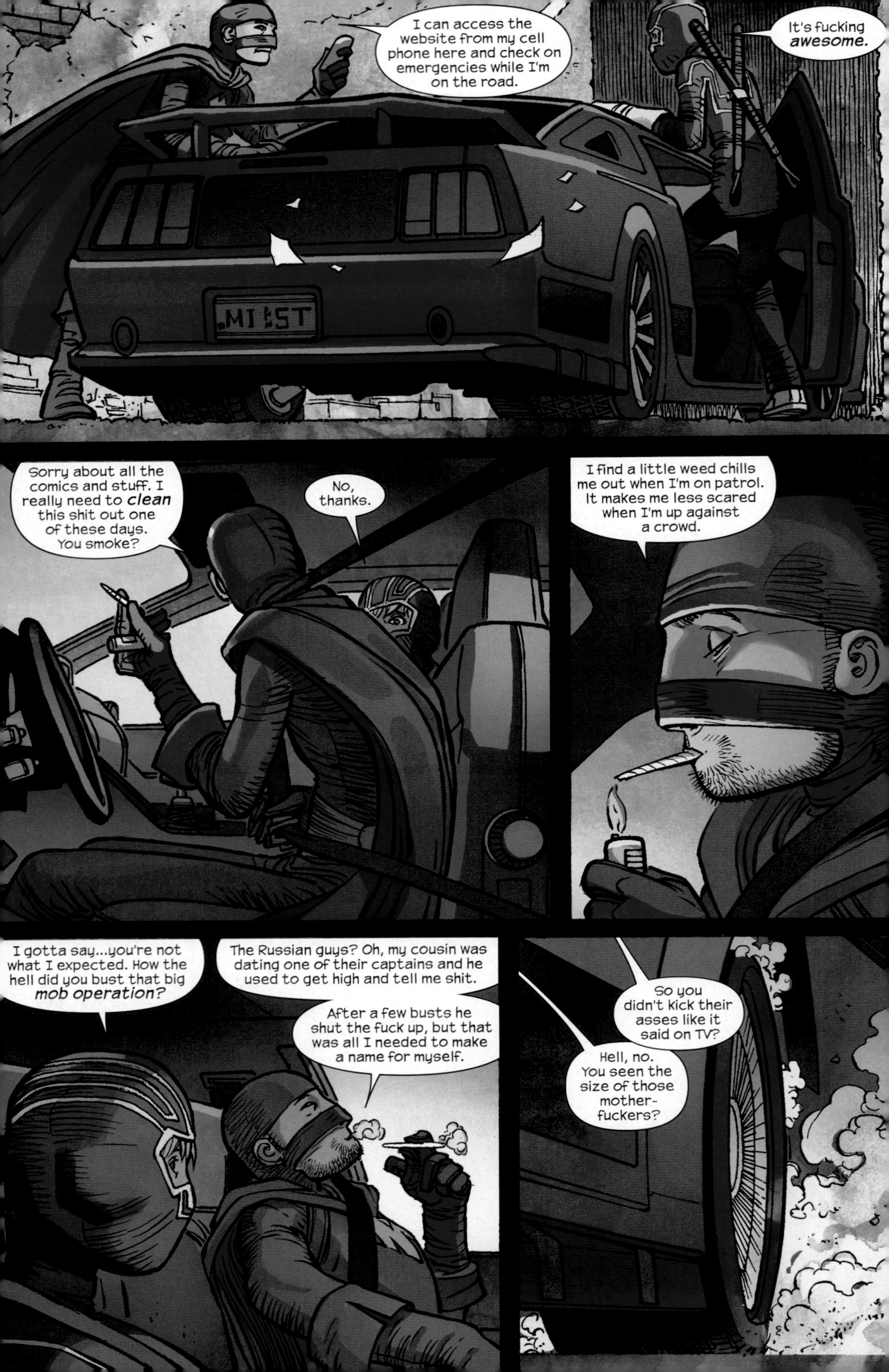
I can access the website from my cell phone here and check on emergencies while I'm on the road.
It's fucking awesome.
MI 1ST
Sorry about all the comics and stuff. I really need to clean this shit out one of these days. You smoke?
No, thanks.
I find a little weed chills me out when I'm on patrol. It makes me less scared when I'm up against a crowd.
I gotta say...you're not what I expected. How the hell did you bust that big mob operation?
The Russian guys? Oh, my cousin was dating one of their captains and he used to get high and tell me shit.
After a few busts he shut the fuck up, but that was all I needed to make a name for myself.
So you didn't kick their asses like it said on TV?
Hell, no. You seen the size of those mother-fuckers?

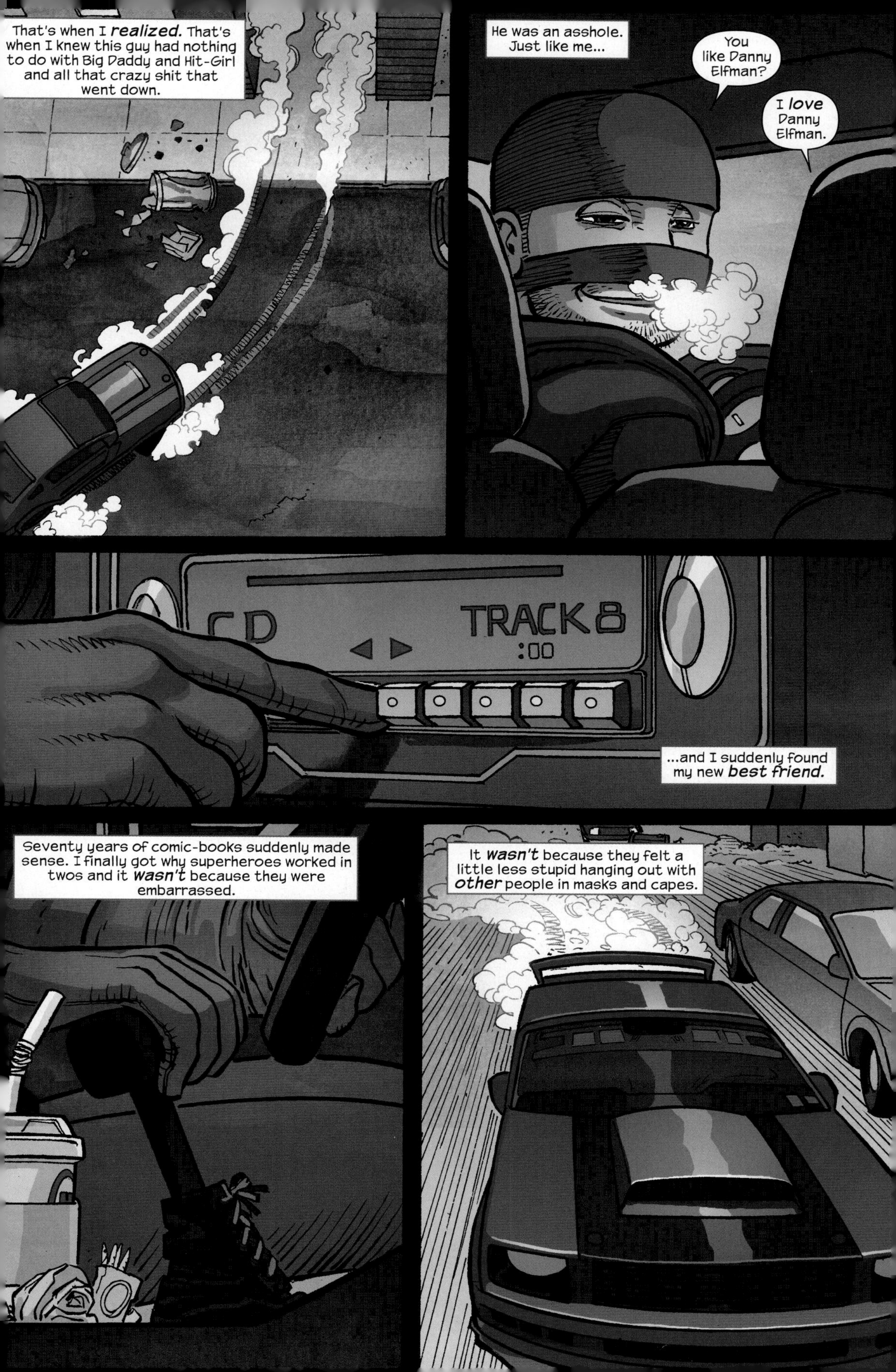
That's when I realized. That's when I knew this guy had nothing to do with Big Daddy and Hit-Girl and all that crazy shit that went down.
He was an asshole. Just like me...
You like Danny Elfman?
I love Danny Elfman.
CD
TRACK 8
:00
...and I suddenly found my new best friend.
Seventy years of comic-books suddenly made sense. I finally got why superheroes worked in twos and it wasn't because they were embarrassed.
It wasn't because they felt a little less stupid hanging out with other people in masks and capes.

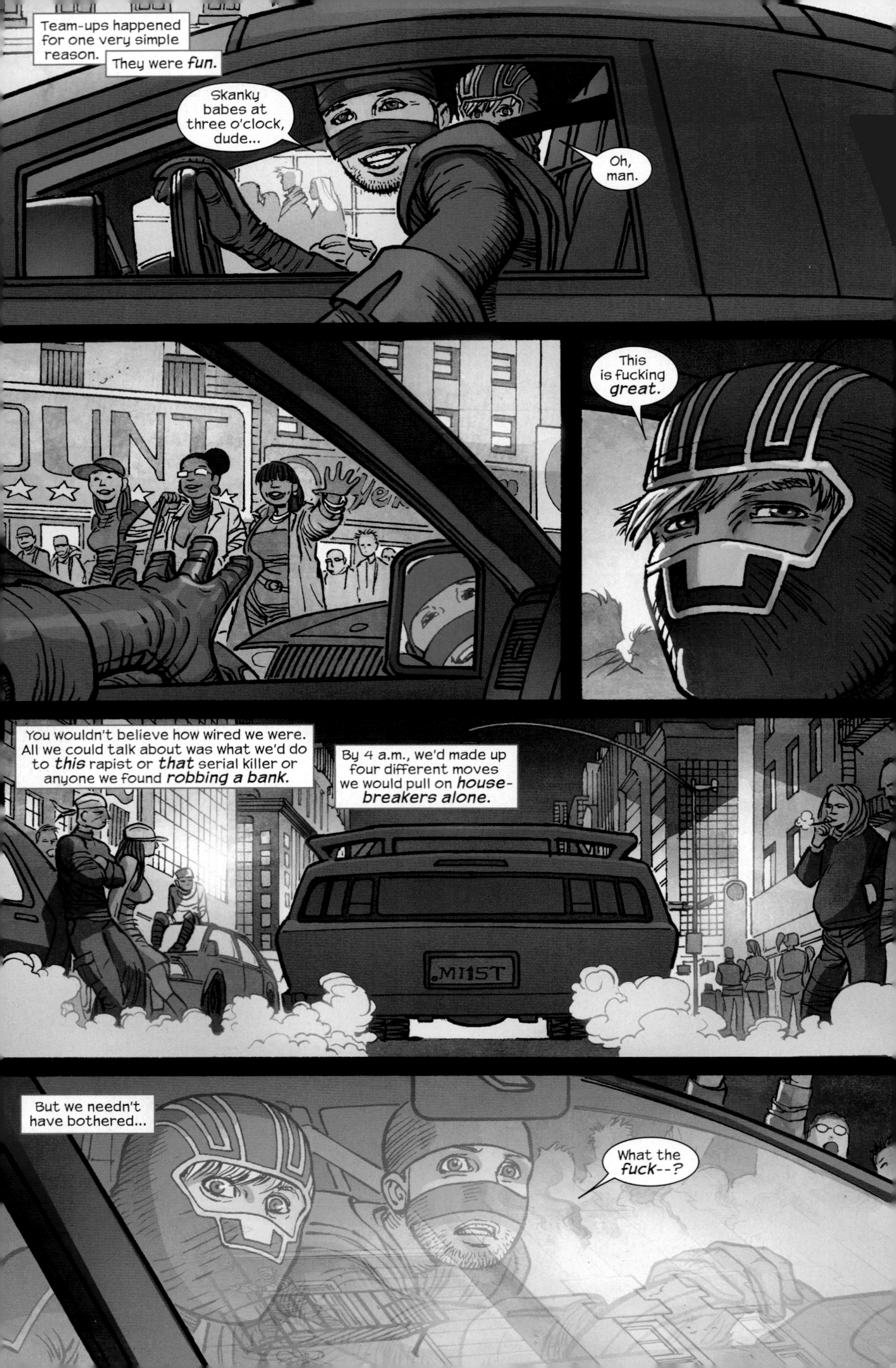
Team-ups happened for one very simple reason.
They were *fun.*
Skanky babes at three o'clock, dude...
Oh, man.
This is fucking *great.*
You wouldn't believe how wired we were. All we could talk about was what we'd do to *this* rapist or *that* serial killer or anyone we found *robbing a bank.*
By 4 a.m., we'd made up four different moves we would pull on *house-breakers alone.*
MI15T
But we needn't have bothered...
What the *fuck*--?

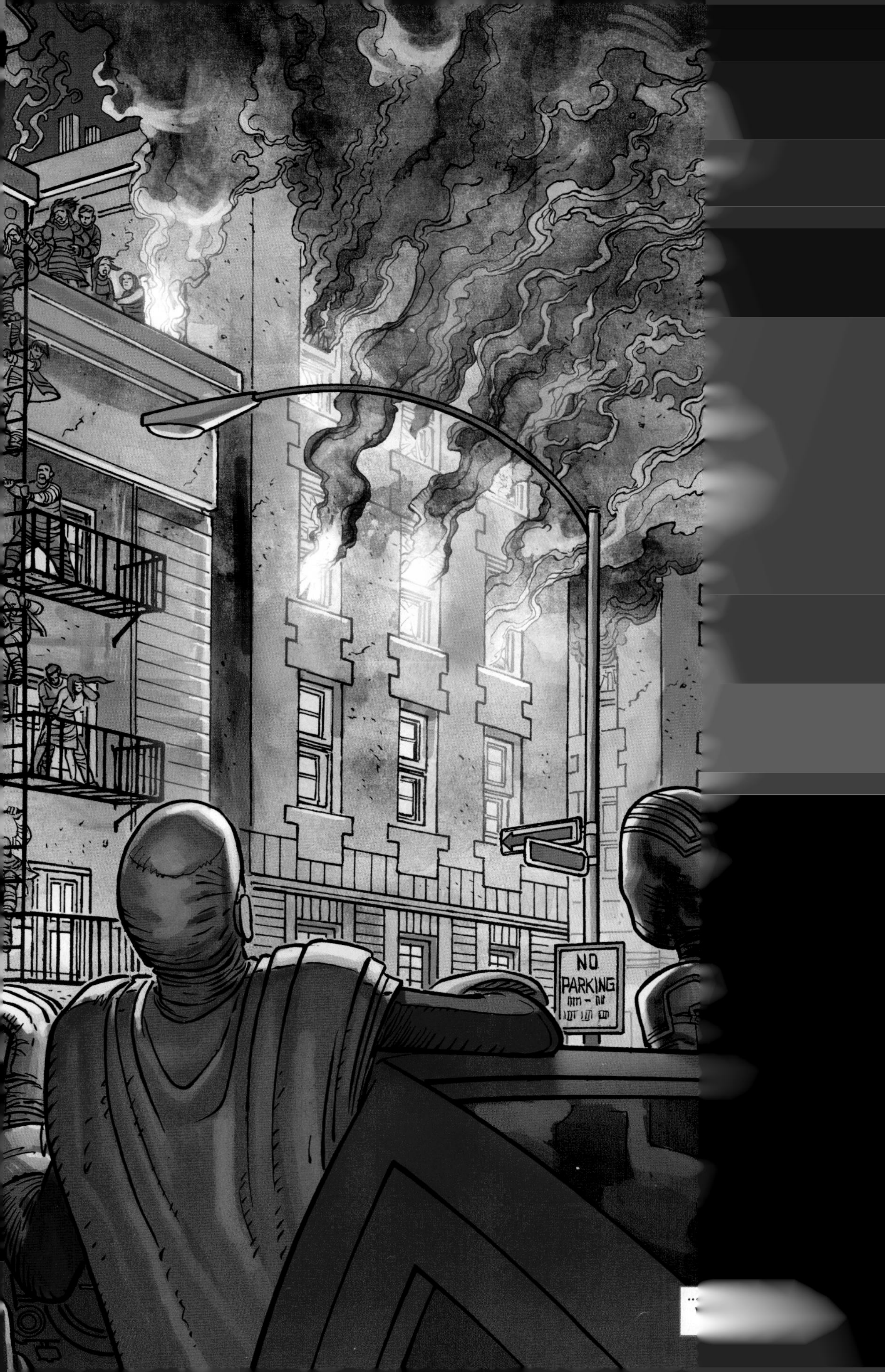
NO PARKING

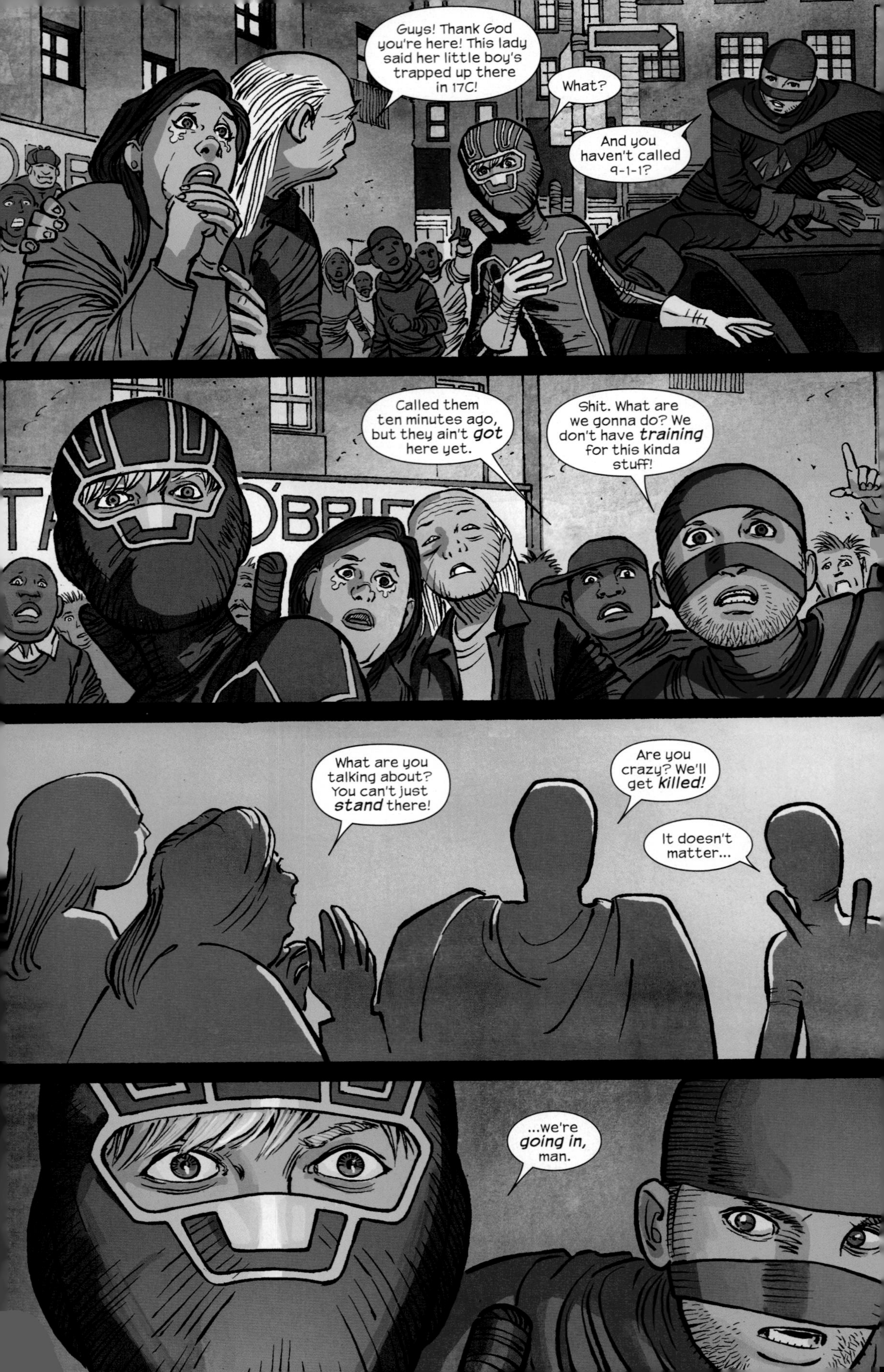
Guys! Thank God you're here! This lady said her little boy's trapped up there in 17C!
What?
And you haven't called 9-1-1?
Called them ten minutes ago, but they ain't got here yet.
Shit. What are we gonna do? We don't have training for this kinda stuff!
What are you talking about? You can't just stand there!
Are you crazy? We'll get killed!
It doesn't matter...
...we're going in, man.

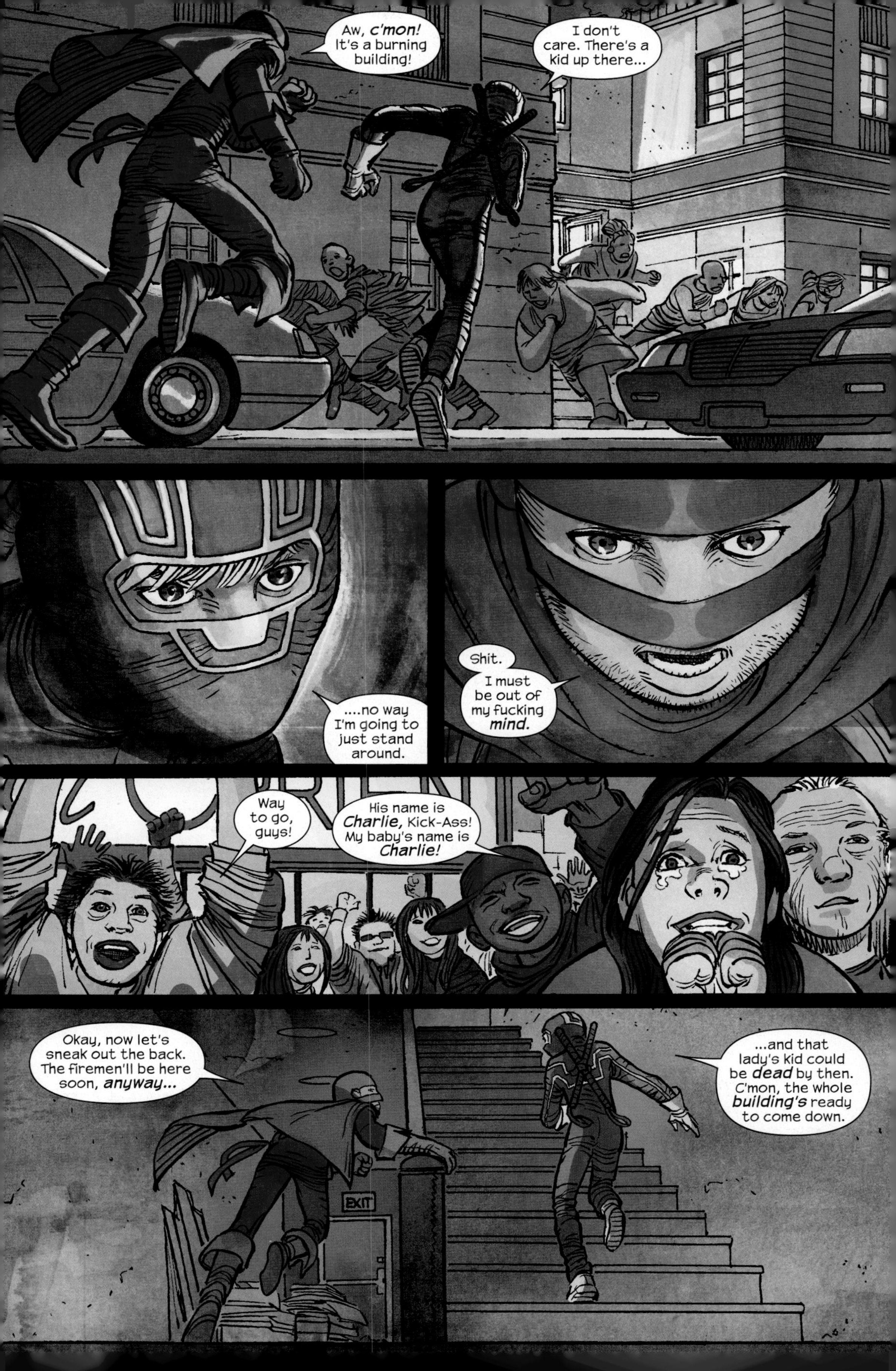

Aw, c'mon! It's a burning building!
I don't care. There's a kid up there...
....no way I'm going to just stand around.
Shit.
I must be out of my fucking mind.
Way to go, guys!
His name is Charlie, Kick-Ass! My baby's name is Charlie!
Okay, now let's sneak out the back. The firemen'll be here soon, anyway...
...and that lady's kid could be dead by then. C'mon, the whole building's ready to come down.
EXIT

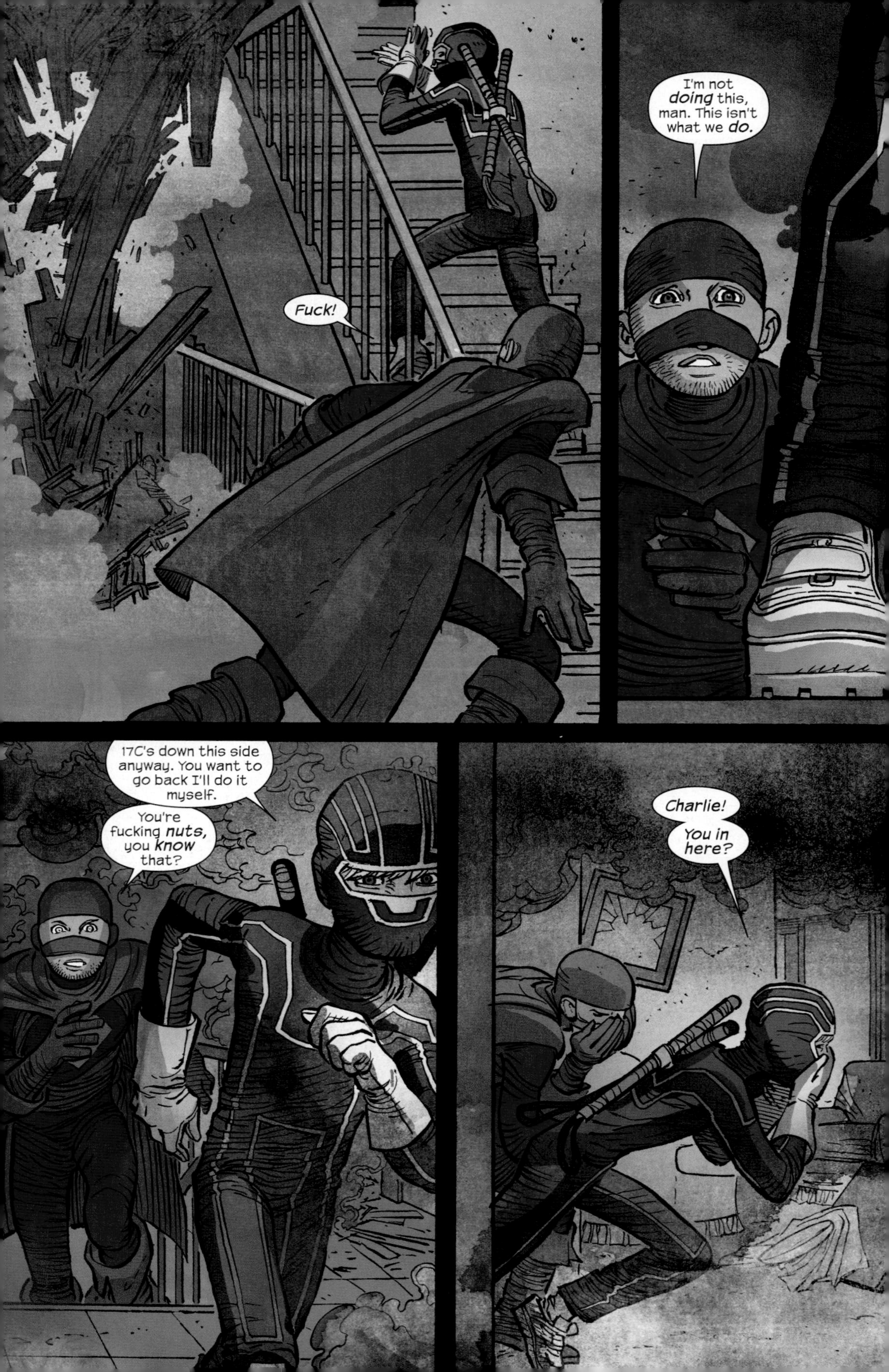
Fuck!
I'm not doing this, man. This isn't what we do.
17C's down this side anyway. You want to go back I'll do it myself.
You're fucking nuts, you know that?
Charlie!
You in here?

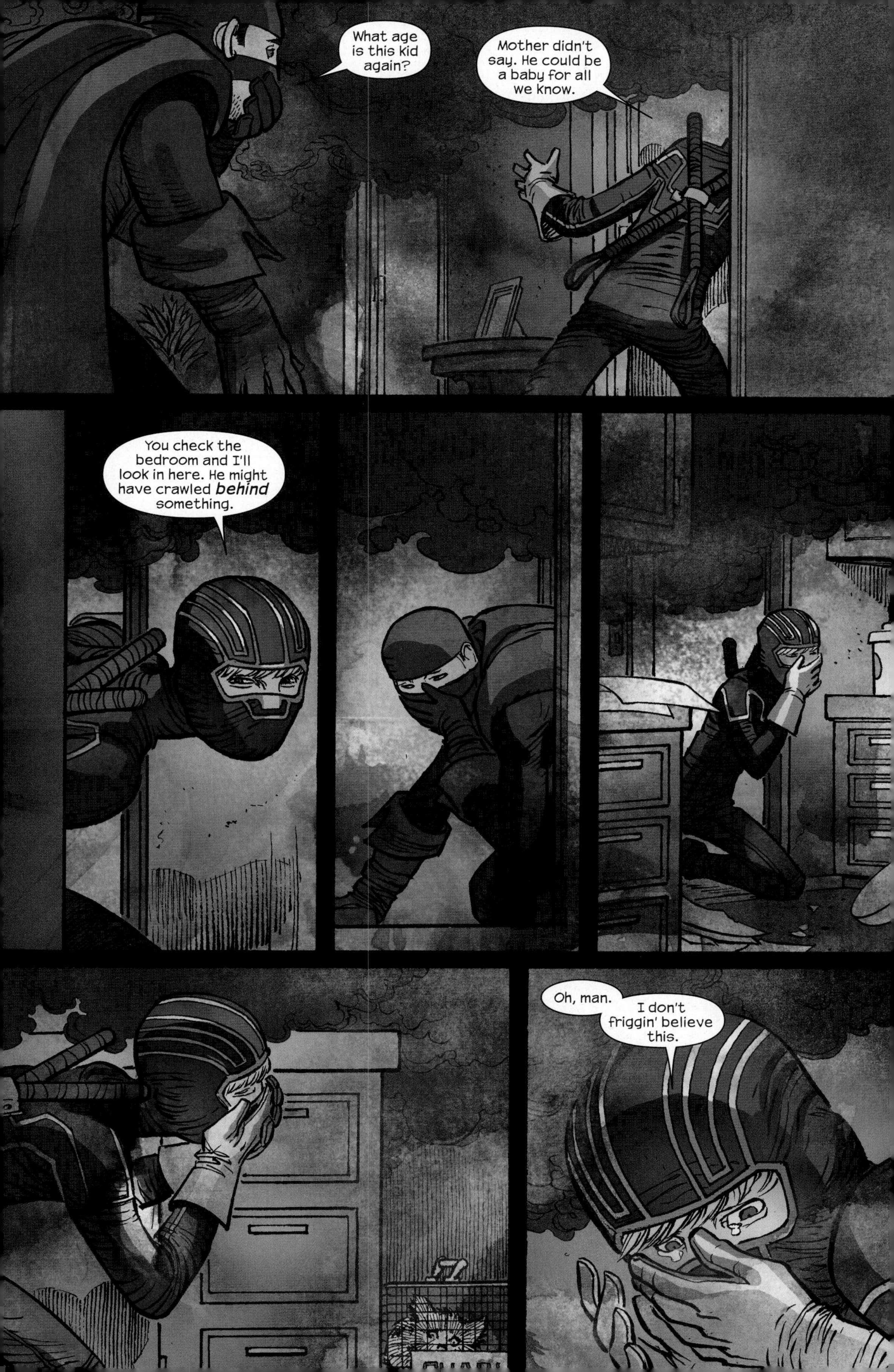
What age is this kid again?
Mother didn't say. He could be a baby for all we know.
You check the bedroom and I'll look in here. He might have crawled *behind* something.
Oh, man.
I don't friggin' believe this.

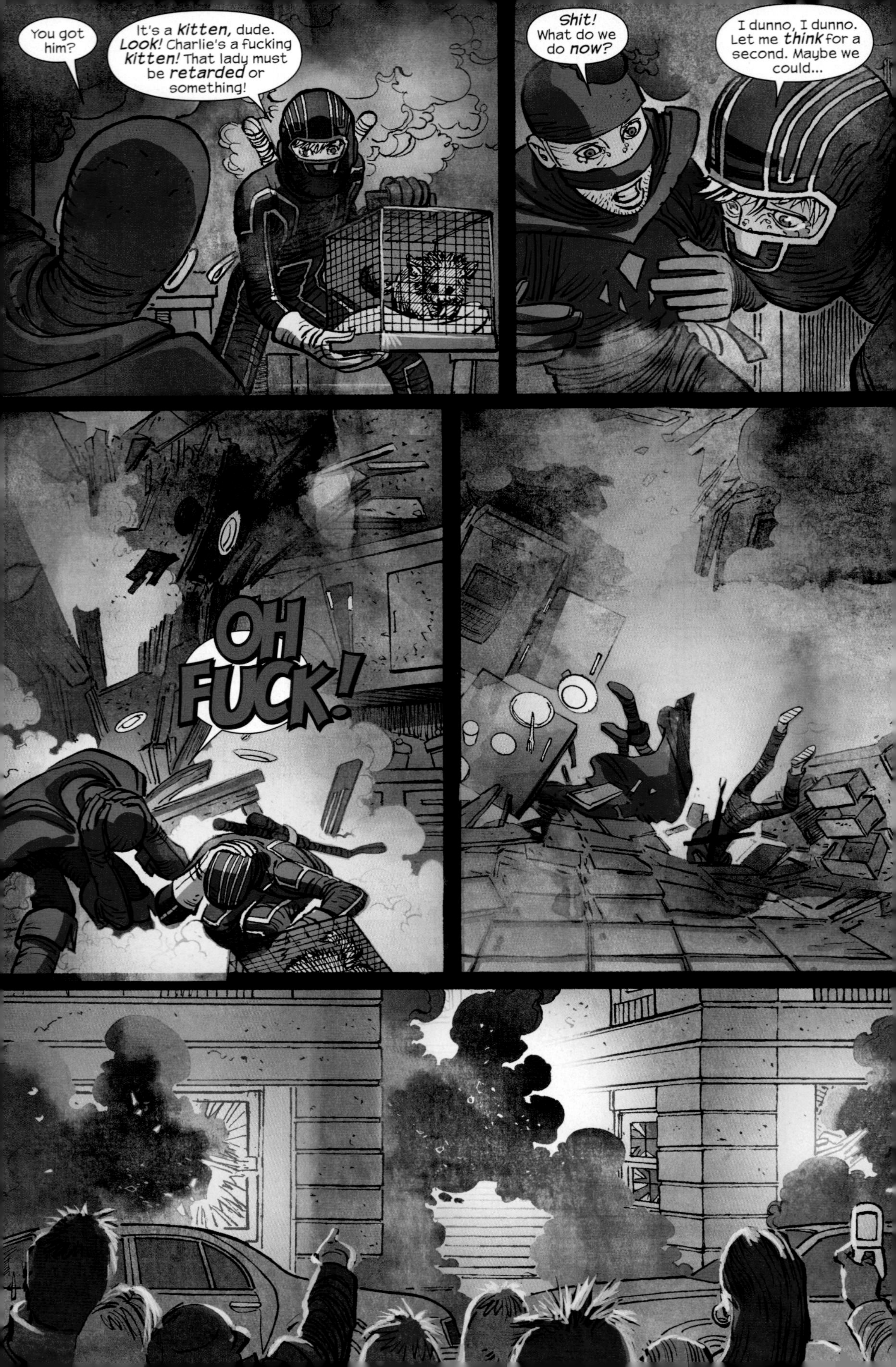
You got him?
It's a *kitten,* dude. *Look!* Charlie's a fucking *kitten!* That lady must be *retarded* or something!
Shit! What do we do *now?*
I dunno, I dunno. Let me *think* for a second. Maybe we could...
OH FUCK!

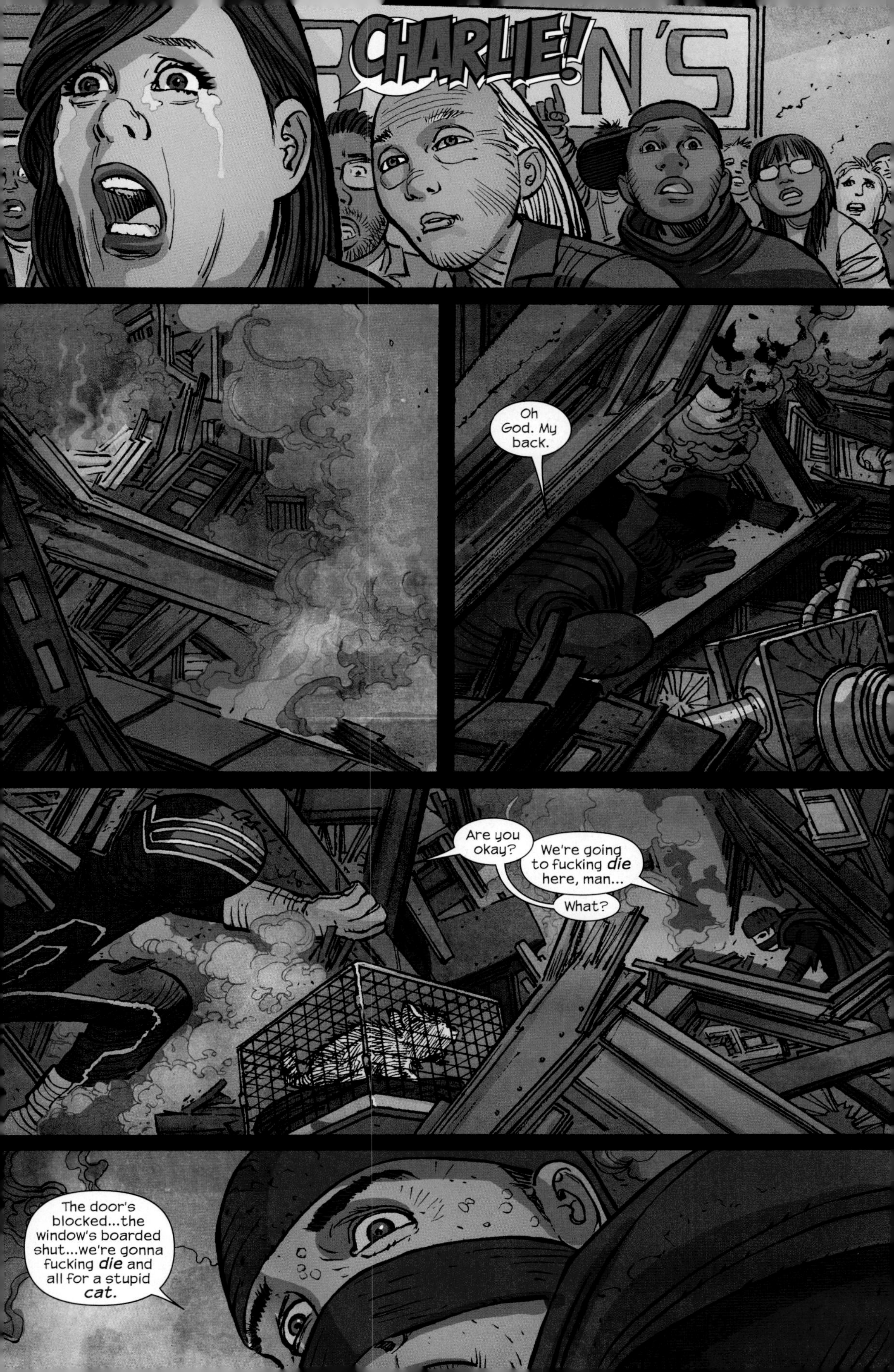
CHARLIE!
Oh God. My back.
Are you okay?
We're going to fucking *die* here, man...
What?
The door's blocked...the window's boarded shut...we're gonna fucking *die* and all for a stupid *cat.*

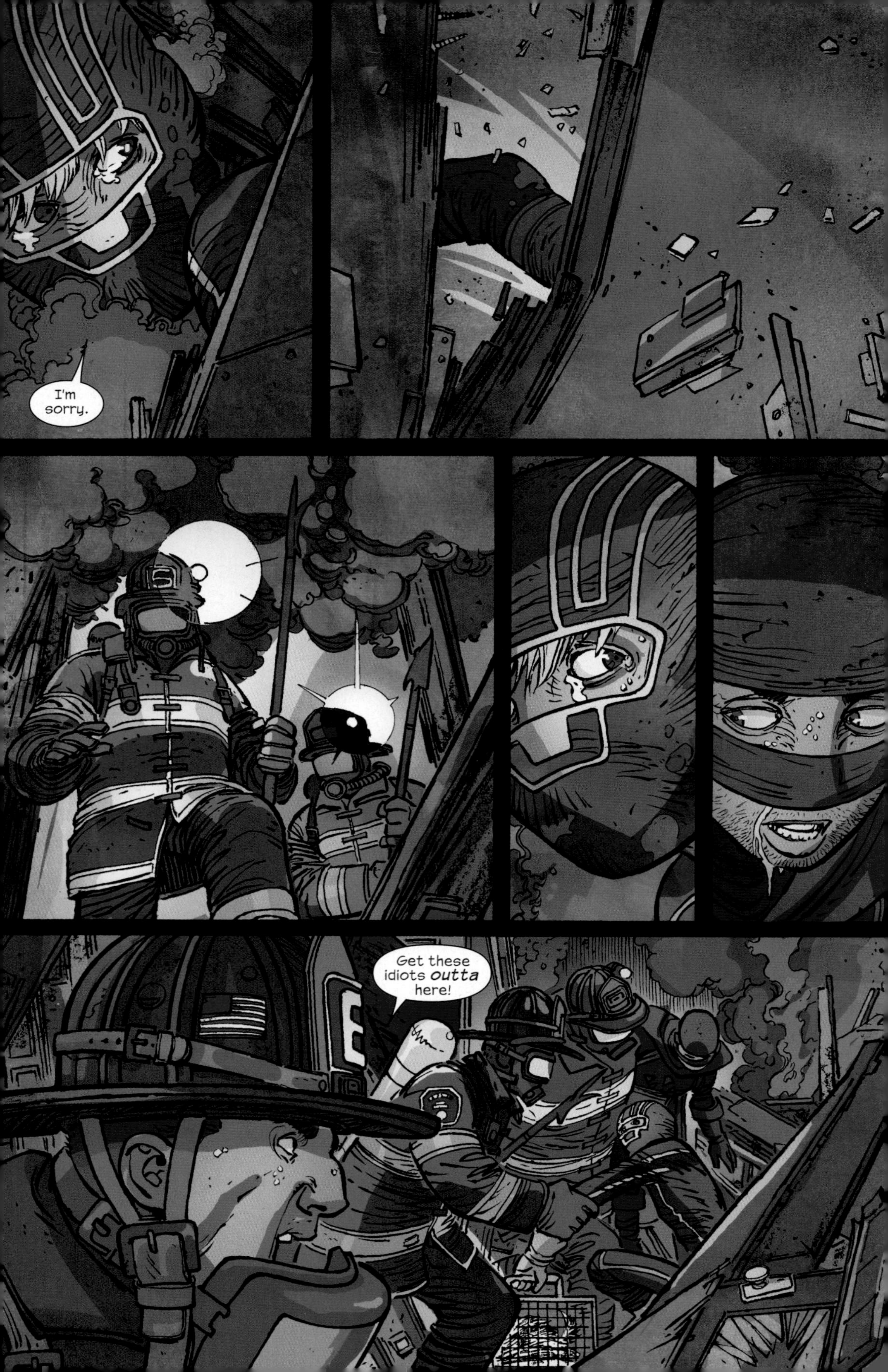
I'm sorry.
Get these idiots *outta* here!

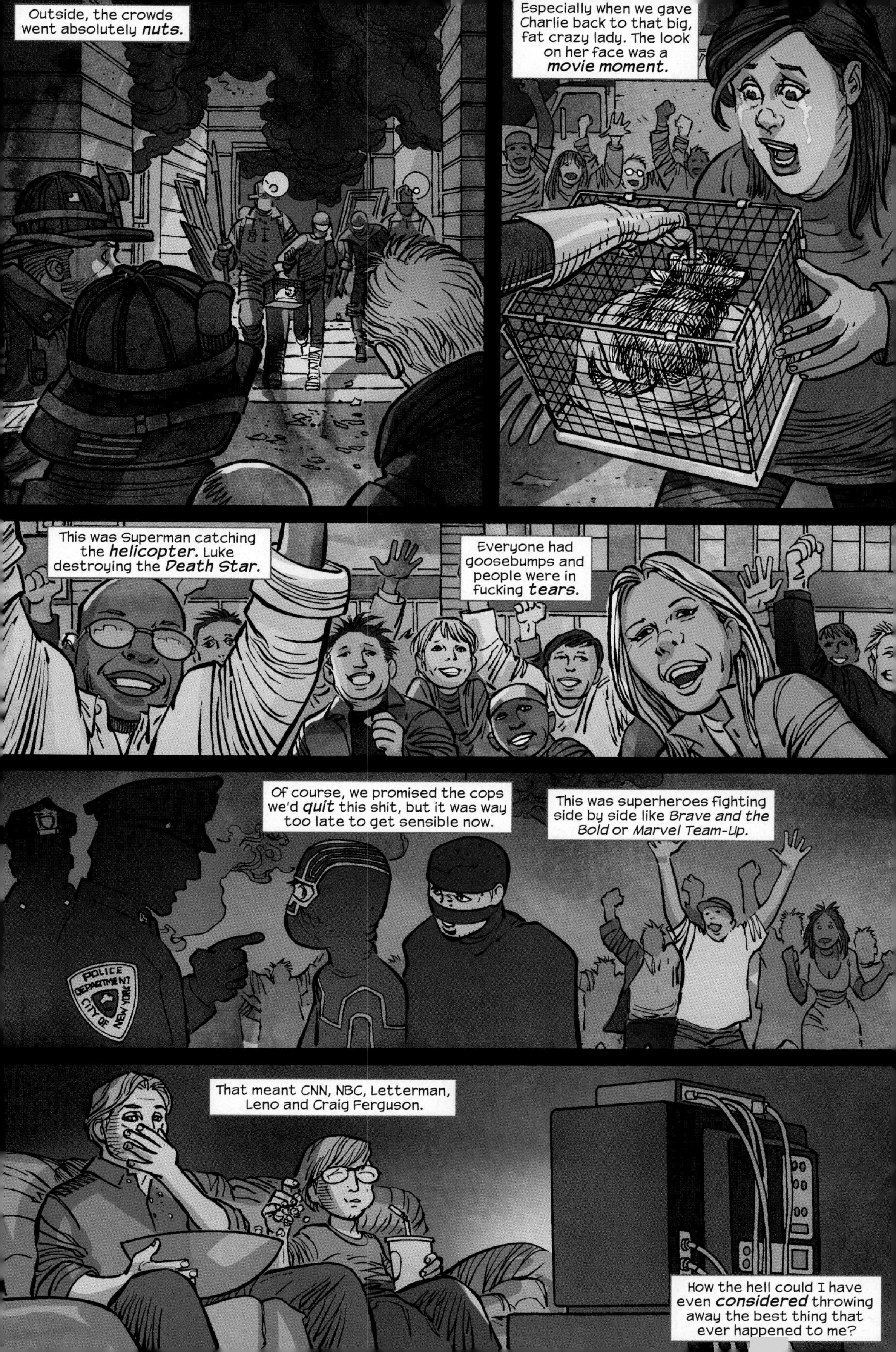
Outside, the crowds went absolutely *nuts.*
Especially when we gave Charlie back to that big, fat crazy lady. The look on her face was a *movie moment.*
This was Superman catching the *helicopter.* Luke destroying the *Death Star.*
Everyone had goosebumps and people were in fucking *tears.*
Of course, we promised the cops we'd *quit* this shit, but it was way too late to get sensible now.
This was superheroes fighting side by side like *Brave and the Bold* or *Marvel Team-Up.*
POLICE DEPARTMENT CITY OF NEW YORK
That meant CNN, NBC, Letterman, Leno and Craig Ferguson.
How the hell could I have even *considered* throwing away the best thing that ever happened to me?

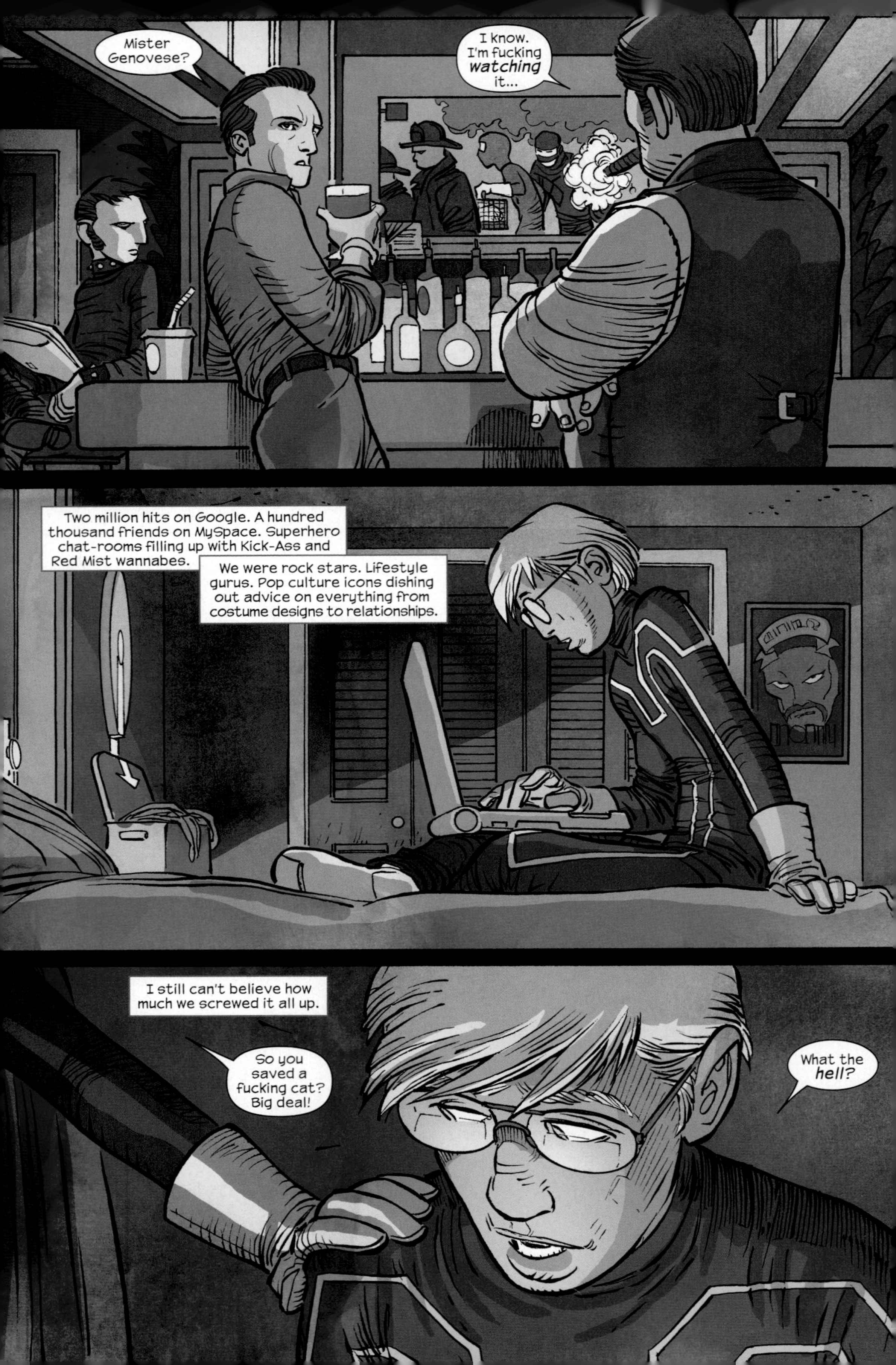
Mister Genovese?
I know. I'm fucking *watching* it...
Two million hits on Google. A hundred thousand friends on MySpace. Superhero chat-rooms filling up with Kick-Ass and Red Mist wannabes.
We were rock stars. Lifestyle gurus. Pop culture icons dishing out advice on everything from costume designs to relationships.
I still can't believe how much we screwed it all up.
So you saved a fucking cat? Big deal!
What the *hell*?

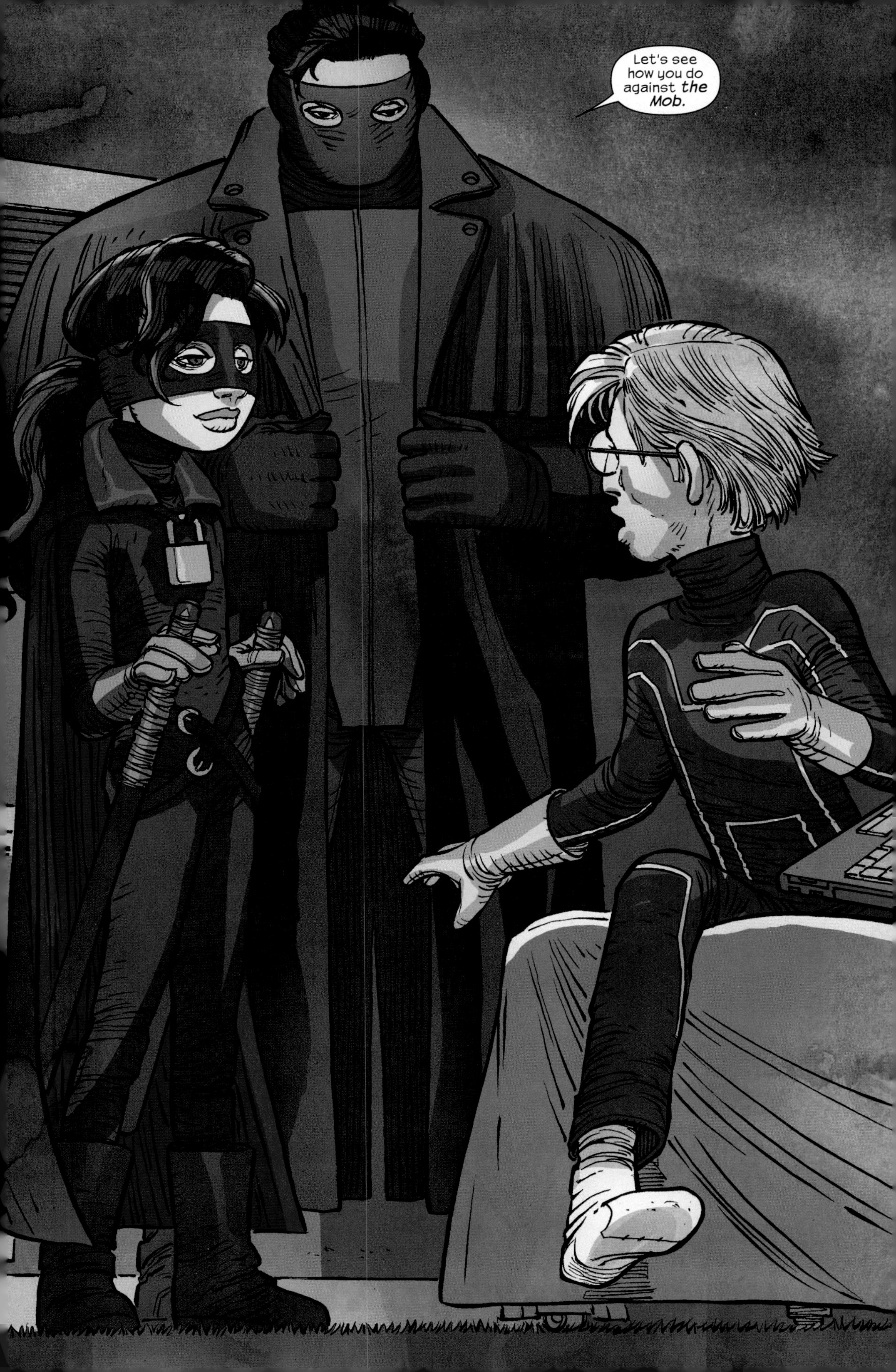
Let's see how you do against *the Mob.*

SIX

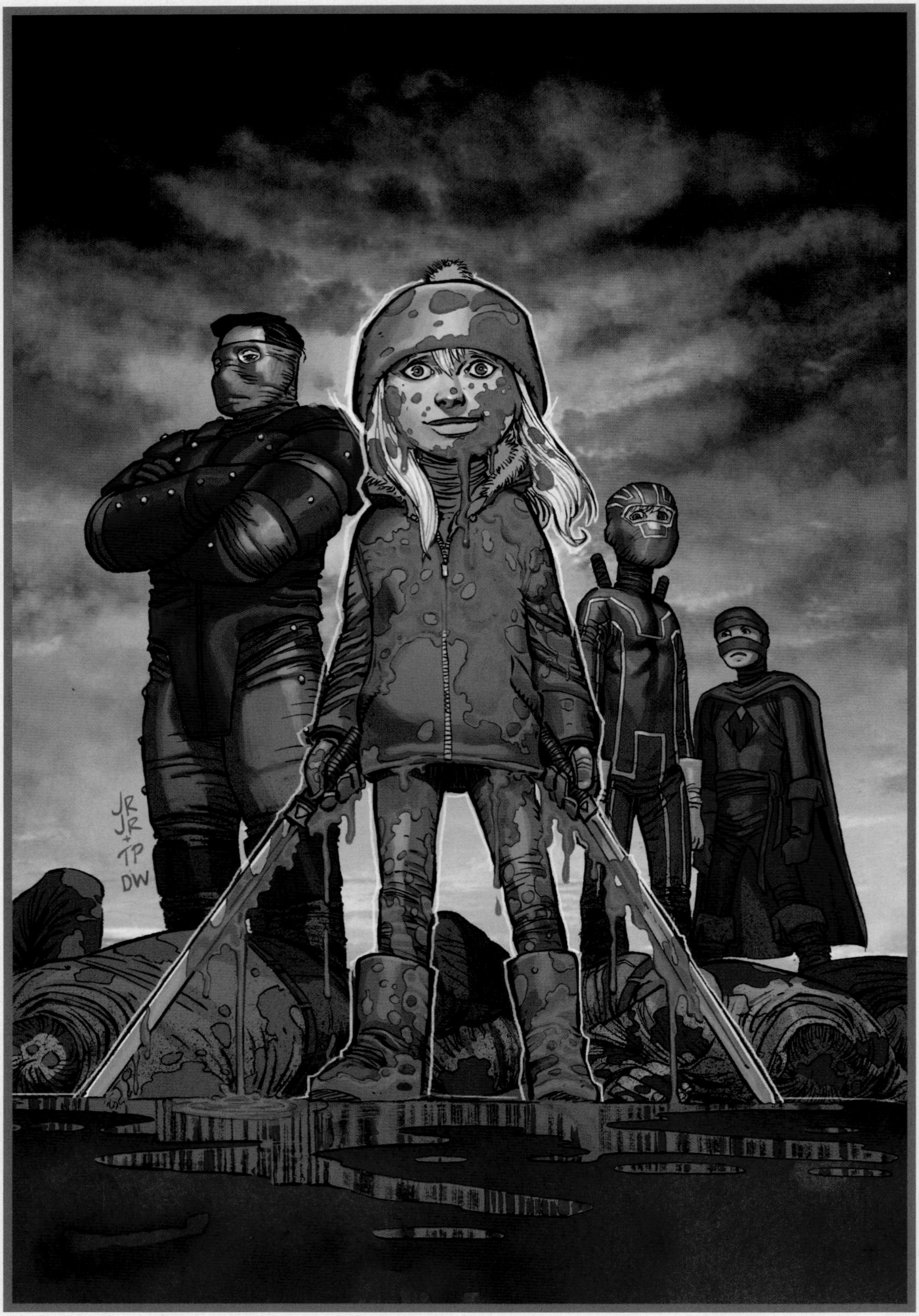
JR JR + TP DW

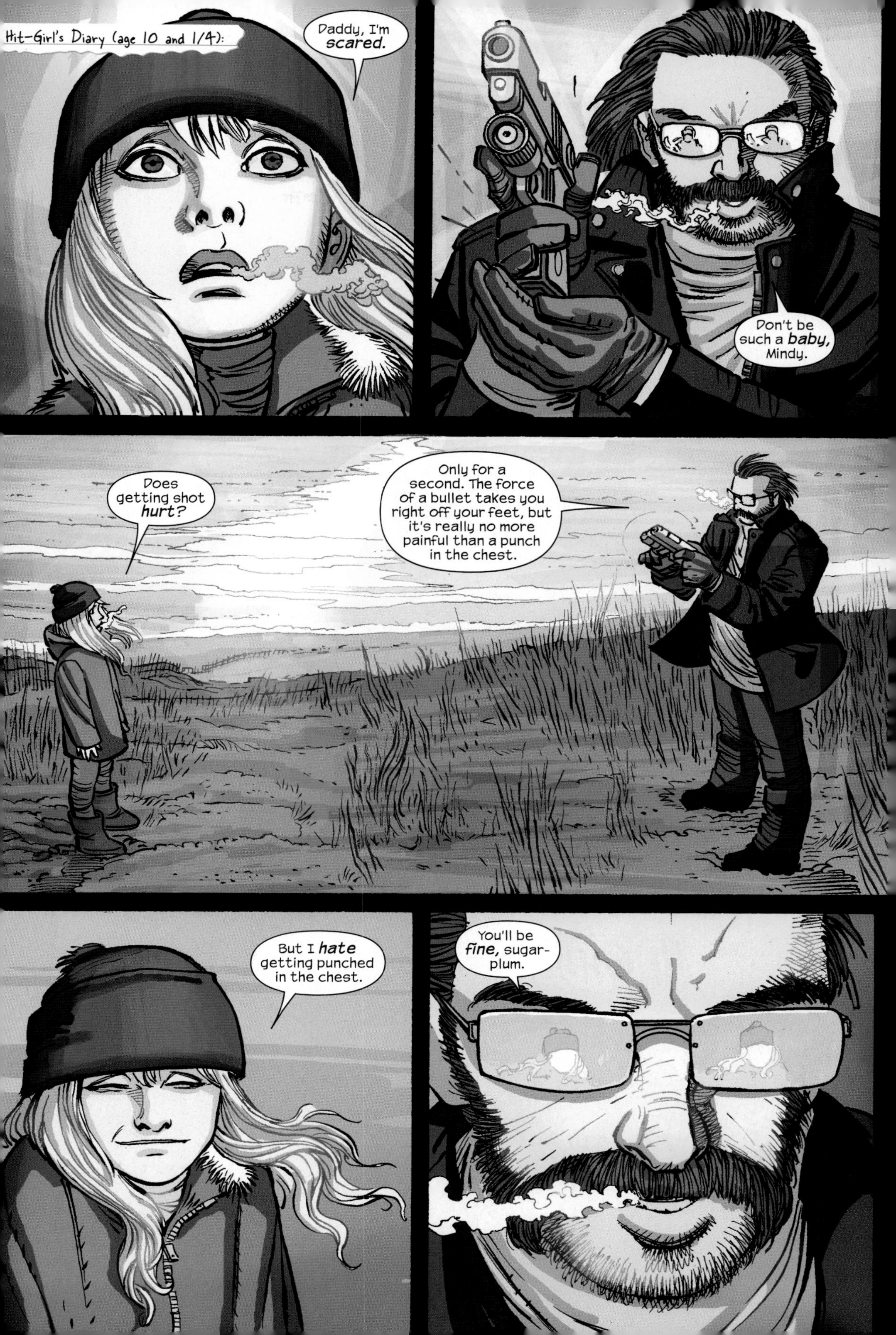
Hit-Girl's Diary (age 10 and 1/4):
Daddy, I'm *scared.*
Don't be such a *baby,* Mindy.
Does getting shot *hurt?*
Only for a second. The force of a bullet takes you right off your feet, but it's really no more painful than a punch in the chest.
But I *hate* getting punched in the chest.
You'll be *fine,* sugar-plum.

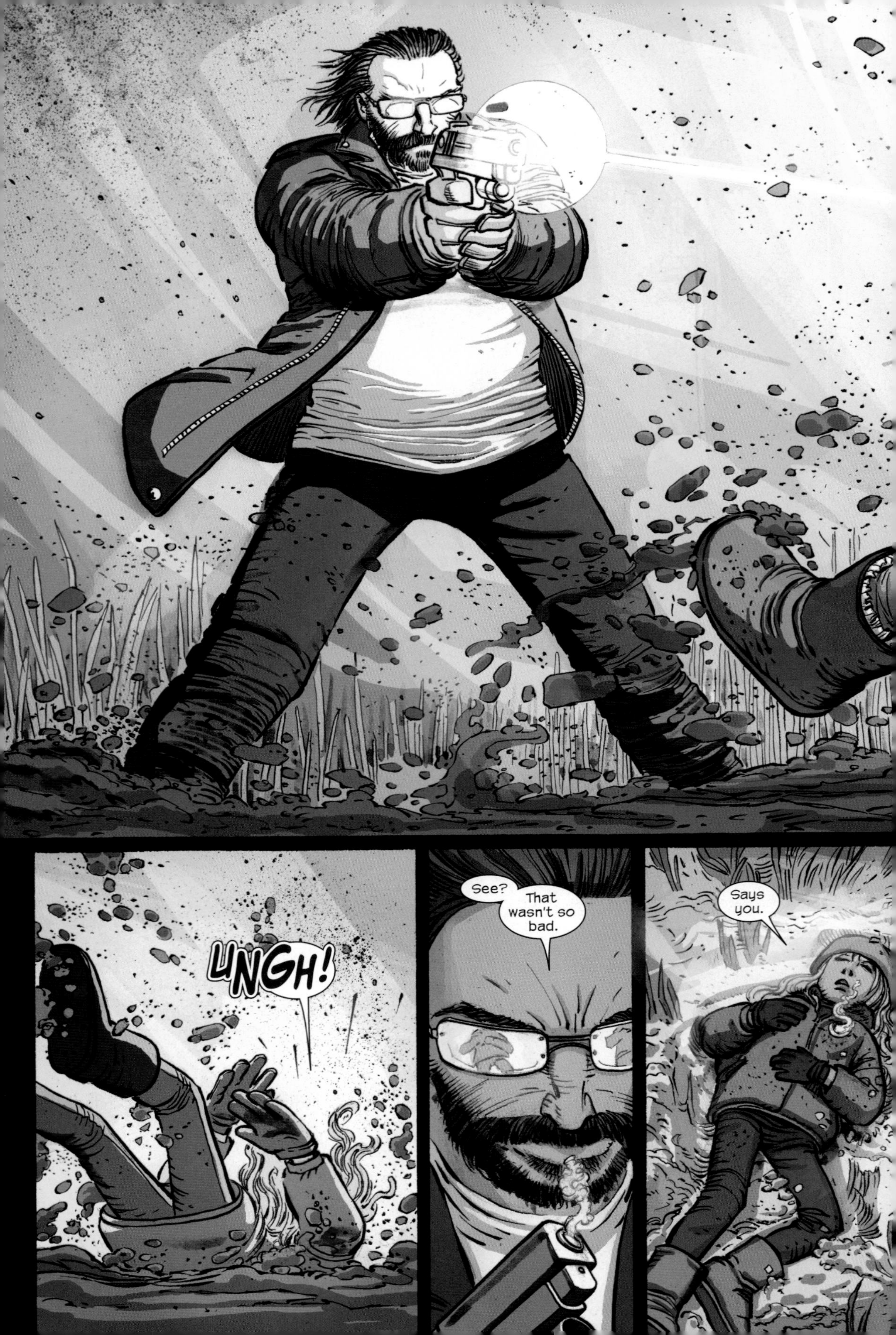
UNGH!
See?
That wasn't so bad.
Says you.

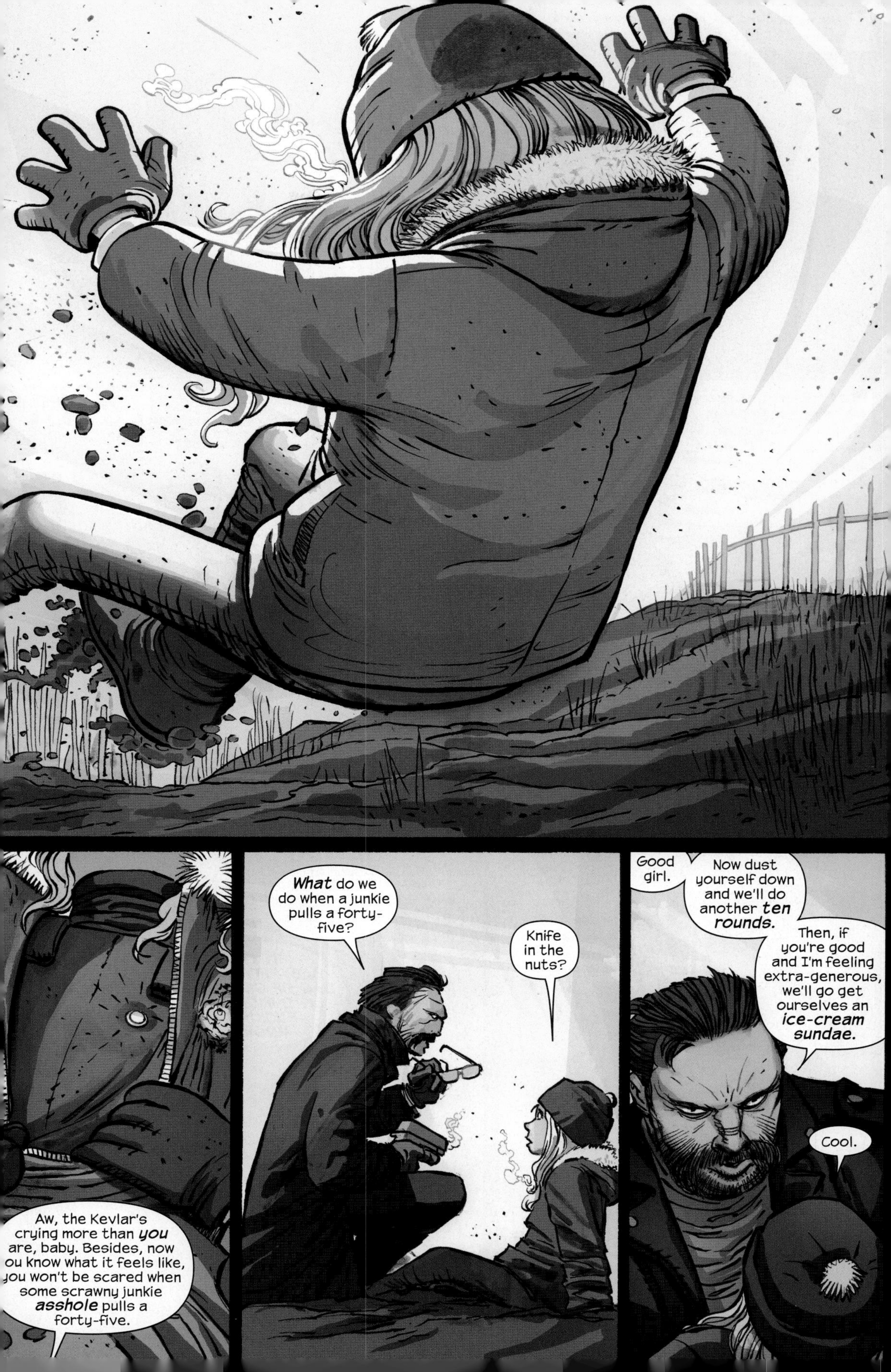
Aw, the Kevlar's crying more than *you* are, baby. Besides, now ou know what it feels like, you won't be scared when some scrawny junkie ***asshole*** pulls a forty-five.
What do we do when a junkie pulls a forty-five?
Knife in the nuts?
Good girl.
Now dust yourself down and we'll do another ***ten rounds.***
Then, if you're good and I'm feeling extra-generous, we'll go get ourselves an ***ice-cream sundae.***
Cool.

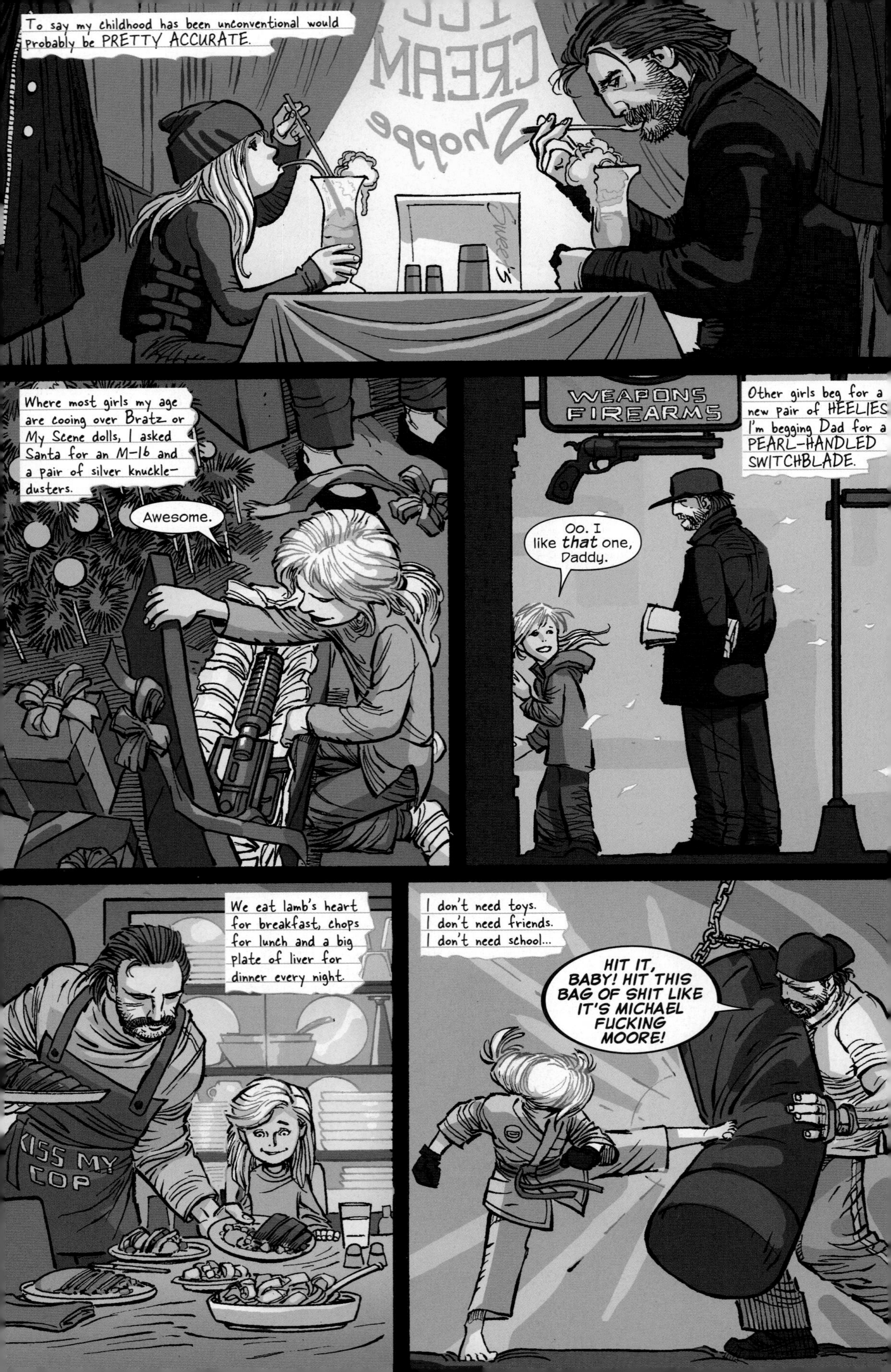
To say my childhood has been unconventional would probably be PRETTY ACCURATE.
ICE CREAM Shoppe
Where most girls my age are cooing over Bratz or My Scene dolls, I asked Santa for an M-16 and a pair of silver knuckle-dusters.
Awesome.
WEAPONS FIREARMS
Other girls beg for a new pair of HEELIES I'm begging Dad for a PEARL-HANDLED SWITCHBLADE.
Oo. I like *that* one, Daddy.
We eat lamb's heart for breakfast, chops for lunch and a big plate of liver for dinner every night.
KISS MY COP
I don't need toys. I don't need friends. I don't need school...
HIT IT, BABY! HIT THIS BAG OF SHIT LIKE IT'S MICHAEL FUCKING MOORE!

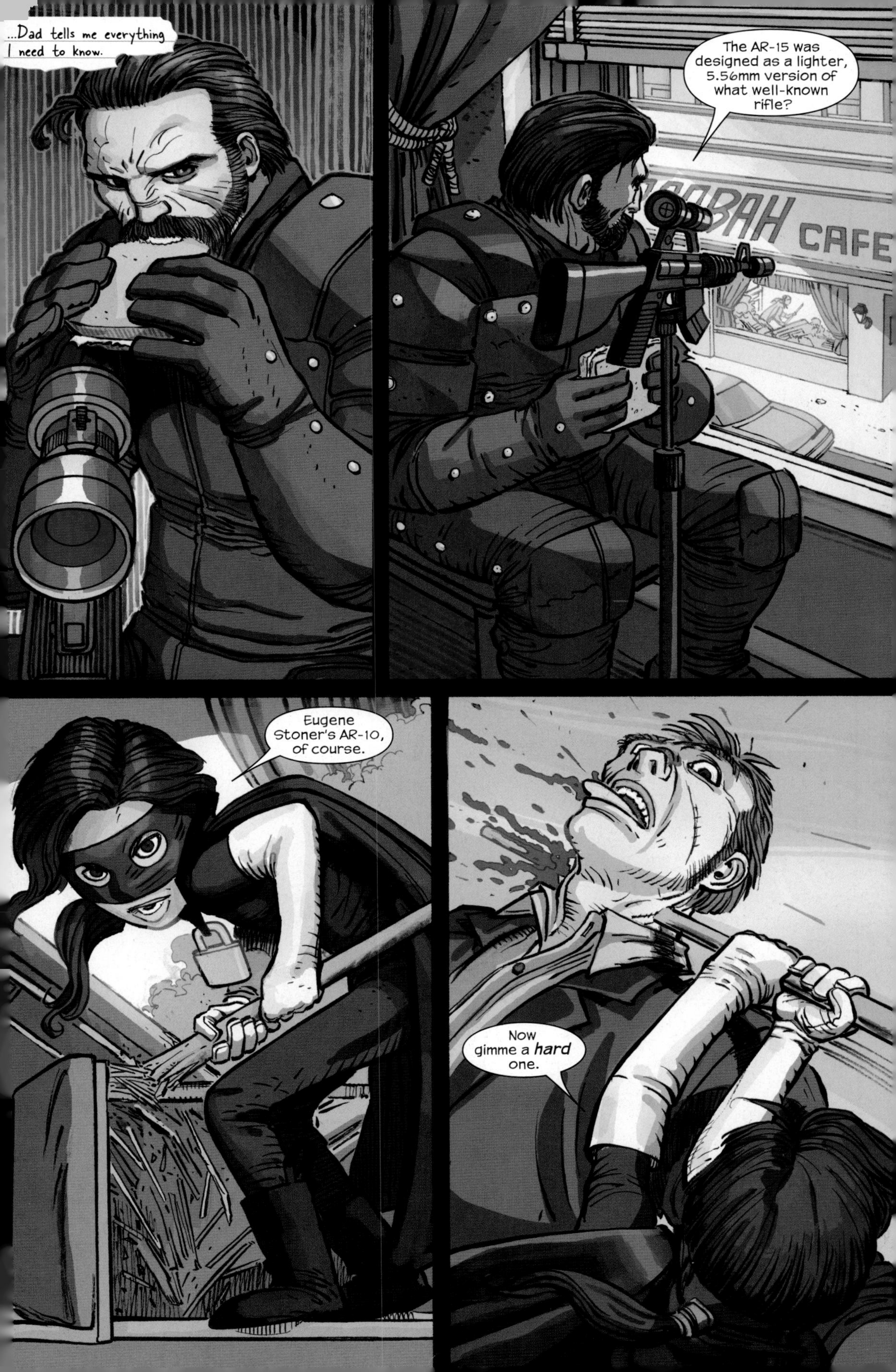
...Dad tells me everything I need to know.
The AR-15 was designed as a lighter, 5.56mm version of what well-known rifle?
BAH CAFE
Eugene Stoner's AR-10, of course.
Now gimme a *hard* one.

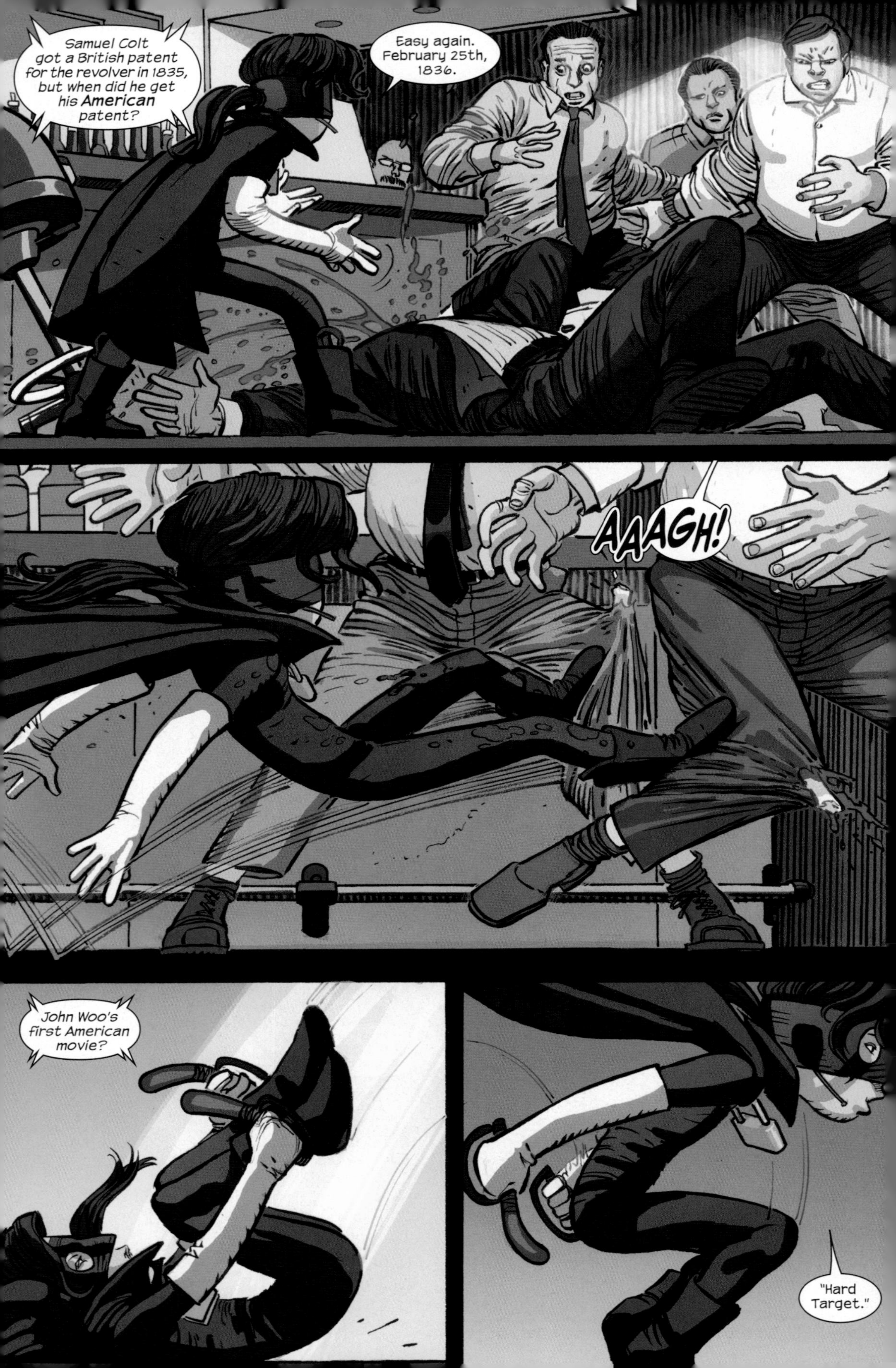
Samuel Colt got a British patent for the revolver in 1835, but when did he get his **American** patent?
Easy again. February 25th, 1836.
AAAGH!
John Woo's first American movie?
"Hard Target."

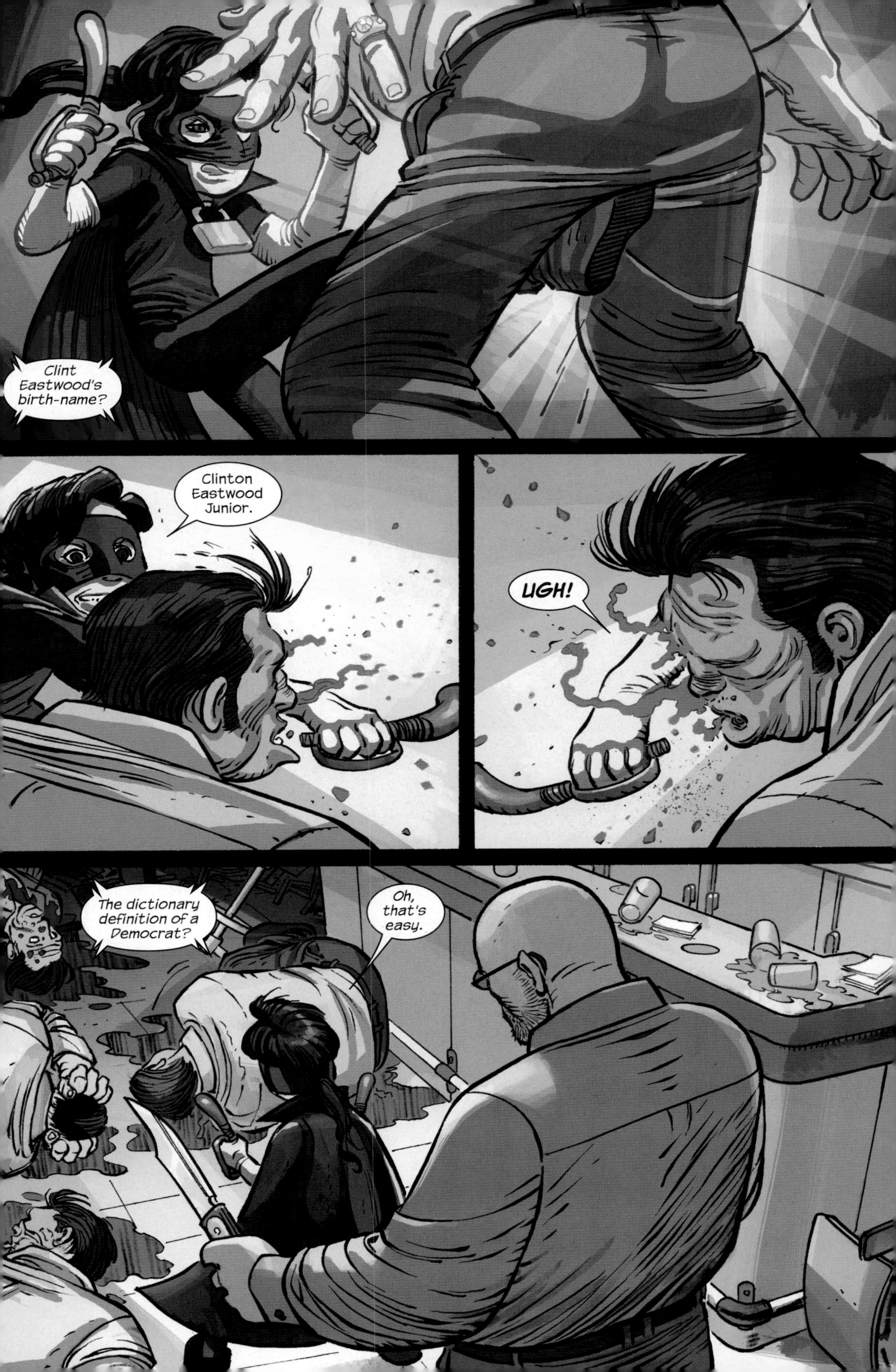
Clint Eastwood's birth-name?
Clinton Eastwood Junior.
UGH!
The dictionary definition of a Democrat?
Oh, that's easy.

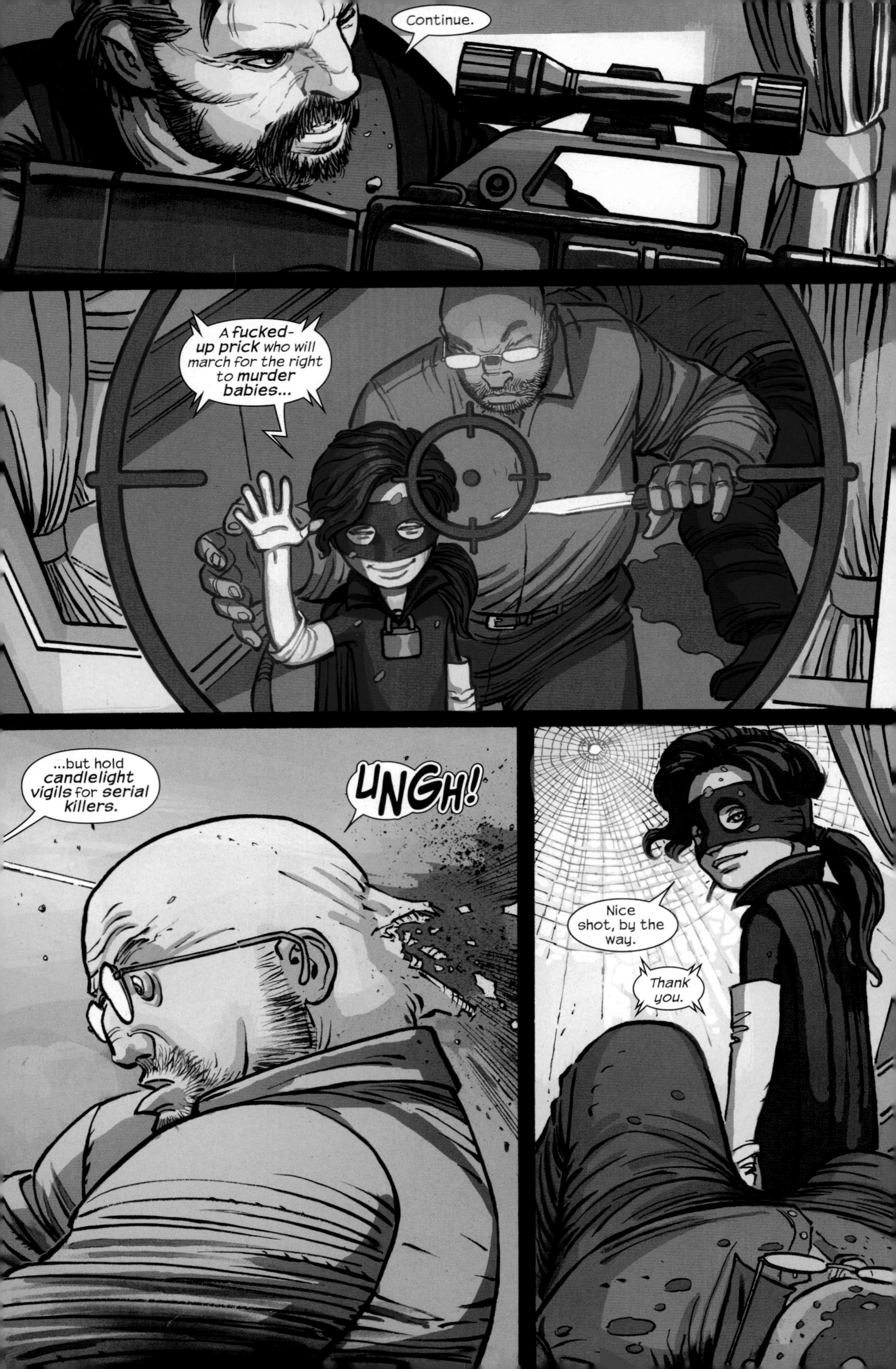
Continue.
A fucked-up prick who will march for the right to murder babies...
...but hold candlelight vigils for serial killers.
UNGH!
Nice shot, by the way.
Thank you.

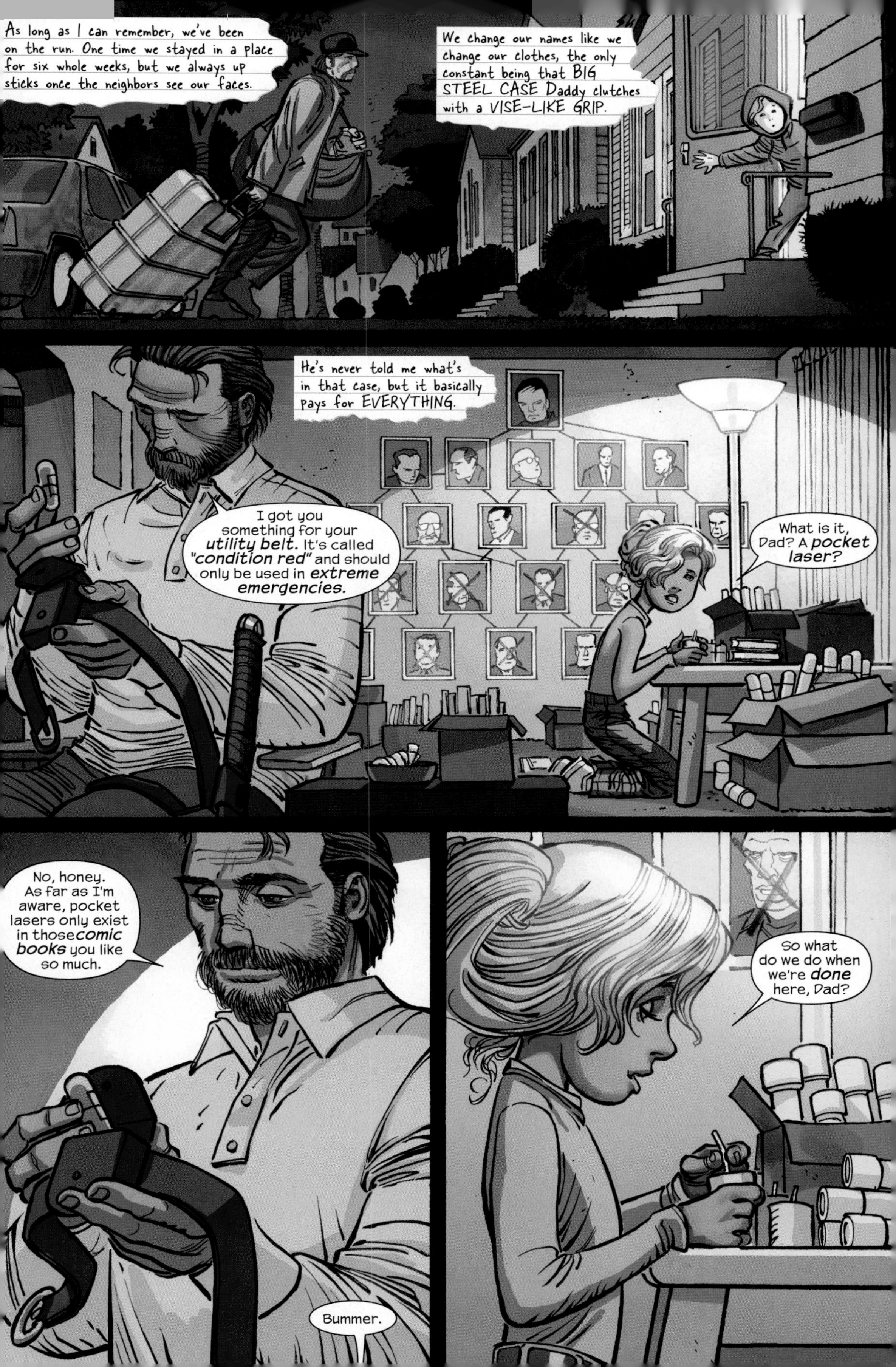

As long as I can remember, we've been on the run. One time we stayed in a place for six whole weeks, but we always up sticks once the neighbors see our faces.
We change our names like we change our clothes, the only constant being that BIG STEEL CASE Daddy clutches with a VISE-LIKE GRIP.
He's never told me what's in that case, but it basically pays for EVERYTHING.
I got you something for your utility belt. It's called "condition red" and should only be used in extreme emergencies.
What is it, Dad? A pocket laser?
No, honey. As far as I'm aware, pocket lasers only exist in those comic books you like so much.
Bummer.
So what do we do when we're done here, Dad?

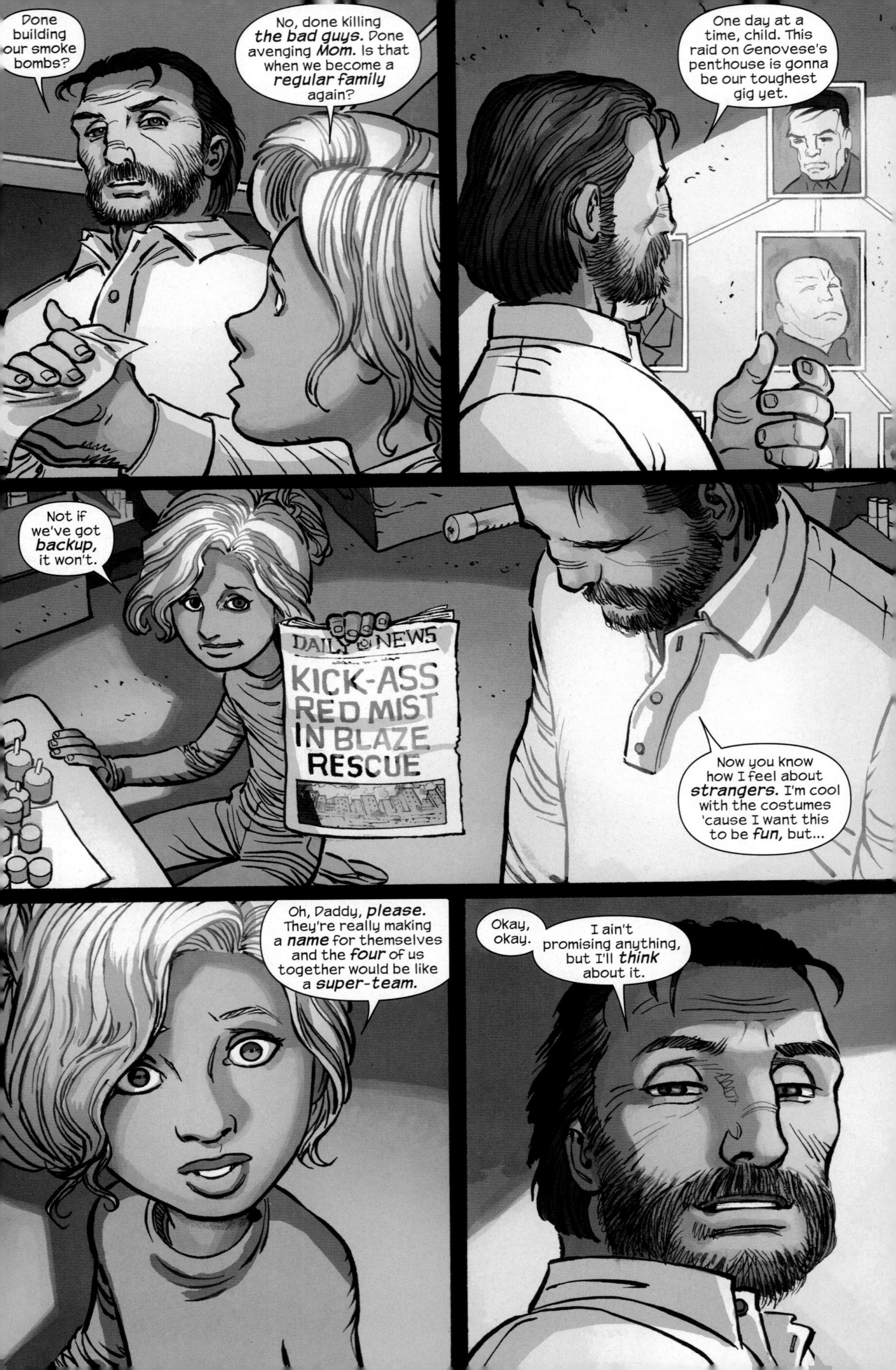
Done building our smoke bombs?
No, done killing the bad guys. Done avenging Mom. Is that when we become a regular family again?
One day at a time, child. This raid on Genovese's penthouse is gonna be our toughest gig yet.
Not if we've got backup, it won't.
DAILY NEWS
KICK-ASS RED MIST IN BLAZE RESCUE
Now you know how I feel about strangers. I'm cool with the costumes 'cause I want this to be fun, but...
Oh, Daddy, please. They're really making a name for themselves and the four of us together would be like a super-team.
Okay, okay.
I ain't promising anything, but I'll think about it.

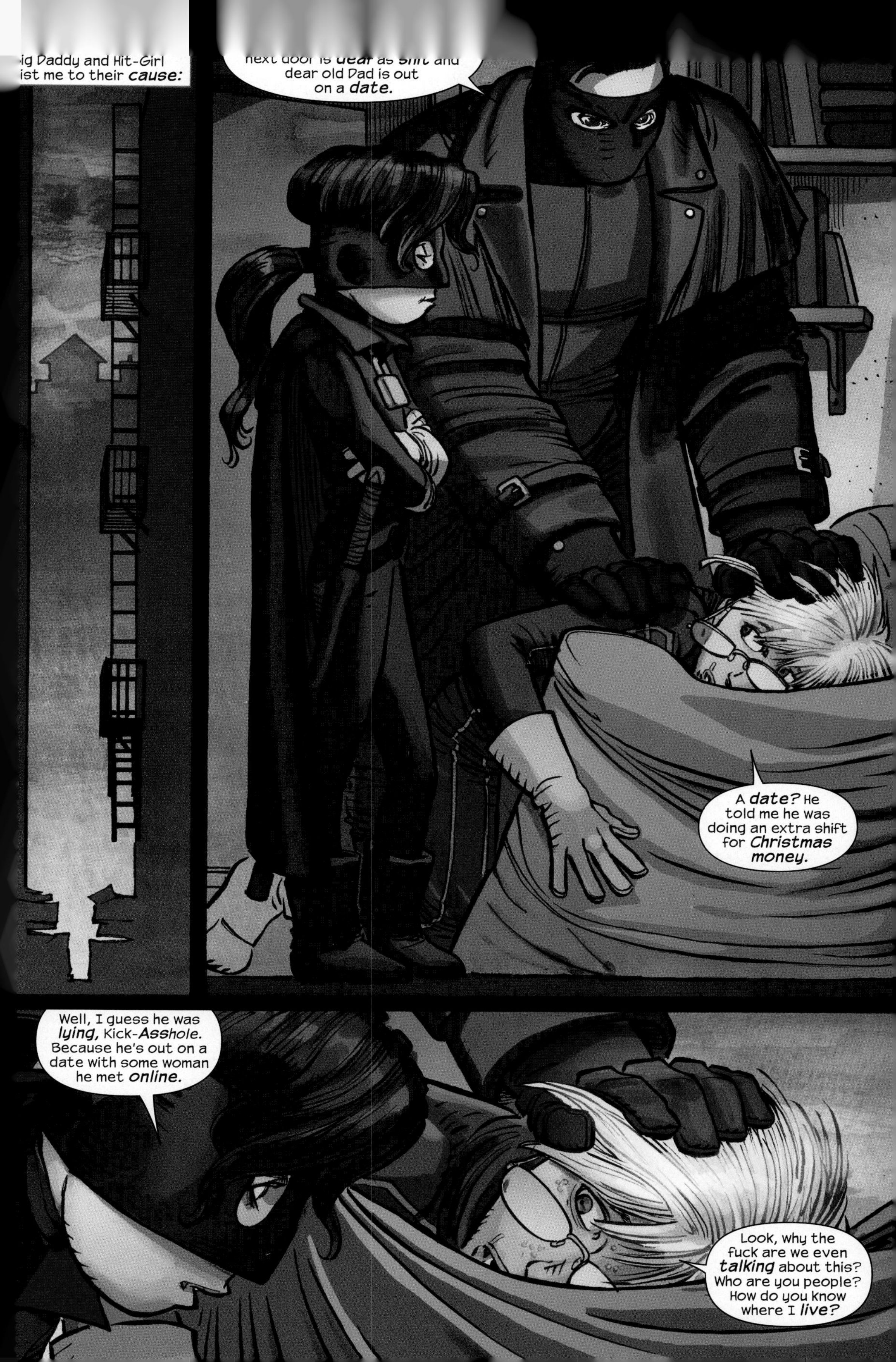
ig Daddy and Hit-Girl
ist me to their cause:
next door is dead as shit and dear old Dad is out on a date.
A date? He told me he was doing an extra shift for Christmas money.
Well, I guess he was lying, Kick-Asshole. Because he's out on a date with some woman he met online.
Look, why the fuck are we even talking about this? Who are you people? How do you know where I live?

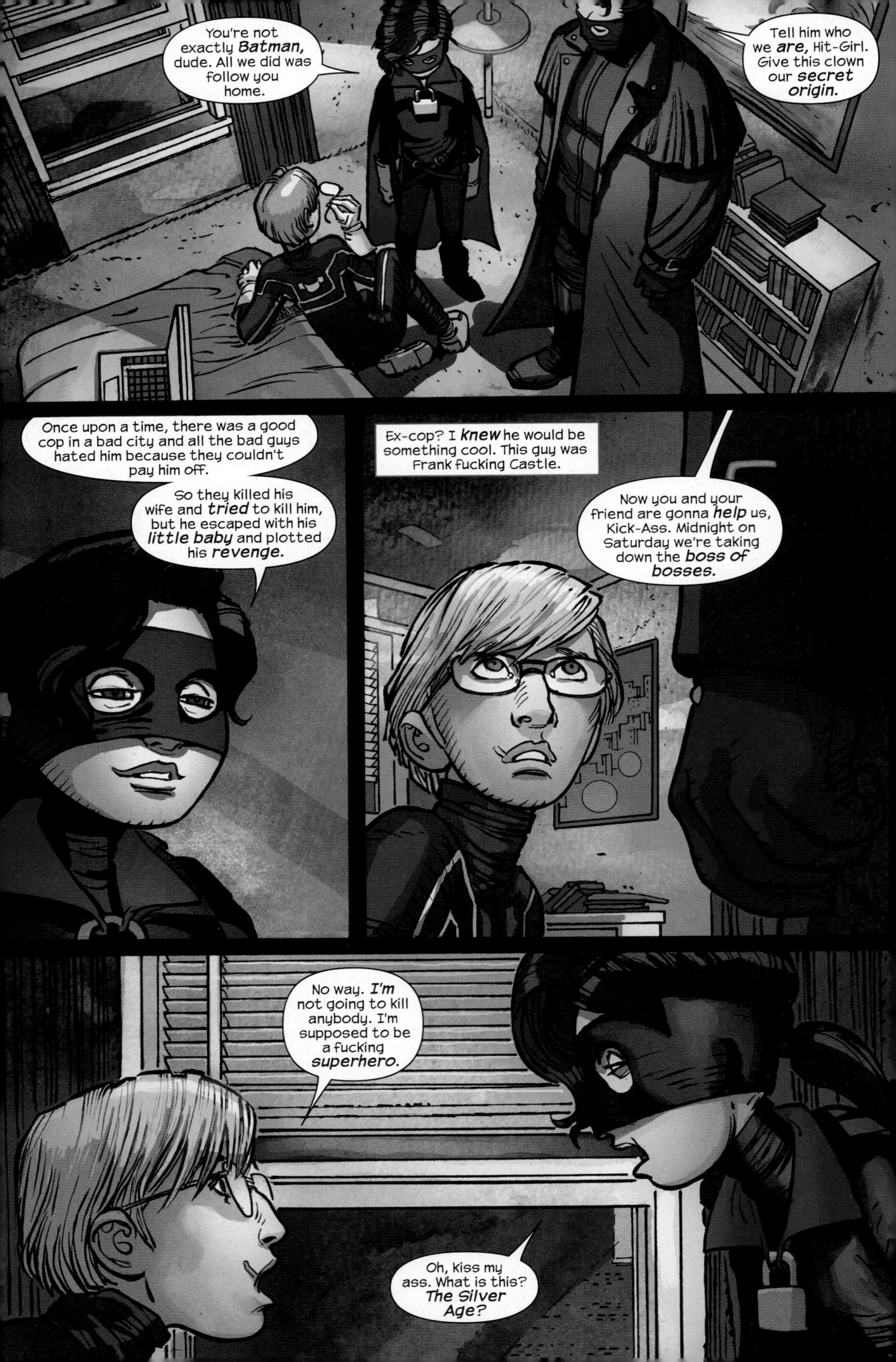
You're not exactly Batman, dude. All we did was follow you home.
Tell him who we are, Hit-Girl. Give this clown our secret origin.
Once upon a time, there was a good cop in a bad city and all the bad guys hated him because they couldn't pay him off.
So they killed his wife and tried to kill him, but he escaped with his little baby and plotted his revenge.
Ex-cop? I knew he would be something cool. This guy was Frank fucking Castle.
Now you and your friend are gonna help us, Kick-Ass. Midnight on Saturday we're taking down the boss of bosses.
No way. I'm not going to kill anybody. I'm supposed to be a fucking superhero.
Oh, kiss my ass. What is this? The Silver Age?

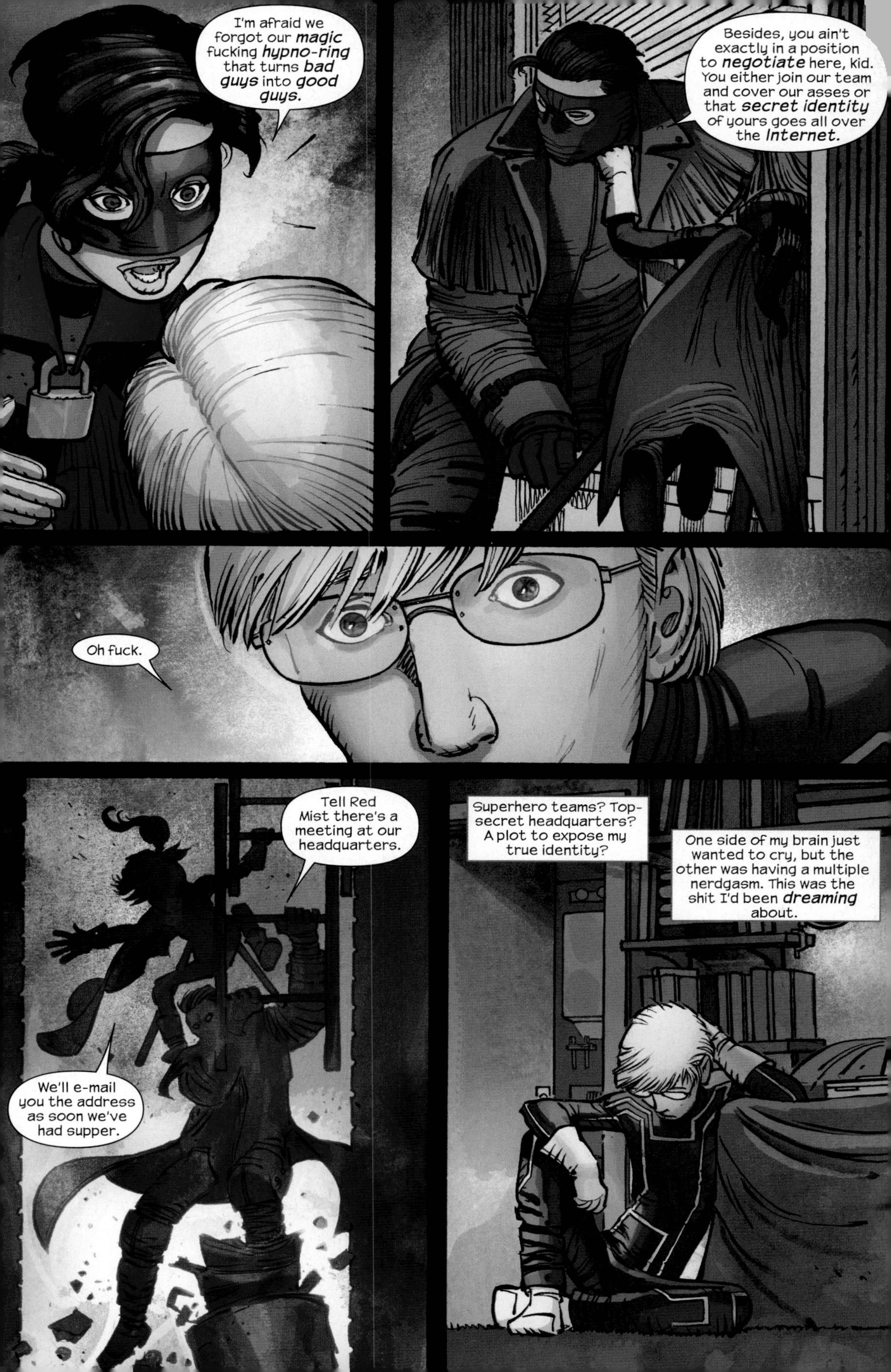
I'm afraid we forgot our magic fucking hypno-ring that turns bad guys into good guys.
Besides, you ain't exactly in a position to negotiate here, kid. You either join our team and cover our asses or that secret identity of yours goes all over the Internet.
Oh fuck.
Tell Red Mist there's a meeting at our headquarters.
We'll e-mail you the address as soon we've had supper.
Superhero teams? Top-secret headquarters? A plot to expose my true identity?
One side of my brain just wanted to cry, but the other was having a multiple nerdgasm. This was the shit I'd been dreaming about.

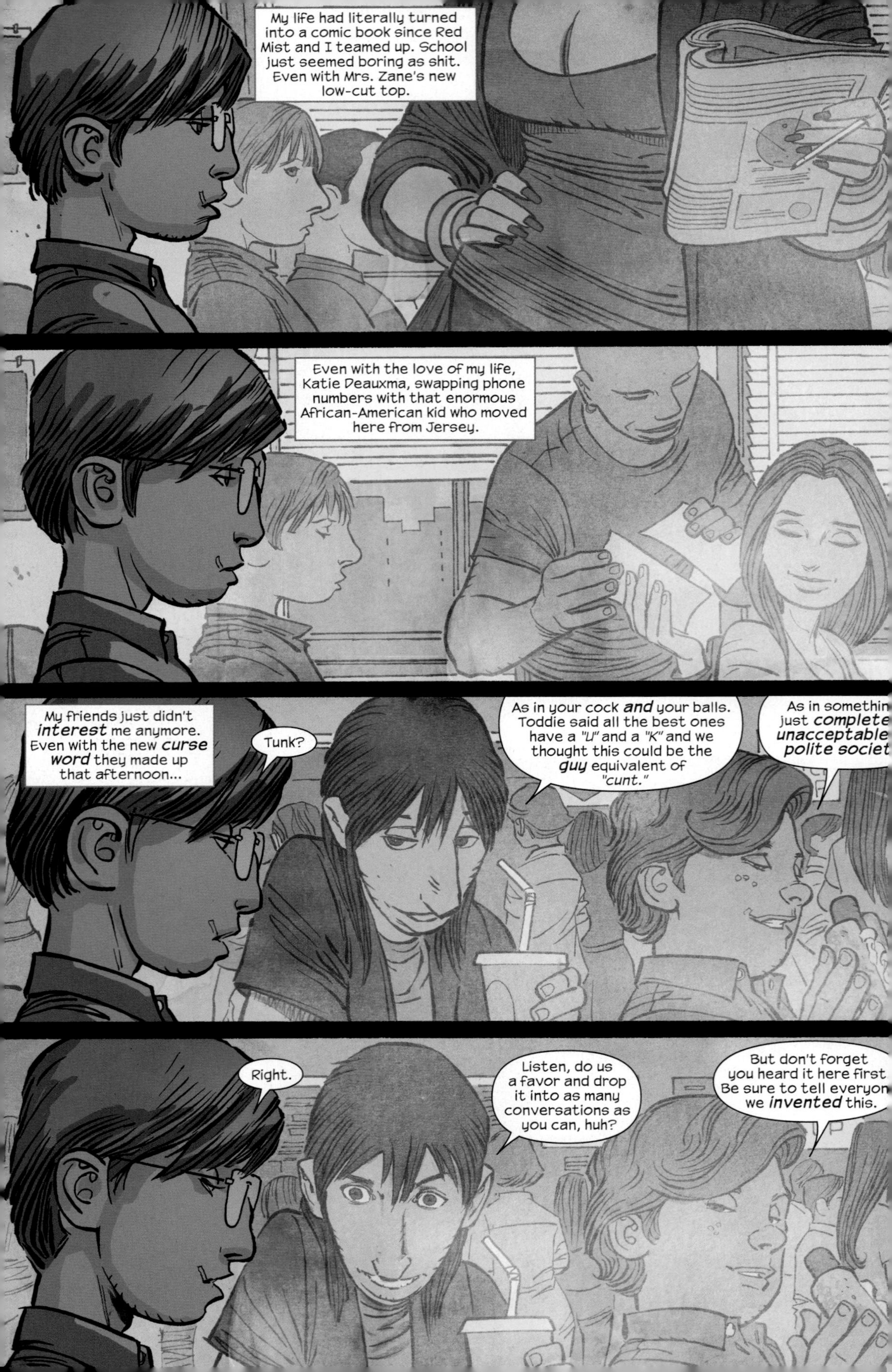
My life had literally turned into a comic book since Red Mist and I teamed up. School just seemed boring as shit. Even with Mrs. Zane's new low-cut top.
Even with the love of my life, Katie Deauxma, swapping phone numbers with that enormous African-American kid who moved here from Jersey.
My friends just didn't *interest* me anymore. Even with the new ***curse word*** they made up that afternoon...
Tunk?
As in your cock ***and*** your balls. Toddie said all the best ones have a *"U"* and a *"K"* and we thought this could be the ***guy*** equivalent of *"cunt."*
As in somethin just ***complete unacceptable polite societ***
Right.
Listen, do us a favor and drop it into as many conversations as you can, huh?
But don't forget you heard it here first Be sure to tell everyon we ***invented*** this.

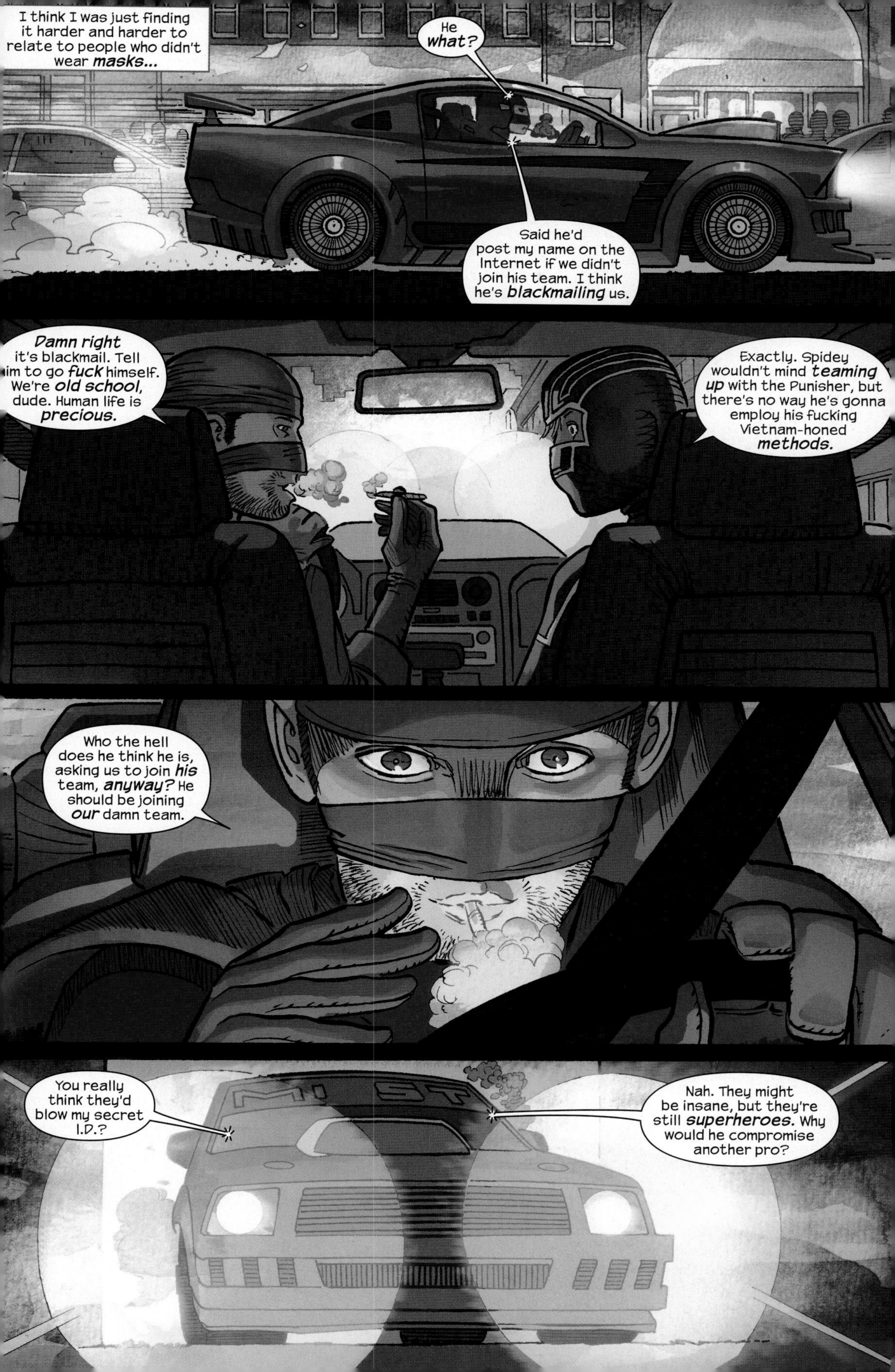

I think I was just finding it harder and harder to relate to people who didn't wear *masks...*
He *what?*
Said he'd post my name on the Internet if we didn't join his team. I think he's *blackmailing* us.
Damn right it's blackmail. Tell im to go *fuck* himself. We're *old school,* dude. Human life is *precious.*
Exactly. Spidey wouldn't mind *teaming up* with the Punisher, but there's no way he's gonna employ his fucking Vietnam-honed *methods.*
Who the hell does he think he is, asking us to join *his* team, *anyway?* He should be joining *our* damn team.
You really think they'd blow my secret I.D.?
Nah. They might be insane, but they're still *superheroes.* Why would he compromise another pro?

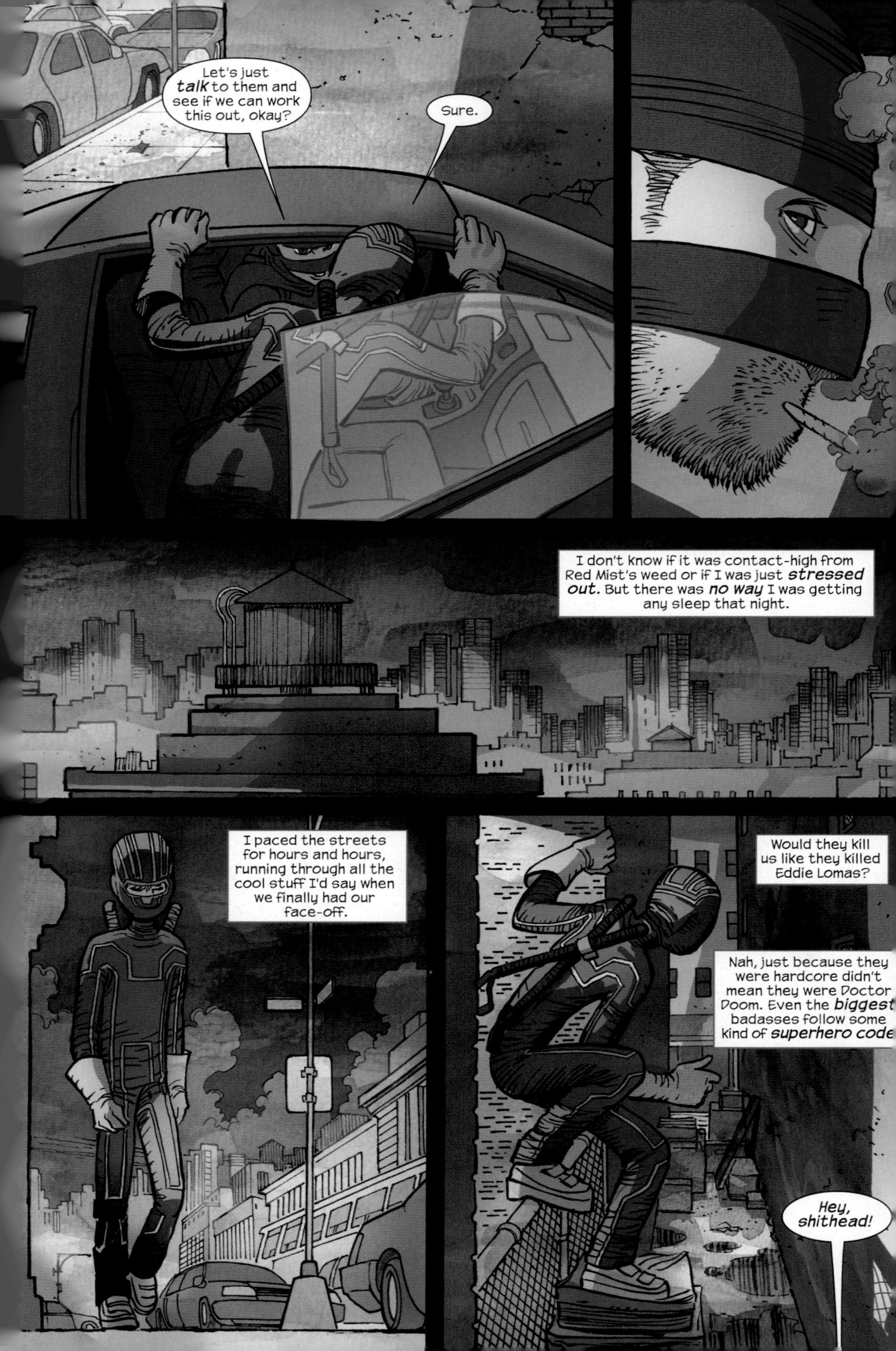

Let's just *talk* to them and see if we can work this out, okay?
Sure.
I don't know if it was contact-high from Red Mist's weed or if I was just *stressed out.* But there was *no way* I was getting any sleep that night.
I paced the streets for hours and hours, running through all the cool stuff I'd say when we finally had our face-off.
Would they kill us like they killed Eddie Lomas?
Nah, just because they were hardcore didn't mean they were Doctor Doom. Even the *biggest* badasses follow some kind of *superhero code*
Hey, shithead!

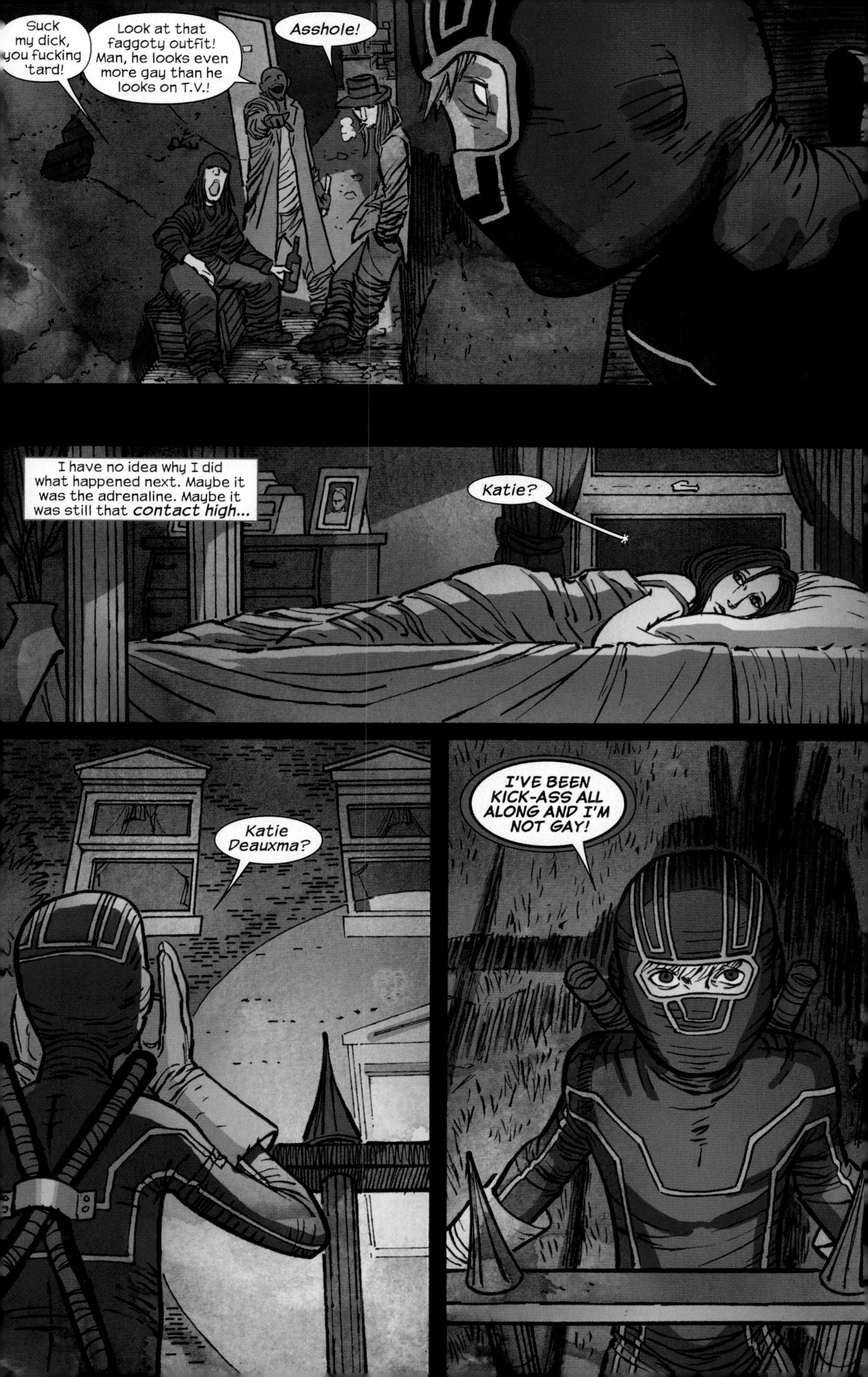
Suck my dick, you fucking 'tard!
Look at that faggoty outfit! Man, he looks even more gay than he looks on T.V.!
Asshole!
I have no idea why I did what happened next. Maybe it was the adrenaline. Maybe it was still that *contact high...*
Katie?
Katie Deauxma?
I'VE BEEN KICK-ASS ALL ALONG AND I'M NOT GAY!

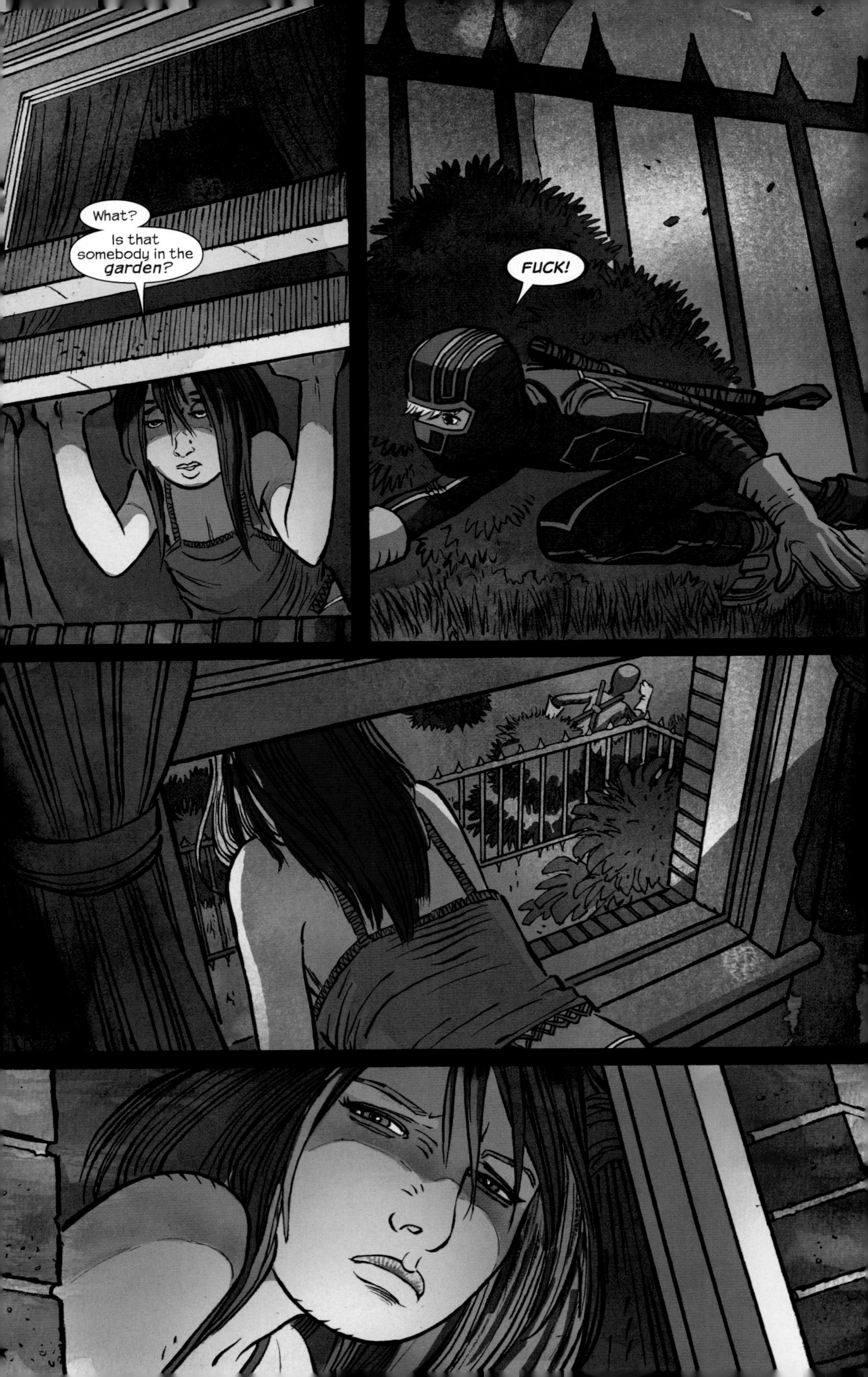
What?
Is that somebody in the *garden*?
FUCK!

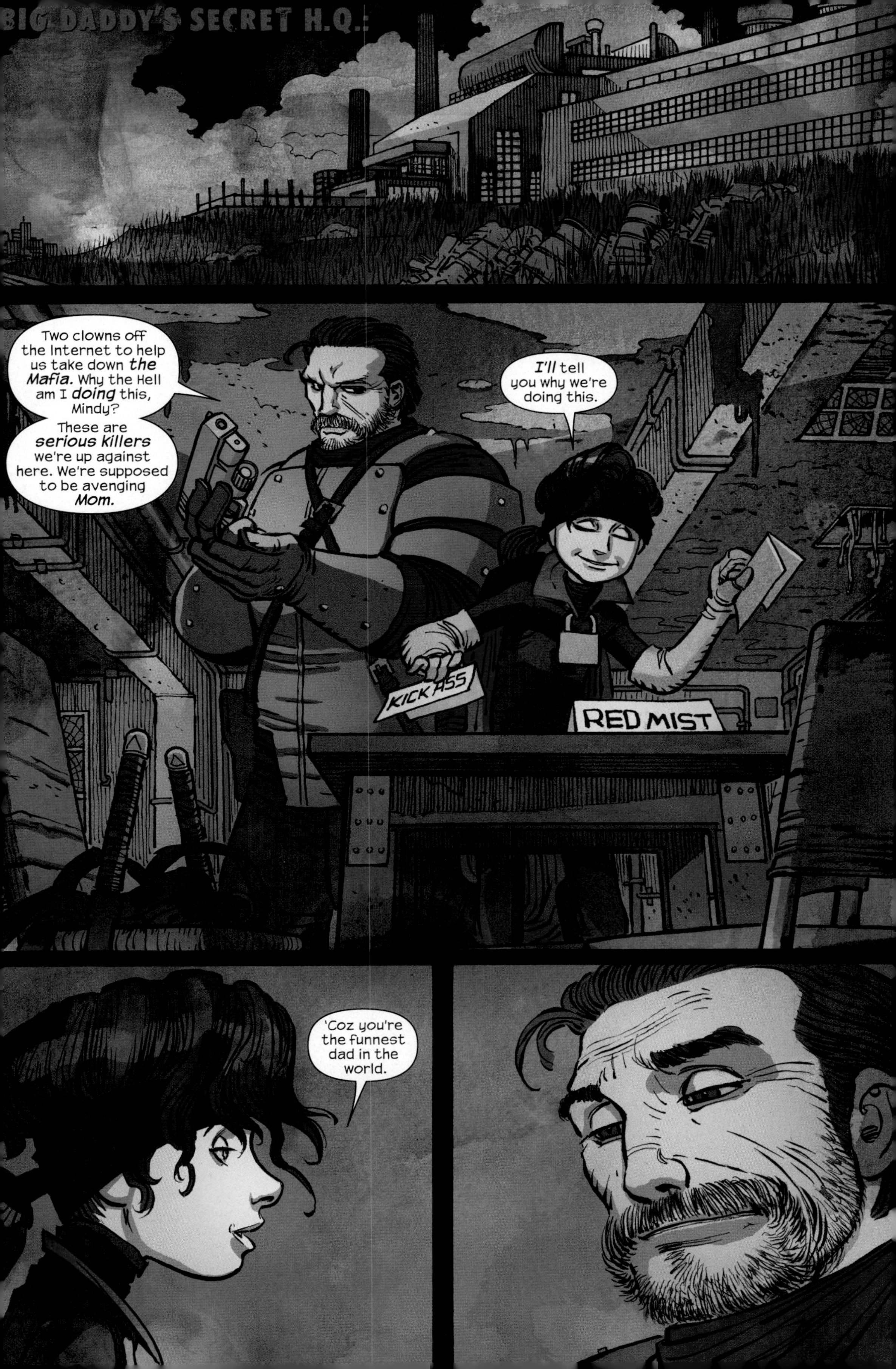
BIG DADDY'S SECRET H.Q.:
Two clowns off the Internet to help us take down *the Mafia.* Why the Hell am I *doing* this, Mindy?
These are *serious killers* we're up against here. We're supposed to be avenging *Mom.*
I'll tell you why we're doing this.
KICK ASS
RED MIST
'Coz you're the funnest dad in the world.

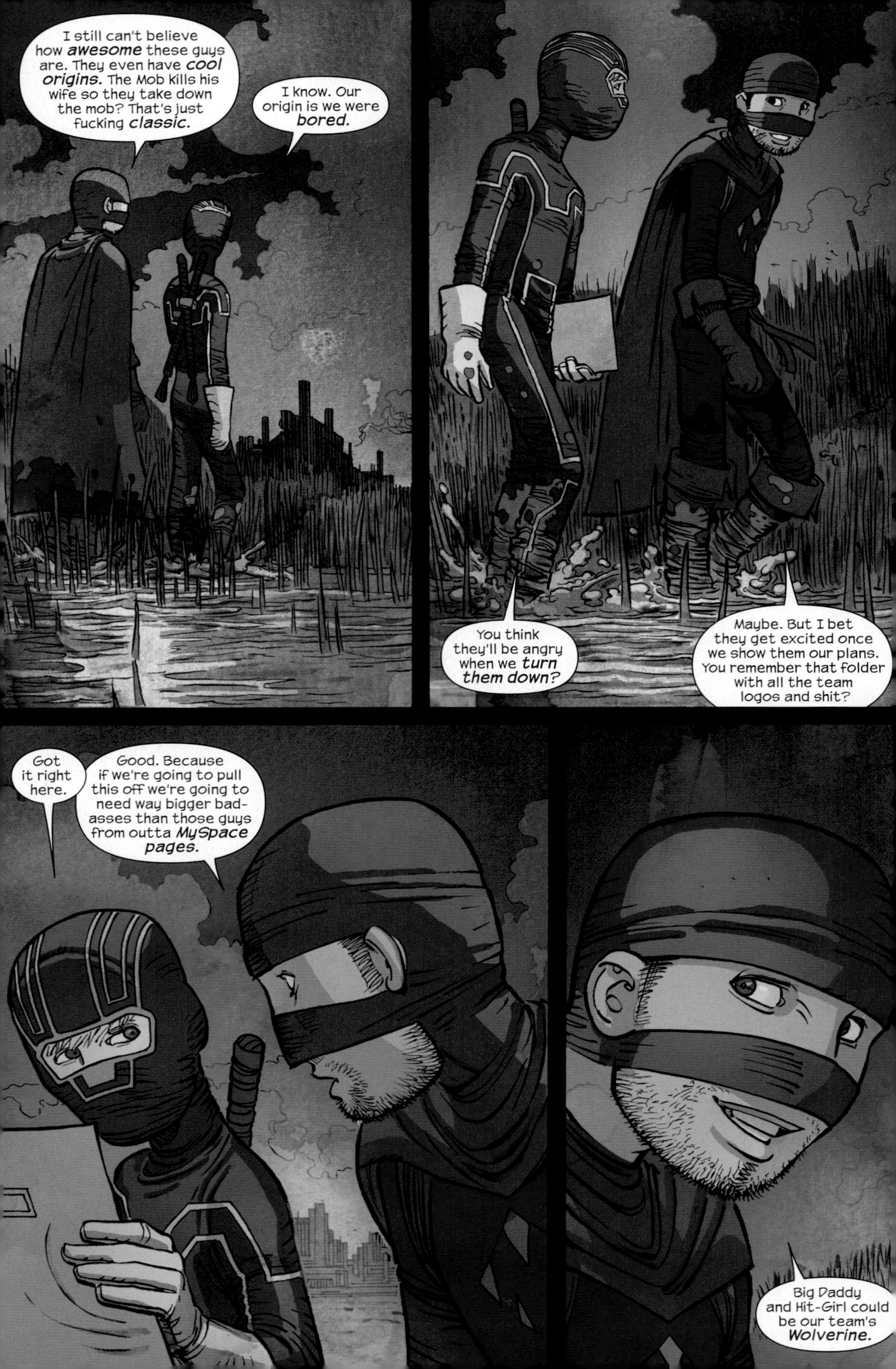
I still can't believe how awesome these guys are. They even have cool origins. The Mob kills his wife so they take down the mob? That's just fucking classic.
I know. Our origin is we were bored.
You think they'll be angry when we turn them down?
Maybe. But I bet they get excited once we show them our plans. You remember that folder with all the team logos and shit?
Got it right here.
Good. Because if we're going to pull this off we're going to need way bigger bad-asses than those guys from outta MySpace pages.
Big Daddy and Hit-Girl could be our team's Wolverine.

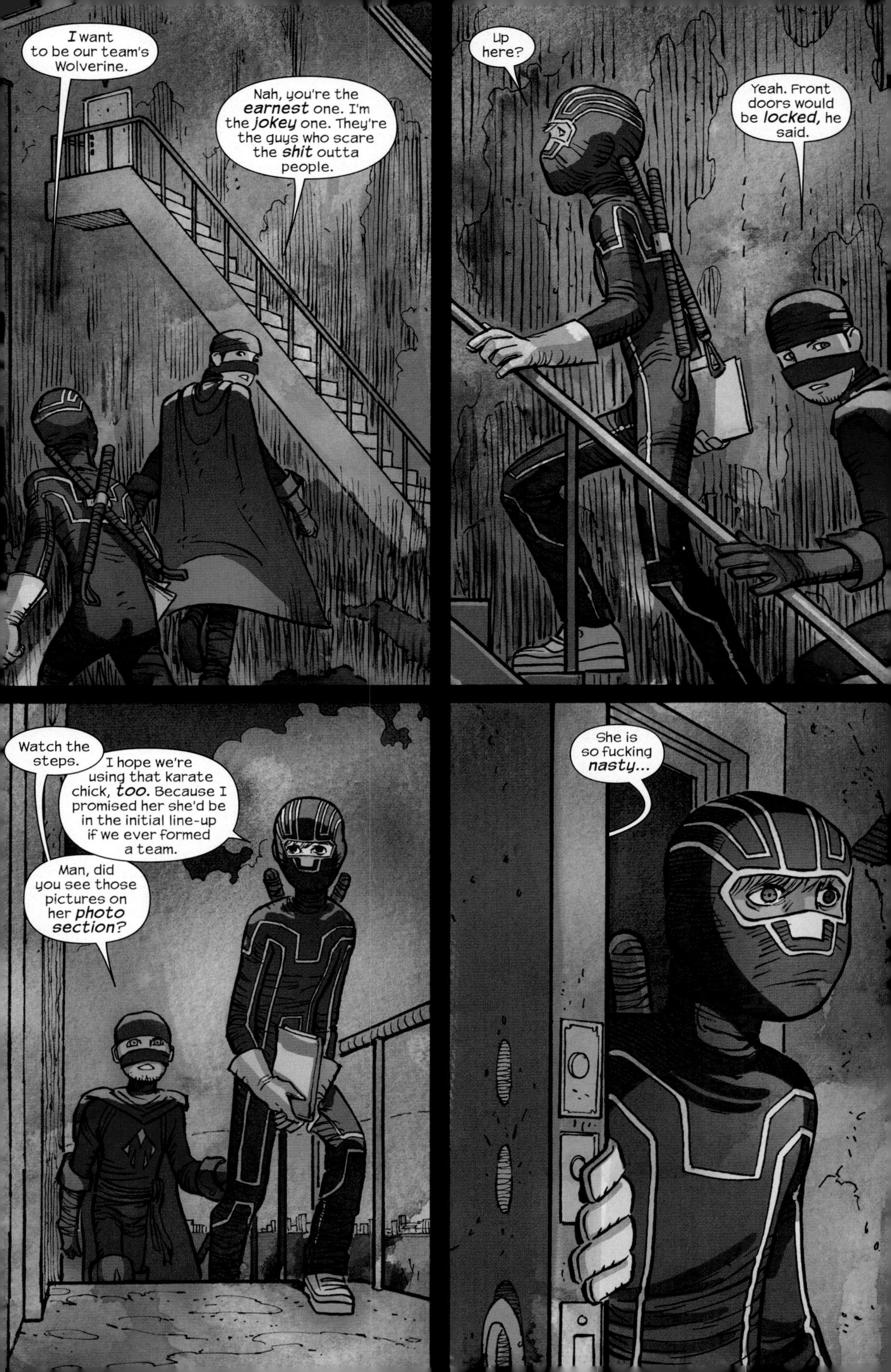
I want to be our team's Wolverine.
Nah, you're the earnest one. I'm the jokey one. They're the guys who scare the shit outta people.
Up here?
Yeah. Front doors would be locked, he said.
Watch the steps.
I hope we're using that karate chick, too. Because I promised her she'd be in the initial line-up if we ever formed a team.
Man, did you see those pictures on her photo section?
She is so fucking nasty...

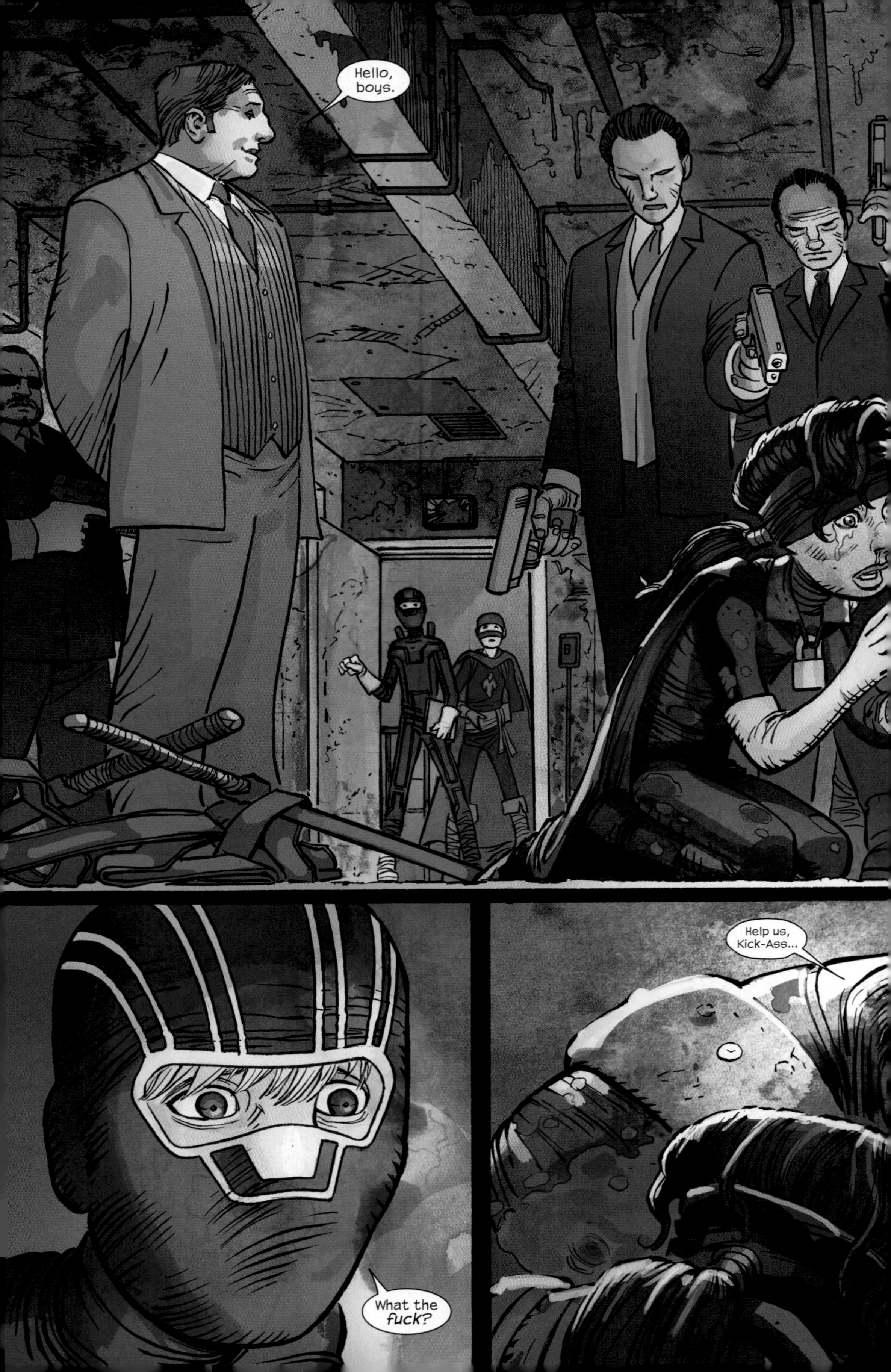

Hello, boys.
What the *fuck*?
Help us, Kick-Ass...

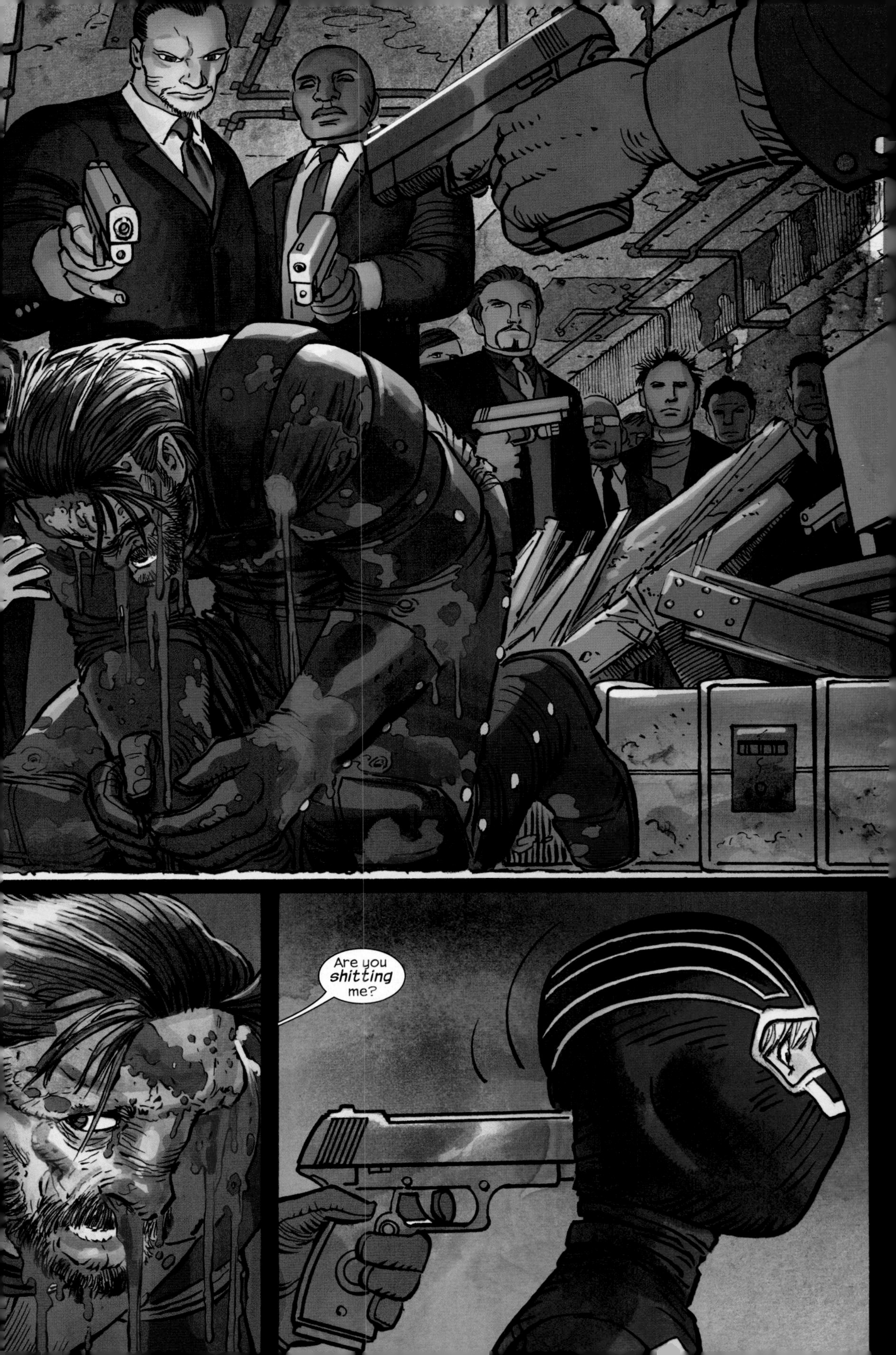
Are you *shitting* me?

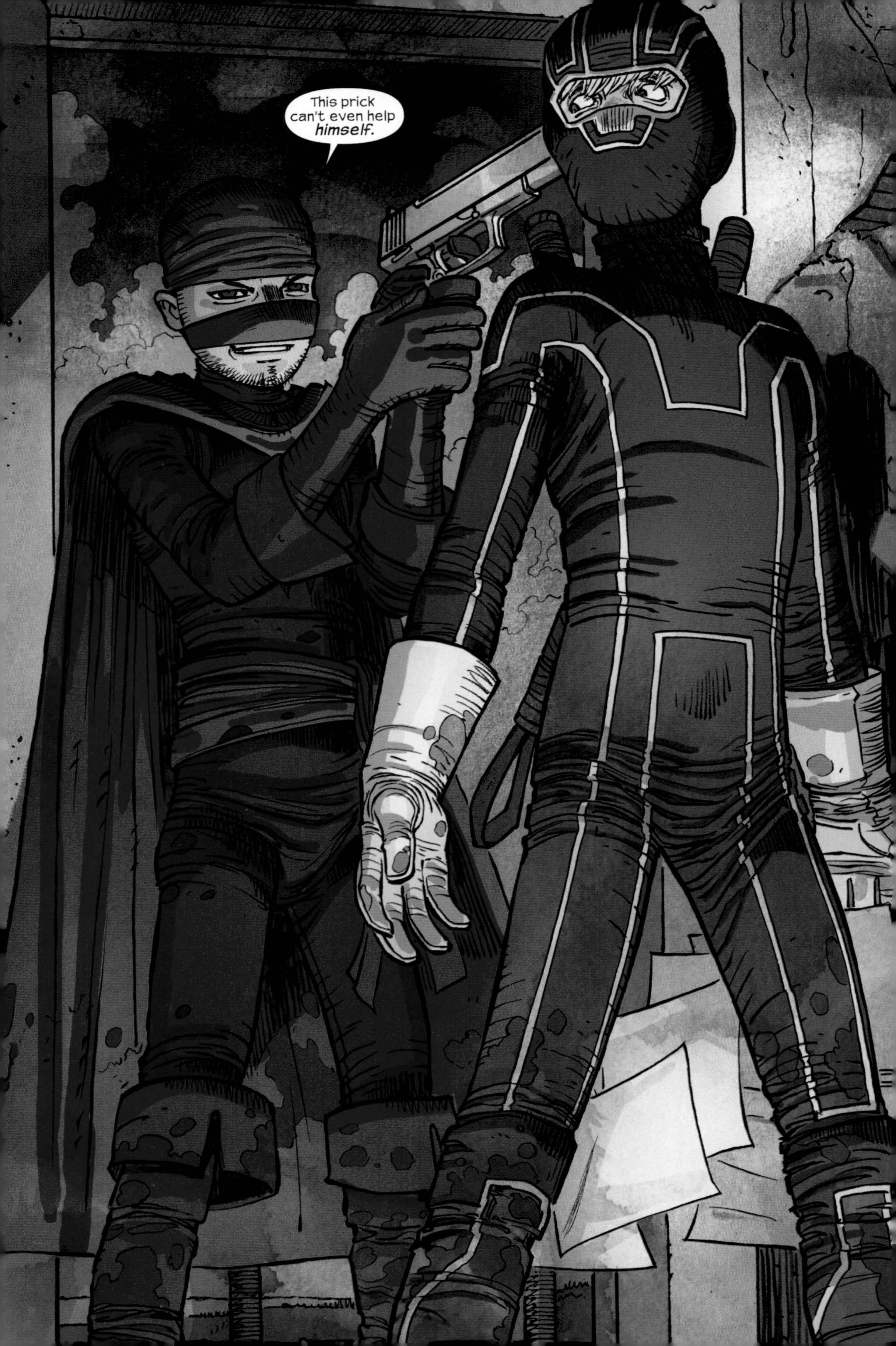
This prick can't even help *himself*.

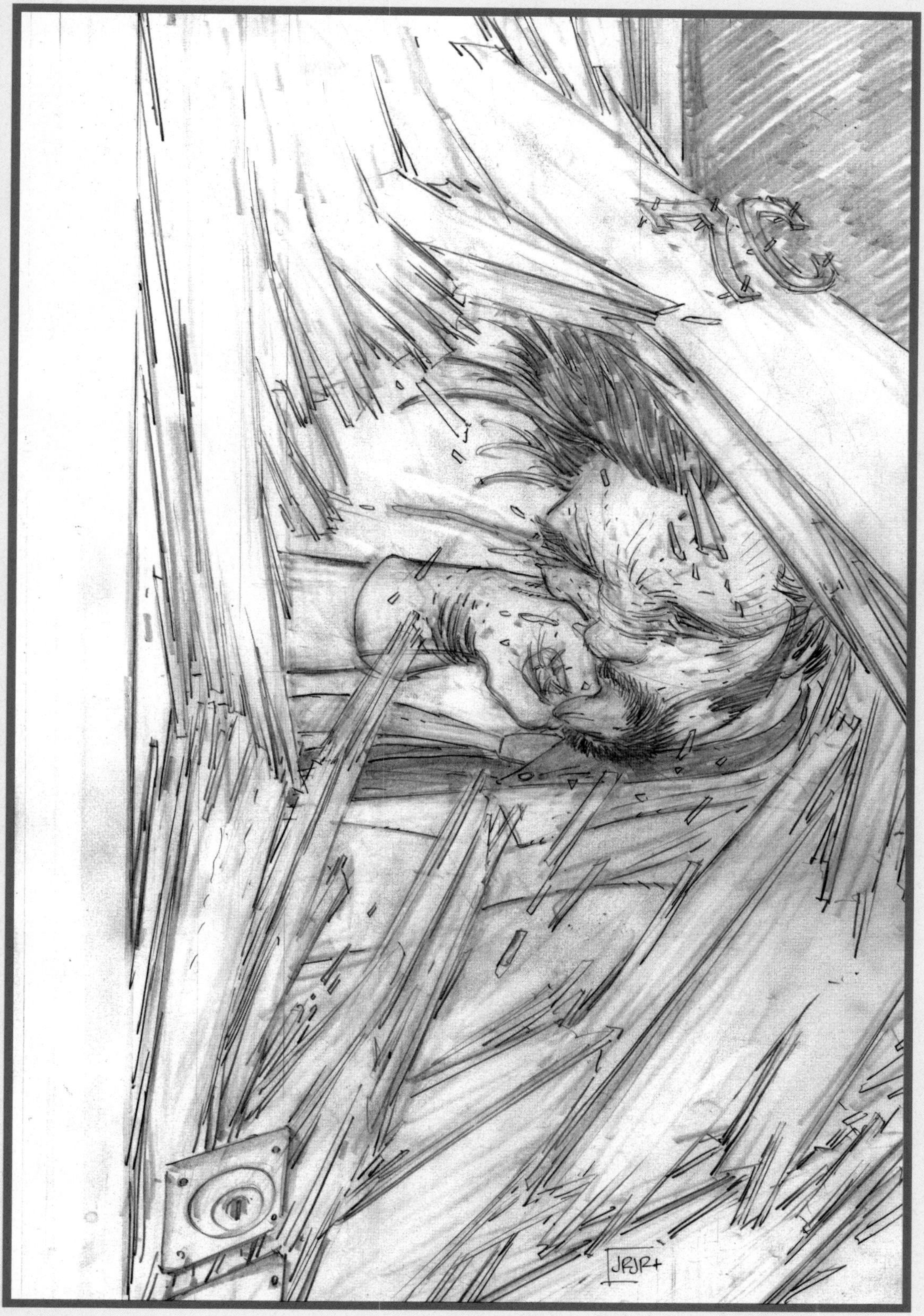
JRJR+

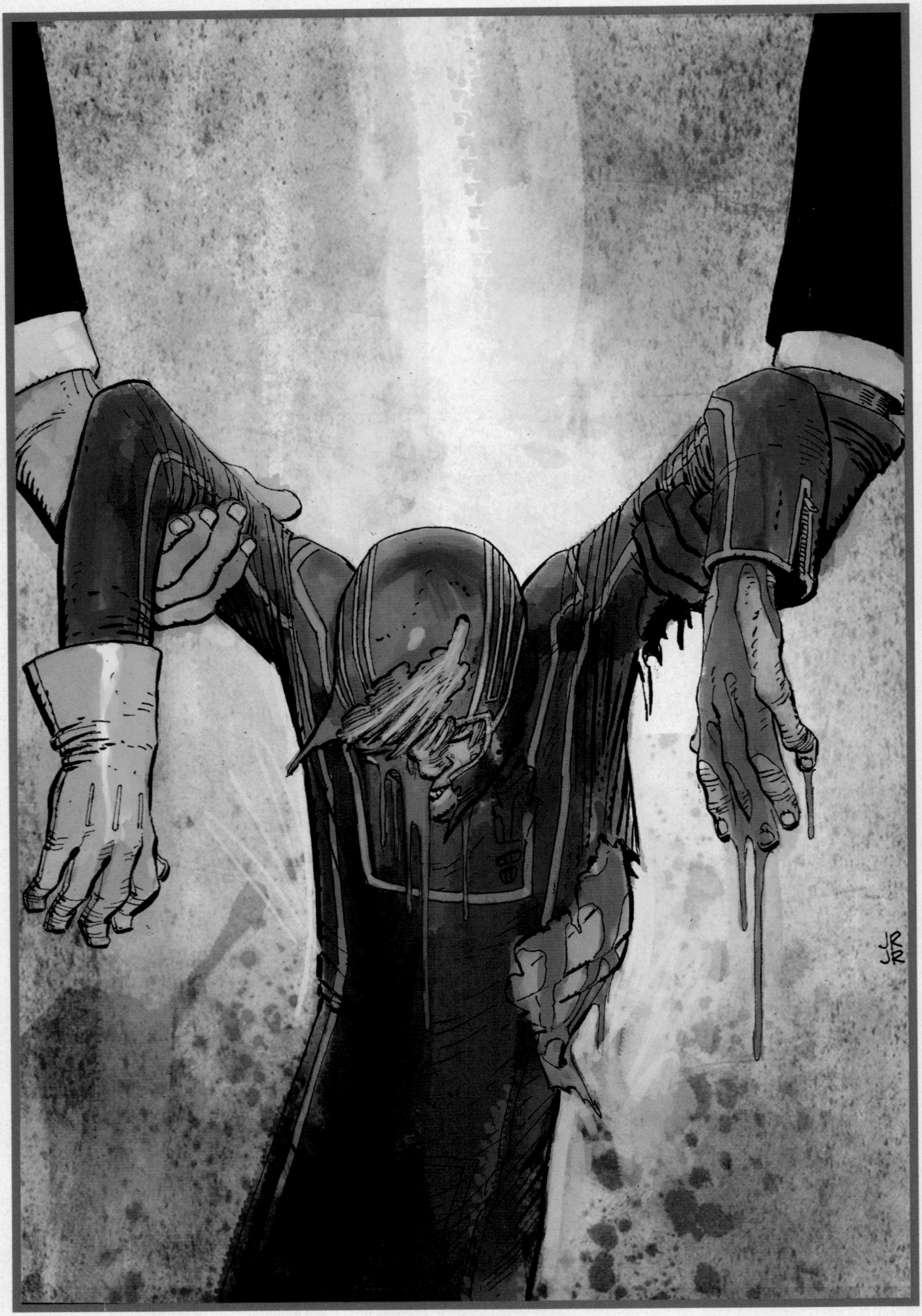
JR
JR

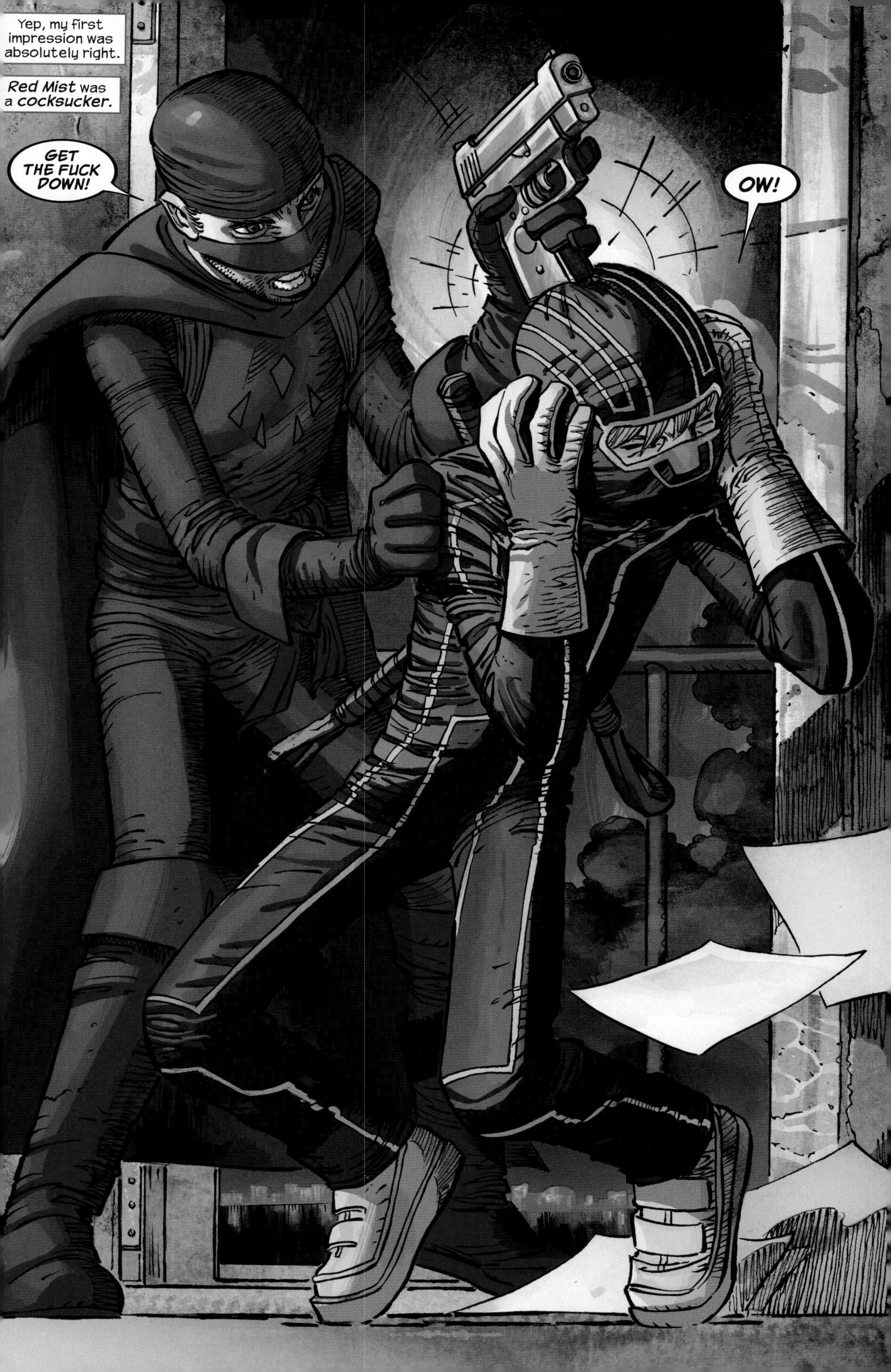
Yep, my first impression was absolutely right.
Red Mist was a cocksucker.
GET THE FUCK DOWN!
OW!

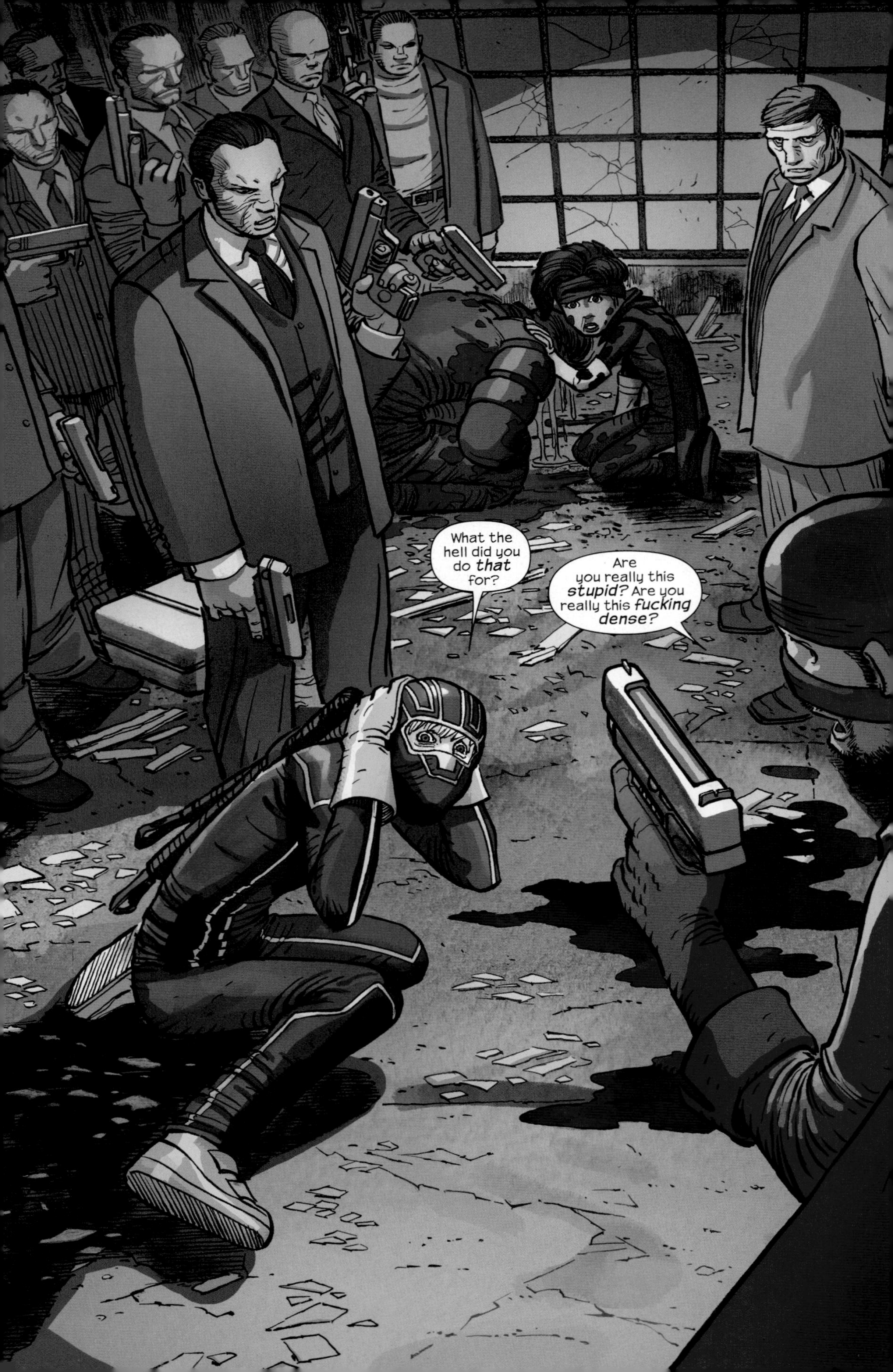

What the hell did you do *that* for?
Are you really this ***stupid?*** Are you really this ***fucking dense?***

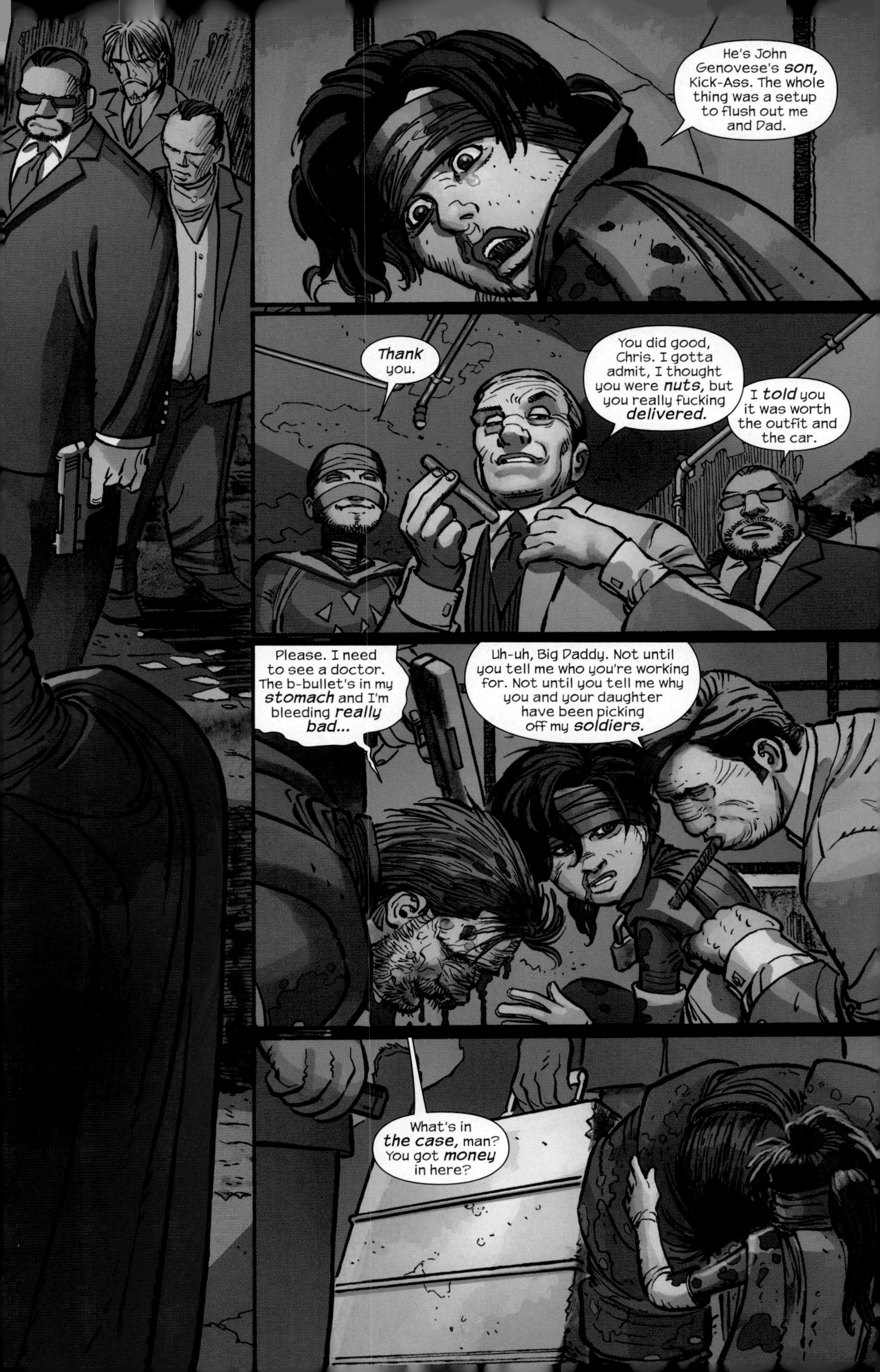
He's John Genovese's son, Kick-Ass. The whole thing was a setup to flush out me and Dad.
Thank you.
You did good, Chris. I gotta admit, I thought you were nuts, but you really fucking delivered.
I told you it was worth the outfit and the car.
Please. I need to see a doctor. The b-bullet's in my stomach and I'm bleeding really bad...
Uh-uh, Big Daddy. Not until you tell me who you're working for. Not until you tell me why you and your daughter have been picking off my soldiers.
What's in the case, man? You got money in here?

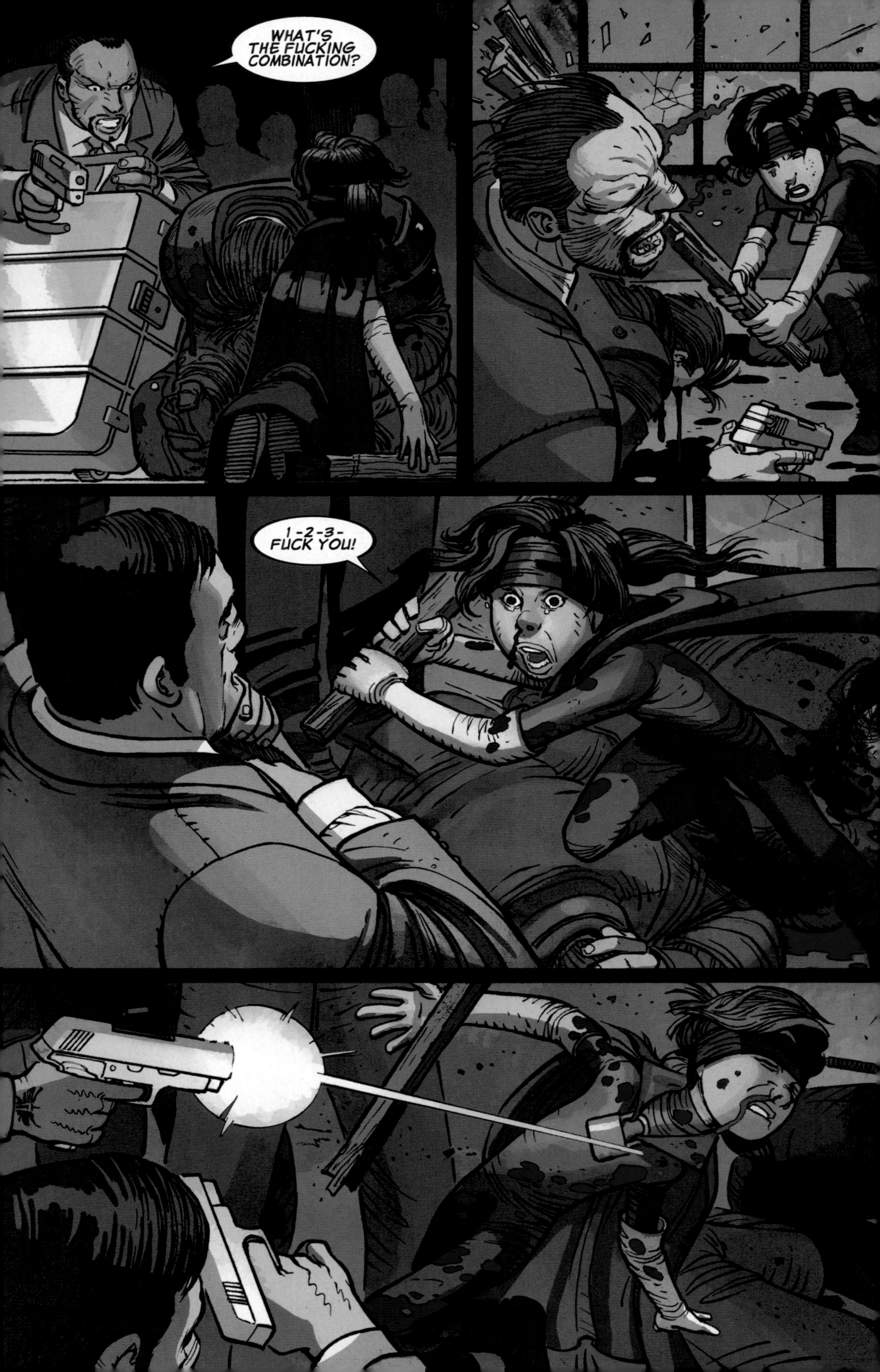
WHAT'S THE FUCKING COMBINATION?
1-2-3- FUCK YOU!

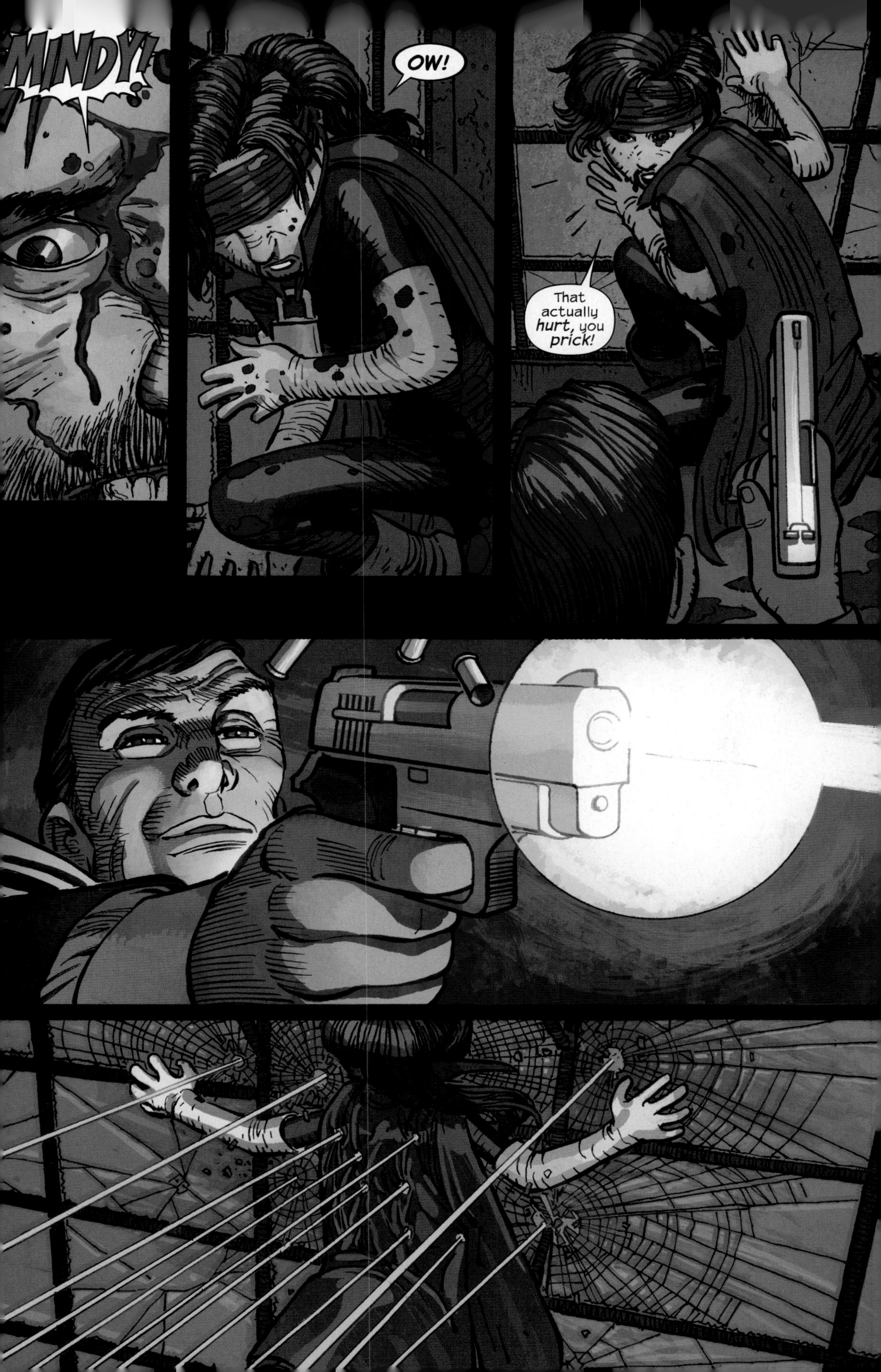

MINDY!
OW!
That actually *hurt*, you *prick!*

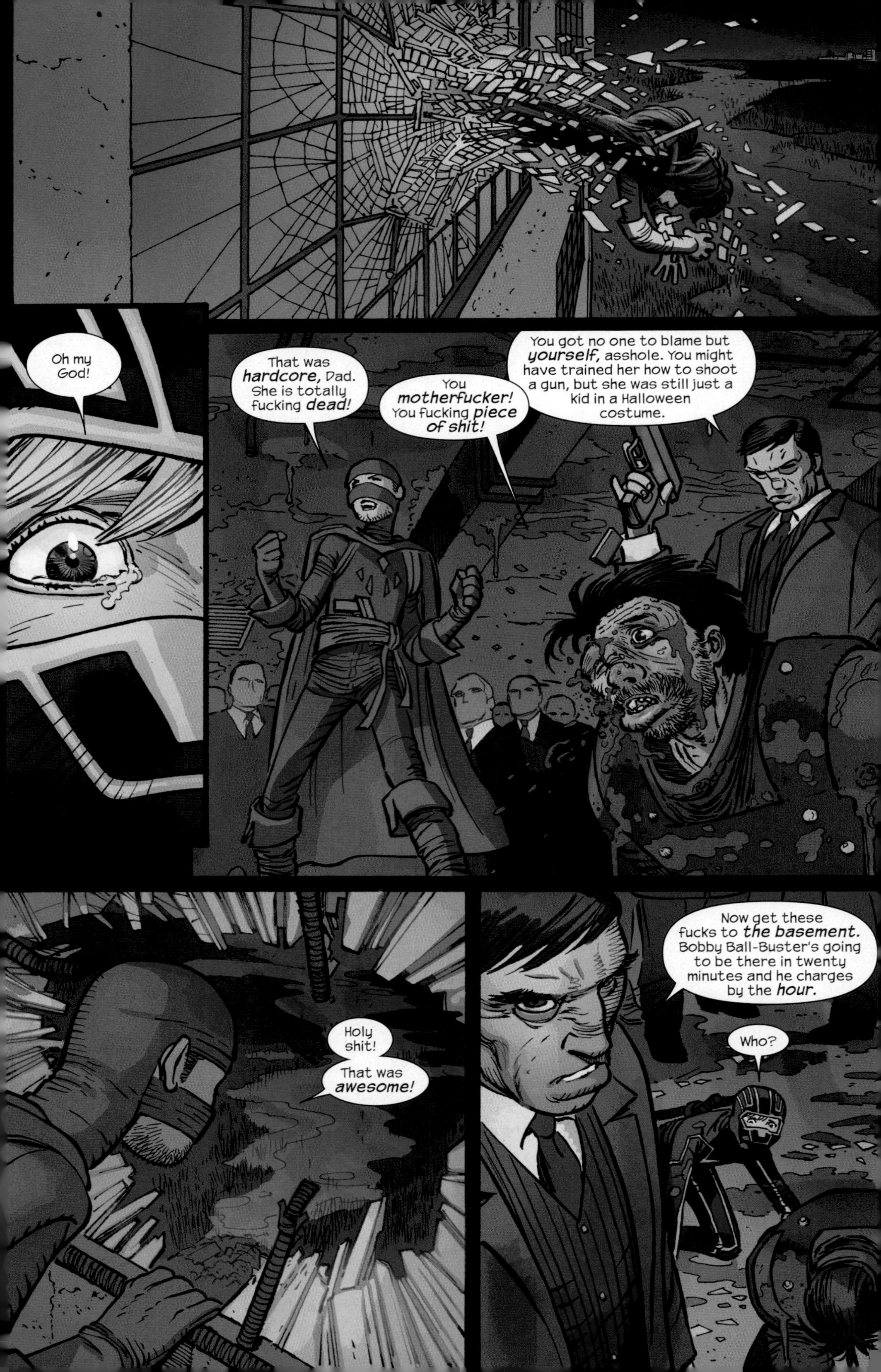
Oh my God!
That was hardcore, Dad. She is totally fucking dead!
You motherfucker! You fucking piece of shit!
You got no one to blame but yourself, asshole. You might have trained her how to shoot a gun, but she was still just a kid in a Halloween costume.
Holy shit!
That was awesome!
Now get these fucks to the basement. Bobby Ball-Buster's going to be there in twenty minutes and he charges by the hour.
Who?

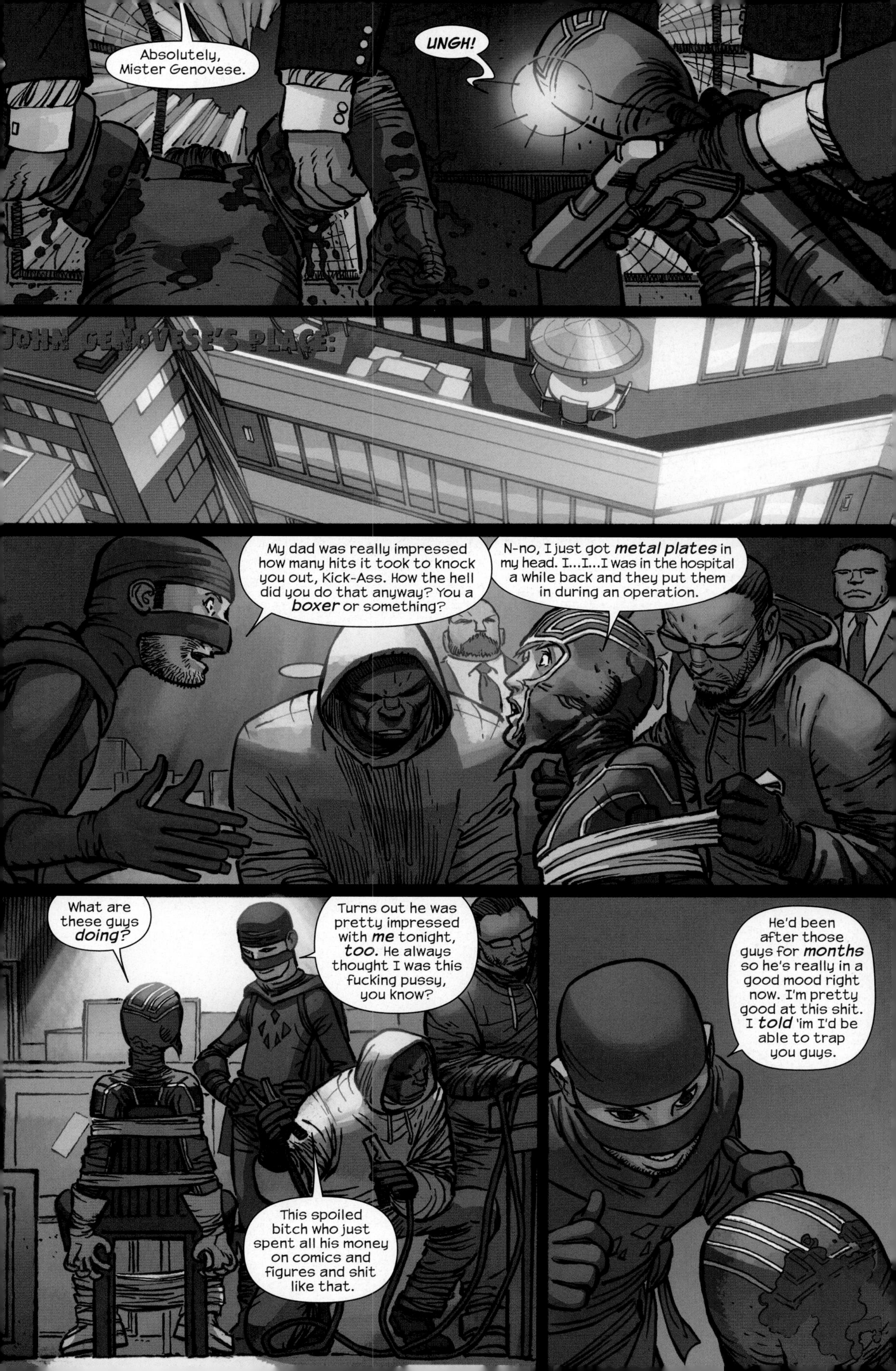
Absolutely, Mister Genovese.
UNGH!
JOHN GENOVESE'S PLACE:
My dad was really impressed how many hits it took to knock you out, Kick-Ass. How the hell did you do that anyway? You a boxer or something?
N-no, I just got metal plates in my head. I...I...I was in the hospital a while back and they put them in during an operation.
What are these guys doing?
Turns out he was pretty impressed with me tonight, too. He always thought I was this fucking pussy, you know?
This spoiled bitch who just spent all his money on comics and figures and shit like that.
He'd been after those guys for months so he's really in a good mood right now. I'm pretty good at this shit. I told 'im I'd be able to trap you guys.

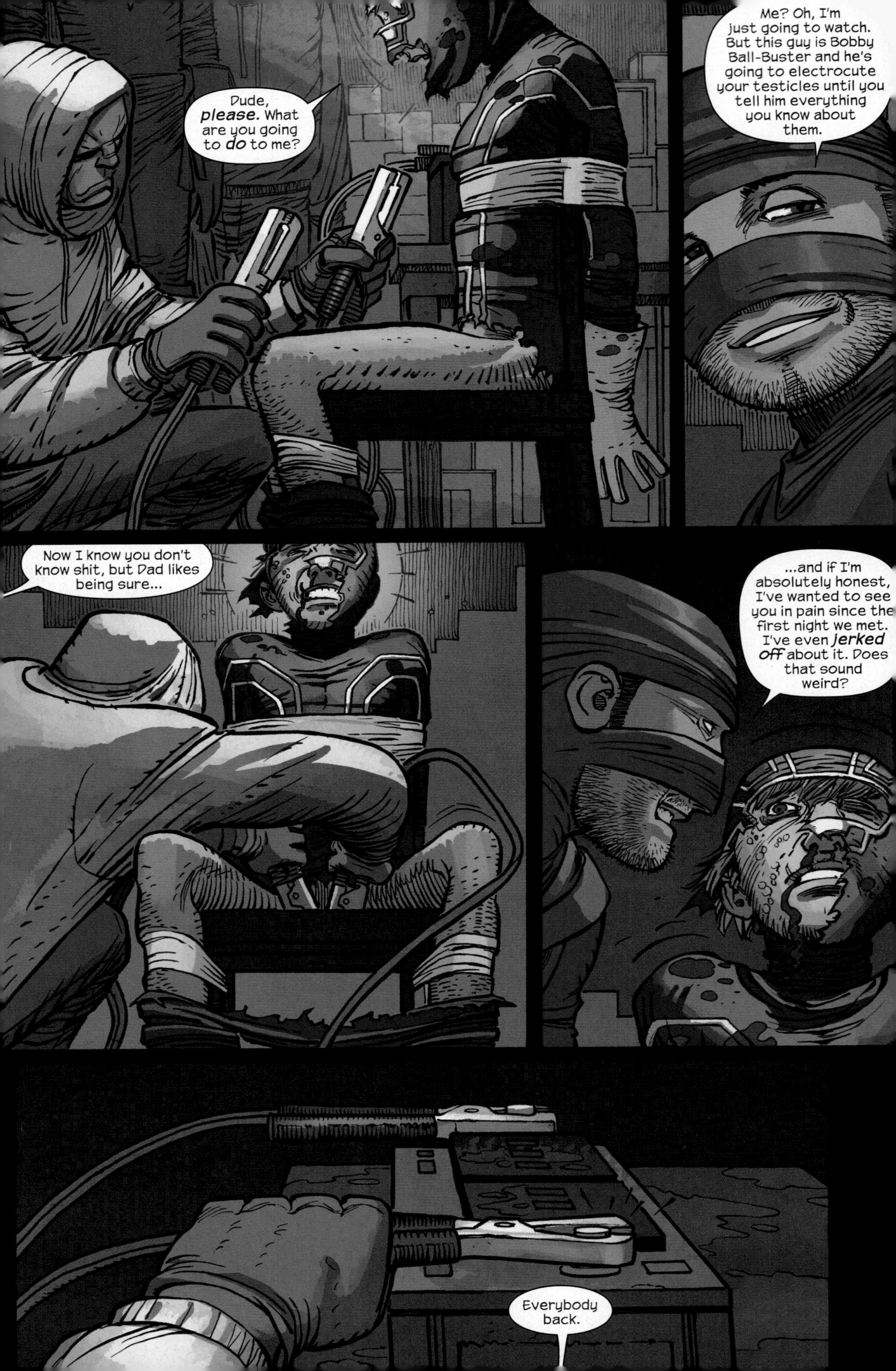

Dude, please. What are you going to do to me?
Me? Oh, I'm just going to watch. But this guy is Bobby Ball-Buster and he's going to electrocute your testicles until you tell him everything you know about them.
Now I know you don't know shit, but Dad likes being sure...
...and if I'm absolutely honest, I've wanted to see you in pain since the first night we met. I've even jerked off about it. Does that sound weird?
Everybody back.

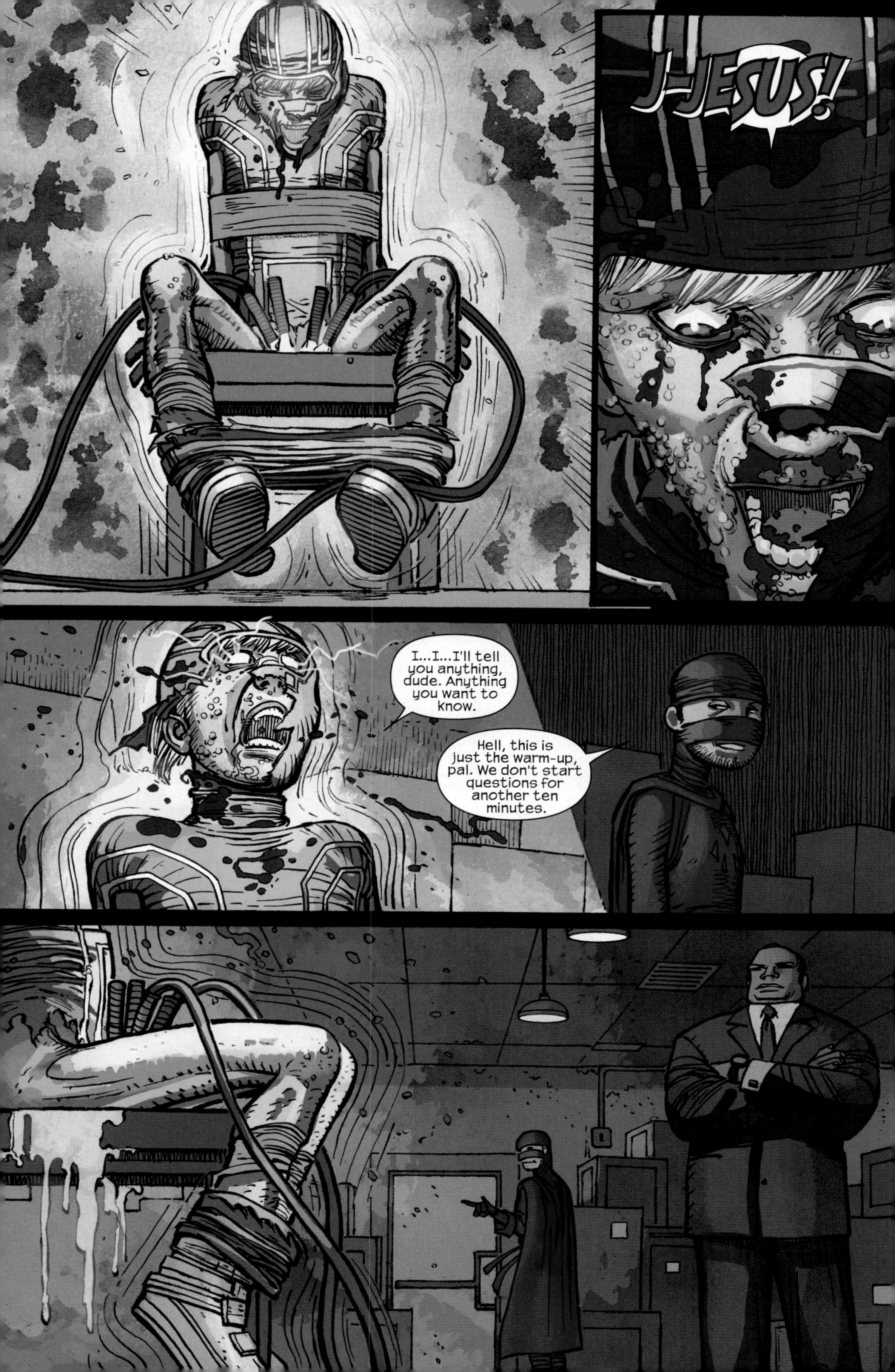
J-JESUS!
I...I...I'll tell you anything, dude. Anything you want to know.
Hell, this is just the warm-up, pal. We don't start questions for another ten minutes.

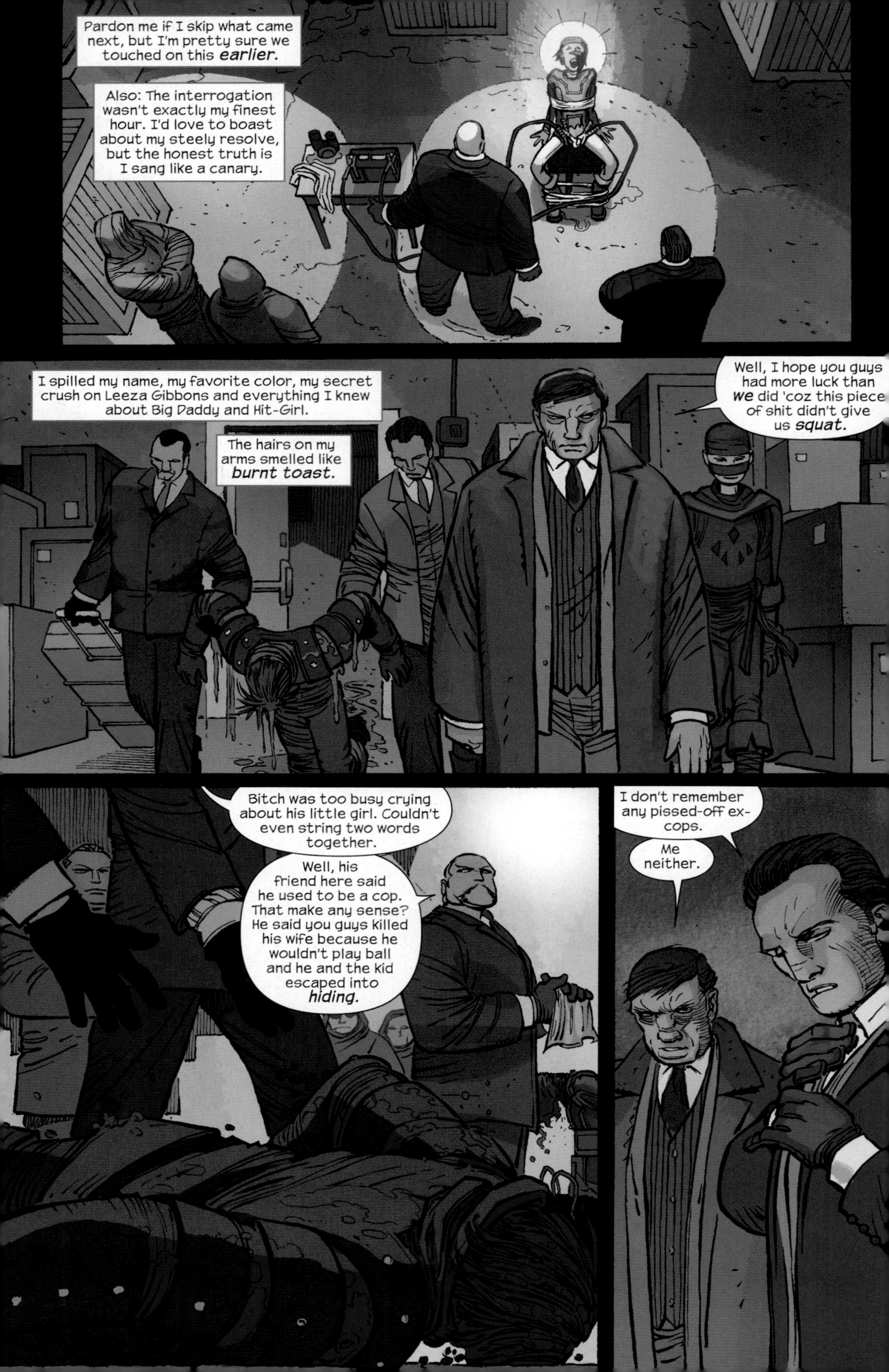

Pardon me if I skip what came next, but I'm pretty sure we touched on this *earlier.*
Also: The interrogation wasn't exactly my finest hour. I'd love to boast about my steely resolve, but the honest truth is I sang like a canary.
I spilled my name, my favorite color, my secret crush on Leeza Gibbons and everything I knew about Big Daddy and Hit-Girl.
The hairs on my arms smelled like *burnt toast.*
Well, I hope you guys had more luck than *we* did 'coz this piece of shit didn't give us *squat.*
Bitch was too busy crying about his little girl. Couldn't even string two words together.
Well, his friend here said he used to be a cop. That make any sense? He said you guys killed his wife because he wouldn't play ball and he and the kid escaped into *hiding.*
I don't remember any pissed-off ex-cops.
Me neither.

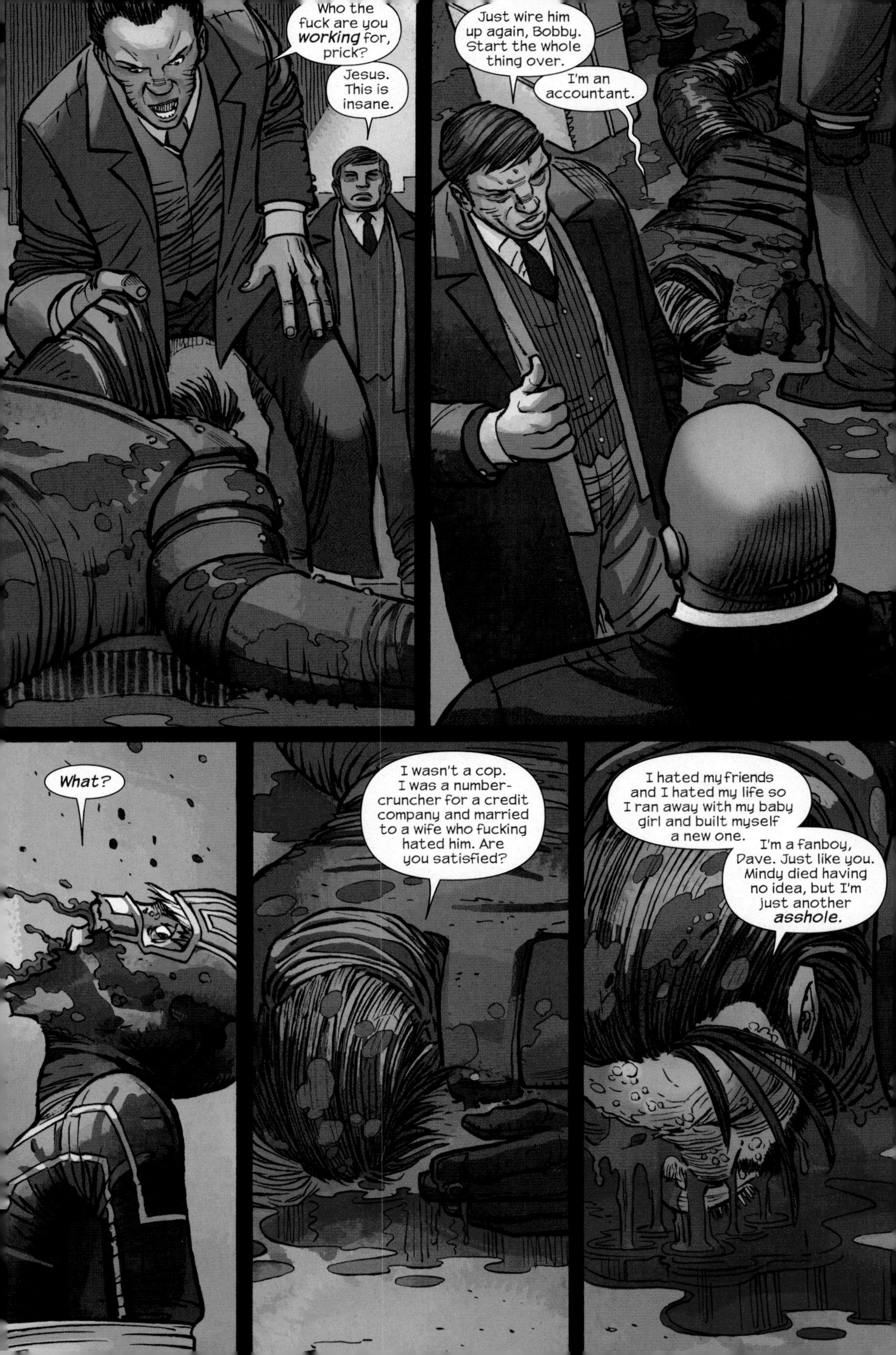
Who the fuck are you *working* for, prick?
Jesus. This is insane.
Just wire him up again, Bobby. Start the whole thing over.
I'm an accountant.
What?
I wasn't a cop. I was a number-cruncher for a credit company and married to a wife who fucking hated him. Are you satisfied?
I hated my friends and I hated my life so I ran away with my baby girl and built myself a new one.
I'm a fanboy, Dave. Just like you. Mindy died having no idea, but I'm just another *asshole*.

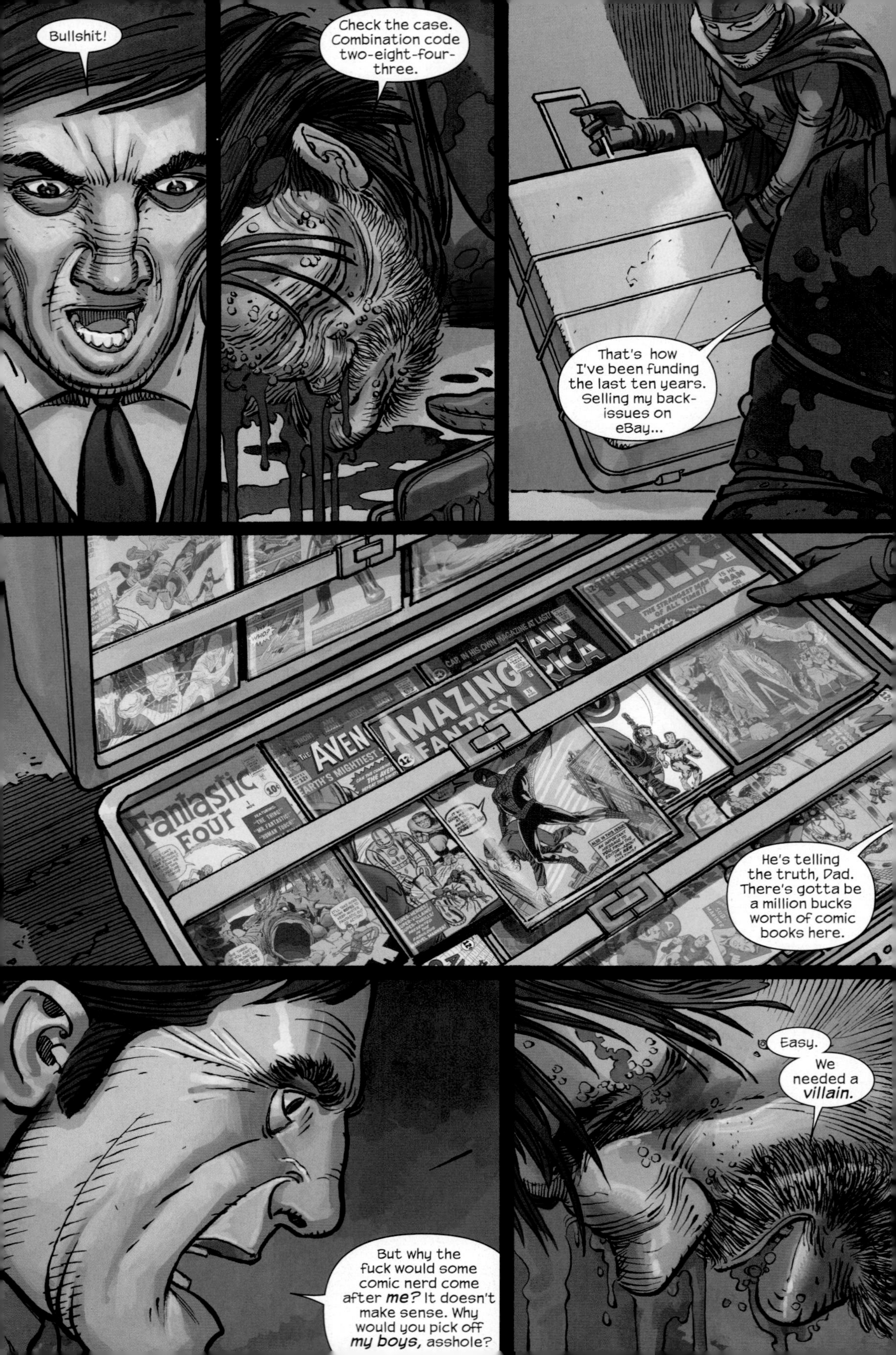
Bullshit!
Check the case. Combination code two-eight-four-three.
That's how I've been funding the last ten years. Selling my back-issues on eBay...
He's telling the truth, Dad. There's gotta be a million bucks worth of comic books here.
But why the fuck would some comic nerd come after *me?* It doesn't make sense. Why would you pick off *my boys,* asshole?
Easy.
We needed a *villain.*

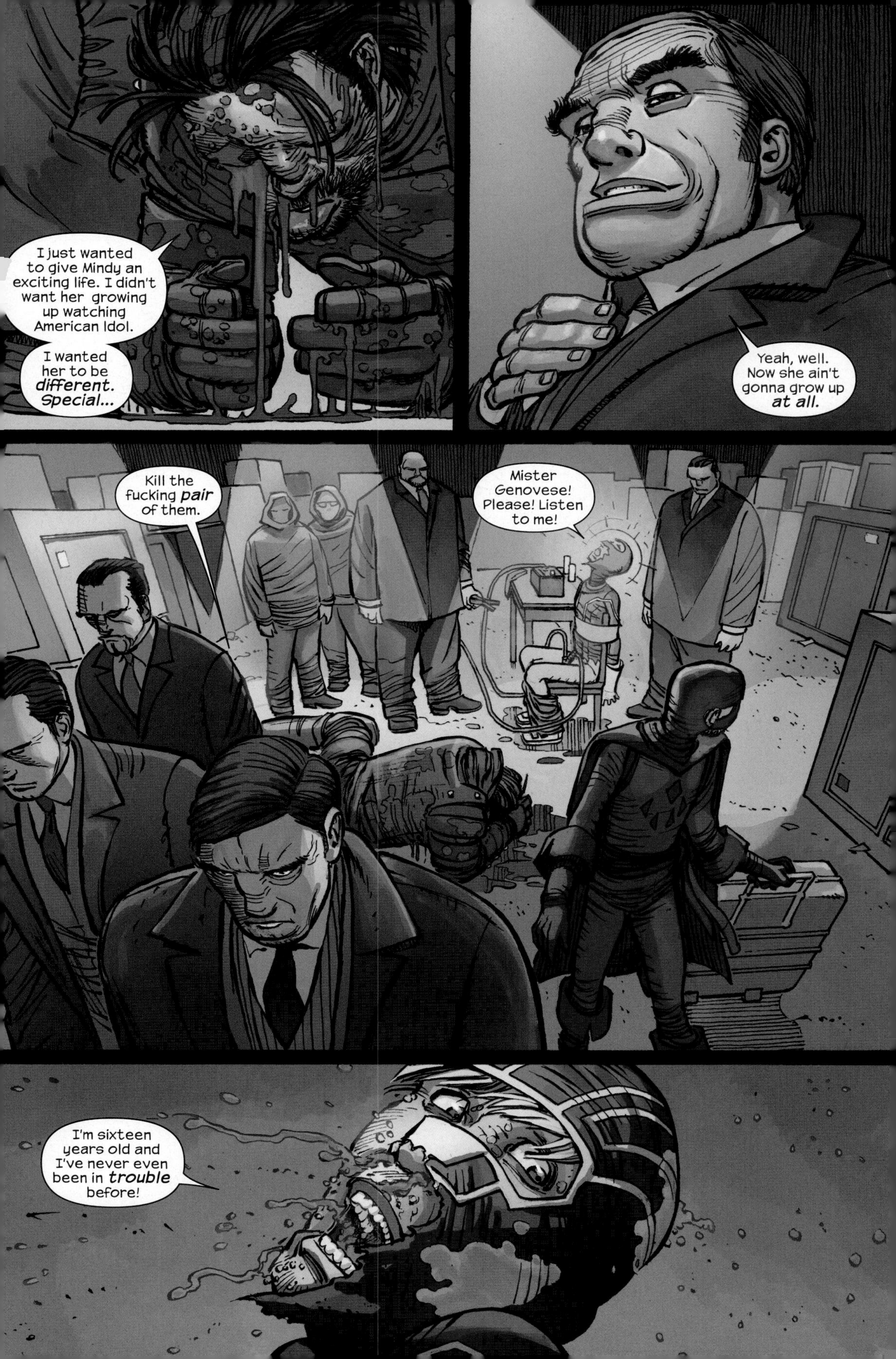

I just wanted to give Mindy an exciting life. I didn't want her growing up watching American Idol.
I wanted her to be *different*. *Special*...
Yeah, well. Now she ain't gonna grow up *at all*.
Kill the fucking *pair* of them.
Mister Genovese! Please! Listen to me!
I'm sixteen years old and I've never even been in *trouble* before!

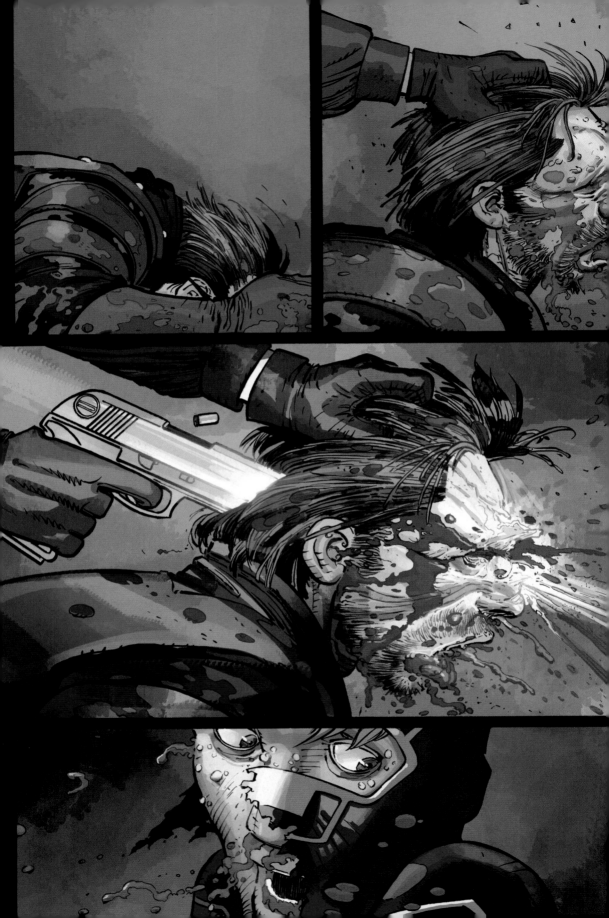

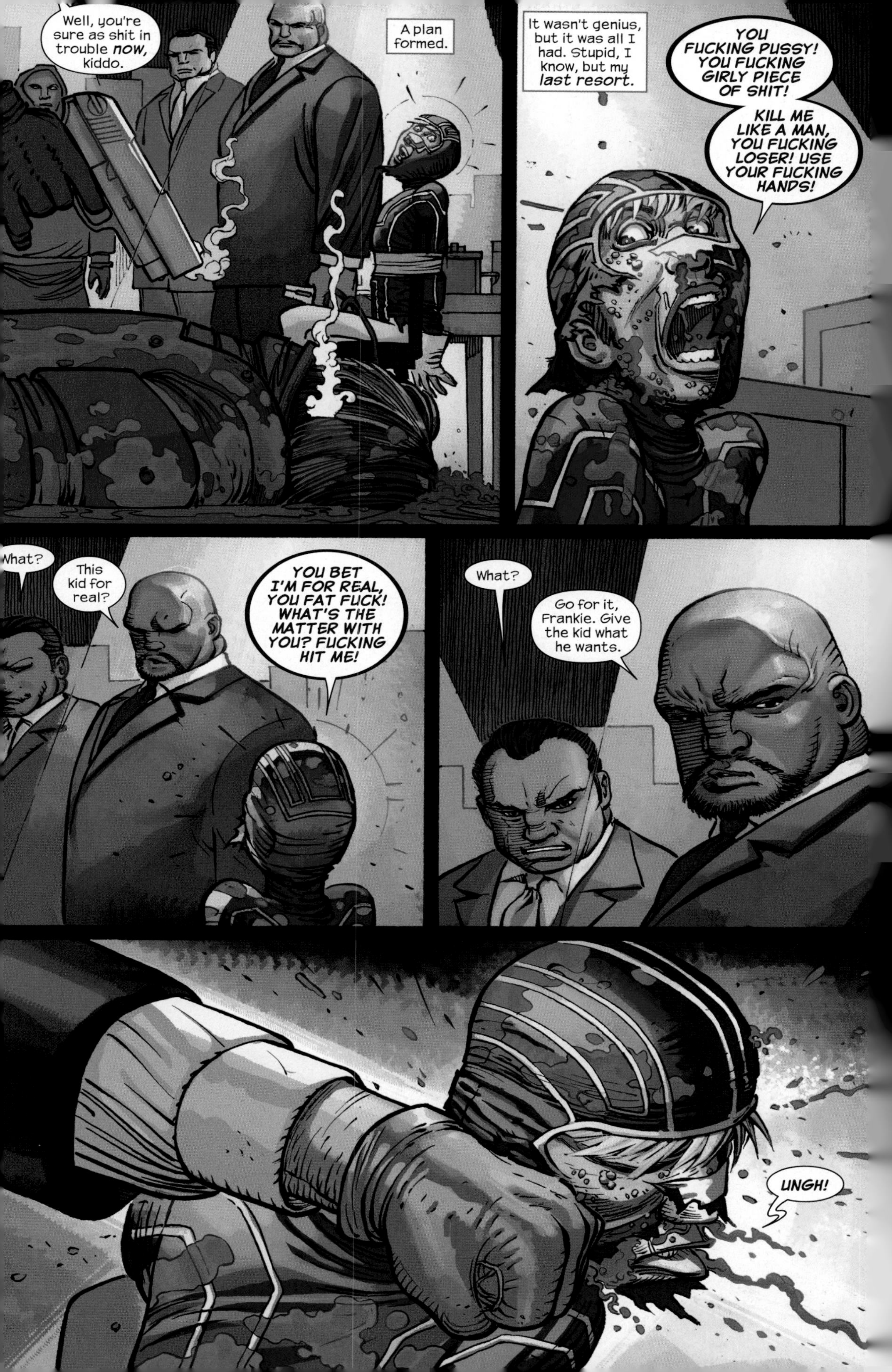

Well, you're sure as shit in trouble *now,* kiddo.
A plan formed.
It wasn't genius, but it was all I had. Stupid, I know, but my *last resort.*
YOU FUCKING PUSSY! YOU FUCKING GIRLY PIECE OF SHIT!
KILL ME LIKE A MAN, YOU FUCKING LOSER! USE YOUR FUCKING HANDS!
What?
This kid for real?
YOU BET I'M FOR REAL, YOU FAT FUCK! WHAT'S THE MATTER WITH YOU? FUCKING HIT ME!
What?
Go for it, Frankie. Give the kid what he wants.
UNGH!

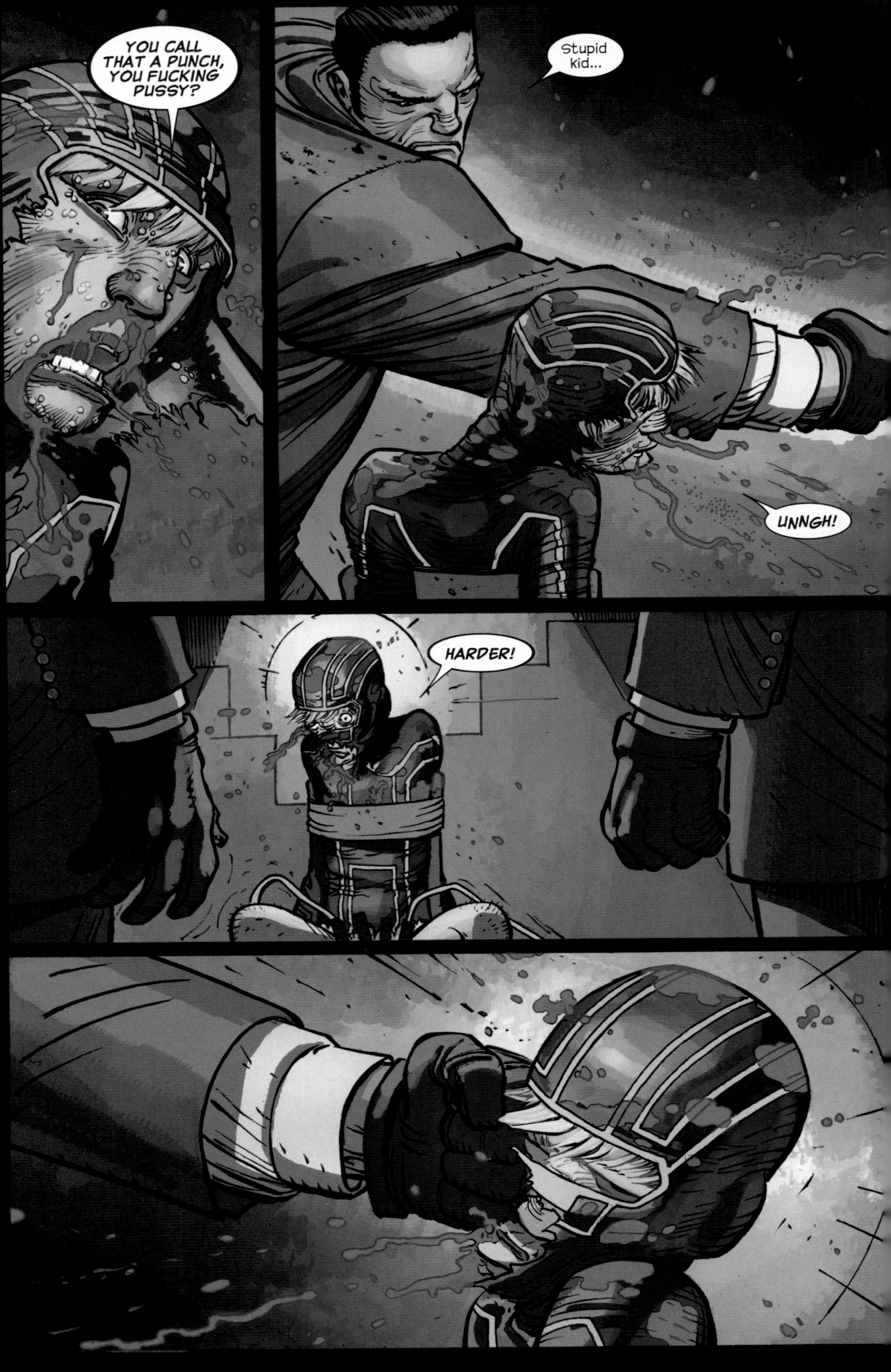
YOU CALL THAT A PUNCH, YOU FUCKING PUSSY?
Stupid kid...
UNNGH!
HARDER!

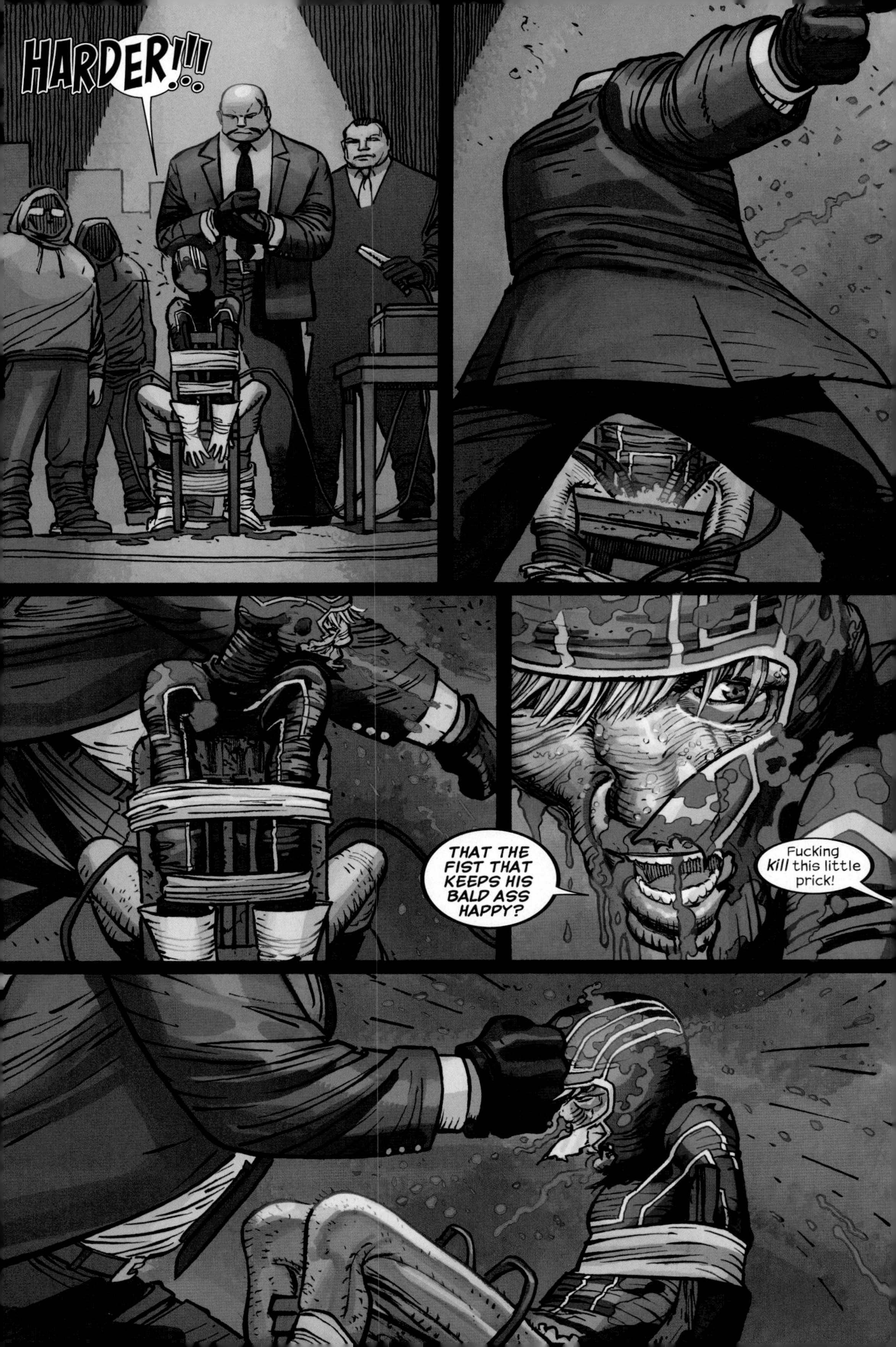
HARDER!!!
THAT THE FIST THAT KEEPS HIS BALD ASS HAPPY?
Fucking *kill* this little prick!

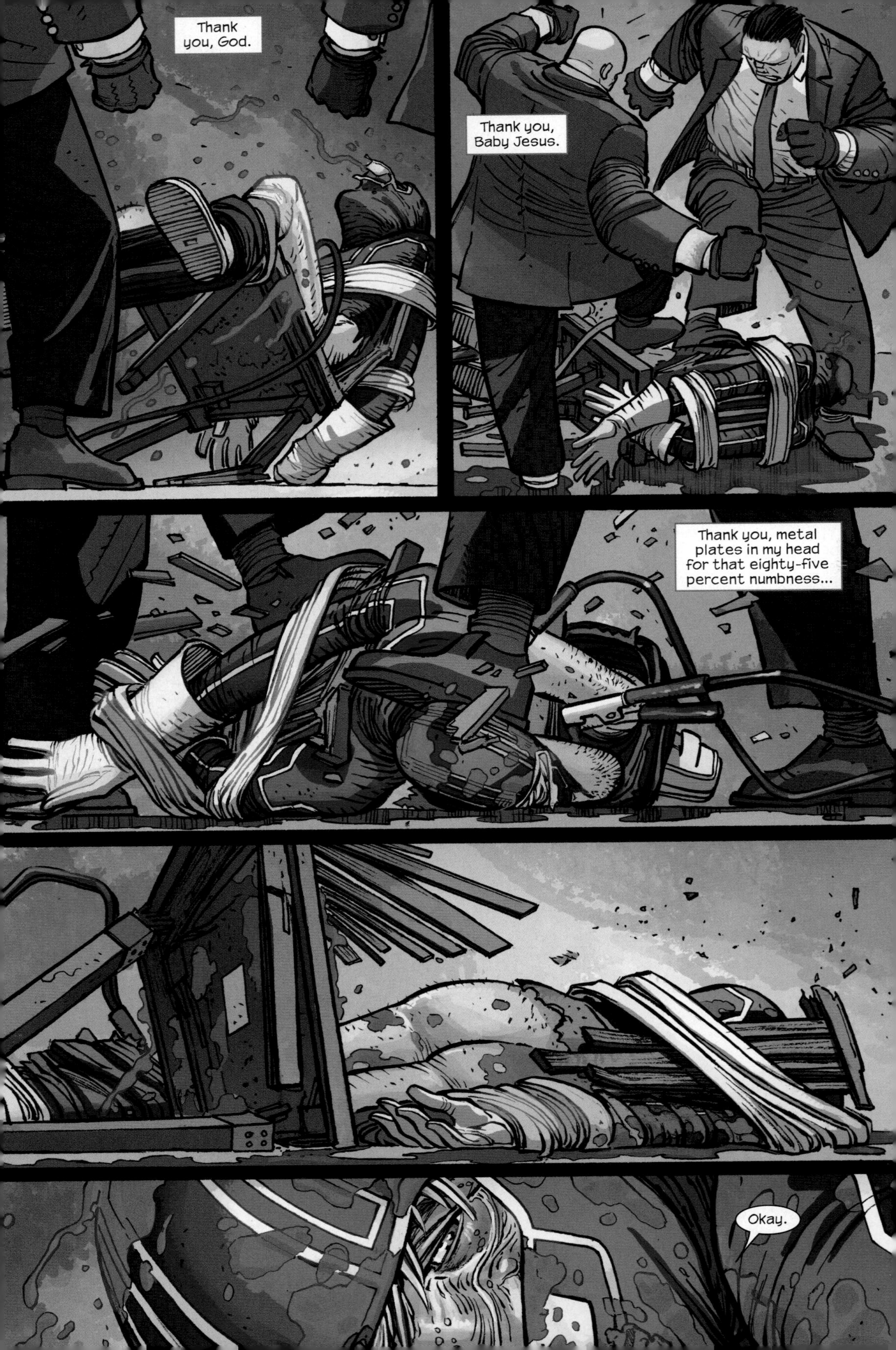
Thank you, God.
Thank you, Baby Jesus.
Thank you, metal plates in my head for that eighty-five percent numbness...
Okay.

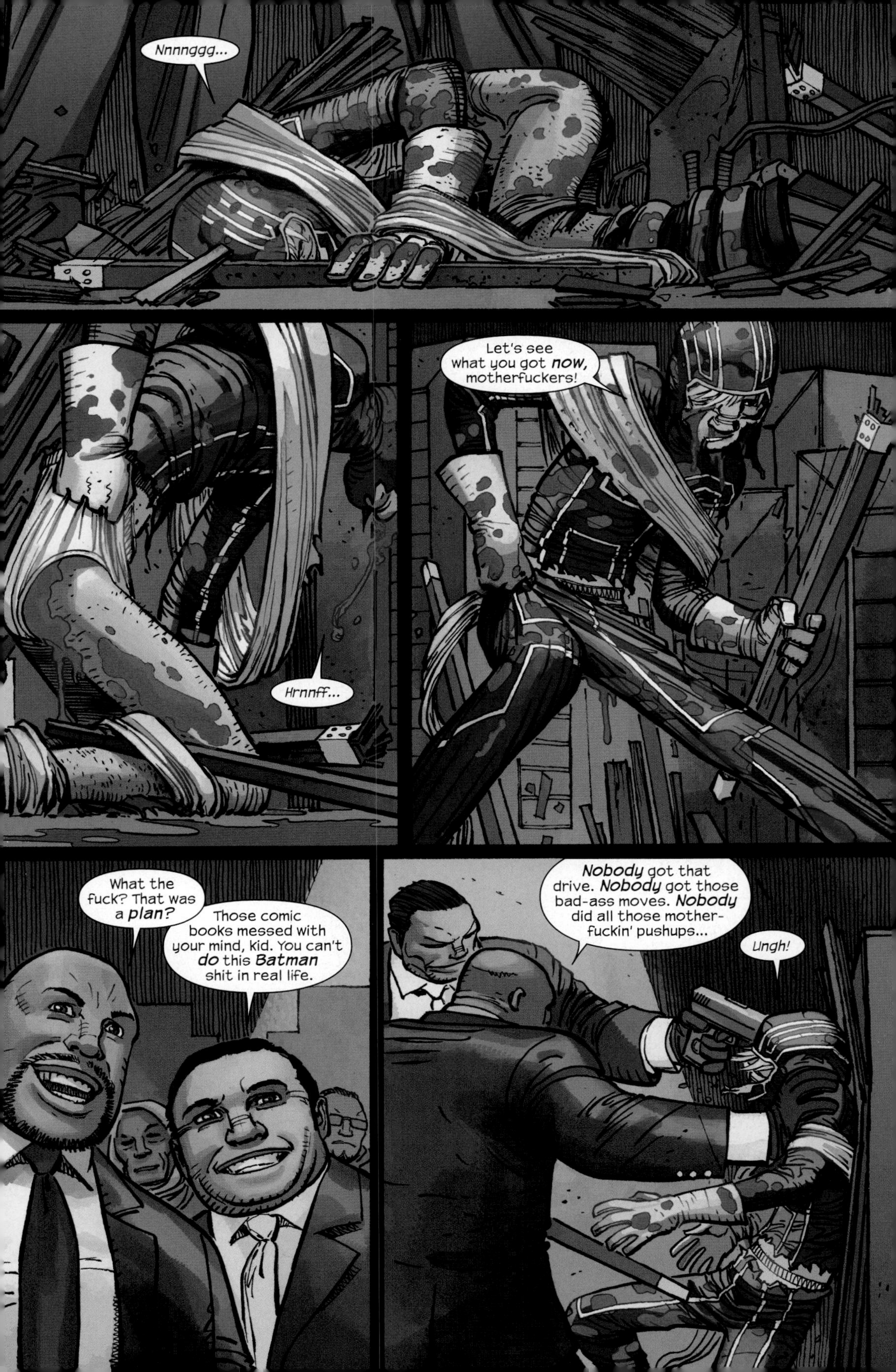
Nnnnggg...
Hrnnff...
Let's see what you got now, motherfuckers!
What the fuck? That was a plan?
Those comic books messed with your mind, kid. You can't do this Batman shit in real life.
Nobody got that drive. Nobody got those bad-ass moves. Nobody did all those mother-fuckin' pushups...
Ungh!

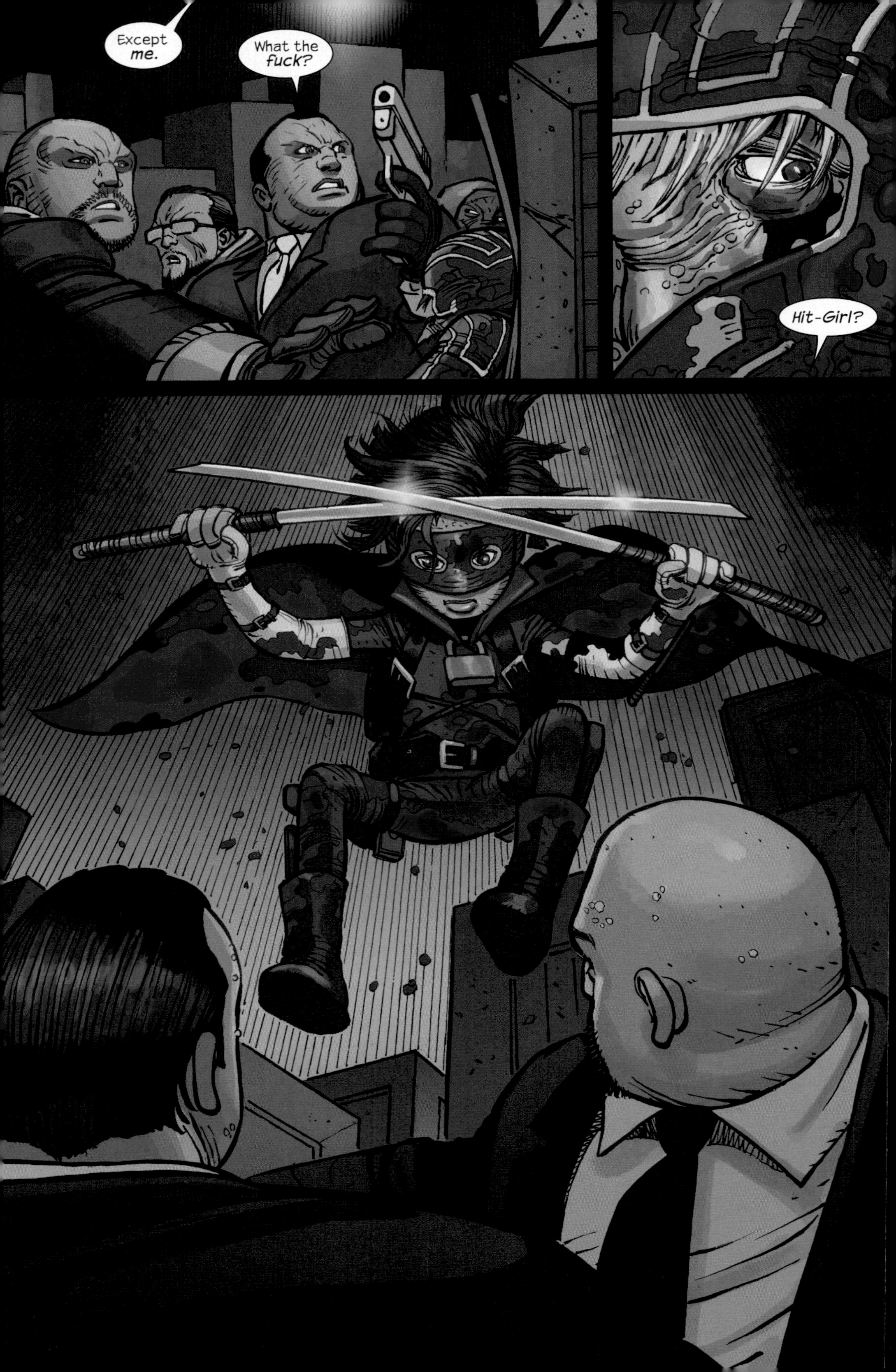
Except me.
What the fuck?
Hit-Girl?

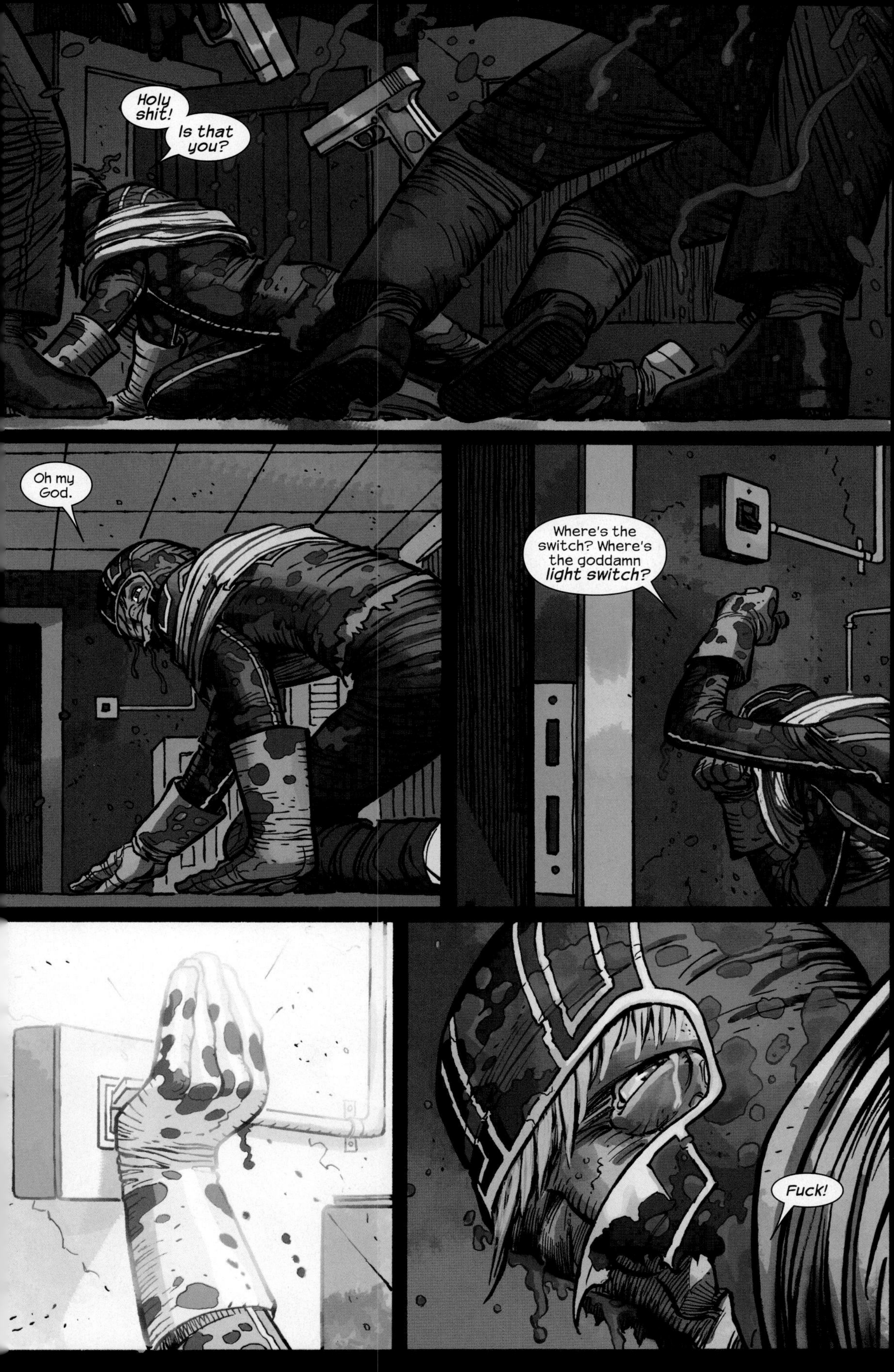
Holy shit!
Is that you?
Oh my God.
Where's the switch? Where's the goddamn *light switch*?
Fuck!

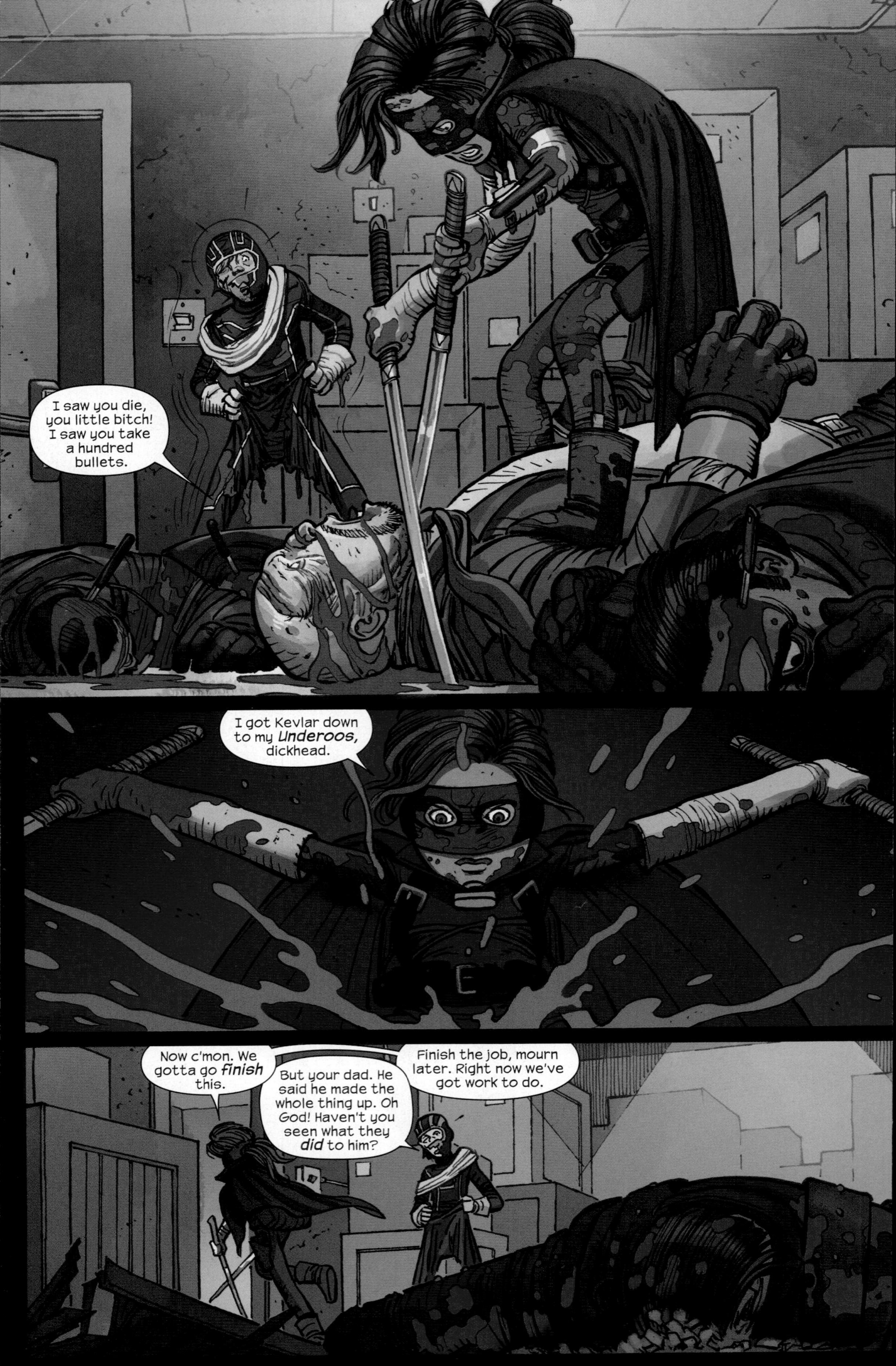
I saw you die, you little bitch! I saw you take a hundred bullets.
I got Kevlar down to my *Underoos,* dickhead.
Now c'mon. We gotta go **finish** this.
But your dad. He said he made the whole thing up. Oh God! Haven't you seen what they **did** to him?
Finish the job, mourn later. Right now we've got work to do.

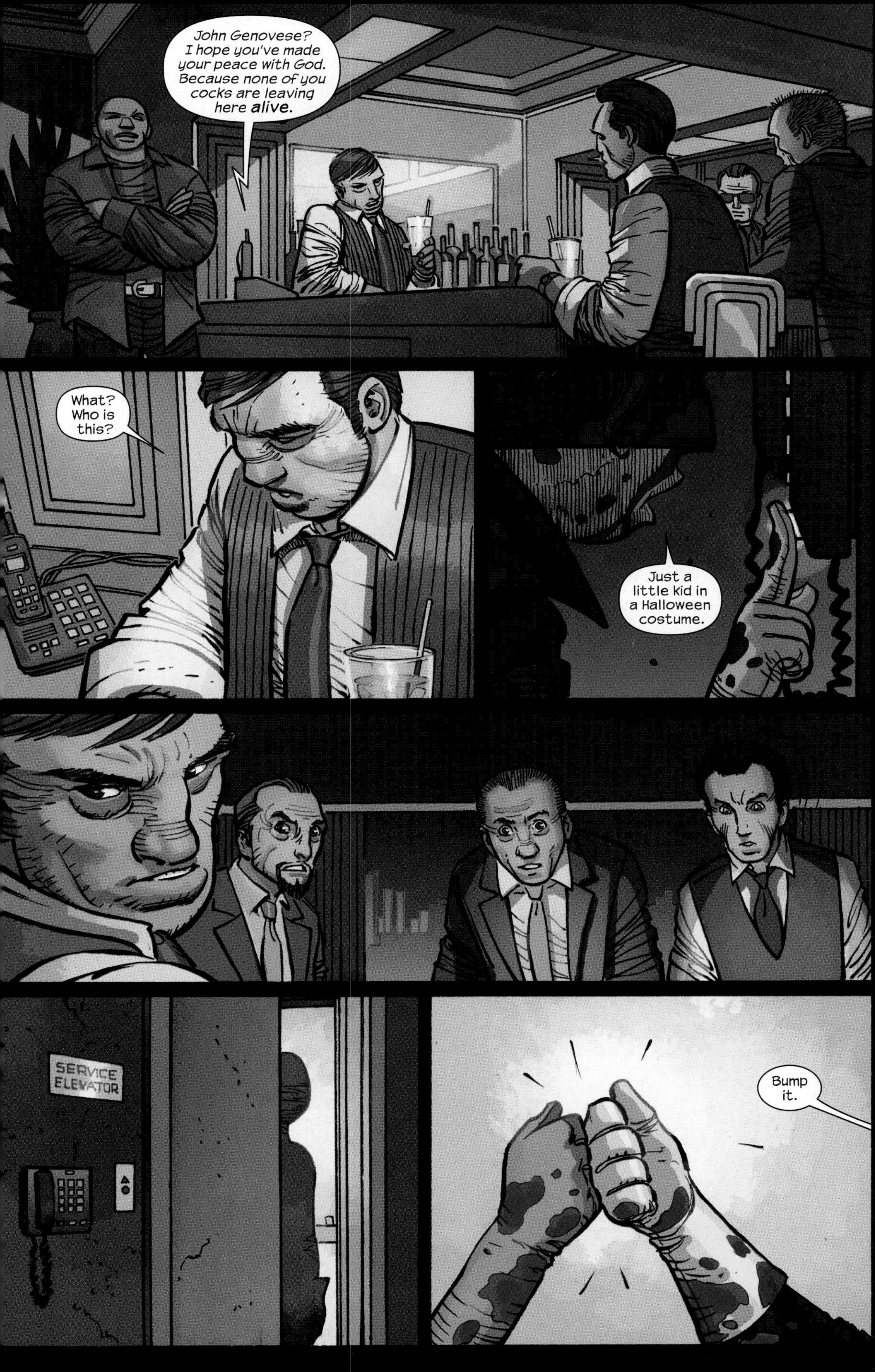
John Genovese? I hope you've made your peace with God. Because none of you cocks are leaving here alive.
What? Who is this?
Just a little kid in a Halloween costume.
SERVICE ELEVATOR
Bump it.

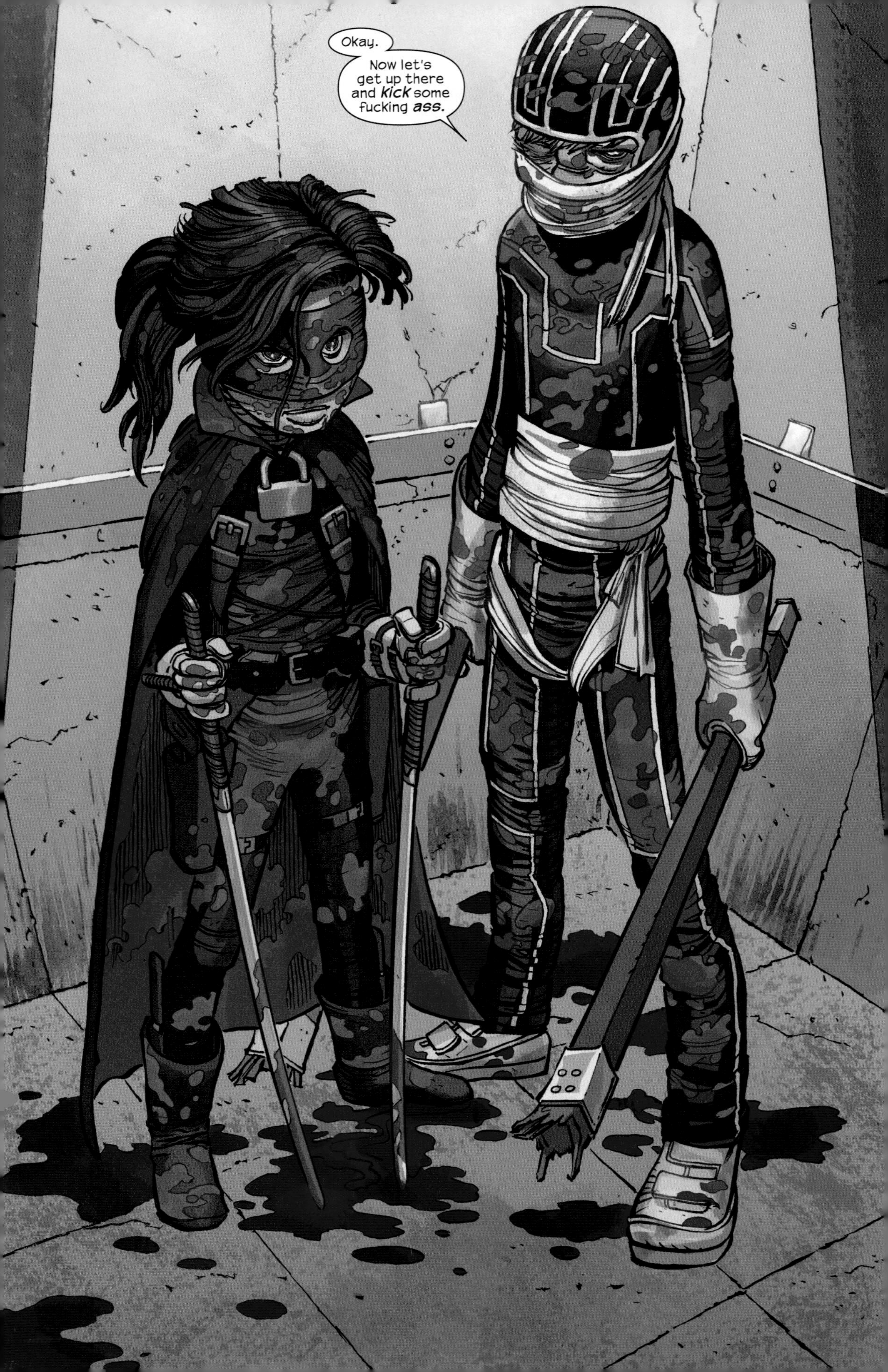
Okay.
Now let's get up there and *kick* some fucking *ass.*

EIGHT

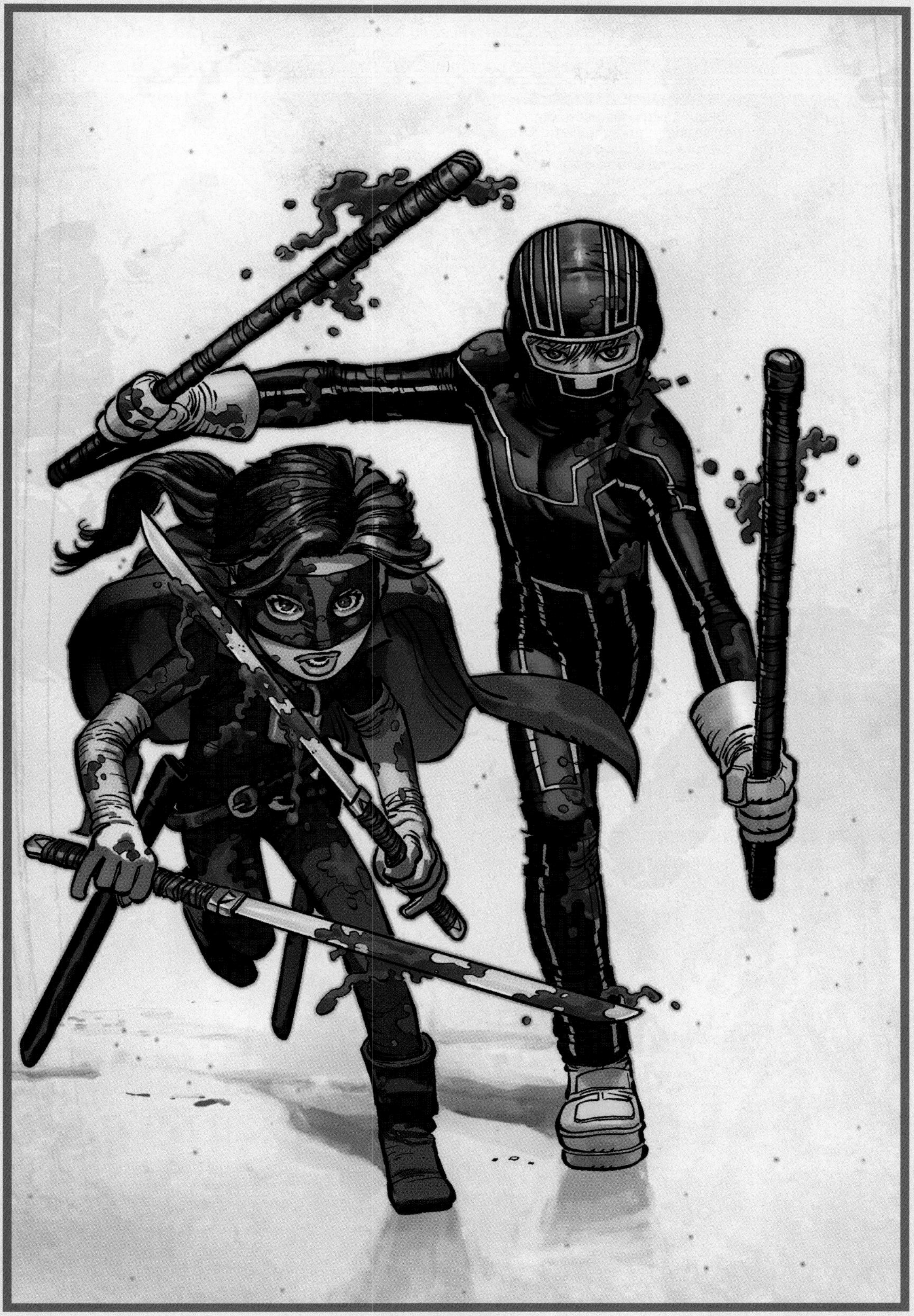

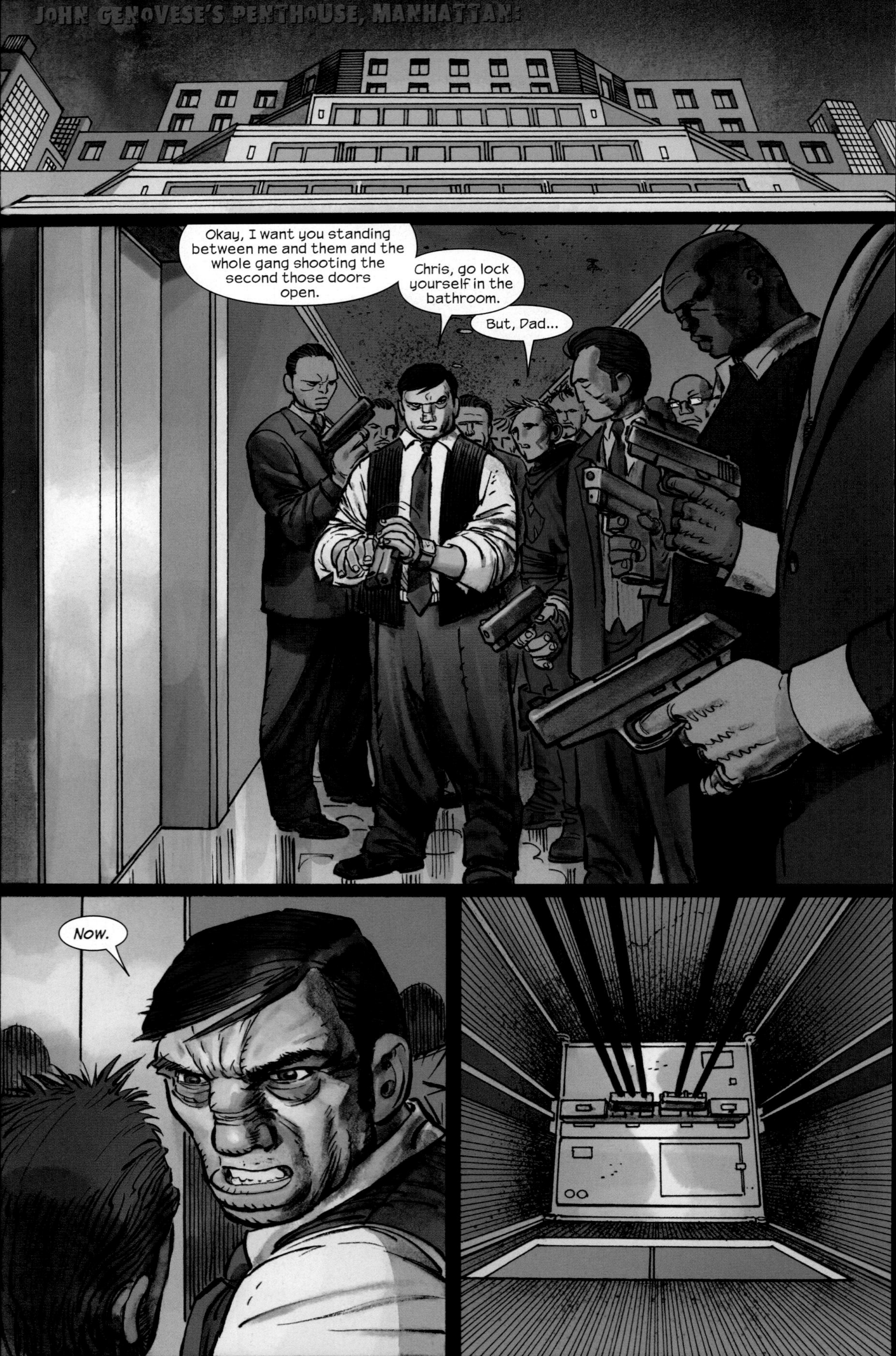

JOHN GENOVESE'S PENTHOUSE, MANHATTAN:
Okay, I want you standing between me and them and the whole gang shooting the second those doors open.
Chris, go lock yourself in the bathroom.
But, Dad...
Now.

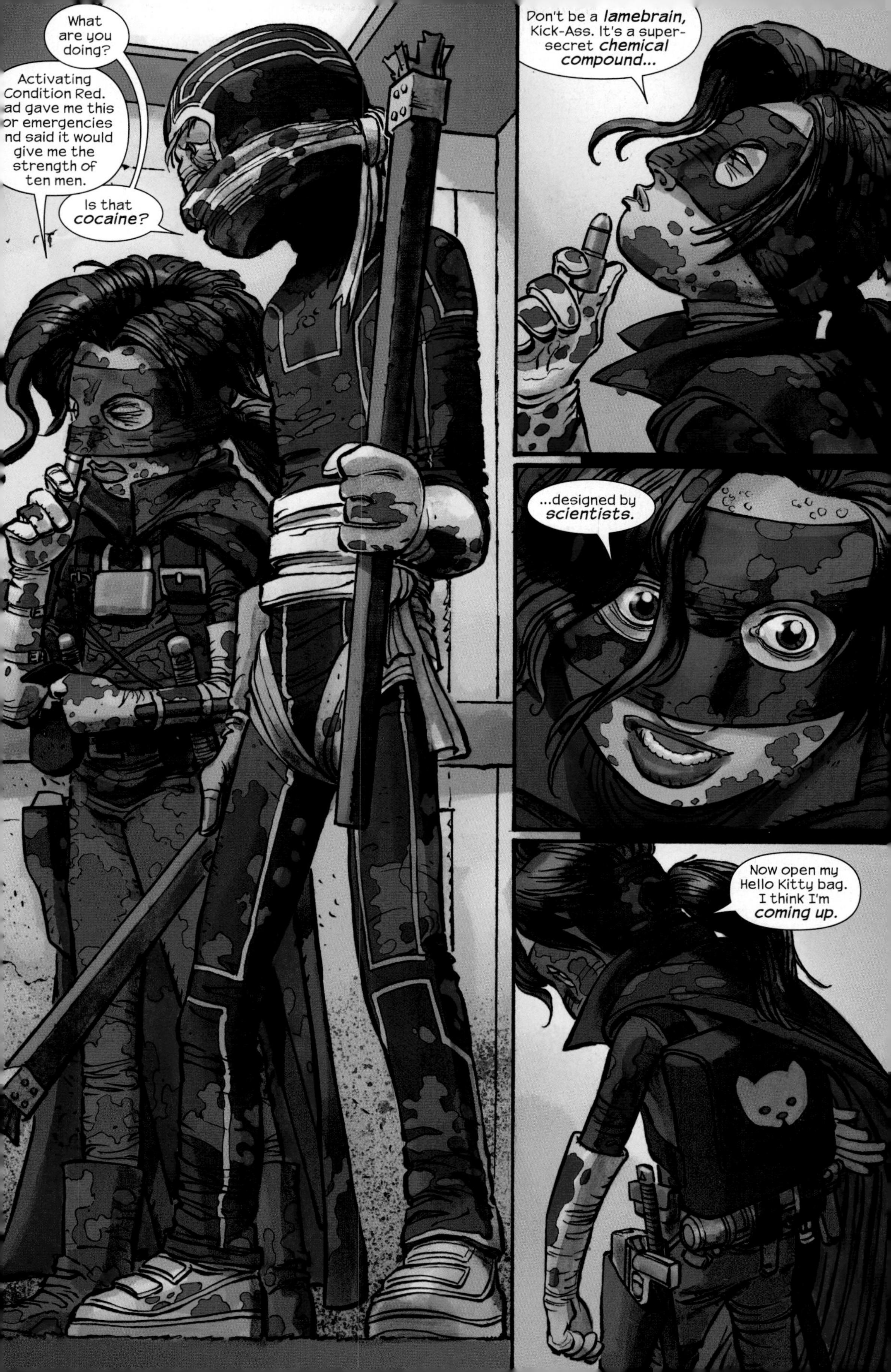
What are you doing?
Activating Condition Red. ad gave me this or emergencies nd said it would give me the strength of ten men.
Is that *cocaine?*
Don't be a *lamebrain,* Kick-Ass. It's a super-secret *chemical compound...*
...designed by *scientists.*
Now open my Hello Kitty bag. I think I'm *coming up.*

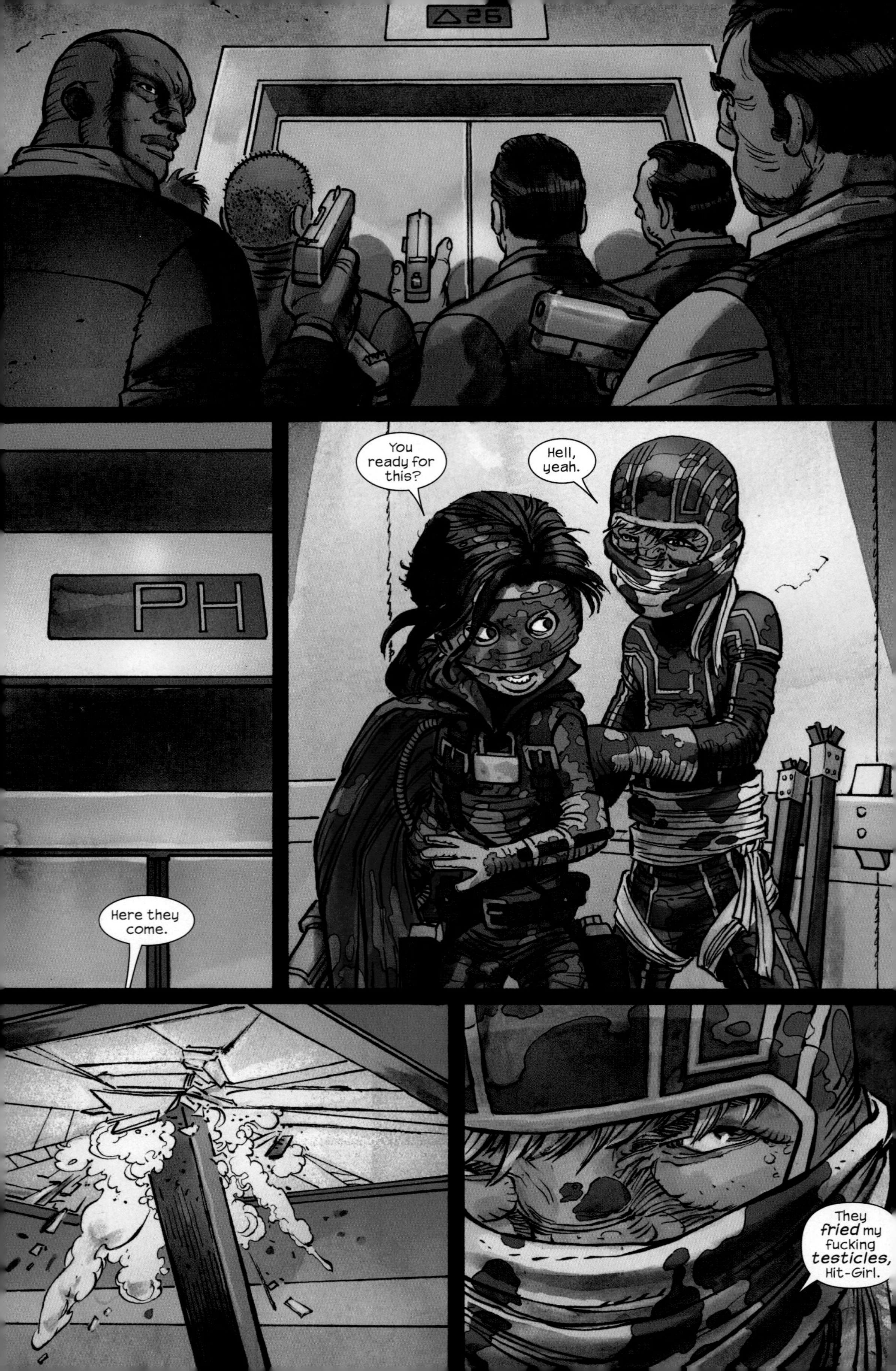

△26
PH
Here they come.
You ready for this?
Hell, yeah.
They *fried* my fucking *testicles,* Hit-Girl.

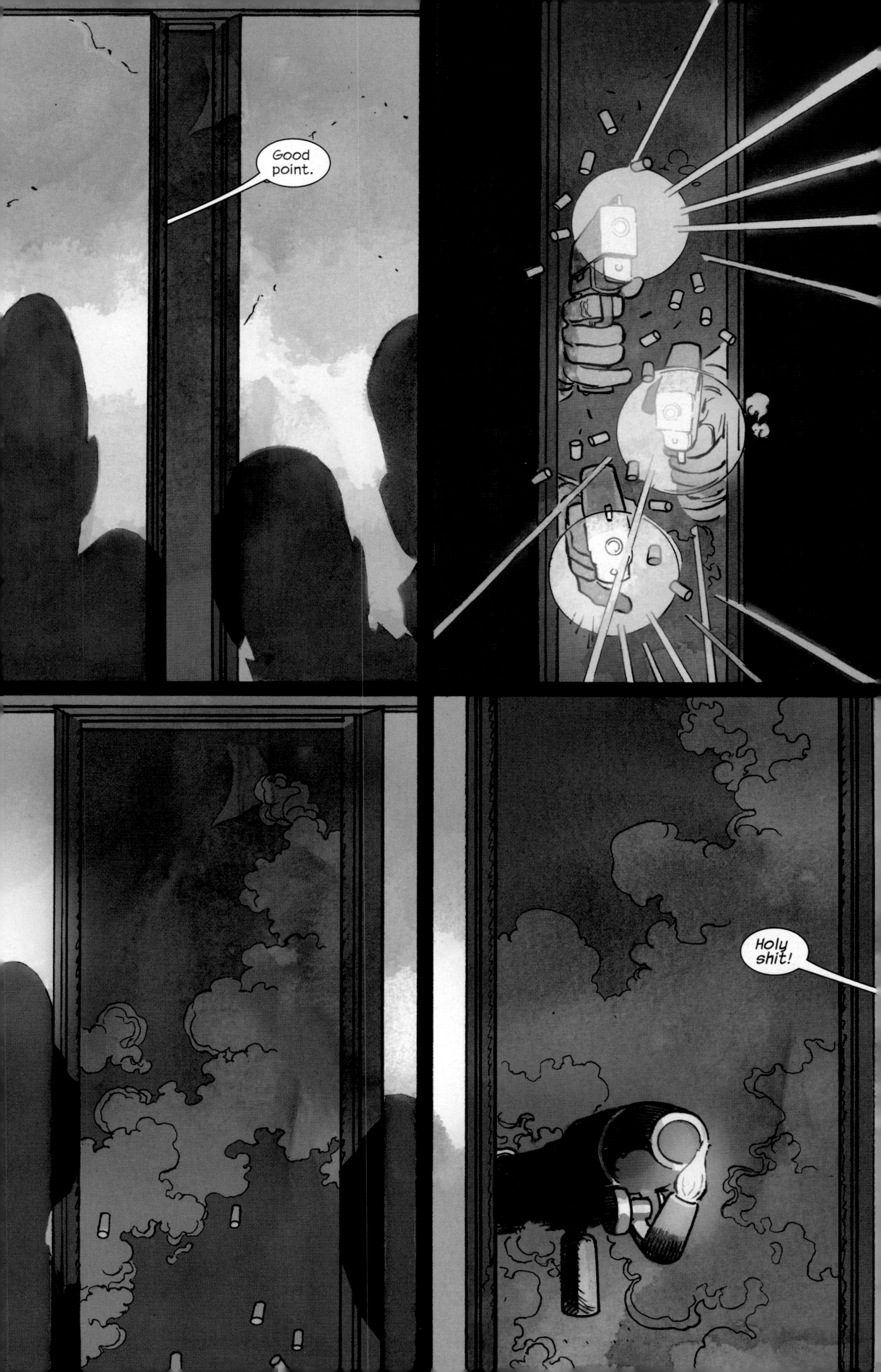
Good point.
Holy shit!

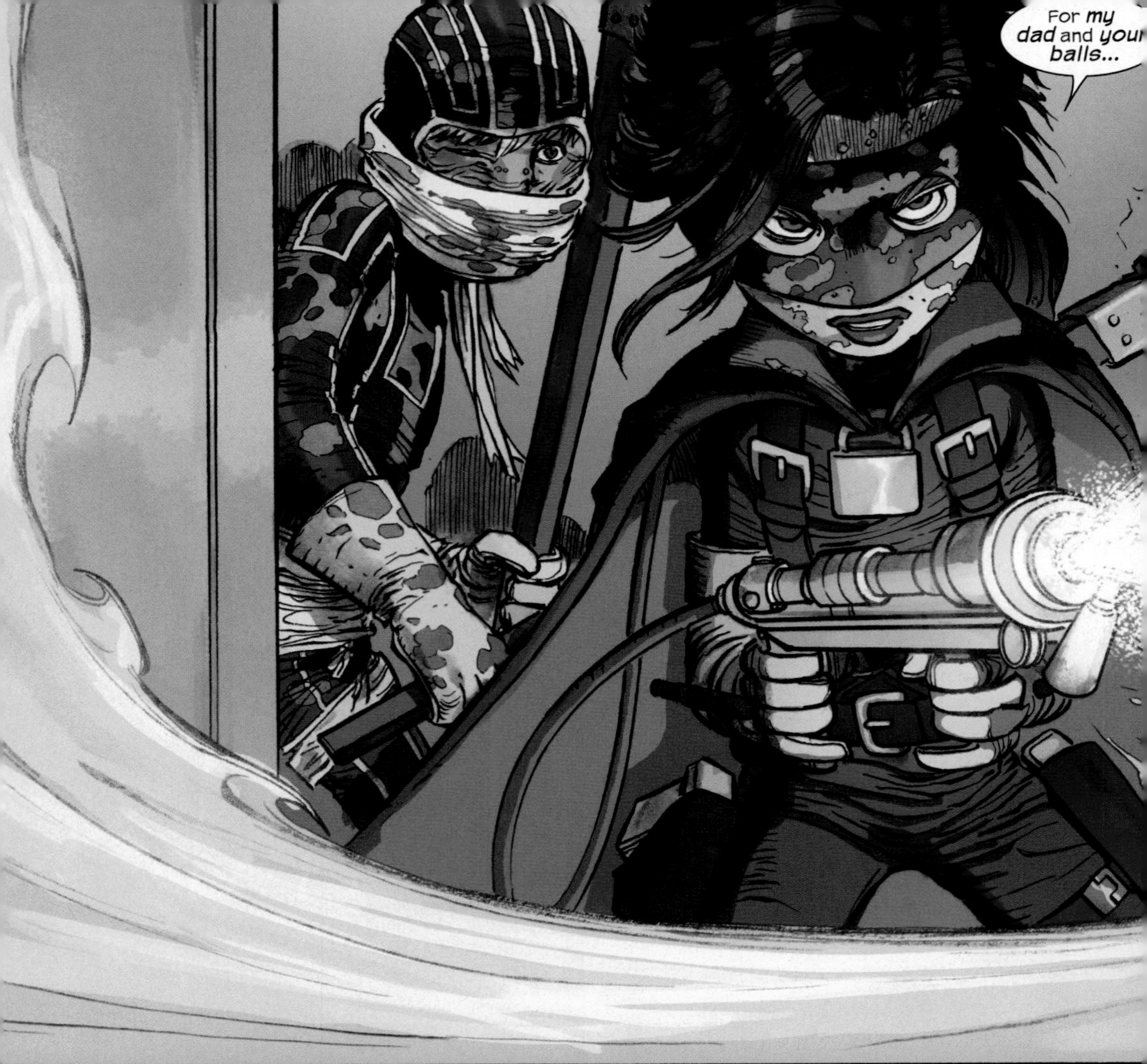
For my dad and your balls...
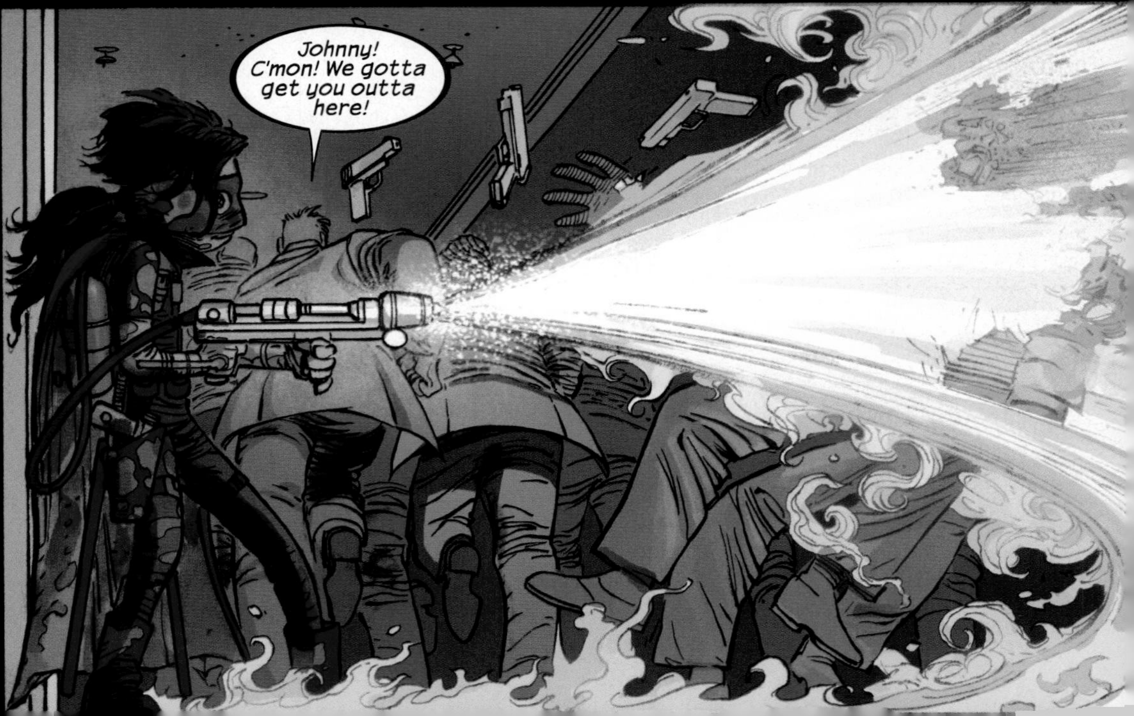
Johnny! C'mon! We gotta get you outta here!

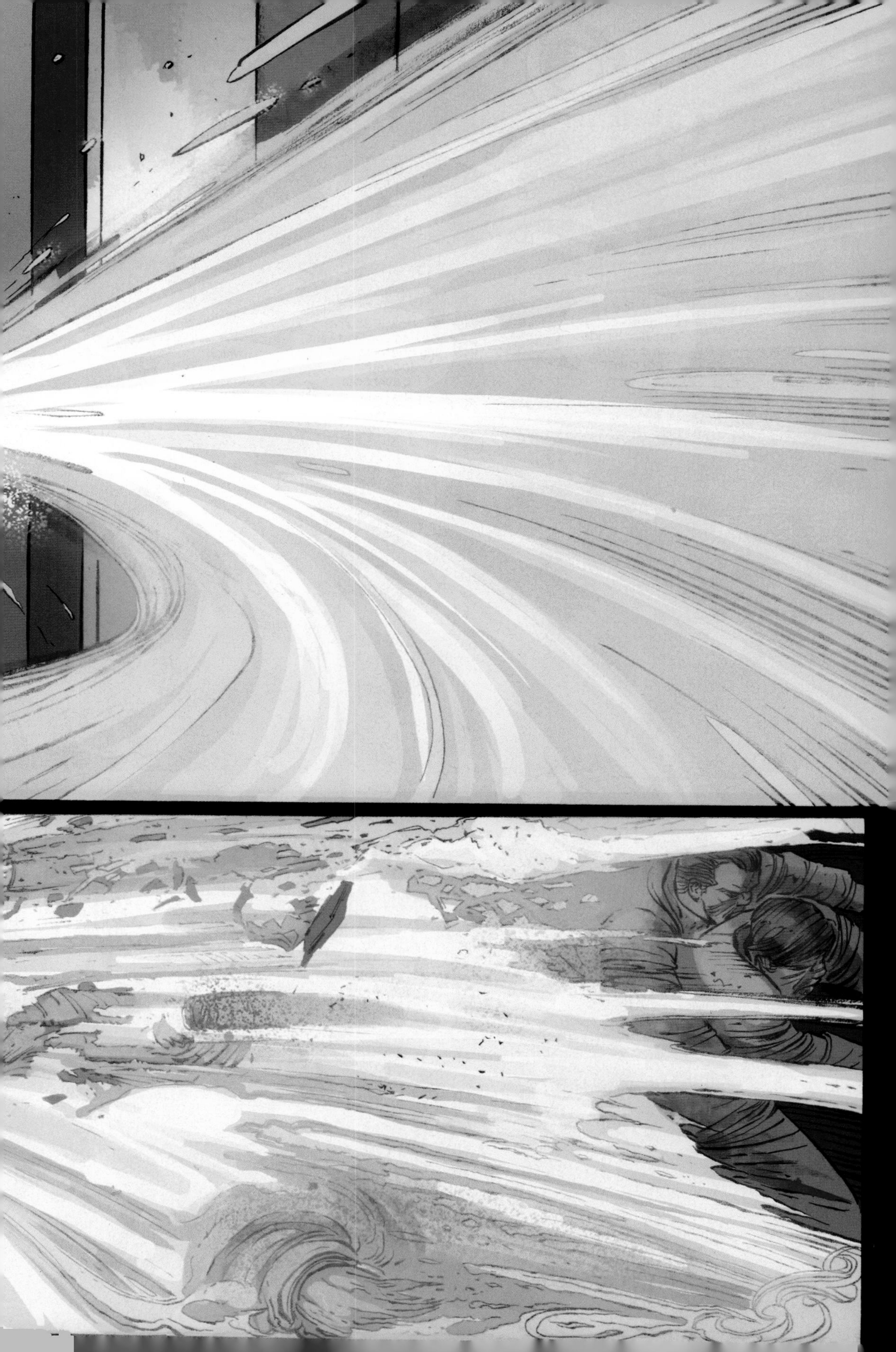

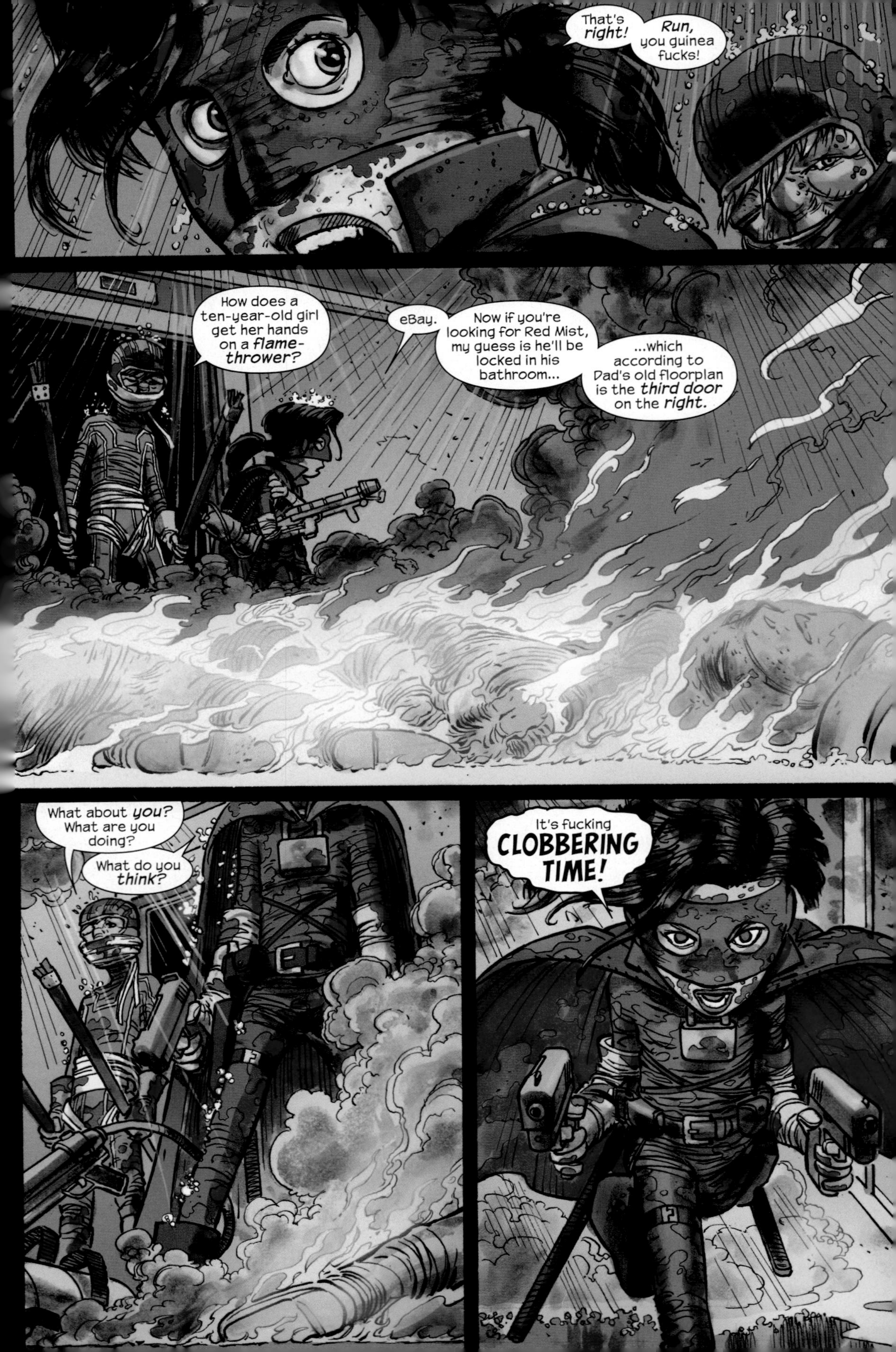
That's *right!*
Run, you guinea fucks!
How does a ten-year-old girl get her hands on a *flame-thrower?*
eBay.
Now if you're looking for Red Mist, my guess is he'll be locked in his bathroom...
...which according to Dad's old floorplan is the *third door* on the *right.*
What about *you?* What are you doing?
What do you *think?*
It's fucking CLOBBERING TIME!

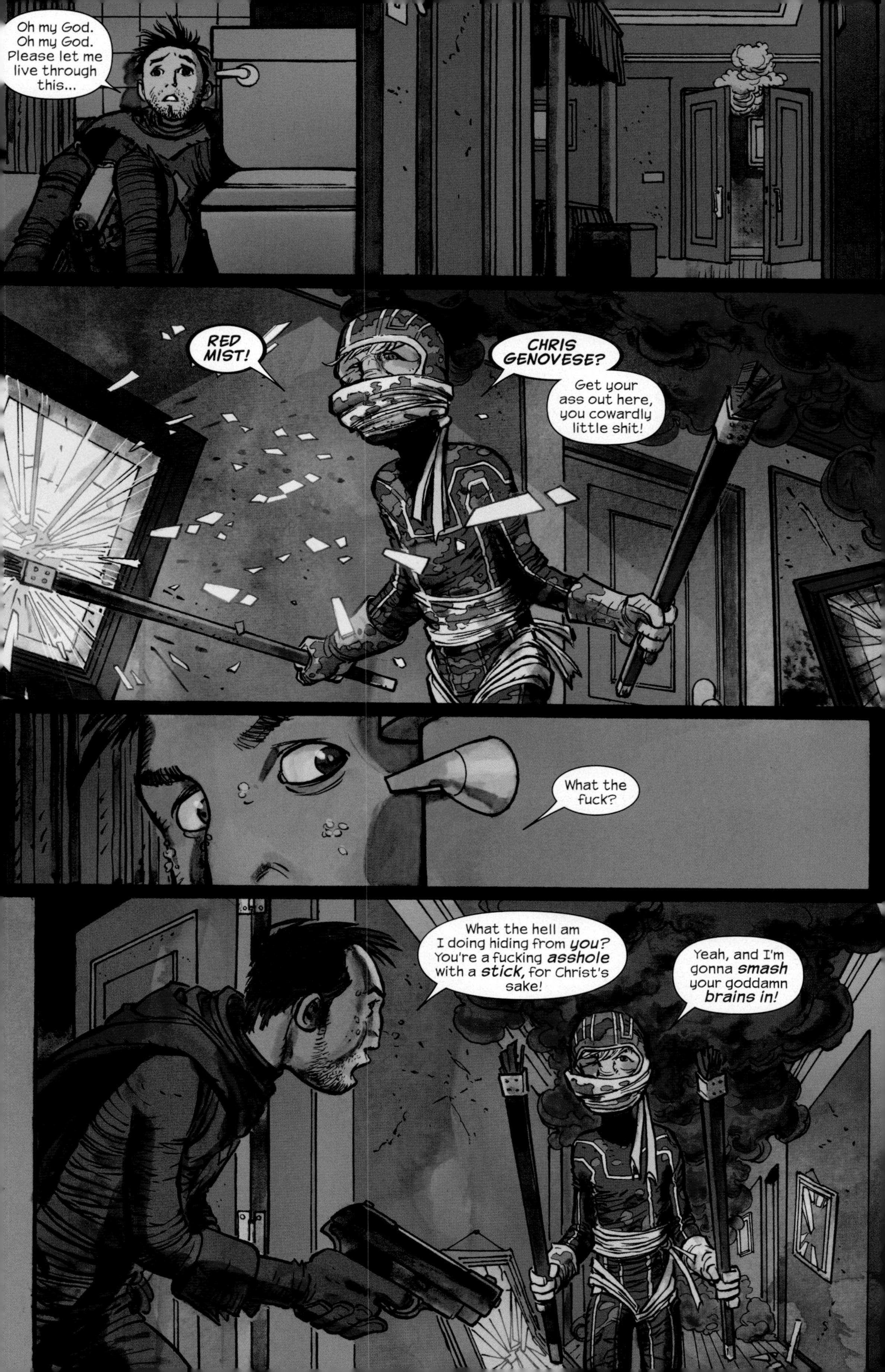

Oh my God. Oh my God. Please let me live through this...
RED MIST!
CHRIS GENOVESE?
Get your ass out here, you cowardly little shit!
What the fuck?
What the hell am I doing hiding from *you*? You're a fucking *asshole* with a *stick,* for Christ's sake!
Yeah, and I'm gonna *smash* your goddamn *brains in!*

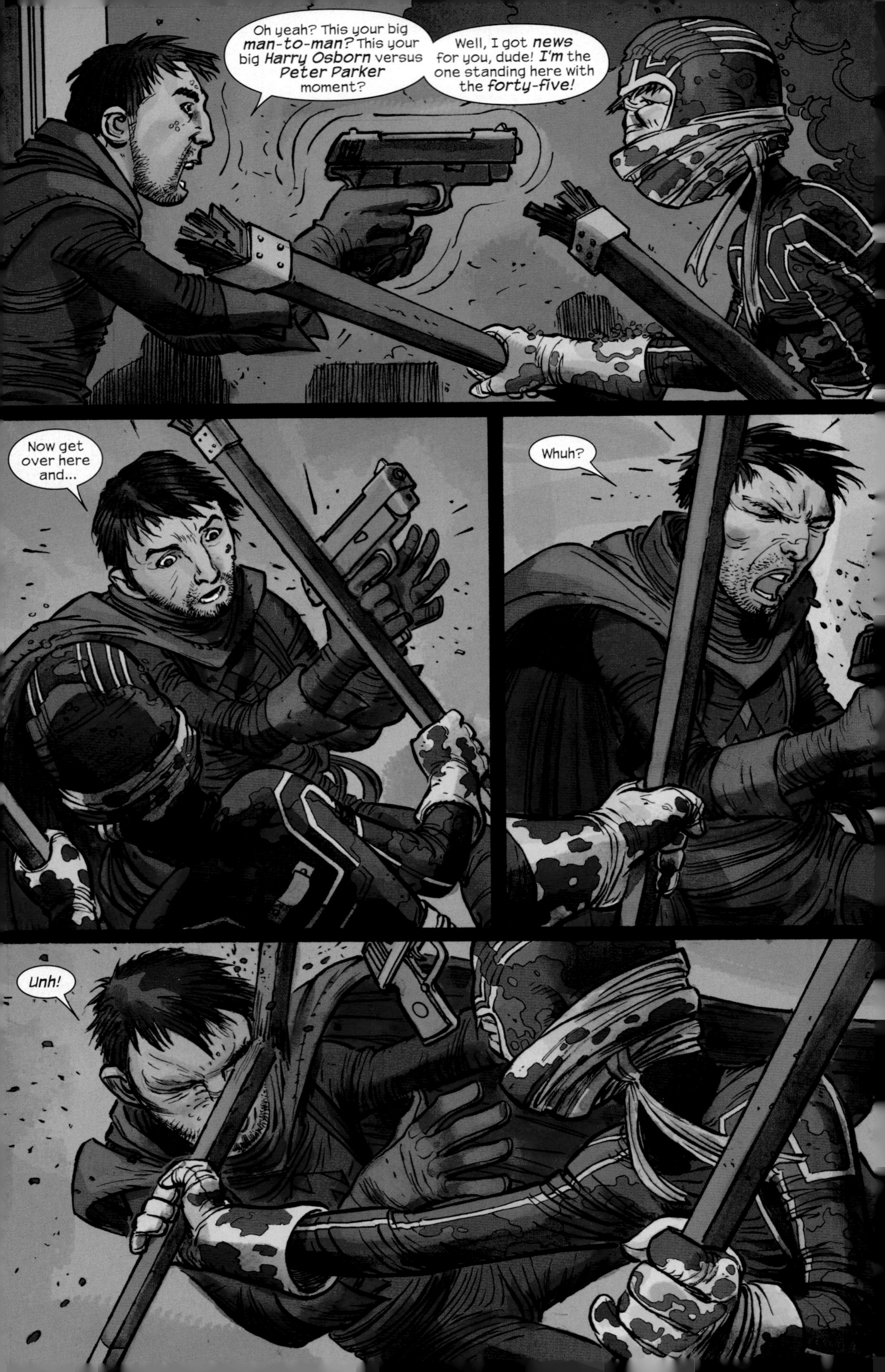
Oh yeah? This your big man-to-man? This your big Harry Osborn versus Peter Parker moment?
Well, I got news for you, dude! I'm the one standing here with the forty-five!
Now get over here and...
Whuh?
Unh!

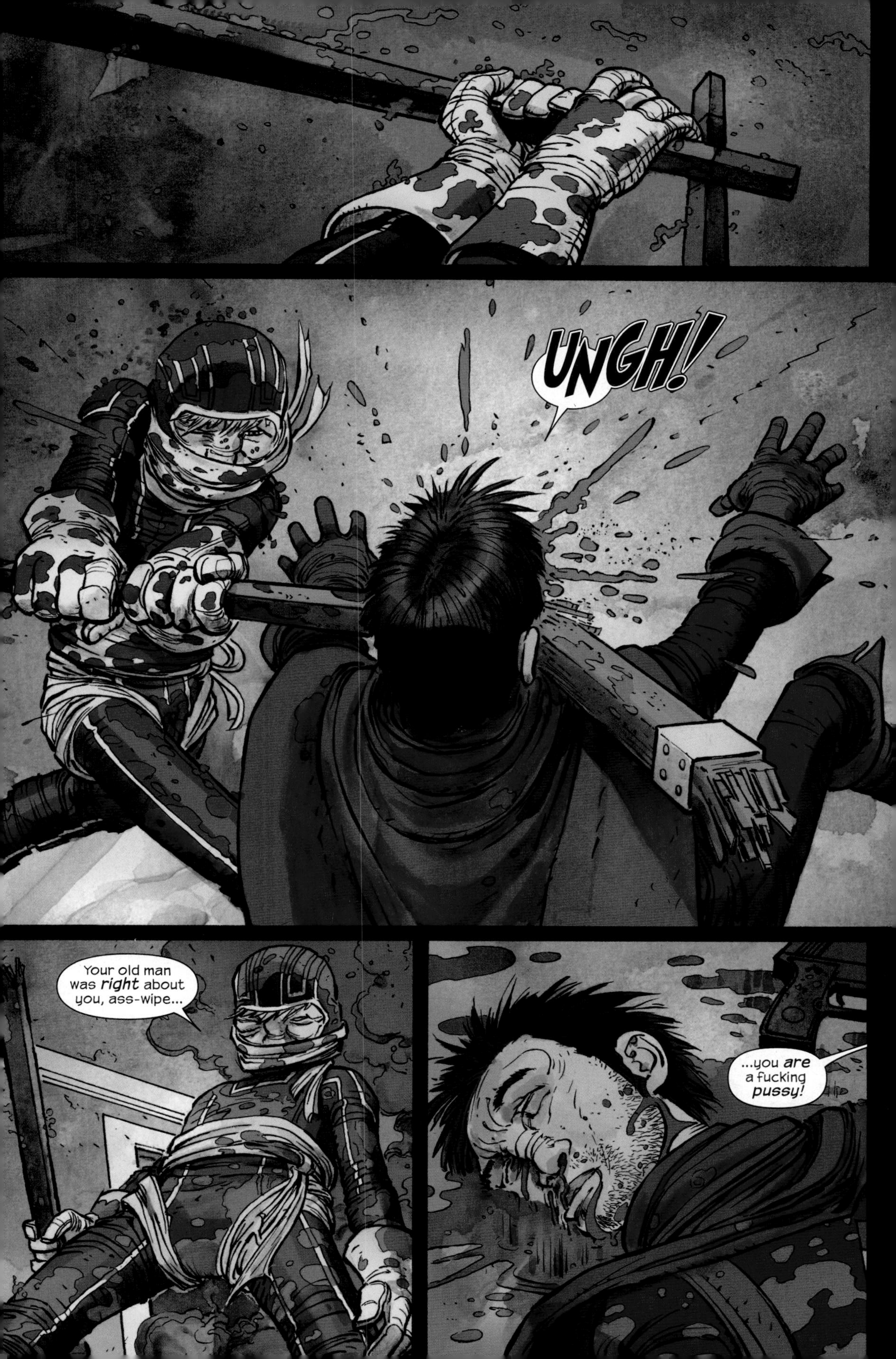
UNGH!
Your old man was right about you, ass-wipe...
...you are a fucking pussy!

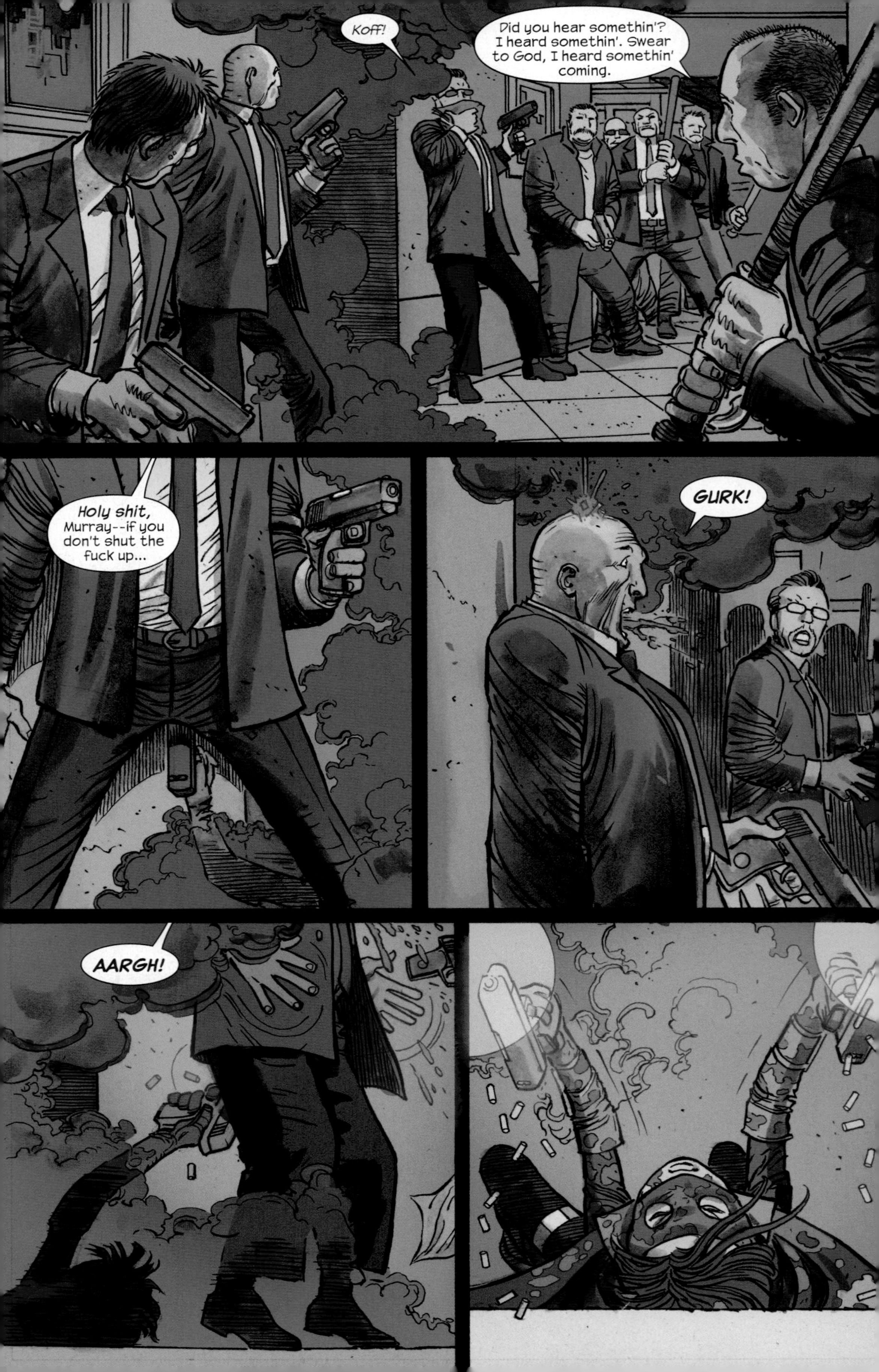
Koff!
Did you hear somethin'? I heard somethin'. Swear to God, I heard somethin' coming.
Holy shit, Murray--if you don't shut the fuck up...
GURK!
AARGH!

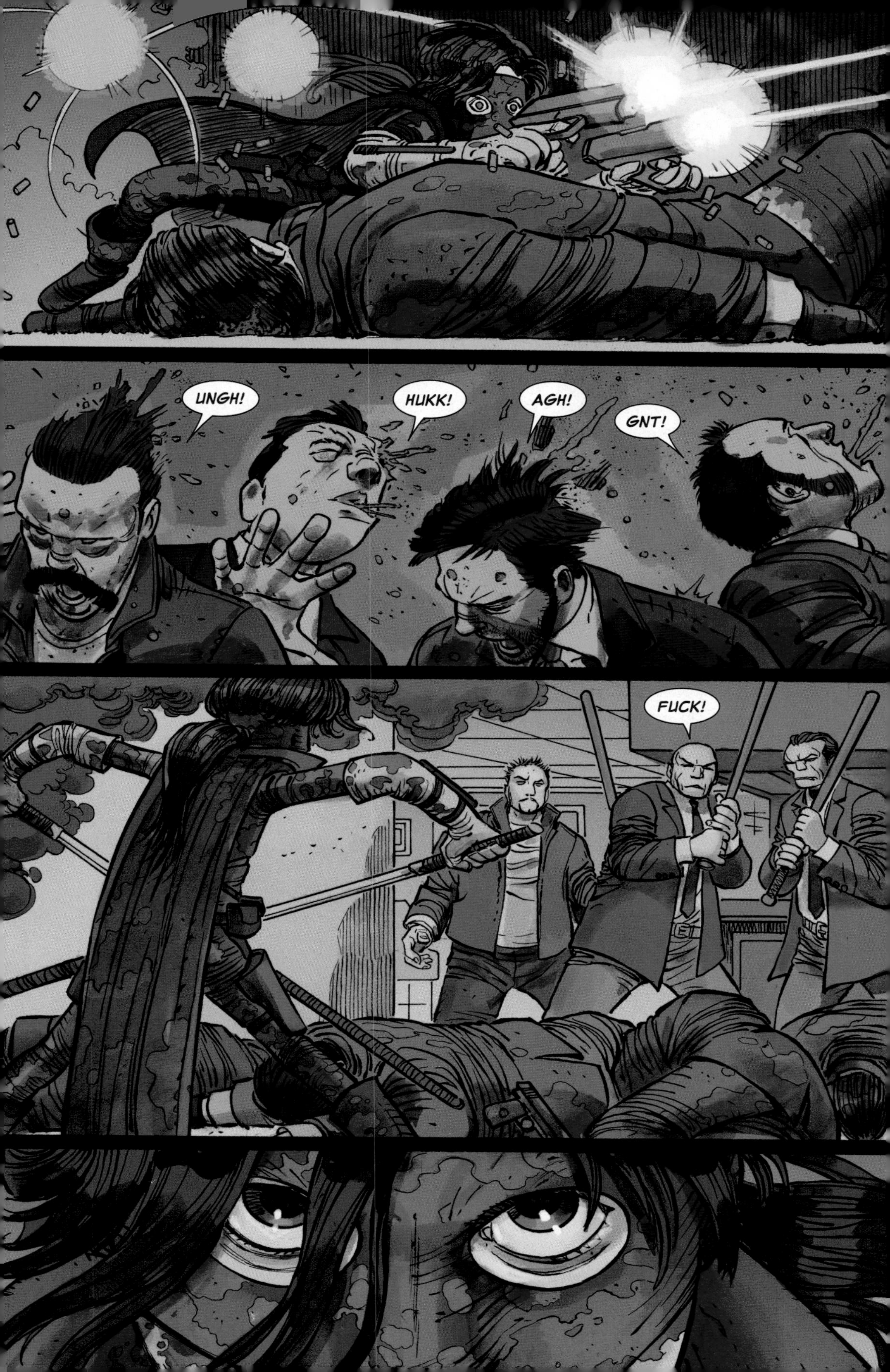
UNGH!
HUKK!
AGH!
GNT!
FUCK!

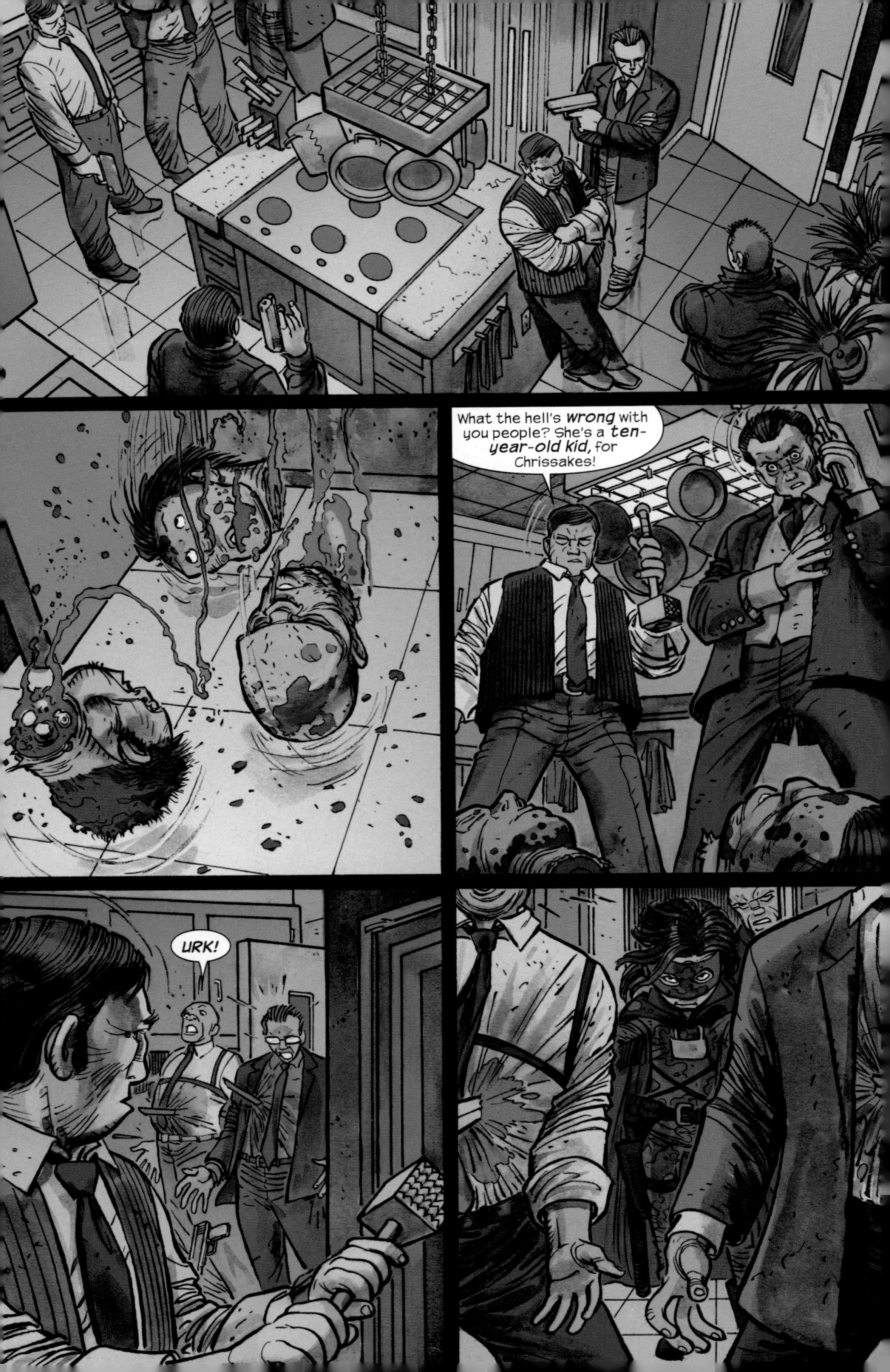
What the hell's *wrong* with you people? She's a *ten-year-old kid,* for Chrissakes!
URK!

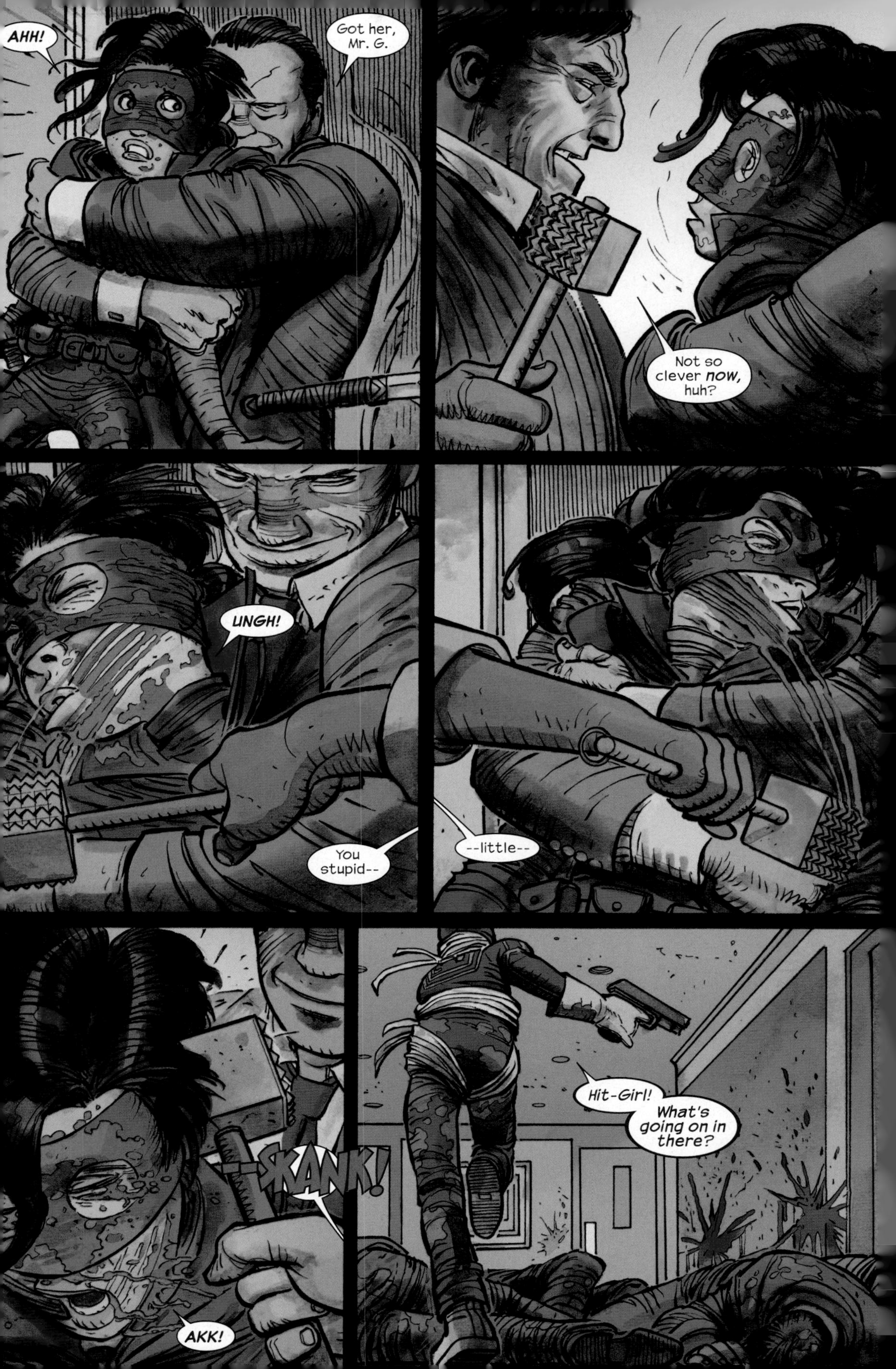
AHH!
Got her, Mr. G.
Not so clever NOW, huh?
UNGH!
You stupid--
--little--
SKANK!
AKK!
Hit-Girl!
What's going on in there?

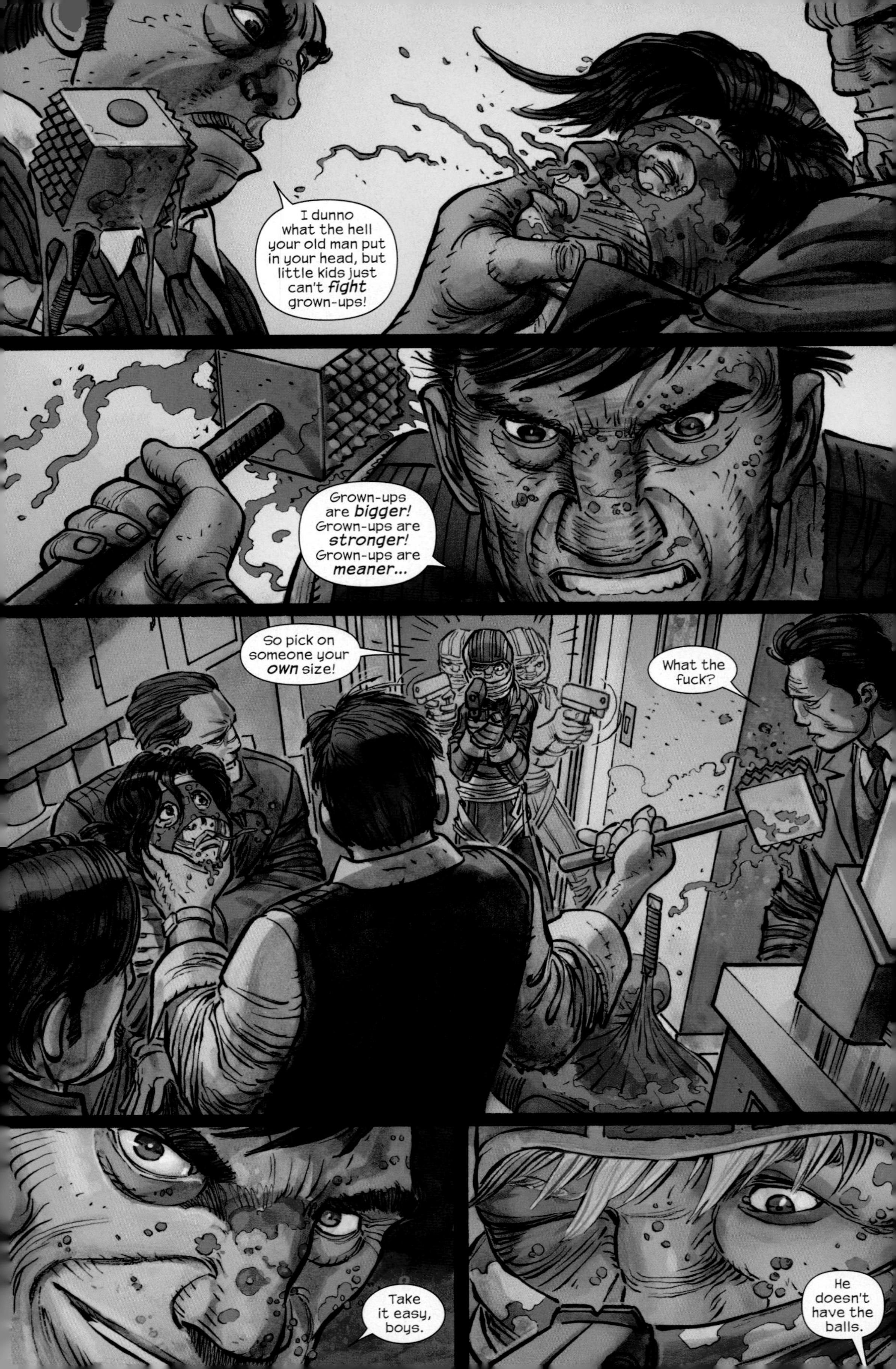
I dunno what the hell your old man put in your head, but little kids just can't *fight* grown-ups!
Grown-ups are ***bigger!*** Grown-ups are ***stronger!*** Grown-ups are ***meaner...***
So pick on someone your ***own*** size!
What the fuck?
Take it easy, boys.
He doesn't have the balls.

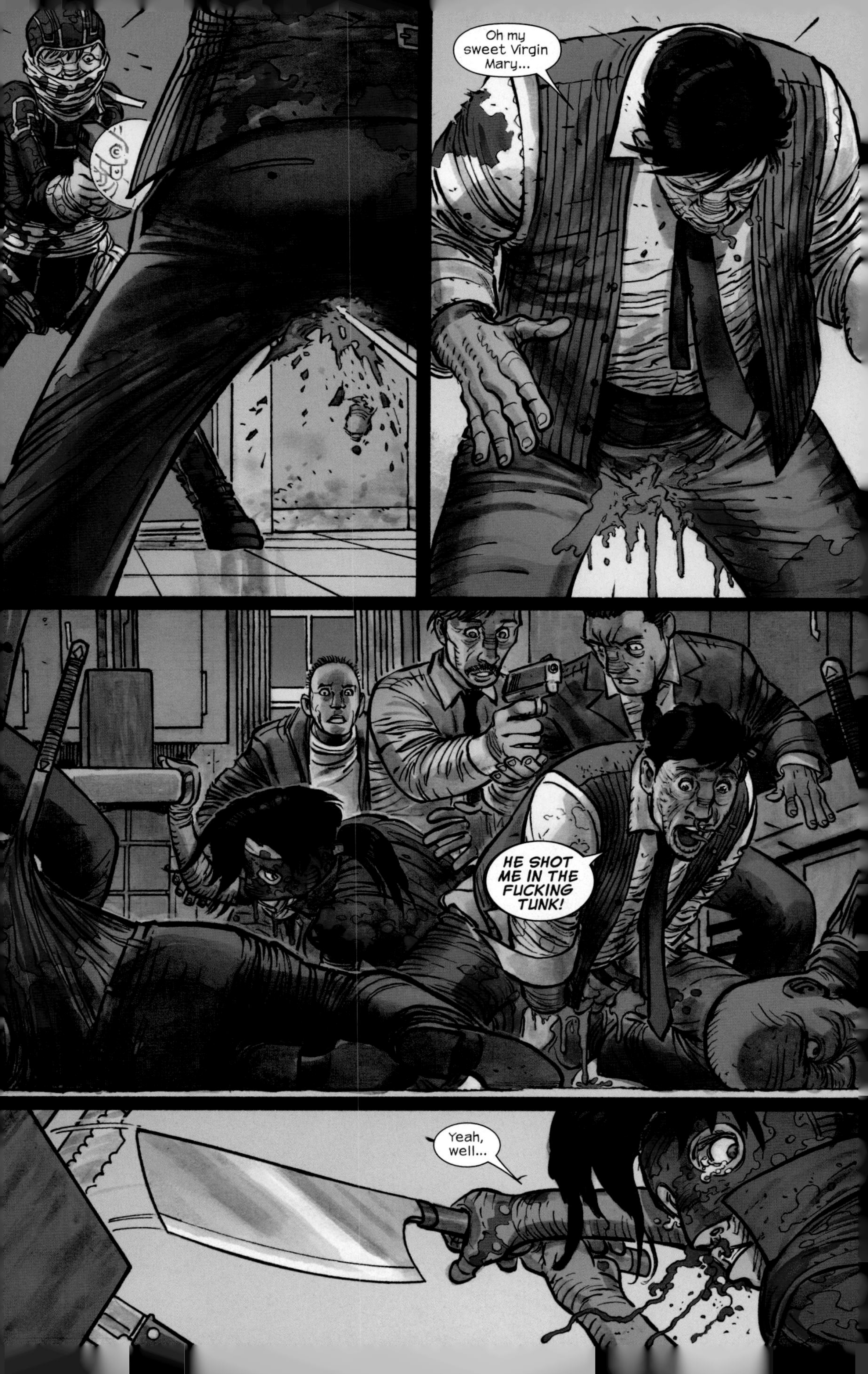
Oh my sweet Virgin Mary...
HE SHOT ME IN THE FUCKING TUNK!
Yeah, well...

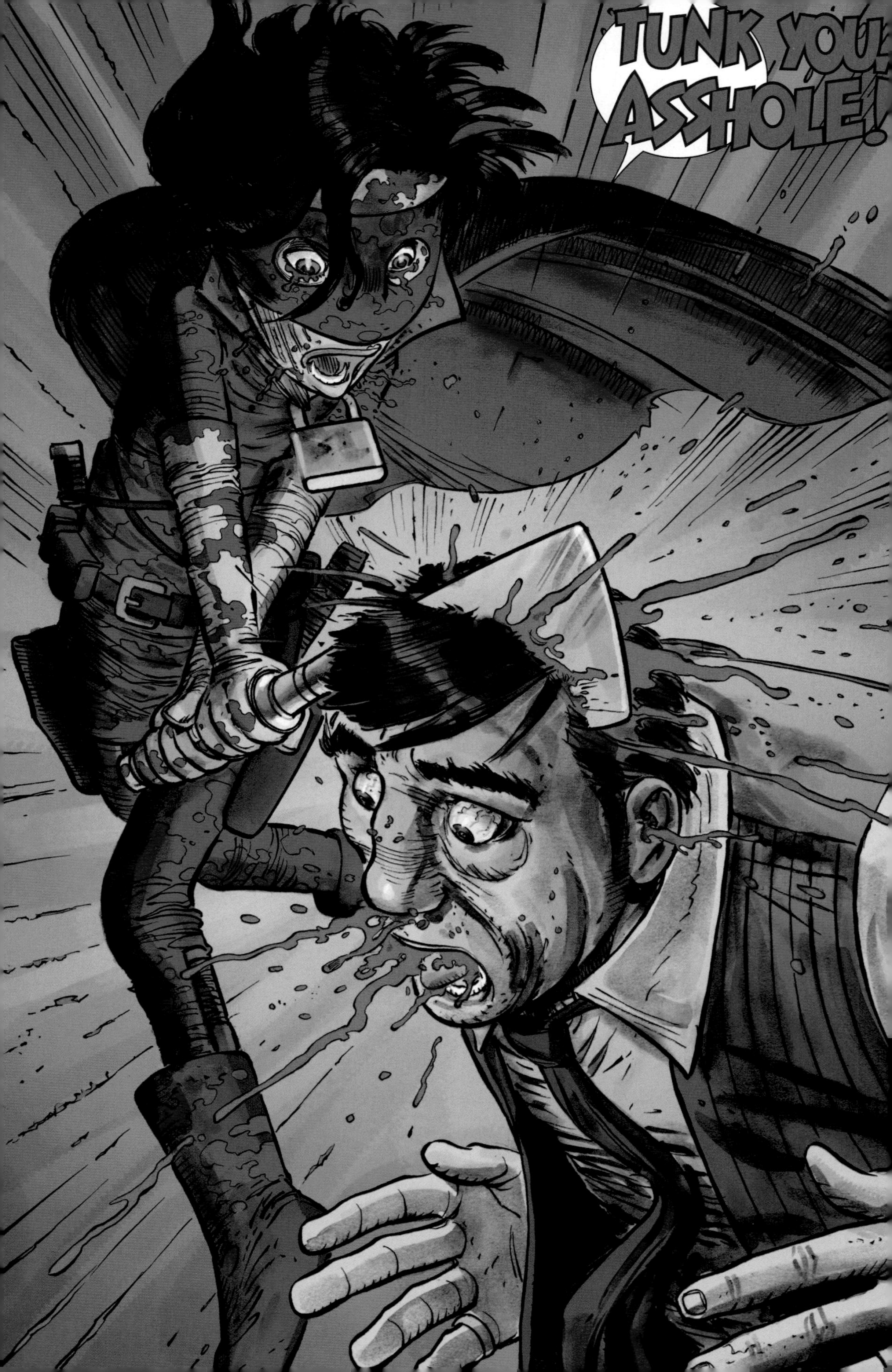
TUNK YOU, ASSHOLE!

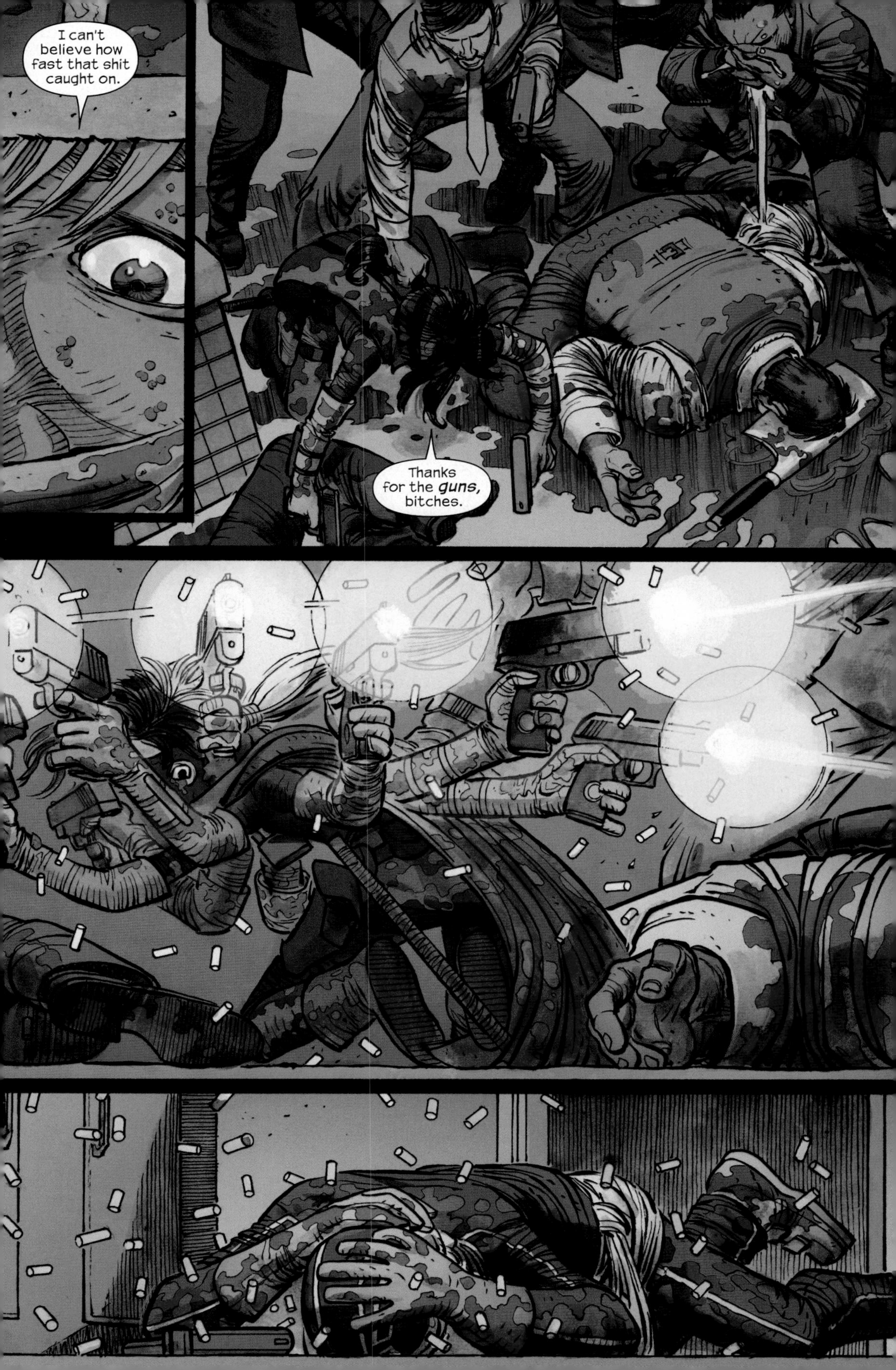
I can't believe how fast that shit caught on.
Thanks for the *guns,* bitches.

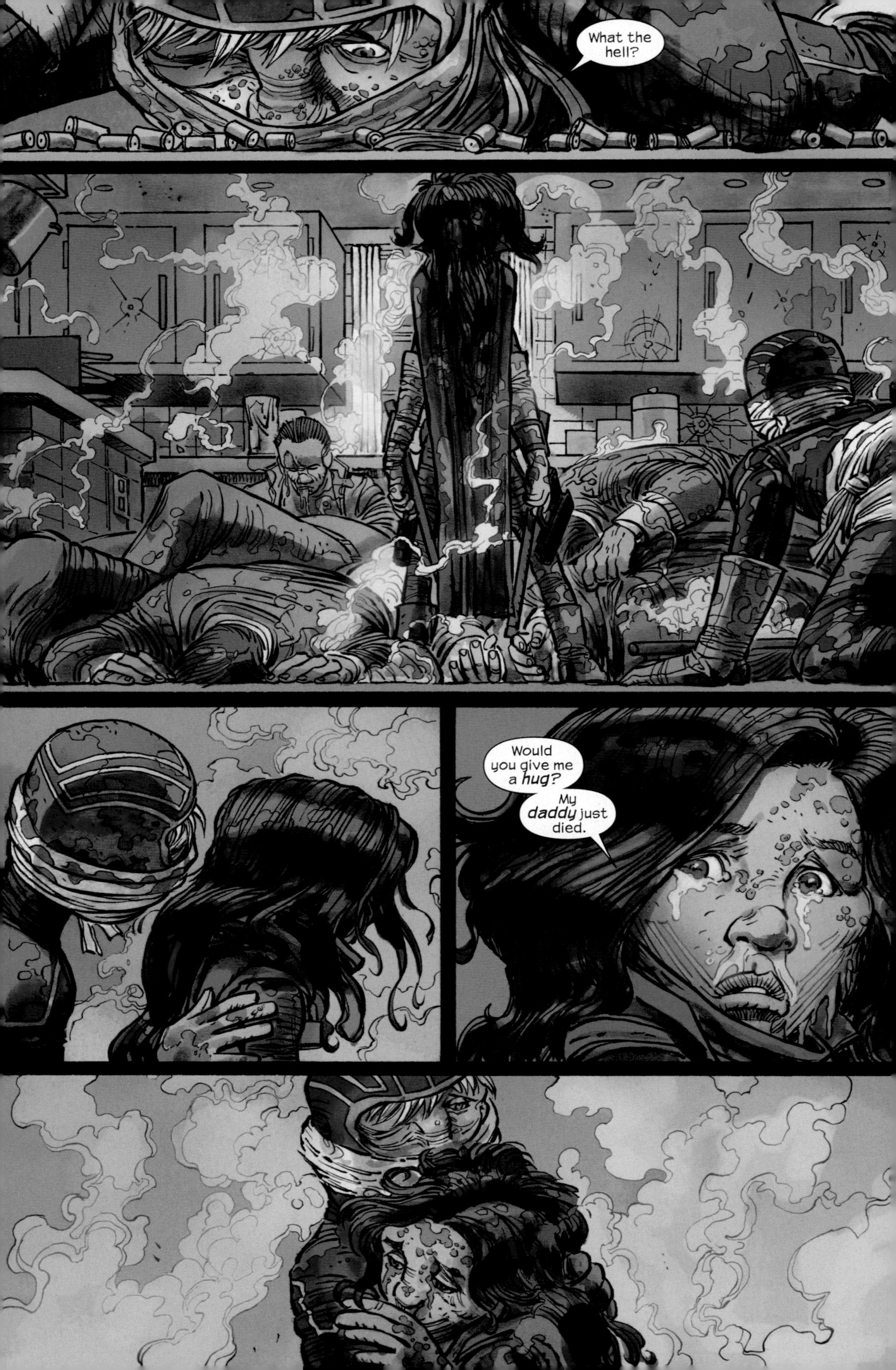
What the hell?
Would you give me a *hug?*
My *daddy* just died.

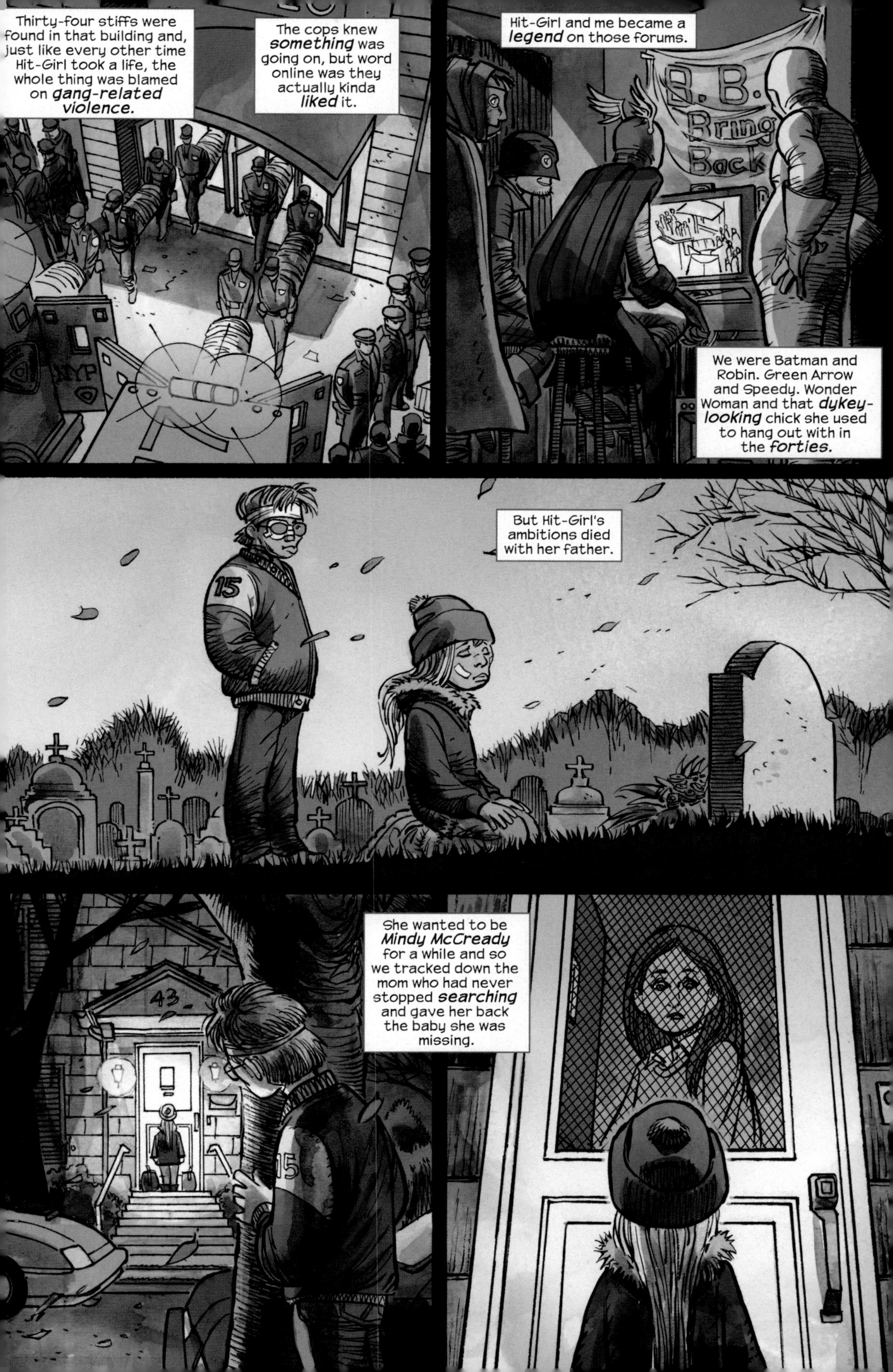
Thirty-four stiffs were found in that building and, just like every other time Hit-Girl took a life, the whole thing was blamed on *gang-related violence.*
The cops knew *something* was going on, but word online was they actually kinda *liked* it.
NYPD
Hit-Girl and me became a *legend* on those forums.
B. B. Bring Back
We were Batman and Robin. Green Arrow and Speedy. Wonder Woman and that *dykey-looking* chick she used to hang out with in the *forties.*
15
But Hit-Girl's ambitions died with her father.
43
She wanted to be *Mindy McCready* for a while and so we tracked down the mom who had never stopped *searching* and gave her back the baby she was missing.
15

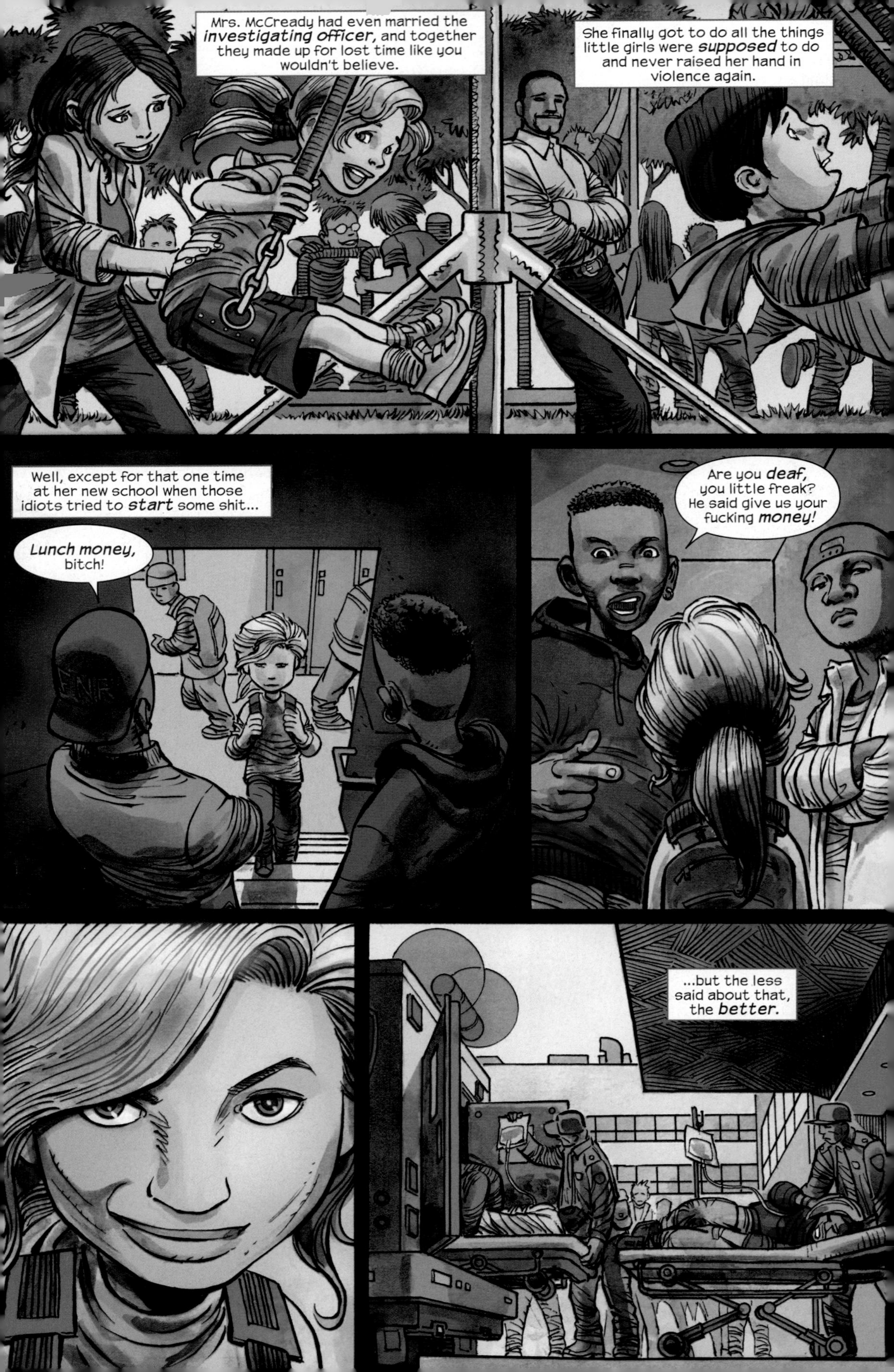

Mrs. McCready had even married the *investigating officer*, and together they made up for lost time like you wouldn't believe.
She finally got to do all the things little girls were *supposed* to do and never raised her hand in violence again.
Well, except for that one time at her new school when those idiots tried to *start* some shit...
Lunch money, bitch!
Are you *deaf,* you little freak? He said give us your fucking *money!*
...but the less said about that, the *better.*

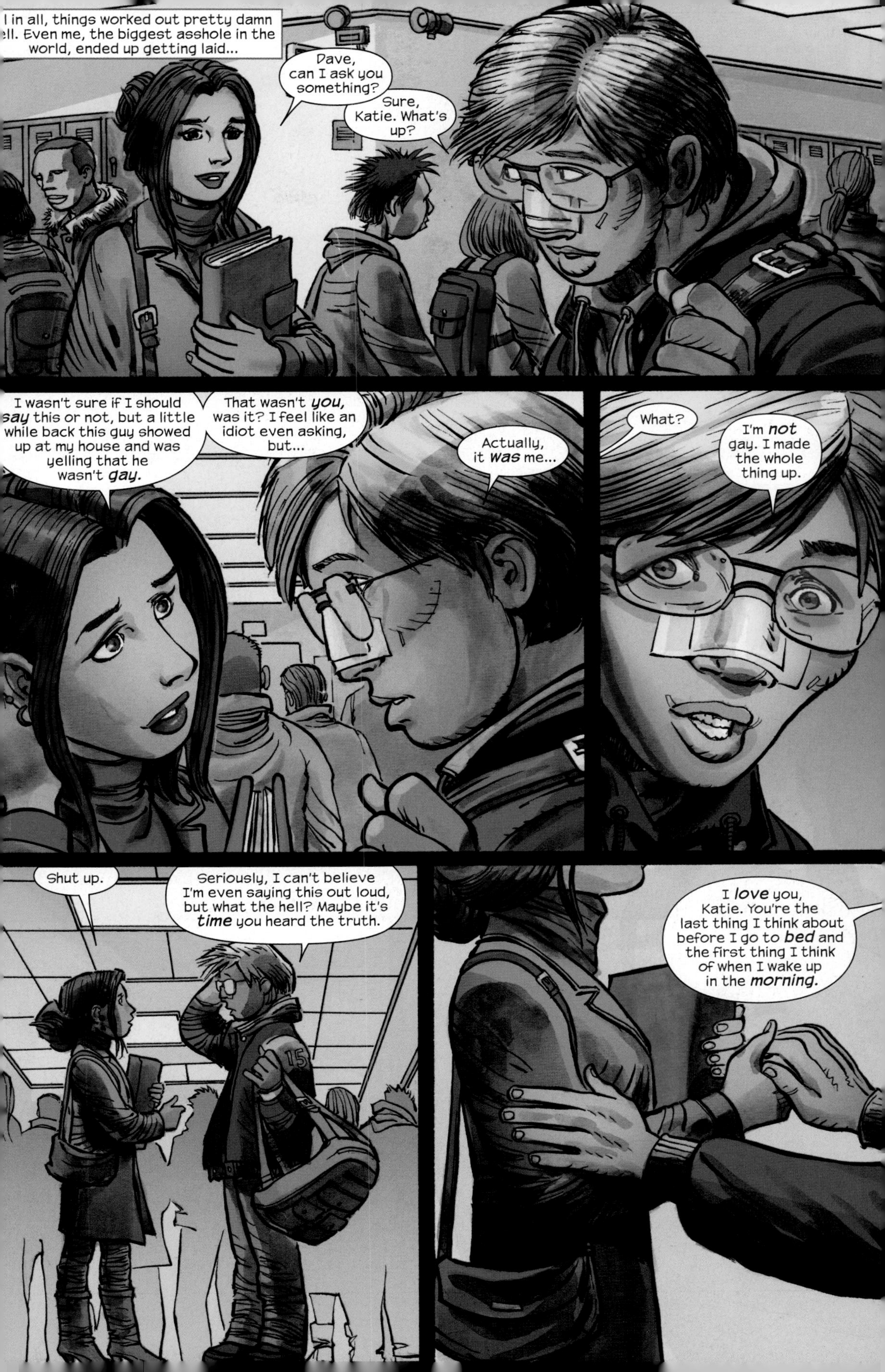
l in all, things worked out pretty damn
ell. Even me, the biggest asshole in the world, ended up getting laid...
Dave, can I ask you something?
Sure, Katie. What's up?
I wasn't sure if I should say this or not, but a little while back this guy showed up at my house and was yelling that he wasn't gay.
That wasn't you, was it? I feel like an idiot even asking, but...
Actually, it was me...
What?
I'm not gay. I made the whole thing up.
Shut up.
Seriously, I can't believe I'm even saying this out loud, but what the hell? Maybe it's time you heard the truth.
I love you, Katie. You're the last thing I think about before I go to bed and the first thing I think of when I wake up in the morning.

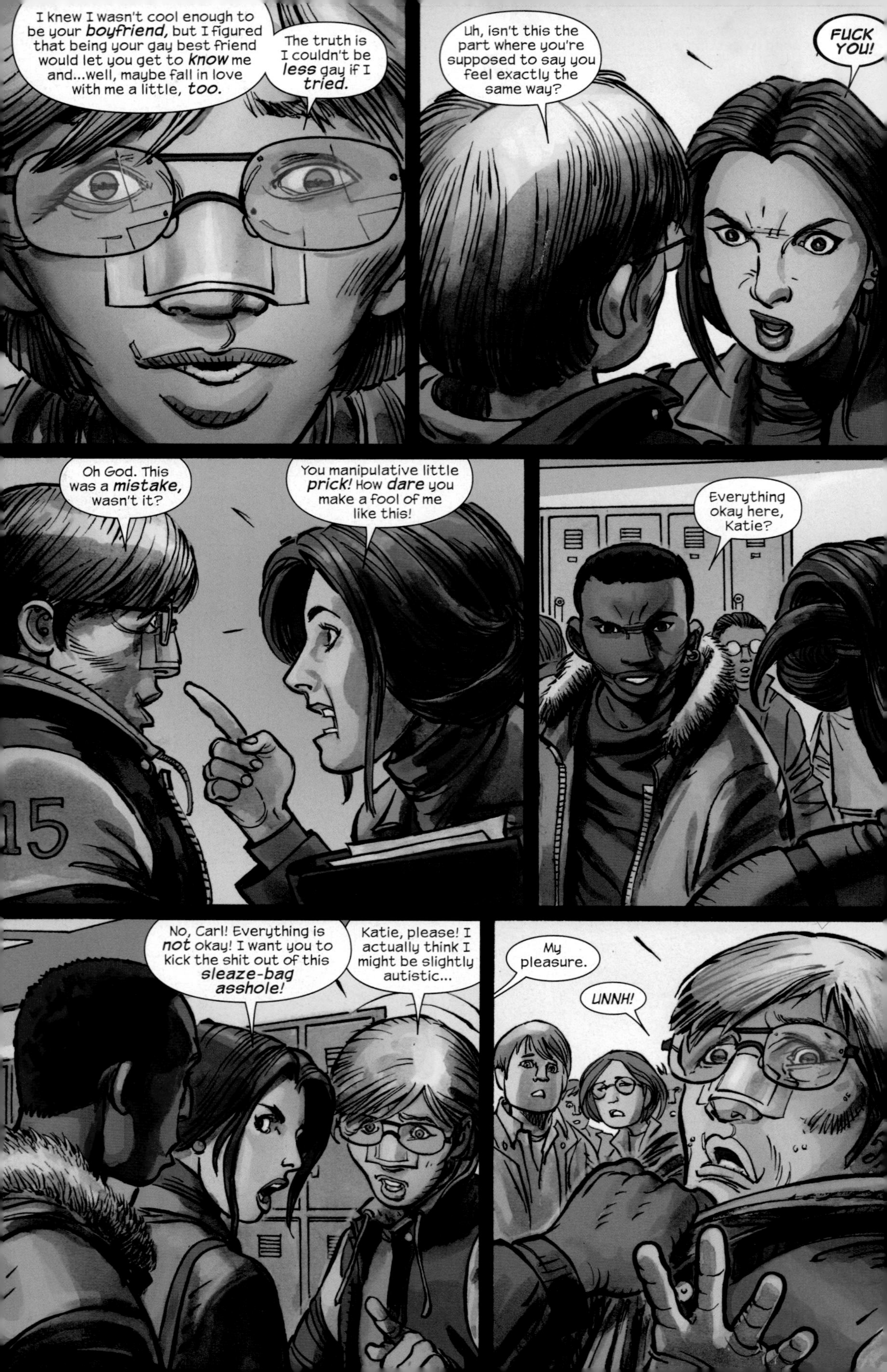
I knew I wasn't cool enough to be your boyfriend, but I figured that being your gay best friend would let you get to know me and...well, maybe fall in love with me a little, too.
The truth is I couldn't be less gay if I tried.
Uh, isn't this the part where you're supposed to say you feel exactly the same way?
FUCK YOU!
Oh God. This was a mistake, wasn't it?
You manipulative little prick! How dare you make a fool of me like this!
15
Everything okay here, Katie?
No, Carl! Everything is not okay! I want you to kick the shit out of this sleaze-bag asshole!
Katie, please! I actually think I might be slightly autistic...
My pleasure.
UNNH!

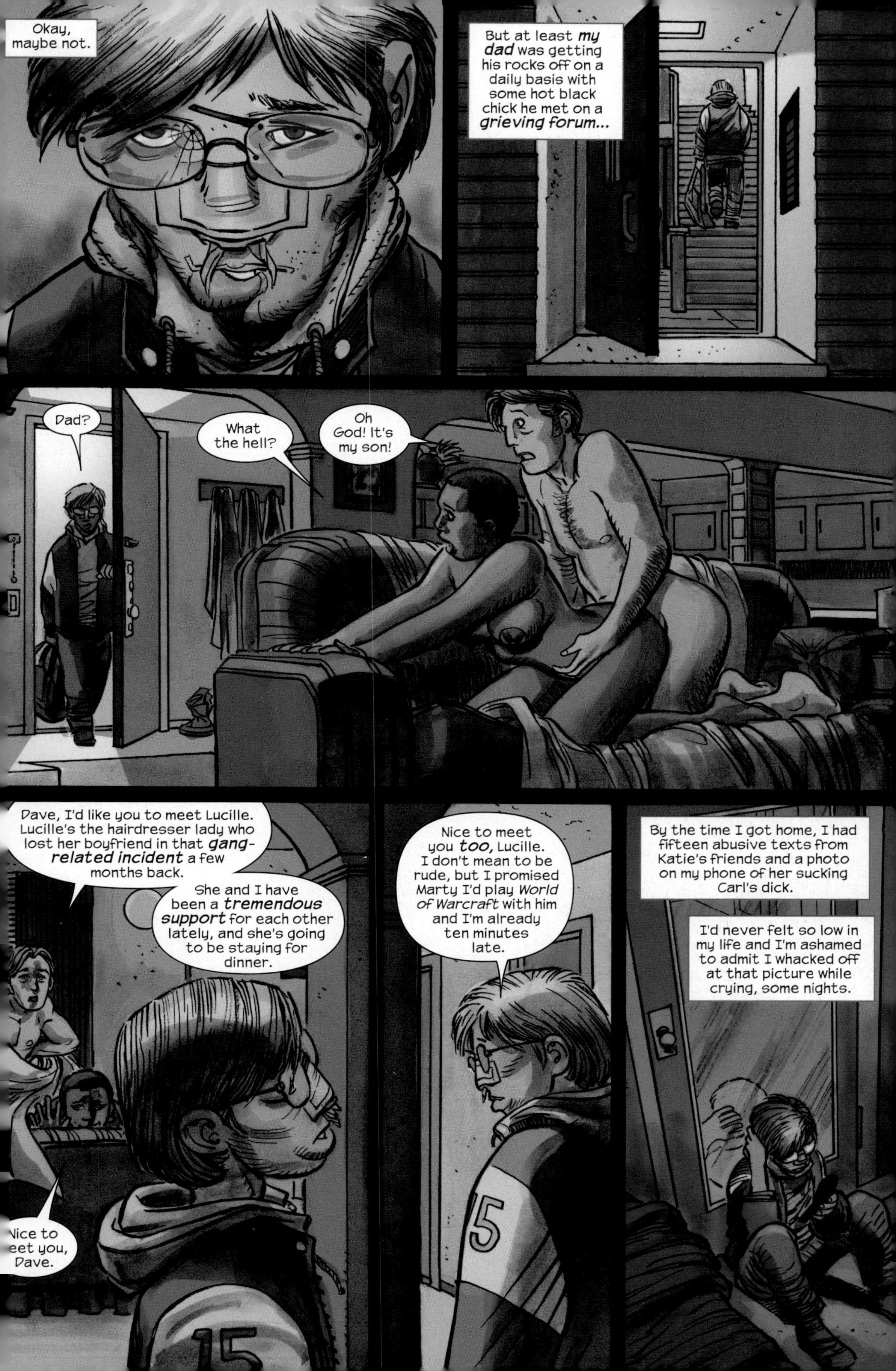
Okay, maybe not.
But at least *my dad* was getting his rocks off on a daily basis with some hot black chick he met on a *grieving forum...*
Dad?
What the hell?
Oh God! It's my son!
Dave, I'd like you to meet Lucille. Lucille's the hairdresser lady who lost her boyfriend in that *gang-related incident* a few months back.
She and I have been a *tremendous support* for each other lately, and she's going to be staying for dinner.
Nice to eet you, Dave.
Nice to meet you *too,* Lucille. I don't mean to be rude, but I promised Marty I'd play *World of Warcraft* with him and I'm already ten minutes late.
By the time I got home, I had fifteen abusive texts from Katie's friends and a photo on my phone of her sucking Carl's dick.
I'd never felt so low in my life and I'm ashamed to admit I whacked off at that picture while crying, some nights.

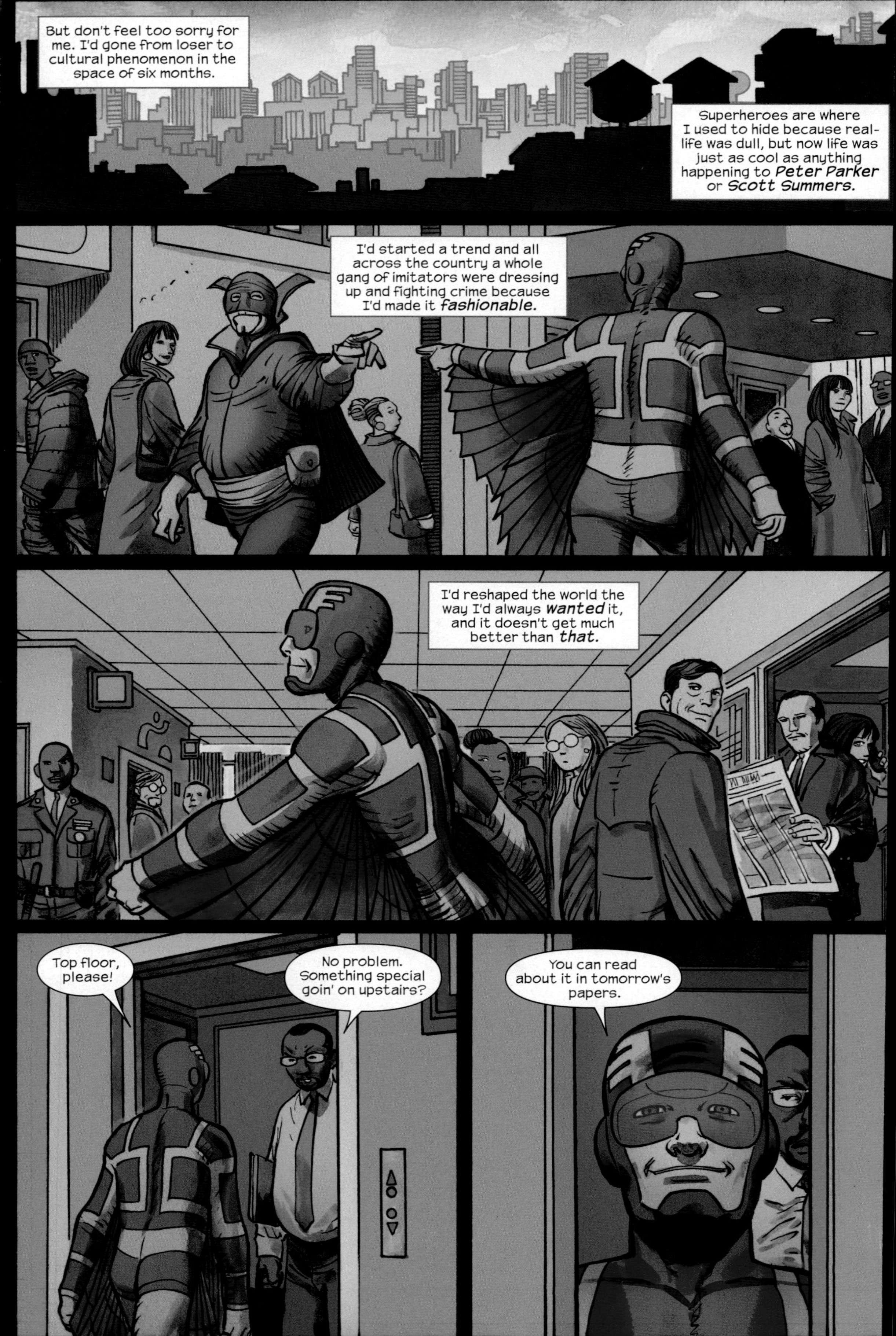
But don't feel too sorry for me. I'd gone from loser to cultural phenomenon in the space of six months.
Superheroes are where I used to hide because real-life was dull, but now life was just as cool as anything happening to *Peter Parker* or *Scott Summers.*
I'd started a trend and all across the country a whole gang of imitators were dressing up and fighting crime because I'd made it *fashionable.*
I'd reshaped the world the way I'd always *wanted* it, and it doesn't get much better than *that.*
Top floor, please!
No problem. Something special goin' on upstairs?
You can read about it in tomorrow's papers.

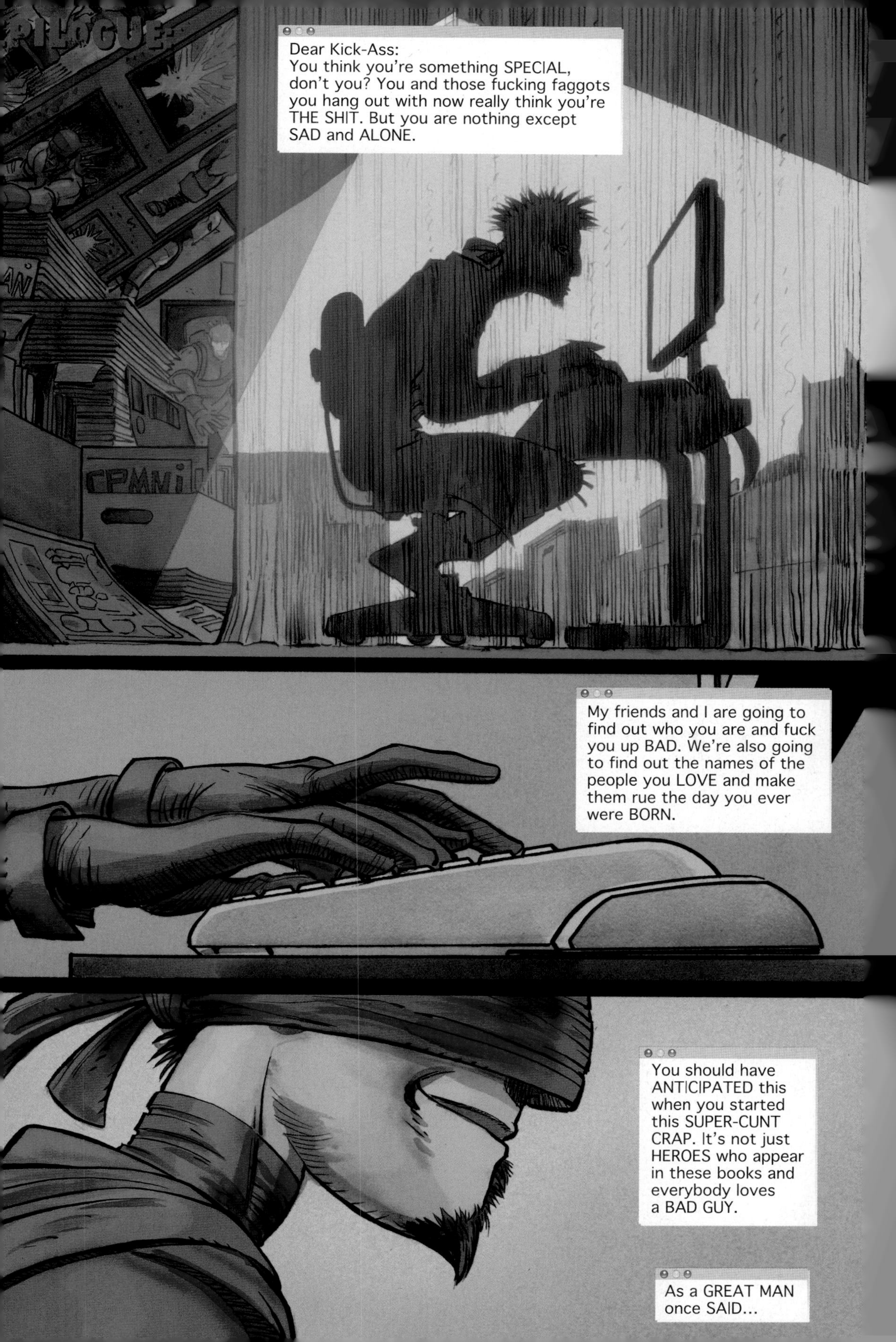
EPILOGUE
Dear Kick-Ass:
You think you're something SPECIAL, don't you? You and those fucking faggots you hang out with now really think you're THE SHIT. But you are nothing except SAD and ALONE.
My friends and I are going to find out who you are and fuck you up BAD. We're also going to find out the names of the people you LOVE and make them rue the day you ever were BORN.
You should have ANTICIPATED this when you started this SUPER-CUNT CRAP. It's not just HEROES who appear in these books and everybody loves a BAD GUY.
As a GREAT MAN once SAID...

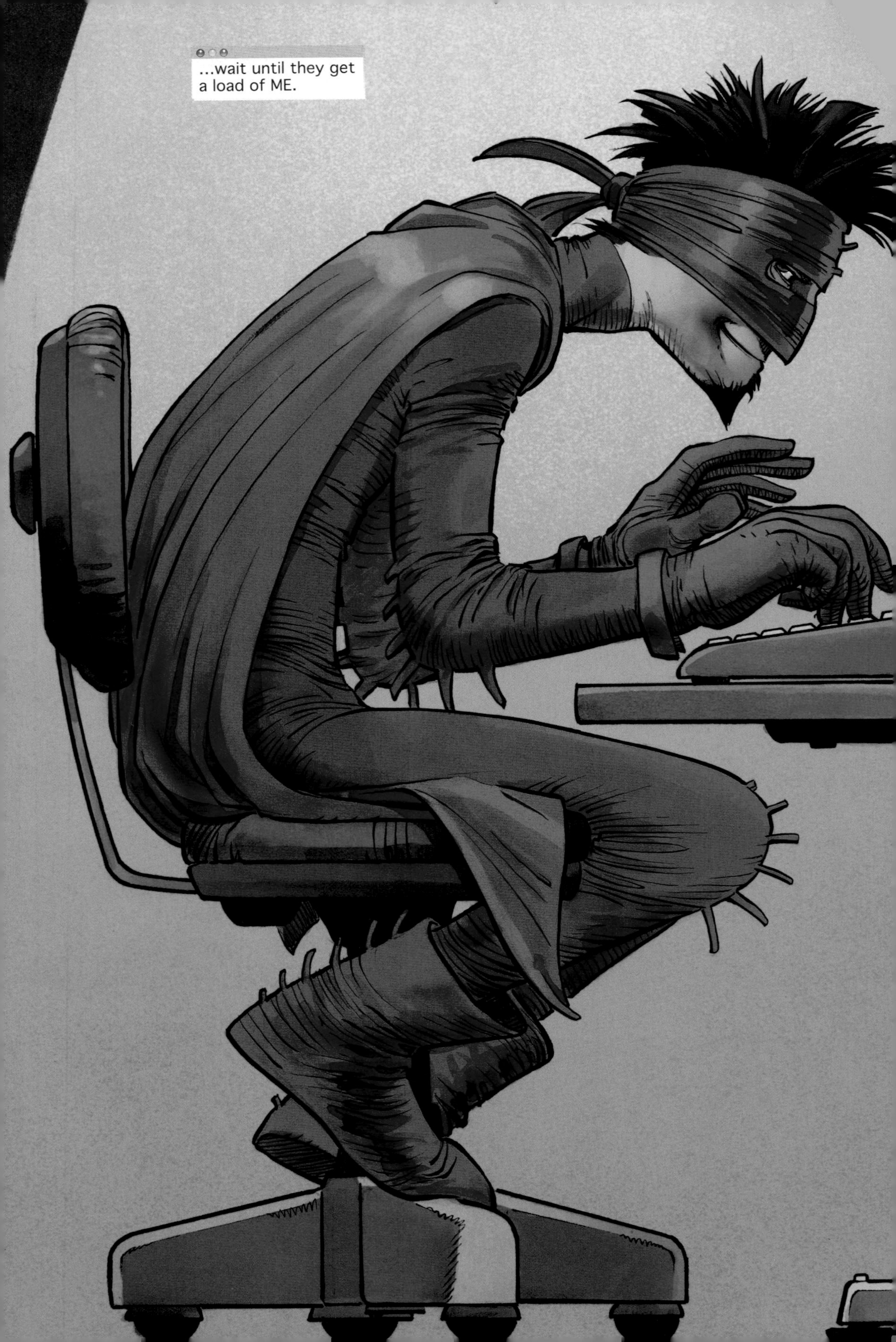
...wait until they get a load of ME.

END OF BOOK ONE

KICK

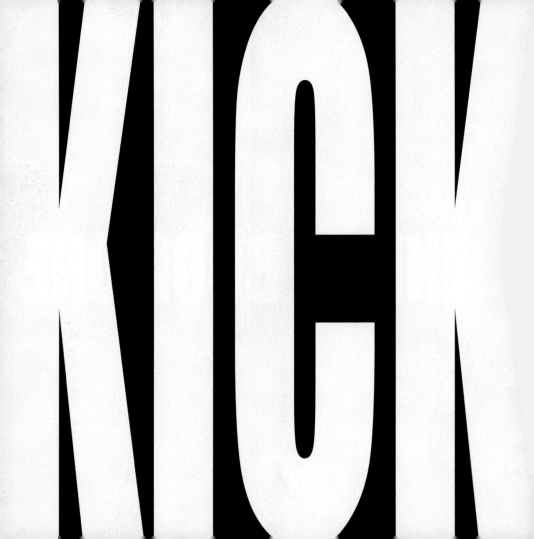

-ASS

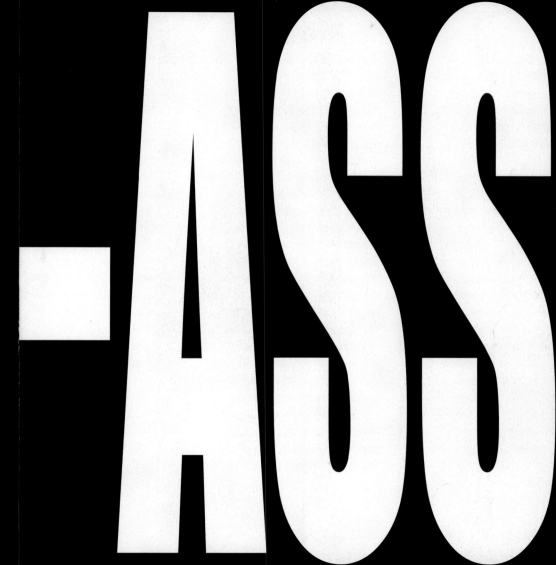

MARK MILLAR has been one of the key writers for Marvel Comics in the 21st century. Millar's first major contribution to Marvel was *Ultimate X-Men*, which achieved great creative and commercial success throughout his two-year run. Working with artist Bryan Hitch on *The Ultimates*, Millar surpassed his own success with that commercial and critical darling. Next, joining up with some of the industry's top creative talent, the Scottish writer took on two of Marvel's most iconic characters: Spider-Man and Wolverine. While working on creator-owned books like *Wanted*, turned into a Hollywood blockbuster staring Angelina Jolie, he penned *Civil War*, the epic miniseries that definitively reshaped the landscape of Marvel's heroes. More recently, Millar has reunited with Hitch on *Fantastic Four* and with *Civil War* artist Steve McNiven in both the pages of *Wolverine* and the upcoming *Nemesis*, as well as returning to the Ultimate Universe with *Ultimate Avengers.*

JOHN ROMITA JR. is a modern-day comic-art legend. A loyal Marvel artist since the late '70s, he has followed in his father's footsteps and helped keep the Romita name on the list of top-shelf talent. Timeless runs on *Iron Man, Uncanny X-Men, Amazing Spider-Man,* and *Daredevil* helped establish him as his own man artistically, and his art on *Wolverine* is arguably the decade's most explosive comic art—trumped perhaps only by his own work on the massive summer blockbuster event *World War Hulk*. JRJR has also paired with renowned writer Neil Gaiman for *The Eternals*, their reworking of the classic Marvel Comics characters, and has recently returned to *Amazing Spider-Man*; he will follow that up with another high-profile Marvel series.

TOM PALMER has worked as an illustrator in the advertising and editorial fields, but he has spent the majority of his career in comic books. His first assignment, fresh out of art school, was on *Doctor Strange*, and he has gone on to lend his inking talents to many of Marvel's top titles, including *X-Men, The Avengers, Tomb of Dracula*, and more recently *Punisher, Hulk,* and *Ghost Rider.* He lives and works in New Jersey.

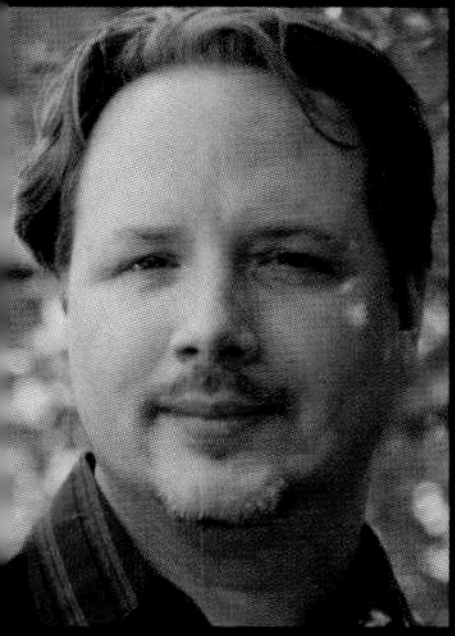

AN WHITE is
e of the comic
dustry's best and
ost sought-after
lor artists. Well-
own for his work
titles such as *The
nazing Spider-
an, Punisher, Dark
engers, Captain
nerica, Black
nther, Wolverine*
d countless more,
an's envelope-
shing rendering
d color palette
ng a sense of
gency and power
every page he
uches.

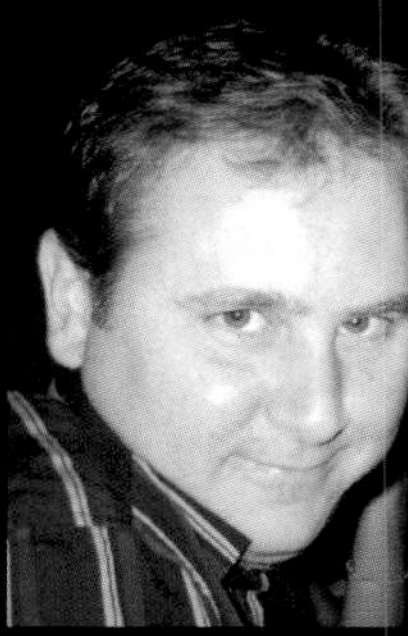

CHRIS ELIOPOULOS is a multiple award-winner for his lettering, having worked on dozens of books during the twenty years he's been in the industry—including Erik Larsen's *Savage Dragon*, for which he hand-lettered the first 100 issues. Along with his success as a letterer, he also publishes his own strip *Misery Loves Sherman*, wrote and illustrated the popular *Franklin Richards: Son of a Genius* one-shots, and writes Marvel's *Lockjaw and the Pet Avengers* series.

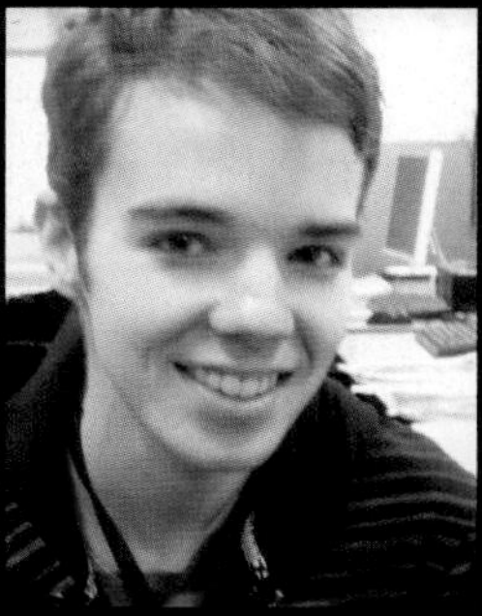

MICHAEL HORWITZ's student thesis (a five minute documentary about the private lives of cabbages) was met with resounding indifference by NYU, forcing the Virginia native to realize a career in experimental film wasn't in the cards. With a résumé padded to the extreme (and omitting a regrettable excursion into the world of go-go dancing), Michael somehow fooled Marvel Comics into hiring him, where he now edits such titles as Laurell K. Hamilton's *Anita Blake* and Stephen King's *The Dark Tower*.

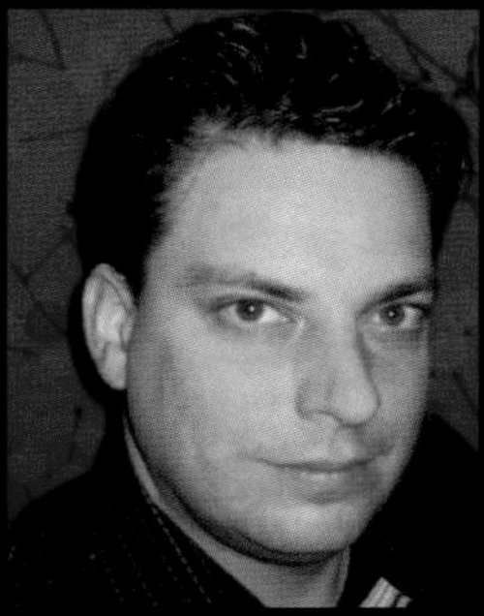

JOHN BARBER self-published his own comics before joining the world of webcomics, and later co-wrote a book called *Webcomics*, with Steven Withrow. In 2003, Barber joined the Marvel Comics editorial team and became editor of the Wolverine franchise, before leaving to pursue a freelance career—including a return to comics on the web (webcomicsnation.com/thejohnbarber). He stuck around on *Kick-Ass*, though, which is a hell of a way to go out, editorially speaking.

KICK-ASS'S GREATEST HITS

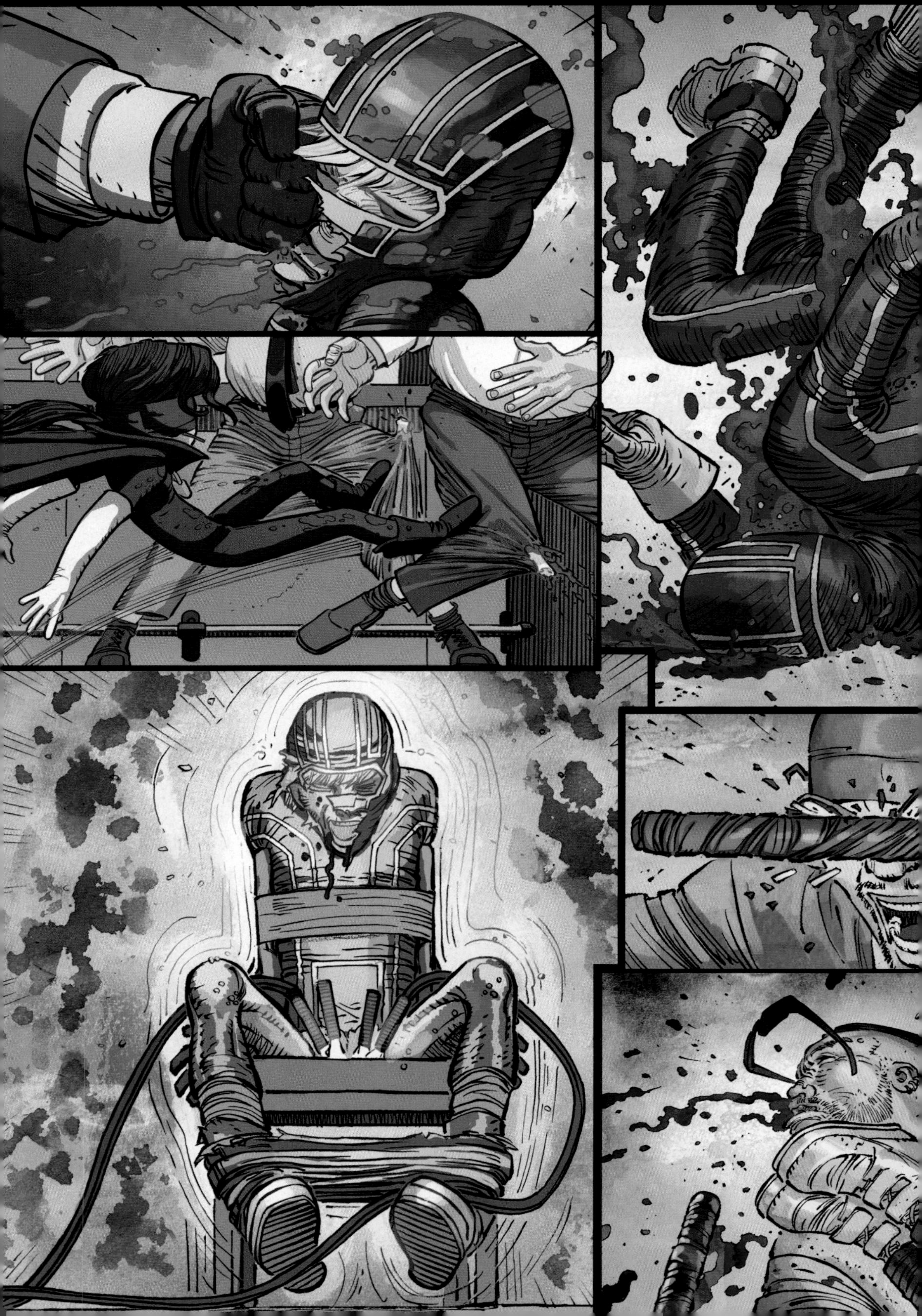

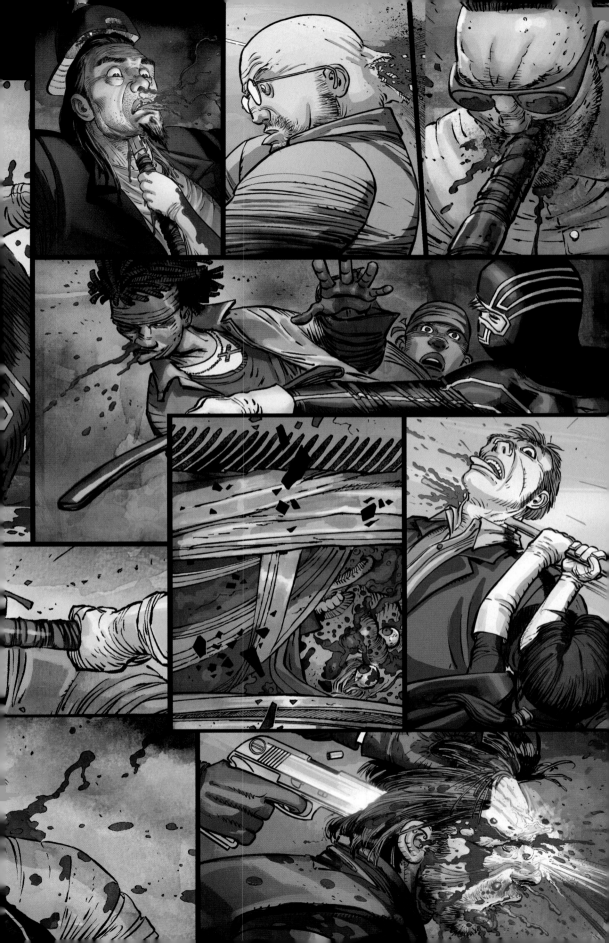

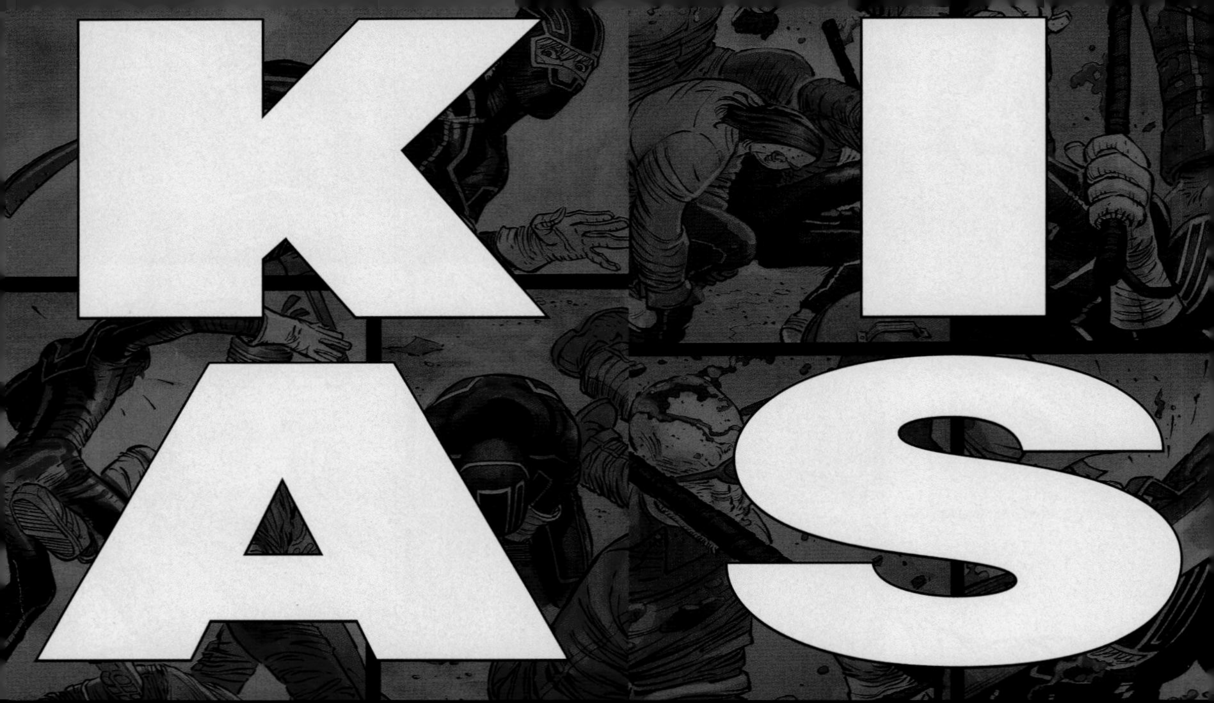
KI
AS

COMBINED CO[illegible]RS FOR ISSUE #1 6TH PRINTING, #2 4TH PRINTING, #3 4TH PRINTING AND #4 3RD PRINTING

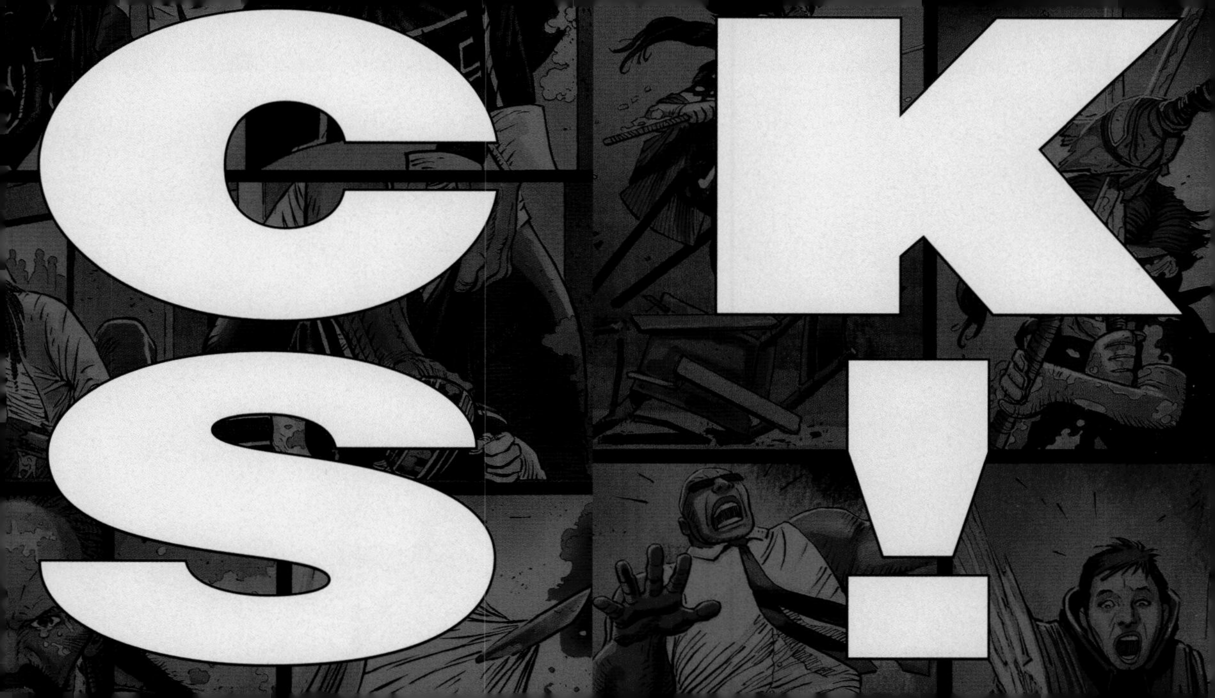
C K
S !

ONE (VARIANT BY MCNIVEN)

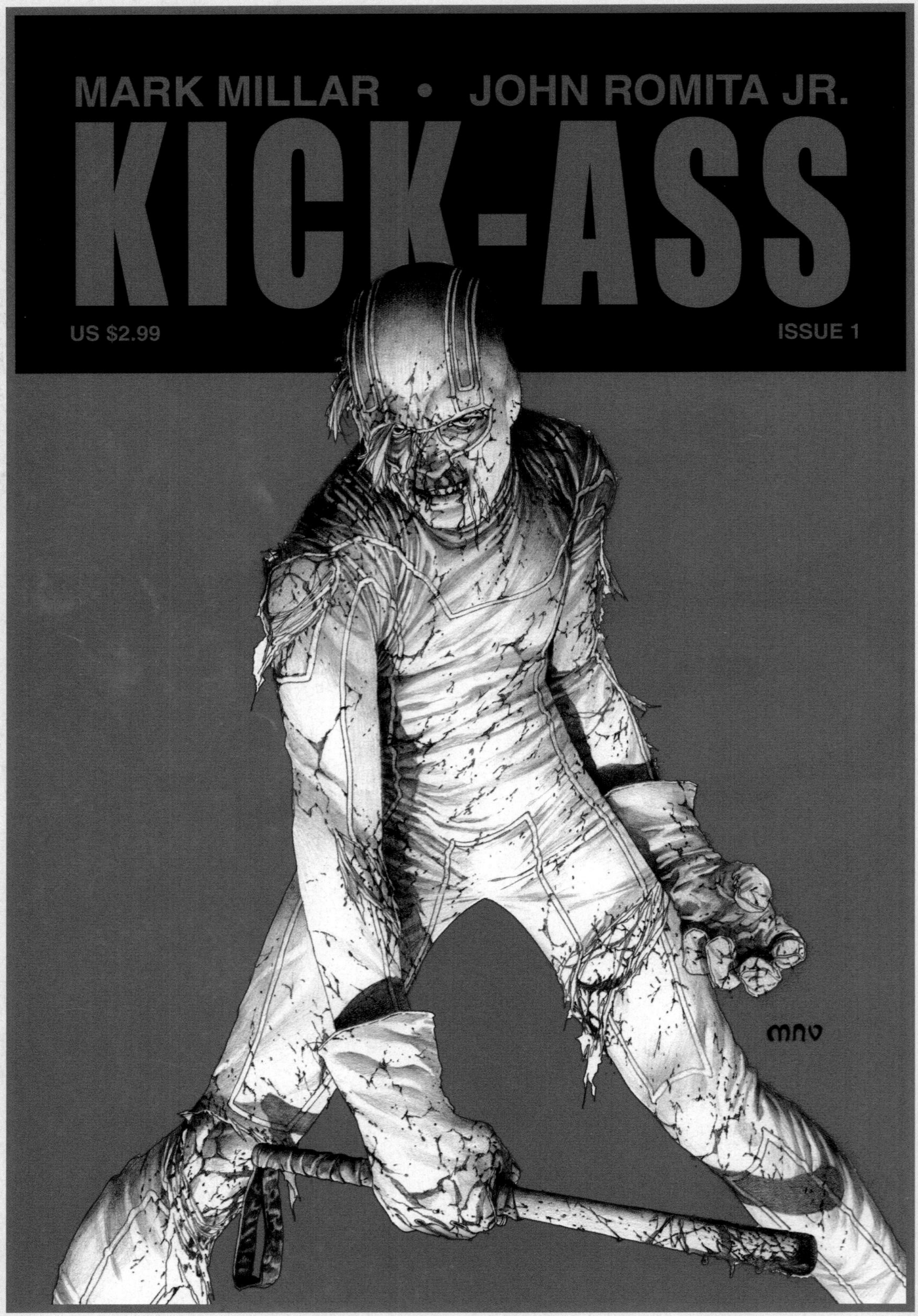
MARK MILLAR • JOHN ROMITA JR.
KICK-ASS
US $2.99
ISSUE 1
MNV

TWO

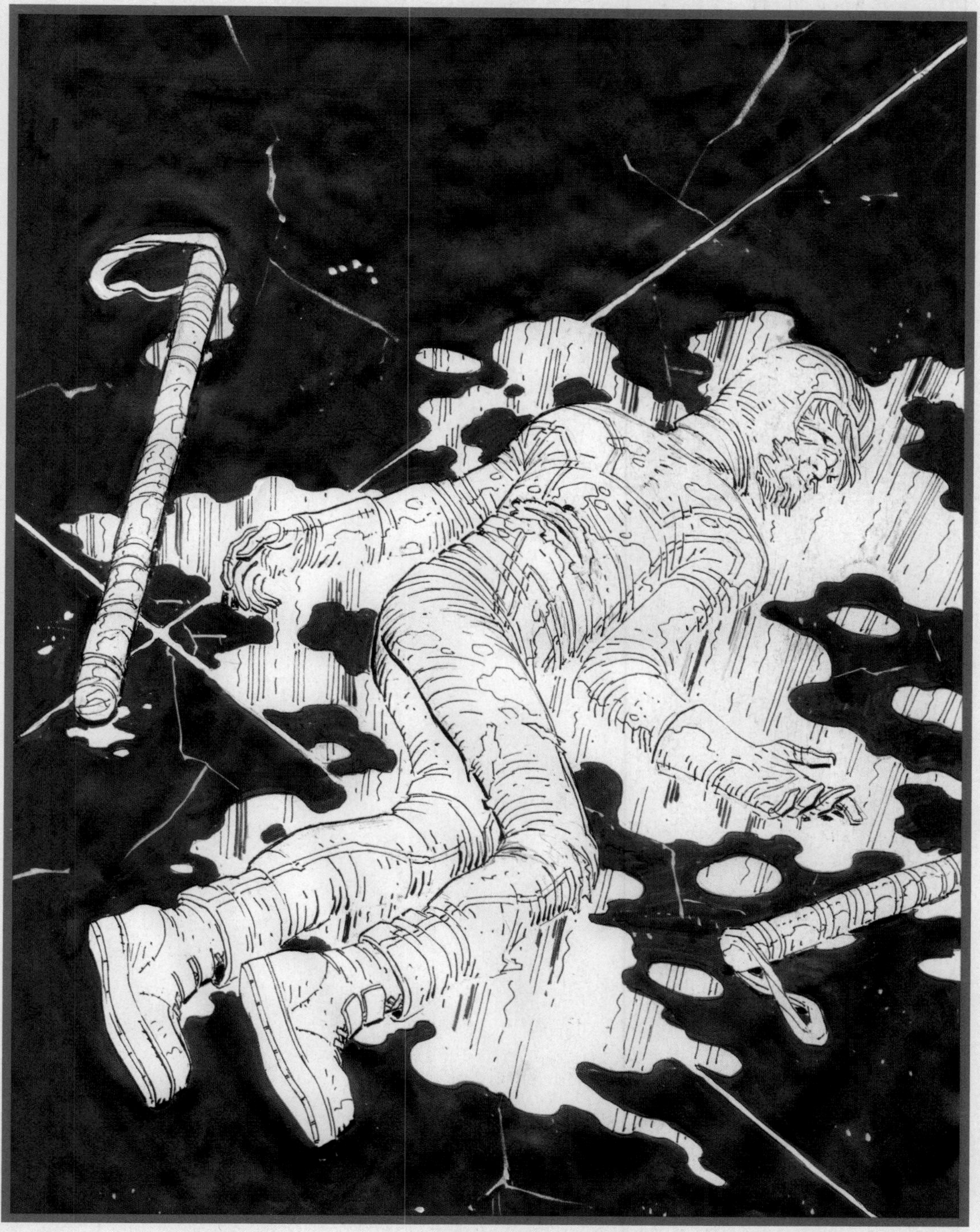

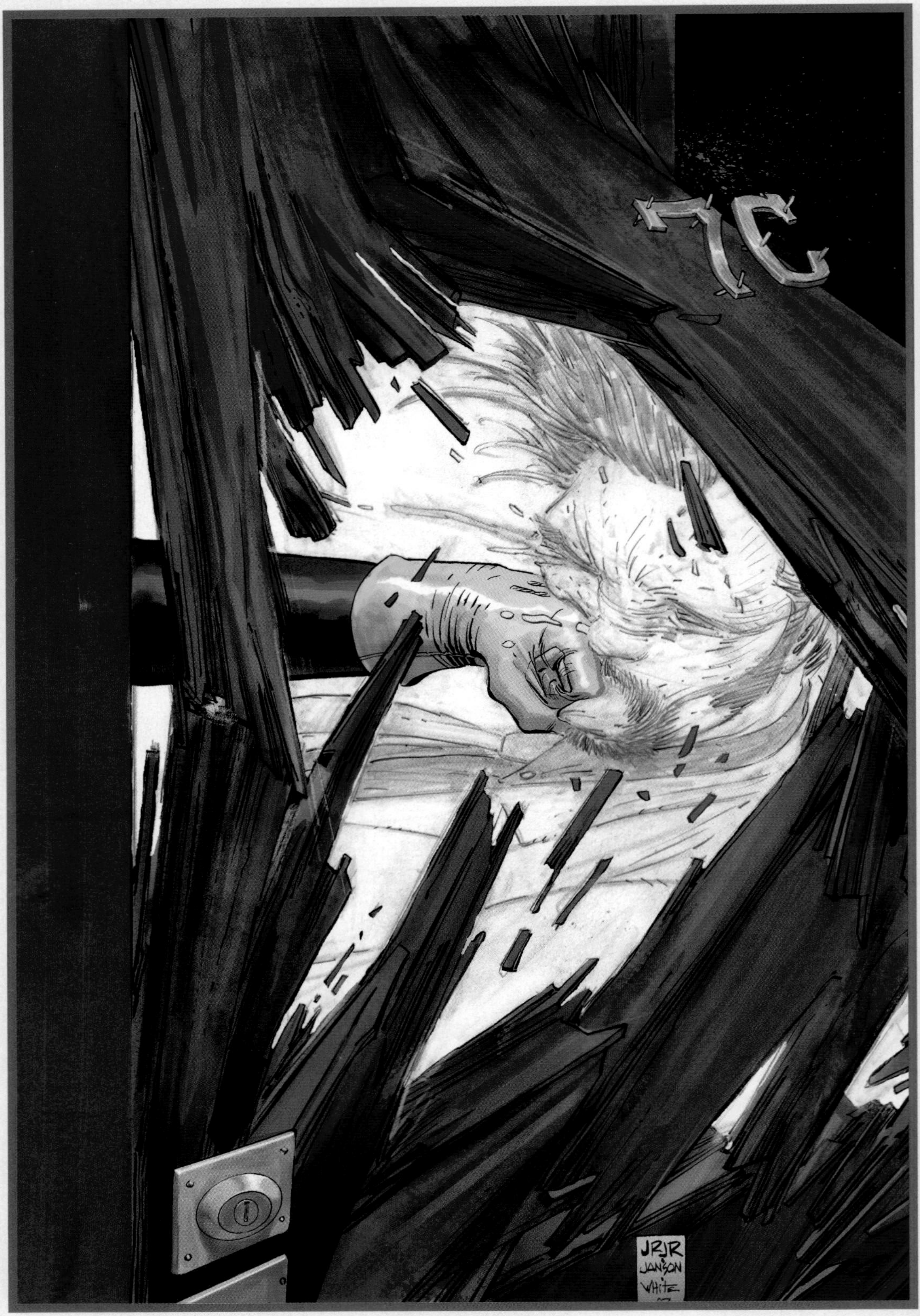
JRJR
JANSON
WHITE

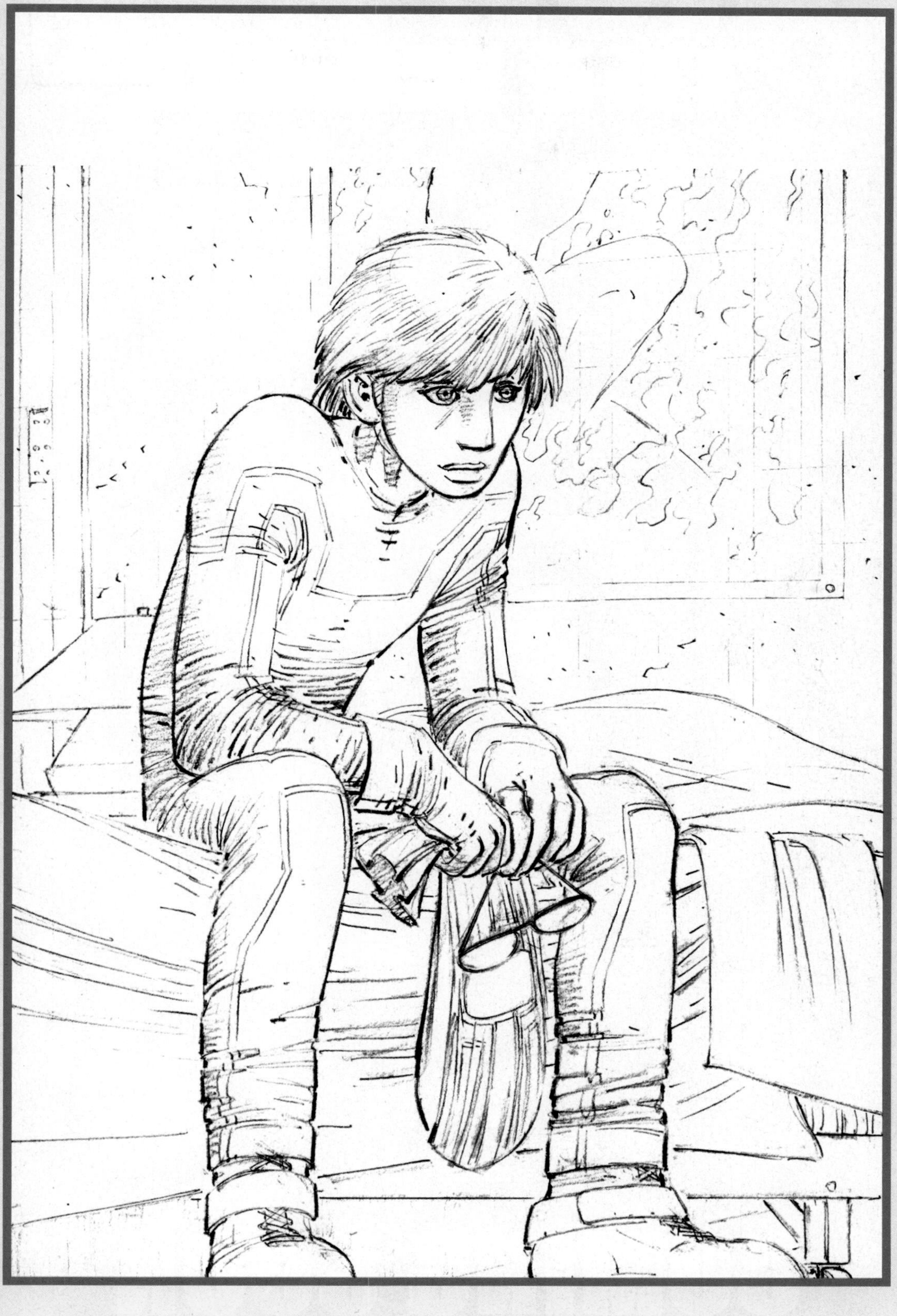

KICK-ASS
THE MOVIE

COMING SOON

PENCILS-JOHN S. ROMITA   INKS-TOM PALMER   COLOR-DEAN WHITE